MIKE MEYERS' CERTIFICATION
Passport ★

A+®
Certification

MIKE MEYERS
TRACEY ROSENBLATH

OSBORNE

New York • Chicago • San Francisco
Lisbon • London • Madrid • Mexico City
Milan • New Delhi • San Juan
Seoul • Singapore • Sydney • Toronto

McGraw-Hill/Osborne
2600 Tenth Street
Berkeley, California 94710
U.S.A.

To arrange bulk purchase discounts for sales promotions, premiums, or fund-raisers, please contact **McGraw-Hill/**Osborne at the above address. For information on translations or book distributors outside the U.S.A., please see the International Contact Information page immediately following the index of this book.

Mike Meyers' A+® Certification Passport

1 2 3 4 5 6 7 8 9 0 DOC DOC 0 1 9 8 7 6 5 4 3 2 1

Book p/n 0-07-219601-7 and CD p/n 0-07-219600-9
parts of
ISBN 0-07-219363-8

Publisher	**Project Editor**	**Indexer**
Brandon A. Nordin	Janet Walden	David Heiret
Vice President &	**Acquisitions Coordinator**	**Design and Production**
Associate Publisher	Jessica Wilson	epic
Scott Rogers		
	Technical Editor	**Illustrators**
Editorial Director	Kevin Vaccaro	Michael Mueller
Gareth Hancock		Lyssa Wald
	Copy Editor	Kelly Stanton-Scott
Acquisitions Editor	Marcia Baker	
Michael Sprague		**Series Cover Design**
	Proofreader	Ted Holladay
	John Schindel	

This book was composed with QuarkXPress™.

Contents

18 Optimizing and Maintaining Windows 9*x*

This book is dedicated to all those who speak the true international language, Geek.

Acknowledgments

We would like to take a moment to acknowledge the many folks who helped make this book possible.

First off, our special thanks to Scott Jernigan, editor *extraordinaire*. Scott put tremendous work into this book: editing, writing, researching, nursemaiding, cursing, cajoling, thwacking ... and blending the wildly differing styles of the authors into a single, solid voice. We'll buy the Guinness, amigo, because you definitely earned it!

To our families, for their patience and support throughout yet another big project.

To the folks at McGraw-Hill/Osborne and epic, for their wonderful input, encouragement, and threats of bodily harm: Michael Sprague, Jessica Wilson, Janet Walden, Marcia Baker, Eric Houts, Andrea Reider, and Qin-Zhong Yu.

To Kevin Vaccaro: Thanks for the excellent suggestions!

To the fine brewers of the Guinness Group, for making the elixir of life, Guinness Stout.

Special thanks also to Robyn Lehmer and Melissa Taylor for help with those last-second read-throughs, doing double duty as proofreaders and sisters! You're the best!

And to the Total Seminars HQ team in Houston—Dudley, Janelle, Roger, Dana, Amber, Martin, Cary, Cindy, Kathy, John H., John D., Chris, and Bambi: You guys rock!

May I see your passport?

What do you mean you don't have a passport? Why, it's sitting right in your hands, even as you read! This book is your passport to a very special place. You're about to begin a journey, my friend, a journey toward that magical place called certification! You don't need a ticket, you don't need a suitcase—just snuggle up and read this passport—it's all you need to get there. Are you ready? Let's go!

Your Travel Agent: Mike Meyers

Hello! I'm Mike Meyers, president of Total Seminars and author of a number of popular certification books. On any given day, you'll find me replacing a hard drive, setting up a web site, or writing code. I love every aspect of this book you hold in your hands. It's part of a powerful new book series called the *Mike Meyer's Certification Passports.* Every book in this series combines easy readability with a condensed format—in other words, the kind of book I always wanted when I went for my certifications. Putting a huge amount of information in an accessible format is an enormous challenge, but I think we achieved our goal and I'm confident you'll agree.

I designed this series to do one thing and only one thing—to get you the information you need to achieve your certification. You won't find any fluff in here. Tracey and I packed every page with nothing but the real nitty-gritty of the A+ Certification exams. Every page has 100 percent pure concentrate of certification knowledge! But we didn't forget to make the book readable, so I hope you enjoy the casual, friendly style.

My personal e-mail address is mikem@totalsem.com and Tracey's e-mail is traceyrosenblath@hotmail.com. Please feel free to contact either of us directly if you have any questions, complaints, or compliments.

Your Destination: A+ Certification

This book is your passport to CompTIA's A+ Certification, the vendor-neutral industry standard certification for PC hardware technicians, the folks who build and fix PCs. To get A+ Certified, you need to pass two exams: A+ Core Hardware and A+ Operating System Technologies. The Core Hardware exam concentrates on the aspects of the PC that aren't operating system-specific. This test is primarily a hardware identification and configuration exam, but it explores everything from basic CPU and RAM topics, to SCSI and networking hardware. The first half of this book handles device installation, troubleshooting, and other hardware-specific topics in detail.

The Operating System Technologies exam concentrates on the organization, operation, function, and troubleshooting of Windows 9*x* and Windows NT/2000 systems, with a significant understanding of the use of command prompt with these operating systems. This exam also includes basic network and Internet configuration questions. The second half of this book delves deeply into OS topics, covering installation, configuration, troubleshooting, and more!

A+ Certification can be your ticket to a career in IT or simply an excellent step in your certification pathway. This book is your passport to success on the A+ Certification exams.

Your Guides: Mike Meyers and Tracey Rosenblath

You get a pair of tour guides for this book, both me and Tracey Rosenblath. I've written numerous computer certification books—including the best-selling *All-in-One A+ Certification Exam Guide*—and I've written significant parts of others, such as the *All-in-One Network+ Certification Exam Guide*. More to the point, I've been working on PCs and teaching others how to make and fix them for a *very* long time, and I love it! When I'm not lecturing or writing about PCs, I'm working on PCs or spanking my friend Scott in *Half-Life* or *Team Fortress*—on the PC, naturally!

Tracey J. Rosenblath is a popular author and computer/networking consultant who resides in Smiths Falls, Ontario, Canada, with her husband and four children. Tracey is a regular contributor to such well-known IT certification web sites as Exam Notes, Certifyd, and Certify Express, where she's published numerous articles, interviews, study guides, and book reviews. In addition, Tracey has contributed countless practice tests to the popular online testing web sites Cert21 and CertifyPro. She has recently published the Windows 2000 Network Design Exam

Cram Personal Test Center for the 70–221 MCSE exam with The Coriolis Group. When she's not busy consulting and writing, Tracey can often be found moderating in the forums on Exam Notes, Certifyd, and Certify Express as Paisleyskye.

Why the Travel Theme?

The steps to gaining a certification parallel closely the steps to planning and taking a trip. All the elements are the same: preparation, an itinerary, a route, even mishaps along the way. Let me show you how it all works.

This book is divided into 21 chapters. Each chapter begins with an *Itinerary* that provides objectives covered in each chapter and an *ETA* to give you an idea of the time involved learning the skills in that chapter. Each chapter is broken down by objectives, either those officially stated by the certifying body or our expert take on the best way to approach the topics. Portable PCs appear in several A+ competencies, for example, but work best as a single chapter. Also, each chapter contains a number of helpful items to bring out points of interest:

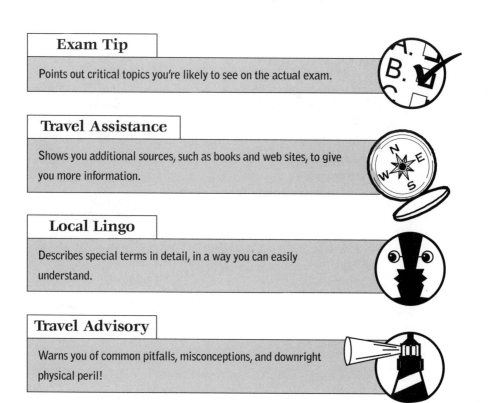

Exam Tip

Points out critical topics you're likely to see on the actual exam.

Travel Assistance

Shows you additional sources, such as books and web sites, to give you more information.

Local Lingo

Describes special terms in detail, in a way you can easily understand.

Travel Advisory

Warns you of common pitfalls, misconceptions, and downright physical peril!

The end of the chapter gives you two handy tools. The *Checkpoint* reviews each objective covered in the chapter with a handy synopsis—a great way to review quickly. Plus, you'll find end-of-chapter questions to test your newly acquired skills.

But the fun doesn't stop there! After you've read the book, pull out the CD and take advantage of the free practice questions! Use the full practice exam to hone your skills and keep the book handy to check answers.

If you want even more practice, log on to http://www.osborne.com/passport and, for a nominal fee, you'll get additional high-quality practice questions.

When you're acing the practice questions, you're ready to take the exam. Go get certified!

The End of the Trail

The IT industry changes and grows constantly, *and so should you.* Finishing one certification is only one step in an ongoing process of gaining more and more certifications to match your constantly changing and growing skills. Read the "Career Flight Path" at the end of the book to see where this certification fits into your personal certification goals. Remember, in the IT business, if you're not moving forward, you're way behind!

Good luck on your certification! Stay in touch!

Mike Meyers
Series Editor
Mike Meyers' Certification Passport

Core Hardware
Service Technician

Ports and Connectors

ETA	NEWBIE	SOME EXPERIENCE	EXPERT
	2.5 hours	1.5 hours	1 hour

Mastering the craft of the PC technician requires you to learn a lot of details about what sometimes seems to be about 14 zillion individual parts, connections, and settings. Even the most basic PC contains hundreds of discrete hardware components, each with its own set of characteristics, shapes, sizes, colors, connections, and so on. But don't panic! It's actually much simpler than it seems! Most of these components fit into certain classes or groups—hard drives, for example, all use basically the same cables and connections. Additionally, the PC industry only uses a few different types of connections for a large number of different devices, so once you learn one type of connector you'll know how to use it all over the PC!

This chapter covers all the major connectors, plugs, and sockets (and spells out the amazing collection of acronyms and abbreviations used by techs). That's a good bit of knowledge to learn as the A+ exams expect you to recognize a particular part simply by seeing what type of connector attaches to that part. It is handy, although certainly not required, to have a PC close by so you can take off the lid and inspect its insides as you progress. So get thee to a screwdriver, grab your PC, take off the lid, and see if you can recognize the various components as you read about them.

Travel Advisory

If you decide to open a PC while reading this chapter, you must take proper steps to avoid the greatest killer of PCs—*electrostatic discharge* (ESD). ESD simply means the passage of a static electrical charge into your PC. Have you ever rubbed a balloon against your shirt, making the balloon stick to you? That's a classic example of static electricity. When that charge dissipates, you may not notice it happening—although on a cool, dry day, I've been shocked so badly by touching a doorknob that I could see a big, blue spark! If you decide to open a PC as you read this chapter, jump ahead to Chapter 2 to read up on ESD and how to prevent it—the life you save may be your PC's!

Objective 1.01   Common Peripheral Ports

Most techs don't go around saying things like, "just plug that there thing into the thingy on the back of the PC," and you shouldn't either! Every cable used with PCs has a *connector* at the end that ultimately plugs into a corresponding *port* on the PC. Connectors and ports can be either male or female, defined as having pins or holes, respectively.

Assigning System Resources: I/O Addresses and IRQs

Everything in your PC gets assigned a series of I/O (input/output) addresses that enable the CPU to give specific, directed commands. Most devices also get an IRQ (for interrupt request, which controls service requests) that enables them to contact the CPU. This should come as no surprise to you if you've worked with PCs for any length of time. What many new techs do not realize, however, is that all of the standard ports on a motherboard are assigned a set of standard resources, and you can usually *change* those resources if you run into a conflict with another component. Further, most CMOS (Complementary Metal-Oxide Semiconductor) setup utilities enable you to disable the serial and parallel ports to free up resources for the newer style ports, such as USB (universal serial bus) ports. Chapter 4 goes into CMOS settings in more detail, and Chapter 10 discusses system resources in depth.

Serial Ports

Serial ports transfer data 1 bit at a time and are used to connect mice, external modems, and other serial devices to the computer. Serial ports can be either 9-pin or 25-pin male ports, as shown in Figure 1-1. All computers have at least one 9-pin serial port, and many still sport a 25-pin serial port. Older 25-pin ports used only 9-pins at any given time, so manufacturers quickly came up with the less-expensive 9-pin serial ports.

Most motherboards have at least one serial port—Serial Port 1—that gets I/O address 3F8 and IRQ 4 (COM1) by default, but most enable you to assign any COM address/IRQ to the serial port. If this doesn't make sense, check out Chapter

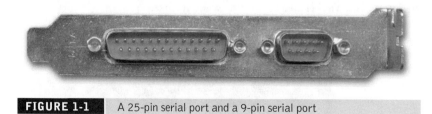

FIGURE 1-1   A 25-pin serial port and a 9-pin serial port

10 for details on I/O addresses and IRQs. Serial ports can communicate with the PC either *synchronously* or *asynchronously*. Synchronous communications send data continuously using dummy bits to keep the data flowing, and asynchronous communications send data intermittently with start and stop bits.

Parallel Ports

Parallel ports are the 25-pin female DB (data bus) ports on the back of your PC, as shown in Figure 1-2. Note the *D* shape of the port, which should help you remember the official term. Parallel ports traditionally get I/O address 278 and IRQ 7 (LPT1), but many modern motherboards give you the option to change these settings. Parallel communications transfers data 8 bits, or 1 byte, at a time.

Exam Tip

Make sure you know that *serial* ports transfer data at a rate of 1 bit at a time, and *parallel* ports transfer data at a rate of 8 bits, or 1 byte, at a time.

Folks often incorrectly refer to parallel ports as printer ports, but many devices other than printers—such as some CD-ROM drives, Zip drives, and scanners—can use parallel ports. Technological advances, such as the ECP (Extended Capabilities Port) and EPP (Enhanced Parallel Port), have kept the parallel port from lumbering into obsolescence. See Chapter 12 for more details.

Objective 1.02

Standard Connectors and Cabling

In addition to the multipurpose serial and parallel ports, many single- or double-function ports appear on the standard PC. These enable you to connect peripherals such as keyboards, monitors, and the like.

FIGURE 1-2   A 25-pin parallel port

The Keyboard

All keyboards enable you to do one thing—give commands to the PC—but they come in an amazing array of styles, configurations, and connections. Keyboards range from simple, flat, 102-key typewriter wannabes to curved, ergonomically correct beauties with 20 extra keys just for daily essentials (such as surfing the Net, kicking off the next MP3 track, and firing up the calculator).

Keyboards connect to the PC with one of three connectors: a round five-pin DIN (for Deutsch Industrie Norm, often called an AT-style connector), an equally round six-pin mini-DIN (also commonly called a PS/2 connector), or a universal serial bus (USB) connector. Figure 1-3 shows the DIN and mini-DIN connectors.

Keyboard connectors are always male and keyboard ports are always female, regardless of the pin type. Many newer PCs can handle several types of keyboard connections through the use of simple adapters. You can plug the keyboard in Figure 1-4, for example, into either a PS/2 port or a USB slot. Even better, the keyboard can act as a USB *hub*. The USB technology is discussed later in this chapter in Objective 1.03.

The Mouse

The mouse also enables you to communicate with your PC. And, like the keyboard, mice come in an array of sizes, shapes, and connectors. Mice connect to the computer with 9-pin or 25-pin serial connectors, called DBs, or with a mini-DIN (PS/2) connector (see Figure 1-5).

Standard serial mice have female connectors that you plug into the male serial port on the back of your PC. Mini-DIN and PS/2 mice have male connectors that you plug into the female mini-DIN port on the back of your PC. USB mice plug into a female USB slot, often located on the back of the PC but sometimes turning up in odd places (such as on the keyboard shown in Figure 1-4).

 **FIGURE 1-3**   A five-pin DIN (top) and six-pin mini-DIN connector

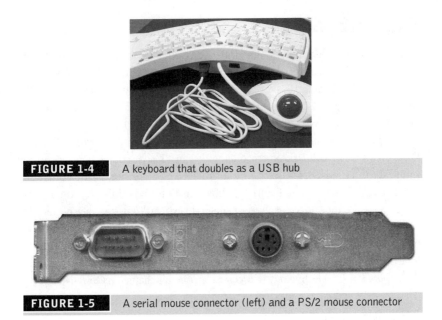

FIGURE 1-4   A keyboard that doubles as a USB hub

FIGURE 1-5   A serial mouse connector (left) and a PS/2 mouse connector

Video

Monitors connect to your PC using a DB video connector. Older CGA (Color/Graphics Adapter) and EGA (Enhanced Graphics Adapter) standard monitors used 9-pin female DB connectors. Most of the monitors you see today are VGA (Video Graphics Adapter), SVGA (Super VGA), or XGA (Extended Graphics Array), and connect to the computer using male DB connectors with 15-pins in three rows, as shown in Figure 1-6.

Exam Tip
VGA, SVGA, and XGA monitors all have the DB connector with 15-pins in three rows.

FIGURE 1-6   A female DB 15-pin connector

Audio

All sound cards have integrated mini-audio ports. Devices such as microphones and speakers connect to the audio ports using mini-audio connectors.

MIDI/Joystick Ports

Many sound cards have a female DB-15 port that supports a joystick or MIDI (Musical Instrument Digital Interface) box for attaching musical instruments to the PC. These devices connect to the port using a male DB connector with 15-pins in two rows.

Exam Tip
Make sure you know that the DB connector with 15-pins in two rows can be used for both MIDI devices and joysticks.

Modems

Modems connect to your telephone line using RJ-11 connectors. RJ-11 connectors use two wires and are identical to telephone connectors (see Figure 1-7). The locking clips on the RJ-11 connectors help secure the cable into the jack, or port. RJ-11 ports look identical to phone jacks and are found on your modem. All modems have at least one RJ-11 port, and many modems have two RJ-11 ports— one for the modem and the other for a telephone, so you can use the telephone line for voice when the modem is not in use.

Network Cards

Network Interface Cards (NICs) enable you to plug network cables into the PC and thus experience one of the fundamentally important sides of computing, the joy of network gaming! Most network cables have either an RJ-45 or BNC connector that connects to the NIC in a corresponding port. Some NICs also have the

FIGURE 1-7 RJ-11 connectors on a modem

older-style AUI (Attachment Unit Interface) ports. RJ-45 connectors are twisted-pair cables that transfer data using four or eight wires. These connectors look like XXL-sized RJ-11 (telephone) connectors and plug in just like a telephone cable. BNC connectors look like cable television connectors. The pin in the center of the BNC connector fits into the hole in the BNC port. After you have connected the BNC connector to its port, you lock it into place by twisting it slightly. The 15-pin AUI ports look exactly like a MIDI or joystick port. Figure 1-8 shows a NIC with both a BNC port (left) and an RJ-45 port.

Exam Tip

Make sure you know the difference between RJ-11 connectors and RJ-45 connectors, and that you can easily differentiate between the two at a glance.

Printers

Printers can use either a Centronics port (shown in Figure 1-9), a USB port, or both. Centronics ports are female ports that look like a slot with two metal clips to lock the connector into place. The male Centronics connector looks like a tab covered with contacts. Technicians often refer to these 36 contacts as *pins*. After

FIGURE 1-8   A NIC with both a BNC port and an RJ-45 port

FIGURE 1-9   A Centronics port

connecting the Centronics connector to the printer, you also need to attach the 25-pin male connector at the other end of the cable to the 25-pin female parallel port on the back of your PC. Techs and users in the know always go with IEEE-1284–compliant parallel cables for attaching parallel devices. Cheap cables can cause problems. See Chapter 12 for the full scoop on printers.

Exam Tip

Use IEEE-1284-compliant cables for laser and ink jet printers.

You can connect USB printers to the PC using a USB cable. The square connector on the USB cable connects to the printer, and the rectangular connector on the USB cable connects to a USB port on the back of your PC, or to a USB hub. USB is discussed in more detail in the following objective.

Objective 1.03

Enhanced Ports and Connectors

Current systems rely heavily on three types of ports for attaching peripherals—USB, FireWire, and SCSI (Small Computer System Interface). Each technology offers dramatic enhancements in plug and play, ease of use, and speed.

USB

USB ports transfer data at speeds up to 12 megabits per second, making them much faster than traditional parallel or serial communications. All Windows operating systems from Windows 95 OEM Service Release 2 (OSR 2) and later support the use of USB. Windows NT does not support USB, but Windows 2000 handles it very well.

Exam Tip

USB is supported by all Windows Operating Systems after Windows 95 OSR 2 but was not supported by the original release of Windows 95 or Windows NT.

USB cables have two connectors. The rectangular Type A connector connects to a USB port or hub. The square shaped Type B connector connects to the USB device.

USB devices are *hot swappable*, which means that you can connect or disconnect them at any time without powering down your PC. USB technology enables you to daisy chain up to 127 devices together using *only one IRQ*. However, for real-life, on-the-job situations it's a bad idea to hit this maximum. Some applications reserve bandwidth, and you could wind up with quite a mess. Too much of a good thing isn't good!

Exam Tip
Remember that you can hot swap USB devices, and can daisy chain up to 127 USB devices together using only one IRQ.

Many current devices connect via USB, such as keyboards, mice, joysticks, microphones, scanners, printers, modems, and cameras. Some devices, such as keyboards, even act as USB hubs with extra USB ports enabling you to connect other USB devices directly to them (that is, daisy chain them).

Travel Assistance
For more information about USB, visit http://www.usb.org.

IEEE-1394

IEEE-1394 (more glamorously known as *FireWire*; the terms can be used interchangeably) is an exciting communications technology created in a joint effort by Apple, Texas Instruments, and the IEEE (Institute of Electrical and Electronics Engineers).

FireWire enables data transfers at speeds up to a blindingly fast 400 megabits per second. Such incredible speeds make this technology perfect for digital video recorders, external hard drives, and other real-time devices. You can add and remove FireWire devices from the PC on the fly, without powering it down.

FireWire technology enables you to daisy chain up to 63 FireWire devices together off a single controller, thus using only one set of IRQs, I/O addresses, and direct memory access (DMA) channels. Moreover, you can interconnect up to 1023 FireWire busses, which in theory means that you could connect 64,449 FireWire devices to a single PC.

FireWire connectors look like slightly smaller USB connectors, but have one rounded side so that you cannot connect them backward, as shown in Figure 1-10.

> **Travel Assistance**
>
> For more information regarding FireWire and the IEEE-1394 standard, visit http://www.ieee.org.

SCSI

Many PCs—especially those on the higher end—have a SCSI (pronounced "skuzzy") connector of one sort or another for attaching SCSI devices. SCSI devices have a variety of interfaces, but the 50-pin SCSI-2 port shown in Figure 1-11 is the most common. The 50-pin connector has fine (read, *easily breakable*) pins that fit only one way into the port. You might also see 68-pin or 25-pin ports on some devices or PCs. To do the amazing variety of SCSI devices and standards justice, they get their own chapter in Chapter 8.

> **Travel Assistance**
>
> For more information on SCSI, check out the SCSI Trade Organization at http://www.scsita.org.

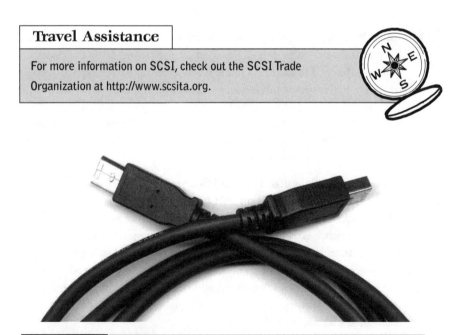

FIGURE 1-10 FireWire, or IEEE-1394, connector

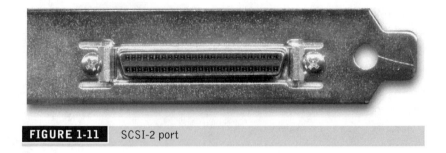

FIGURE 1-11   SCSI-2 port

CHECKPOINT

✔ **Objective 1.01:** Common Peripheral Ports The 9-pin and 25-pin serial ports and the 25-pin parallel ports are used for connecting serial and parallel devices, respectively, to the PC. Serial devices such as mice and modems transfer data 1 bit a time, whereas parallel devices such as printers, scanners, and Zip drives transfer data 8 bits at a time.

✔ **Objective 1.02:** Standard Connectors and Cabling Keyboards connect to the motherboard with 5-pin DIN (AT-style), 6-pin mini-DIN (PS/2), or USB connectors. Mice connect to the 9-pin serial bus in older systems; PS/2 or USB in newer systems. Make sure you remember the 15-pin, three-row DB port is for video; whereas the 15-pin, two-row port is for MIDI devices or joysticks (if on a sound card) or for the ancient AUI network connector. Finally, know the difference between the RJ-11 connectors for modems and the RJ-45 connectors for NICs.

✔ **Objective 1.03:** Enhanced Ports and Connectors USB enables you to hot swap devices and daisy chain up to 127 devices in one PC running Windows 95 OSR 2 or later. The Type A connector goes into the port; the Type B connector goes into the device. FireWire completely eclipses the USB data transfer rate of 12 Mbps, transferring data at a blazing 400 Mbps! Plus, you can hot swap IEEE 1394 devices and daisy chain up to 63 devices off one controller. Finally, the 50-pin port used by SCSI-2 devices and the 68-pin SCSI devices are the most common ones seen on the many SCSI technologies available today.

REVIEW QUESTIONS

1. Which of these connectors can you use to connect a keyboard to a PC? (Select all that apply.)

   A. Mini-DIN
   B. 9-pin serial
   C. 25-pin parallel
   D. USB

2. Which of these connectors can you use to connect an SVGA monitor to a PC?

   A. 25-pin serial
   B. 9-pin serial
   C. 15-pin DB in two rows
   D. 15-pin DB in three rows

3. Which of the following ports can be found on network cards? (Select all that apply.)

   A. BNC
   B. RJ-45
   C. Parallel
   D. USB

4. How many pins does a Centronics connector have?

   A. 10
   B. 25
   C. 36
   D. 34

5. How is data transferred in serial communications?

   A. 10 bits at a time
   B. 1 bit at a time
   C. 1 byte at a time
   D. 16 bits at a time

6. How is data transferred in parallel communications? (Select all that apply.)

    A. 8 bits at a time

    B. 1 byte at a time

    C. 1 bit at a time

    D. 8 bytes at a time

7. If you daisy chain 63 USB devices together, how many IRQs do you need?

    A. 63

    B. 21

    C. 1

    D. 2

8. If you try to connect a USB printer to a friend's PC, and the PC will not recognize the printer, what is most likely the problem?

    A. Your friend is using the first release of Windows 95.

    B. Your friend is using the latest version of Windows, which is incompatible with USB.

    C. The printer is out of ink.

    D. The system files on the PC are corrupted, and Windows needs to be reinstalled.

9. To what does a Type A USB connector connect?

    A. To a USB port on the PC

    B. To a USB device

    C. To a serial port on the back of your PC

    D. To a USB modem

10. What is the top data transfer speed possible under the IEEE-1394 standard?

    A. 50 megabits per second

    B. 100 megabits per second

    C. 400 megabits per second

    D. 400 megabytes per second

11. How many devices can you daisy chain on a single FireWire connection?

    A. 65

    B. 127

    C. 63

    D. 1023

REVIEW ANSWERS

1. **A** **D** Keyboards can use a USB or mini-DIN connector.

2. **D** An SVGA monitor cable has a 15-pin connector in three rows.

3. **A** **B** Network cards can have BNC ports, RJ-45 ports, or both.

4. **C** Centronics connectors have 36 pins or contacts.

5. **B** Serial communications transfer data 1 bit at a time.

6. **A** **B** Parallel communications transfer data 8 bits (1 byte) at a time.

7. **C** Regardless of the number of USB devices that you daisy chain together, you need only one IRQ—that is one of the biggest advantages of USB.

8. **A** Out of all of the possible answers, A is the most likely. The first release of Windows 95 did not support USB.

9. **B** The Type A connector on a USB cable connects only to the USB device. The USB ports on the back of your PC use the flatter Type B connector.

10. **C** The FireWire standard enables data transfers of up to 400 megabits per second.

11. **C** You can daisy chain up to 63 devices on a single FireWire controller.

Maintenance and Safety Precautions

ETA	NEWBIE	SOME EXPERIENCE	EXPERT
	3 hours	2 hours	1 hour

Maintaining a well-functioning PC requires that you do a lot more than running an occasional ScanDisk or deleting temporary Internet files. You need to follow some fairly extensive physical maintenance routines, such as cleaning, bathing, shampooing...err...you get the idea. This chapter goes through the important routines.

Further, although the PC might look like a benign beige box connected to a nice monitor and a quiet laser printer, it can reach out and bite an unwary tech—sometimes with deadly effect. This chapter examines the most dangerous areas of the PC and peripherals, teaching you what to avoid and how to avoid damaging you or the PC. Let's get started.

Objective 2.01   Preventative Maintenance Procedures

To prolong the life of your PC, you simply must inspect and clean it regularly. Cleaning your PC on a regular basis can prevent overheating and ESD.

Local Lingo

ESD   Electrostatic discharge is a quick electrical charge that occurs when two objects with different electrical potentials come into contact with each other. More on this subject in Objective 2.05, later in this chapter.

During the inspection process, look for damaged or cracked components, improperly seated components, frayed cables, and loose connections.

Exam Tip

Make sure you know that regular cleaning of the PC will prolong the life of your components, help to prevent ESD, and help to prevent overheating.

Liquid Cleaning Compounds

Before using any liquid cleaning compound, make sure that your computer is turned off. If the PC has power when you use liquid cleaners, you run the risk of frying or shorting out your components, which is an expensive risk to take. Also make sure that the component you have cleaned with a liquid cleaner is thoroughly dry before turning your computer back on!

Clean or Soapy Water and a Damp Cloth

In some cases, you need only a bit of water and a damp cloth for cleaning chores, such as when cleaning the mouse ball, the outside of the mouse, or the exterior of the monitor or computer case. If water alone cannot do the job thoroughly, you can use mild soapy water on your damp cloth. Make sure that the cloth is damp and not wet and that you do not splash or drip water into your components.

If the keys on your keyboard start to stick or you've spilled a cup of coffee into your keyboard, or, for that matter, you just know that there is a lot of grunge under the keys, you can clean the keyboard with distilled water. Some techs will use a light silicone spray lubricant, but I find that water does nearly as good a job. Keep in mind that if you want your keyboard to work again, you need to make sure that it is unplugged before you clean it and that it is thoroughly dry before you plug it in again. As a general rule, wait at least 48 hours before re-attaching the keyboard to your system.

Denatured Alcohol

The best thing to use for cleaning floppy drive heads is denatured alcohol. But how do you get it in there? You can't just pour it in! You need to use a lint free swab dipped in the alcohol to clean the floppy drive heads, or you can purchase a floppy drive cleaning kit, which almost always comes complete with denatured alcohol. Don't clean the mechanical mechanism with alcohol because the parts are lubricated and the alcohol will dissolve the lubricant.

When cleaning your mouse, you can use a damp cloth to clean the cover and ball, as mentioned earlier, but what about the rollers? Some people pick at the rollers with their fingernails to get all of the grunge off of them, but if you want to keep your fingernails clean you can use a cotton swab dipped in denatured alcohol to help loosen and remove the dirt.

Glass Cleaner

You need to turn your monitor off before cleaning to avoid damage to the screen. Many technicians clean the monitor screen with regular glass cleaner. Under most circumstances, however, water and a damp cloth will do the job just fine. Water is the safest cleaning liquid you can use on a monitor. When cleaning the LCD display screen of a laptop, do *not* use glass cleaner at all. You will melt the screen!

Fabric Softener

Some technicians like to use a mixture of 1 part fabric softener to 10 parts water to clean the plastic casing of their computer components. As a cleaning solution it's not as good as mild soap and water, but as an anti-static solution it's excellent! Use it after the cleaning process to help protect your computer from the harmful effects of static electricity.

Cleaning Contacts and Connectors

To protect your contacts and connectors from becoming dirty, avoid touching them with your hands. Your skin contains natural oils that can leave a residue on contacts and connectors, and that residue needs to be cleaned off. Leaving the contacts untouched will reduce the amount of residue and make them easier for you to clean.

Denatured Alcohol

You should regularly inspect your contacts and clean them with denatured alcohol. Denatured alcohol is the best solution for cleaning the oily residue caused by human oil secretions, and it evaporates, leaving no residue behind.

Erasers

Some technicians use an eraser to rub residue off contacts, but this leaves a residue of its own and may actually rub the contacts right off. If you absolutely must use erasers, make sure you use the white ones, and immediately clean any rubber residue off of the contacts. Never, ever use pink erasers to clean contacts as these contain acids that have the potential to destroy your contacts.

Non-Static Vacuums

Common household dust kills PCs. Throw in some dog and cat hair and you might as well call a priest right now. A dust buildup can cause dreaded static and can cause your components to overheat and become useless. When removing dust buildup from your keyboard, inside your computer's case, and from your components, use a non-static vacuum (shown in Figure 2-1). Many hand-held vacuums are designed specifically for use on PCs. Note that you should definitely *not* use a common household vacuum cleaner. These create static electricity and can toast your PC!

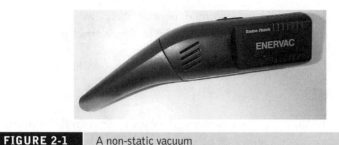

FIGURE 2-1   A non-static vacuum

Compressed Air

Compressed air works well for getting the dust out of power supply fans, expansion slots, and keyboards, but you need to exercise care in using it for blowing the dust off components and the inside of the case. It is not uncommon to blow the dust off one component right onto another component.

You also need to exercise extreme care when using compressed air, because the liquid that compresses the air sits in the bottom of the can and is usually not released unless you turn the can upside down or sideways. This liquid can damage or destroy your components.

Lint-Free Cloths

Lint-free cloths are excellent for removing dust from your computer. The cloths used for cleaning eyeglasses work the best, because they will not scratch surfaces or leave lint behind.

> **Travel Advisory**
>
> Make sure you never use "dry dusting" lint-free cloths and the like for cleaning anything in or on your computer. Cloths such as the *Swiffer Sweeper* do wonders for dusting those hard-to-reach places in your house, but they use static electricity to collect the dust. As you probably know by now, static electricity is computer enemy number one!

Objective 2.02   # Component Protection and Storage

You need to protect your computing environment from any kind of power surges or power sags, as either of these events can cause severe damage to your system. Many things outside the control of normal folks cause sags and surges, such as electrical brownouts and blackouts, spikes on the electrical grid, lightning, and electromagnetic interference.

Brownouts

Power sags are usually caused by brownouts, where your lights may flicker or grow dimmer. In other words, a power sag occurs when the supply of electricity drops dramatically but does not go out completely. When the power or electricity returns to its original level, your computer cannot handle the quick and drastic change and damage may occur.

Blackouts

Power surges are caused when the power or electricity goes out completely and comes back on suddenly. In the event of a power surge, any files that you have not saved will most likely become corrupted or lost forever.

Power Spikes

A power spike is a lot more powerful than a power surge and will almost definitely result in the damage of computer components. The damage caused by a power spike can irreparably affect one or several components.

Lightning Storms

Any time you use your computer, or even leave it plugged in, during a lightning storm you are asking for damage to occur. No commonly available PC accessory can protect your PC from the damage caused by electrical storms. You need to unplug your PC and peripherals with power cords until the storm ceases. Leave no stones unturned: make sure you unplug even your modem, because lightning can travel through the phone lines and cause damage to computers and their components through the modem.

Exam Tip
Make sure you know that in the event of an electrical storm, the only way to protect your system is to completely unplug it, plus all peripherals with external power cords.

EMI

EMI, or *electromagnetic interference,* is caused not by storms, but by noise created by high voltage between two cables or excessively long cables. When EMI occurs, your PC may experience sags and surges in the amount of electricity that is provided to it. The threat of EMI can be combated through the use of cables with a Mylar coating and through a noise filter, which will control the amount of electricity that reaches your PC and remove the EMI. Noise filters can be purchased as stand-alone products or can be incorporated into an uninterruptible power supply (more on those in the next section).

Local Lingo
EMI   Electromagnetic interference occurs when two signals are close enough to each other to interfere with each other.

Saving Your PC from Electrical Problems

Any kind of power failure, sag, surge, or spike can cause irreversible damage to your PC and its components. So you simply must protect your PC from these events! Fortunately, many products on the market can help you prevent these events from damaging your PC. These products are called *uninterruptible power supplies* (UPS) and *surge suppressors.*

Uninterruptible Power Supplies

A UPS helps in blackout situations, during which the electricity cuts off completely for a period of time, and brownouts, during which the electrical supply sags well below the level needed to run your PC. Every UPS has batteries that provide backup power, thus enabling you to save your work and shut down your PC properly. A UPS is thus sometimes called a *battery backup.* Note that a UPS *does not* provide unlimited power so you can keep working while the city lights are out. What it does provide you is a short window of a couple of minutes to save and shut down.

Exam Tip
Don't plug a laser printer into a UPS. They use way too much electricity and will interfere with the primary function of a UPS—shutting down safely.

UPSs come in two main varieties, *standby power systems* (SPS) and *online UPS*. Both of these will protect your system in the event of a power outage or sag, but they work differently and provide different levels of protection.

Standby Power Systems

An SPS has a battery that begins generating power as soon as the unit detects a sag in the supply of electricity. It takes a split second for the SPS to come online, however, and therein lies the main disadvantage to using an SPS. The brief lapse of time could result in your files being damaged before the UPS has kicked in.

Online UPSs

An online UPS, in contrast to an SPS, provides electricity to the PC all the time, using the electricity from the AC outlet simply to recharge its batteries. If you have an electrical brownout or blackout, your PC does not even flinch, and you'll have plenty of time to save and shut down properly. As an added bonus, most online UPS boxes act as *power conditioners* that help your PC run better. Electricity coming from the power company does not come in a single stream of electrons at constant pressure, but rather in gentle fluctuations. Because the online UPS runs the PC from its batteries, the UPS can provide a much smoother flow of electricity than the typical wall socket. An online UPS costs more than an SPS, but in the long run its benefits justify the expense.

Surge Suppressors

Surge suppressors help to absorb power surges so that your computer does not feel their effects. They come as either separate modules or incorporated with a UPS. The best suppressors to purchase are the ones with the lifetime or 10-year guarantee. When purchasing a stand-alone surge suppressor, avoid the cheapest ones. They are usually little more than power strips and provide minimal protection against power spikes.

Exam Tip

It is essential that you know that these suppressors will not prevent power spikes in the event of an electrical storm, and in those instances the best thing you can do to protect your system is to unplug your PC and all peripherals with power cords. Don't forget to unplug the phone line from the modem!

Power surges and sags can wreak havoc on an unprotected PC, and not just in the obvious ways. ("Hey, my PC got struck by lightning and it's a smoking ruin. Do you think it still works?") Common surges and sags can damage power supplies and components, and they can even cause file corruption. The cost of a good UPS and surge suppressor is nothing compared to the cost in time and money caused by lost components or corrupted files that you may have to endure if you don't use either one.

Storing Components for Future Use

When storing your computer components for future use, you still need to prevent them from the hazards of ESD, corrosion, and other damage. You should store your computer components in cool, dry places. Heat or warmth can cause premature aging of your components in much the same way that the sun can cause premature aging of your skin. Moreover, heat can also destroy data that has been stored magnetically and dampness can cause corrosion to your components.

It is important that you store your components away from high-voltage devices, and never store batteries of any kind for long periods of time. Old batteries can leak or corrode.

The safest place to store your components for future use and to protect them from ESD is in an anti-static bag, and for the ultimate in component safety, store the components in their manufacturers' original boxes and packaging.

Exam Tip

Make sure you know that the safest place to store components for future use is in their original packaging or in an anti-static bag.

Objective 2.03   ## Potential Hazards and Proper Safety Procedures

While power issues can cause damage to your PC, many hazards can injure the technician, such as high-voltage shocks or electrical fires. You need to make yourself aware of these hazards and of ways to prevent them from occurring.

High-Voltage Equipment

The capacitors in PC power supplies, monitors, and laser printers carry very high voltages that can easily cause severe bodily injuries. Fortunately, in most cases you will not have to worry about identifying high-voltage equipment because it is usually marked by a bright yellow warning sticker that will leave no question about the voltage levels of the components.

Whenever you work with a piece of high-voltage equipment, always make sure the device is unplugged and that you have removed your anti-static wrist strap (for more information, see "Anti-Static Wrist and Ankle Straps," later in this chapter).

Power Supplies

Whenever you work on your computer, you need to make sure it is unplugged. In the old days, you could leave the PC plugged in and thus ensure excellent electrical grounding, but modern PC motherboards always have a small voltage running when the PC is plugged in. Unplug the PC or you'll likely toast something.

When it comes to power supplies, though, even unplugging them does not make them safe to fix. The safest method of repairing power supplies is not to repair them at all. Better to throw them into the recycling bin and install a brand new power supply. It is extremely risky even to open the case of a power supply, because the capacitors can hold a serious charge even when the power supply is unplugged.

If you *must* work on a power supply, make sure you remove your anti-static wrist strap and discharge the capacitors on the power supply. A little static electricity won't bother a power supply at all, but the metal resistor in the strap can attract voltage (or, more importantly, *amperage*) and lead to bad things—massive jolts through your body can kill, so be careful!

Exam Tip

As the electricians will tell you, it's the amperage (the amount of electricity) that'll get you, not the voltage. Power supplies have relatively low voltages, but high amperage.

Use caution when working on power supplies. You might have the brilliant idea of rewiring a power supply to make it last just a little bit longer until you can get to a store to purchase a replacement. After carefully twisting all the wires and wrapping them in electrical tape, you plug the power supply back into the PC and into the wall. The result would likely be sparks flying from the wall, blue flames coming out of the power supply plug, and a jolt that knocks you clear across the room. (Not that *I've* ever done that!)

Monitors

Never open a monitor unless you know exactly what you are trying to accomplish. The voltages inside can kill you. The capacitors in a typical PC monitor also carry extremely high voltages even when unplugged. In addition to the line voltage and capacitors, the flyback transformer is a dangerous part of the monitor. Don't know what that is? That's a good reason to keep out!

Most adjustments are accomplished through controls on the front of the monitor. Internal adjustments are rare and require plastic tools and schematic layouts. A technician who hasn't been trained in monitor repair should not open one.

Local Lingo

CRT   Cathode ray tubes are used in monitors and television screens and move a beam of light across the back of the screen to produce the image on the screen. Most techs use the terms *CRT* and *monitor* interchangeably.

If you *must* work on a CRT, you have two options. First, you can unplug and discharge the monitor. (Talk to a television repair person for details.) Make your fixes, and then plug in the monitor and turn it on. Repeat as necessary. Or second, you can simply leave the monitor powered up so you can see what you're doing and hopefully *fear* will keep you from doing anything incorrectly. Both methods leave a tad do be desired, don't you think?

Travel Advisory

In either case, never wear your anti-static wrist strap when working on a CRT to avoid the possibility of the voltages being transferred to your body from the CRT. If this happens, you will most likely die.

Fires

Most of us will never experience a PC fire, but we may experience an electrical fire in our homes. It is important that you realize that just as smoke can harm you, it can also harm your PC and its components.

If you do experience a computer fire, or any electrical fire for that matter, never, ever throw water on it, because throwing water on an electrical fire can cause the electrical current to travel up the water and straight into you! Instead, if you experience an electrical fire, make sure you use a type C or a type ABC fire extinguisher.

Exam Tip

Make sure that you know that you need to use a type C or type ABC fire extinguisher to put out a fire in a computer.

In fire situations, people have a tendency to panic, so you need to know the safety procedure at your workplace ahead of time and know the precise locations of the fire extinguishers in case you ever need to use them.

Objective 2.04

Disposal Procedures and Environmental Guidelines

Many computer components, such as batteries, CRTs, chemical solvents, and toner kits (for printers), contain harmful ingredients. Don't throw these items in the garbage! Many of these items can be recycled, and a hazardous waste program can remove most.

Exam Tip

Make sure you know the proper disposal procedures for each of the following items prior to taking the exam.

Batteries

Batteries for the computer often contain lithium, mercury, or nickel-cadmium, which means that if they were to be thrown in the garbage and carried off to a landfill site, they could contaminate the water and soil. You can take batteries to a recycling depot or, in some cases, send them back to the manufacturer.

CRTs

Many CRTs contain lead. If you dump them in the trash (and ultimately in a landfill), you may contaminate the soil and water in your area and poison people. Don't do it! For this reason, CRTs must be recycled or turned over to a hazardous waste program.

Toner Kits and Cartridges

The main concern about the disposal of toner kits and cartridges is that there are so many of them. Most people go through several a year, and if they were all thrown in the garbage, they would fill a landfill site. There are many ways of dealing with toner kits and cartridges.

You can now refill these cartridges, which saves on environmental wear but wreaks havoc on your printer. The printing quality from refilled cartridges is often less than that of new cartridges and the refilled ink can cause the bubble jets on ink-jet printers to clog.

Many manufacturers of these cartridges will buy back the used cartridges, refill them, and then resell them, which is probably the best solution.

Chemical Solvents and Cans

Chemical solvents or cans for PC use (or for any other use, for that matter) contain many harmful chemicals that should not be placed in the ground. For this reason, you simply cannot throw these in the garbage or they may damage the soil and water supply. Instead, chemical solvents and cans must be picked up through a hazardous waste program.

Material Safety Data Sheet

Most compounds, chemicals, and components come with a *Material Safety Data Sheet* (MSDS) that contains information about the product as well as any warnings, safe disposal requirements, and safe methods of transportation. If an item comes without an MSDS, you can obtain one from the manufacturer or locate one on the Internet.

> **Travel Assistance**
>
> For more information about MSDSs, or to search for an MSDS, visit http://www.msdssearch.com/.

Electrostatic Discharge Precautions and Procedures

This chapter has mentioned numerous times about the dangers of ESD, but now it's time for some details. Dust and ESD are the two main enemies of your computer. To maintain your computer and to prolong the life of components, you need to learn about the effects of ESD and how to protect your computer from those effects.

How ESD Is Apparent or Hidden

A prime example of ESD, or electrostatic discharge, is the small shock you receive when you walk across a carpeted floor and then touch an object or a person. Zap! The electrical discharge doesn't do you any lasting damage, but such a seemingly harmless shock will destroy computer components. In fact, even discharges well below the level that you can feel will still damage or destroy PC components—and you won't even know! ("Hey, that modem worked just fine a minute ago.... What could have happened?")

> **Travel Advisory**
>
> To learn more about ESD, visit http://www.ce-mag.com/ esdhelp.html.

Hidden ESD

A real concern, and another good reason to clean your computer regularly, is that the dust buildup on PC components can cause an electrical charge that you probably will not be aware of at the time. In most cases, you will not even be aware that a problem exists until a component begins to behave erratically, and by that point it will be extremely difficult or impossible to pinpoint the original source of the problem.

Catastrophic ESD

Catastrophic ESD causes a computer component to fail immediately. When catastrophic ESD occurs, it will be obvious. You can remove the component and replace it with a new one, and it most likely will not affect any other components.

Degradation

Degradation occurs when the effects of ESD are not immediately apparent in their full force, and the effects gradually get worse and worse. Degradation will cause your components to work erratically and can make the original problem hard to recognize. This condition can affect your other system components and cause their failures also.

Common ESD Protection Devices

Many devices are available that can help to protect your system from the effects of ESD to ensure a longer life for your components. These devices include anti-static wrist and ankle straps, anti-static mats, anti-static floor mats, anti-static bags, and anti-static sprays.

> **Exam Tip**
>
> Make sure you know what ESD is and what devices can protect your system from its effects.

You can help prevent the effects of ESD by grounding yourself by touching the exterior of the PC power supply before touching any of your system's components. Remember, though, that you are only at the potential of the system as long as you hold on to the chassis. When you let go, you can build up potential and cause an ESD event.

> **Local Lingo**
>
> **Electrical potential**   Everything has a certain electrical potential, or how charged it is relative to the *zero ground* of the Earth. Note the term *relative*. If your body has a +3000-volt charge and you touch a component that also has a +3000-volt charge (working in the International Space Station, perhaps?), no damage will occur. As far as you and the component are concerned, you're at the same electrical potential. Touch a component that has a −3000 volt charge, on the other hand, and watch the sparks fly!

Anti-Static Wrist and Ankle Straps

Anti-static wrist and ankle straps are composed of a wire with a 1 megaohm resistor. They keep you at the same relative electrical ground level as the computer components on which you're working, as long as you set them up properly.

Anti-static devices have a strap that you wrap around your wrist or your ankle on one end. Some anti-static straps have a clip on the other end that you can attach to a metal device to ground yourself (see Figure 2-2), or a prong at the other end that you plug into the ground wire of an electrical wall outlet. If you are going to use a strap with a prong, make sure that you fully understand that the grounding wire in the outlet is the round hole—the other two slots are for electricity, and you do not want to plug your ankle or wrist strap into them!

Travel Advisory

If you use a wrist strap, make sure that you remove it before working on or near high-voltage components or devices to avoid a potentially deadly situation.

Anti-Static Mats

Anti-static mats are conductive mats that dissipate ESD. They look much like place mats or those baby-changing mats that come with diaper bags, except they have a small clip attached to them that you can attach to a wrist strap to provide a conductive surface for grounding out ESD. These mats make an excellent place to place your tools and your components when you work on a system.

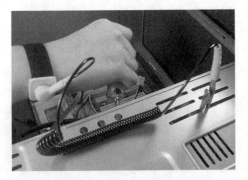

FIGURE 2-2   An anti-static wrist strap grounded to a computer

Anti-Static Floor Mats

Anti-static floor mats look similar to anti-static mats, and they also have the clip that you can attach to a metal object for the purposes of grounding. The main difference is that you need to stand on the floor mats to ground yourself and protect against ESD.

Anti-Static Bags

Placing components in anti-static bags, as mentioned earlier in this chapter, will greatly help your efforts to prevent ESD. Anti-static bags have a special coating or contain small filaments that help dissipate any static charge present when you pick up a component wrapped in such a bag. Better bags resist moisture as well. Always put PC cards and components (drives, RAM, and so on) in anti-static bags. Note that regular plastic or paper bags will *not* protect your components. In fact, if you put a PC component in a plastic baggie, you will almost invariably damage that component. Don't do it!

Anti-Static Spray

Anti-static spray is normally used to avoid static charges in your clothing. Although many people use these sprays to help protect their work areas from the effects of ESD, it is not recommended. If any of the spray touches your components, it could cause damage.

Fabric Softener

As mentioned earlier in this chapter, a mixture of 1 part fabric softener to 10 parts water is an excellent solution to use on a damp cloth to wipe down the plastic surfaces of your PC and monitor. This can protect them from the harmful effects of static.

Potential Dangerous or Hazardous Situations

Temperature and the level of humidity *outside* can dramatically affect the risk of ESD *inside.* If it's cold and dry outside, like an Alaskan winter, and the heater's blowing inside, you are basically a PC-smoking ZAP! waiting to happen. You need to take precautions.

You can protect your system against the effects of ESD by wearing natural fiber clothes (cotton, linen, wool, horsehair) when working on computers. Synthetic fabrics have a tendency to produce static electricity, and you should avoid wearing them. Slinky polyester might be back in style, but save it for the clubs, not the workbench!

You should also wear shoes with rubber soles when working on PCs, and have a work area with a linoleum or uncarpeted floor, because walking on rugs and carpets can generate a great deal of static electricity.

Long hair is another concern when working around computers. If you wear your hair long, you should tie it back before working on a machine so that it does not accidentally get caught or stuck in any components. You should also try to use anti-static smoothing lotions that are now available to reduce the amount of static in your hair. If you don't like the anti-static smoothing lotions, hairspray can help to prevent this problem to a certain extent. One of the authors of this book— the one with the long hair—accidentally took down a whole row of PCs just by walking through an office because of the static electricity in her hair.

If you wear rings and other jewelry, you need to remember to remove them before working on a PC, as these can cause electrical current problems. Another risk of wearing jewelry while working inside machines is that a ring may become stuck on pins or components, which can cause cuts and scratches to your fingers or break off the pins or components.

Finally, to prevent dangers or hazards to yourself, remove your anti-static wrist strap when working on components with high voltages, and never touch a high-voltage device at the same time that you touch a low-voltage device—the two devices could use your body as a conductor to pass electricity.

CHECKPOINT

✔ **Objective 2.01: Preventative Maintenance Procedures**   A solution of mild soap and water does a great job of cleaning plastic surfaces. You should regularly inspect and clean the contacts of your components. The contacts get dirty from the oily residue from your fingers, so you should exercise care in handling components. Denatured alcohol is the best solution to use for cleaning drives and contacts.

✔ **Objective 2.02: Component Protection and Storage**   A UPS protects your system against power sags, and a surge suppressor protects your system from power surges. In the event of a lightning storm, make sure you completely unplug the PC and any peripherals with external power cords. When storing components for future use, make sure to store them in a cool, dry place in anti-static bags or in their original packaging.

✔ **Objective 2.03: Potential Hazards and Proper Safety Procedures**   The capacitors in PC power supplies, monitors, and laser printers carry very high voltages that can cause severe bodily injuries. Don't touch them inside the cases! This is especially true for CRT monitors, which carry deadly levels of electricity even after being unplugged for days.

✔ **Objective 2.04: Special Disposal Procedures and Environmental Guidelines**   Batteries contain nasty chemicals, CRTs contain lead, and even innocuous seeming toner cartridges have environmentally unfriendly chemicals. Always be sure to recycle batteries, monitors, and toner cartridges, or at least have them picked up as hazardous waste.

✔ **Objective 2.05: Electrostatic Discharge Precautions and Procedures**   To help protect your system from the effects of ESD, always use an anti-static wrist strap or ankle strap. Anti-static mats, floor mats, and sprays can protect your work area.

REVIEW QUESTIONS

1. What should you use to clean a mouse ball?

    A. Glass cleaner
    B. Mild soapy water and a damp cloth
    C. Denatured alcohol
    D. Pencil erasers

2. What should you use to clean a keyboard?

    A. Mild soapy water
    B. Tap water
    C. Glass cleaner
    D. Distilled water

3. What will do the best job of completely removing the dust from your computer?

    A. Lint-free cloths
    B. Compressed air

C. Non-static vacuums

D. Paint brushes

4. What type of fire extinguisher should you use to put out a PC fire?

   A. Type A

   B. Type B

   C. Type C

   D. Type D

5. When should you always remove your anti-static wrist strap?

   A. When working around high-voltage devices such as power supplies and CRTs

   B. When cleaning your PC

   C. When changing a toner cartridge in your printer

   D. You should never remove your anti-static wrist strap

6. If you use an anti-static wrist strap with a prong, where do you attach the prong?

   A. In the grounding wire of a wall outlet

   B. In the slot of a wall outlet

   C. In a special hole that is incorporated into every PC case

   D. Into the back of the power supply

7. If you do not receive an MSDS with a product, where can you obtain one? (Select all that apply.)

   A. The Internet

   B. The outside of the box the product came in

   C. The manufacturer

   D. Any good technical book

8. Why should you never wear an anti-static wrist strap when working on power supplies?

   A. The high voltages could injure or kill you

   B. They may get tangled in components

   C. You should always wear an anti-static wrist strap when working on power supplies

   D. The power supply may experience a power surge

9. What are two proper ways to dispose of CRTs?

A. Throw them in the garbage
B. Recycle them
C. Have them picked up by a hazardous waste program
D. There is no proper way to dispose of a CRT

10. What should the conditions be like in the area where you store computer components? (Select all that apply.)

A. Cool
B. Warm
C. Humid
D. Dry

11. When is ESD most likely to occur? (Select all that apply.)

A. When it is cold
B. When it is dry
C. When it is hot
D. When it is cool

12. How can you protect your PC in the event of a lightning storm?

A. With a UPS
B. With a suppressor
C. By unplugging the PC and all of its components
D. By turning off the PC

REVIEW ANSWERS

1. **B** You can clean a mouse ball with mild soapy water on a damp cloth. Make sure the mouse ball is dry before you put it back in the mouse.

2. **D** You should clean a keyboard with distilled water. Tap water may contain iron or other minerals that would be harmful to the circuitry of the keyboard.

3. **C** Non-static vacuums are designed to remove the dust from your system. Using compressed air or dusting with paintbrushes may only move the dust around.

4. **C** You would use a type C fire extinguisher to put out a PC or other electrical fire. If a choice on the exam is a type ABC, that type of fire extinguisher can be used also.

5. **A** You should always remove your anti-static wrist strap when working around CRTs and power supplies. The wrist strap provides a connection from the PC to your body, and wearing a wrist strap while working on either of these components could cause your body to absorb extremely high electrical charges, which could harm or kill you.

6. **A** If you are using an anti-static wrist strap with a prong, the prong should be attached in the wire ground of a wall outlet. The wire ground is the round hole—never place the prong in one of the slots because they contain electricity.

7. **A** **C** If you do not receive an MSDS with a product, you can obtain one from the manufacturer or you can find one on the Internet. Technical books won't have MSDS information, and you won't find it on the outside of the box.

8. **A** You should never wear an anti-static wrist strap when working on power supplies because the voltages are enough to injure or kill you. Wrist straps remove the static charges from the PC and allow your body to absorb them, which means that you could absorb the high electrical voltages of the power supply.

9. **B** **C** The proper way to dispose of CRTs is to either recycle them or have them picked up by a hazardous waste program. CRTs often contain lead, so you can't throw them in a landfill because they could contaminate the water supply.

10. **A** **D** The area where you store computer components should be kept cool and dry. PC components do not like extreme heat, and condensation could cause corrosion.

11. **A** **B** ESD is most likely to occur when it is cold and dry.

12. **C** The only way to protect your system in the event of an electrical storm is to unplug it and all of its components. Simply turning off the machine or using a suppressor will not fully protect your system.

Motherboards, Buses, and Power Supplies

CHAPTER 3

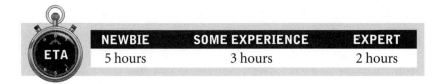

	NEWBIE	SOME EXPERIENCE	EXPERT
ETA	5 hours	3 hours	2 hours

At the heart of every personal computer lives certain core components. The *motherboard* provides the basic structure upon which everything else builds. The *expansion bus* enables you to add cards (and thus functions) to the PC, ranging from the basics of video and networking to the wildest science-fiction components. The *power supply* provides DC current to feed the hungry motherboard and components and makes everything chug along happily. Every good tech needs to understand these three basic ingredients of the PC, including their common variants. Ready?

Common Motherboards: Components and Architecture

Every device in your PC connects either directly or indirectly to the motherboard, the foundation of your computer. Technicians often refer to the motherboard as the systemboard. Both terms are completely interchangeable, and questions on the exam may be worded either way.

Motherboards come in several standardized configurations—called *form factors*—that define the size, location of expansion slots, and so on. Numerous form factors have come and gone, but you need to know about three of them for the A+ exams: AT (Advanced Technology), Baby AT, and ATX (AT Extended).

The form factor of your motherboard also determines the type of case you need for your computer. AT motherboards fit into AT cases, and ATX motherboards fit into ATX cases. When you replace an AT motherboard with an ATX motherboard, you must also replace the case.

Full AT and Baby AT Form Factors

AT motherboards were introduced in 1984 and measure 12×13 inches. The AT motherboard's processor socket is located near the front of the board. The only integrated port on this motherboard is for the keyboard. All other devices connect to the motherboard via cards and expansion slots.

The Baby AT motherboard, shown in Figure 3-1, measures 8.5×13 inches and is laid out exactly like the AT motherboard. Through both AT form factor generations, the location of the screw holes and keyboard port (the same 5-pin DIN socket used as far back as the ancient XT motherboards!) have remained constant, which enables you to fit any AT board into nearly any AT case.

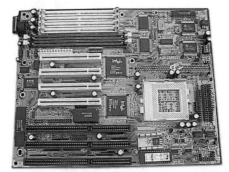

FIGURE 3-1   Baby AT motherboard

> **Exam Tip**
>
> Although vendors sell few AT motherboards today, many systems humming away in offices and homes still have AT motherboards. You need to know about them for common tech work and, consequently, for the A+ Certification exams.

AT power supplies connect to the AT or Baby AT motherboard with one P8 connector and one P9 connector. Each connector has two black ground wires that must be kept together with the other connector's black ground wires when the connectors are plugged in. In other words, all four black wires sit together in the center when the plugs are properly inserted. For more information regarding power supplies, refer to Chapter 11.

> **Travel Advisory**
>
> Keep the black ground wires of the P8 and P9 connectors together or you could damage your motherboard.

ATX

Intel created the ATX motherboard in 1996. The ATX motherboard, shown in Figure 3-2, measures 12×9.6 inches. Although approximately the same size as the Baby AT, the ATX motherboard layout is rotated 90 degrees, and the processor sits

FIGURE 3-2   The ATX motherboard

near the back of the board. ATX boards commonly have numerous integrated ports, including two serial ports, a parallel port, universal serial bus (USB) ports, and mini-DIN connectors for the keyboard and mouse. In fact, the PS/2 connectors provide one of the quickest visual ways to distinguish between ATX and AT motherboards, because the latter use the larger 5-pin DIN.

ATX differs from AT motherboards in a trio of power issues. First, ATX power supplies connect to the motherboard via a single P1 connector, rather than P8 and P9. Second, ATX motherboards implement *soft power*, a trickle of voltage always on the motherboard so you can set them up to do some cool things, such as activate the PC over a LAN or via a modem. Soft power also enables you to turn off the hardware by shutting down the operating system. Very slick! Finally, ATX motherboards introduced support for power management controlled by the system BIOS.

SIMMs and DIMMs

Most form factors contain *Single Inline Memory Module* (SIMM) or *Dual Inline Memory Module* (DIMM) memory slots; some motherboards designed for the Pentium III and Pentium 4 processors have *Rambus Inline Memory Module* (RIMM) slots. For more information regarding RAM and memory slots, please refer to Chapter 6.

Processor Sockets

Every AT, Baby AT, and ATX motherboard has a processor socket or slot to attach a processor to the motherboard. For more information regarding processors and their sockets, please refer to Chapter 5.

External Cache Memory

CPUs use Level 2 (L2) cache memory to store frequently accessed commands and data. Current CPUs have an L2 cache incorporated into the microprocessor package, or *die*, but earlier systems had an L2 cache on the motherboard. Some pre-Pentium systems enabled you to add an L2 cache in slots on the motherboard; early Pentium systems generally had the cache soldered directly on the motherboard.

Objective 3.02

Common PC Expansion Buses

A *bus* is a pathway on the motherboard that enables the components to communicate with the CPU. The A+ certification exams test you on the common buses, plus you need to know these for day-to-day tech stuff: ISA, EISA, VESA local bus, PCI, AGP, and USB. These acronyms and initials are spelled out and described in the following sections.

ISA

IBM introduced what became the *Industry Standard Architecture* (ISA) I/O bus with its first mainstream PC, the 8088. The initial ISA bus was 8-bits wide and offered IRQs 0–7. The 16-bit ISA bus came out in 1984. This newer ISA bus runs at 8.3 MHz and supports IRQs (interrupt requests) 0–15. Although both ISA cards are different sizes, both can be used in a 16-bit ISA slot. Figure 3-3 shows a motherboard with both 8-bit and 16-bit ISA slots. You can still see ISA slots in many computers today that support both 8- and 16-bit cards.

> **Exam Tip**
>
> The 16-bit ISA slots support the use of either 8-bit or 16-bit ISA cards.

EISA

Compaq formed the committee that created the *Extended Industry Standard Architecture* (EISA) as an open standard for bus architecture to compete with IBM's proprietary *microchannel architecture* (MCA). The EISA bus is 32-bits wide, has an

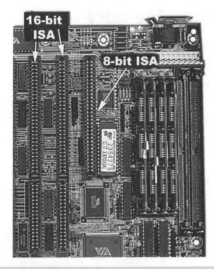

FIGURE 3-3 ISA expansion slots

8.3-MHz bus speed, and supports bus mastering. EISA slots look similar to ISA slots, as you can see in Figure 3-4, and in fact support ISA cards as well as EISA cards.

Back in EISA's heyday, techs loved working with pure EISA systems, because EISA could automatically configure expansion cards when you ran the configuration program. No manual configuration of IRQs or I/O addresses made EISA a sweet bus for its time.

Exam Tip

EISA slots are compatible with both 8-bit and 16-bit ISA cards, although ISA cards do not support burst mode.

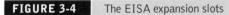

FIGURE 3-4 The EISA expansion slots

VESA Local Bus

The Video Electronics Standards Association created the VESA local bus (VL-bus) technology in 1992 as an enhancement of the ISA bus. The 32-bit–wide VL-bus works with hard drive controllers and increases video performance. The introduction of Windows created the need for more advanced graphics, and running at incredible speeds of 33 MHz, the VL-bus is up to the challenge.

VL-bus slots are similar in size to 16-bit ISA slots and have an extra brown slot at the end. ISA cards are compatible with the VL-bus technology and can be placed in the ISA portion of VL-bus slots (see Figure 3-5).

**VL-Bus
Slots**

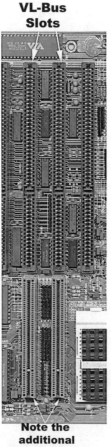

**Note the
additional
32-bit sockets**

FIGURE 3-5   VESA local bus

VL-bus technology has a few quirks, such as a limit to the number of slots on a motherboard and no self-configuration. The VL-bus was built around the 486 processor architecture and ended with that architecture. It went away quickly with the introduction of a new bus architecture, PCI.

PCI

Peripheral Component Interconnect (PCI) was introduced in 1993 and quickly made its way into the hearts of techs. The 32-bit–wide PCI bus runs at half the speed of the processor (up to 33 MHz), which at the time of its creation made this bus an excellent choice for graphics and video. Manufacturers began creating peripherals that could take advantage of these increased speeds. Better still, the PCI bus automatically configures PCI cards, which means the end of messing with manual configuration of IRQs and other resources.

The small, white PCI slots, as shown in Figure 3-6, accept only PCI cards. The PCI bus, however, supports older technologies on the same motherboard. For a few years, it was not uncommon to find motherboards with 8-bit ISA, 16-bit ISA, a couple of VL-bus slots, *and* a few PCI slots!

Nowadays, 3-D graphics and video require even more than the 32-bit PCI bus can offer; manufacturers introduced 64-bit PCI bus to handle the load. Today, primarily only modern server network interface cards (NICs) use the 64-bit PCI bus, because for mainstream video, the bus has been eclipsed by a new bus technology called AGP.

AGP

Accelerated Graphics Port (AGP) was designed specifically for video. A subset of PCI and thus completely plug and play, AGP provides a direct connection between processor and the video card. AGP connects directly to the North Bridge of the Intel 800 series chipset. The bus comes in 32-bit– and 64-bit–wide bus widths. The

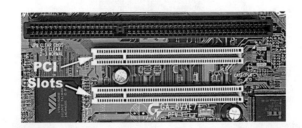

FIGURE 3-6   PCI Expansion slots

32-bit–wide AGP bus operates at the speed of the processor's memory bus (up to 66 MHz) making it perfect for 3-D graphics. The 64-bit AGP 4x bus operates at the speed of the system bus up to 133 MHz. AGP 4x can move data at a rate of 1.07 GB per second using the maximum transfer rate formula.

AGP slots are brown and similar in size to PCI slots, as shown in Figure 3-7. But AGP and PCI cards cannot use the same slots.

Exam Tip

The most common bus architectures that you will see on modern computers are the ISA, PCI, and AGP.

USB

USB differs from the buses discussed so far; it is an external bus that works with the PCI internal bus. Most ATX motherboards have built-in USB ports, or you can install a PCI card that offers the ports. USB (specification 1.0) transfers data at rates of 12 Mbps and enables you to daisy chain up to 127 USB devices together. The newer USB 2.0 specification is even faster.

USB is hot-swappable and supports the Plug and Play technology. You can add and remove USB devices on the fly without opening the case—you simply plug them in and you can use them right away. (For more information on the USB technology, please refer back to Chapter 1.)

Basic Compatibility Guidelines

As a rule, each type of I/O slot requires a specific matching type of expansion card, but some notable exceptions apply. You can install 8-bit ISA cards, for example,

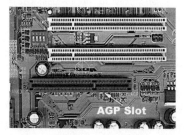

FIGURE 3-7   AGP expansion slot

into 8-bit ISA, 16-bit ISA, EISA, and VL-bus slots. On the other hand, PCI cards and AGP cards, although similar in size, cannot use the same slots. Table 3-1 shows you which expansion cards go with which I/O busses.

TABLE 3-1	Expansion Slot and Card Compatibility						
	8-bit ISA	**16-bit ISA**	**EISA**	**VL-bus**	**PCI**	**AGP**	**USB**
8-bit ISA cards	yes	yes	yes	yes	no	no	no
16-bit ISA cards	no	yes	yes	yes	no	no	no
EISA cards	yes	yes	yes	no	no	no	no
VL-bus cards	no*	no*	no	yes	no	no	no
PCI cards	no	no	no	no	yes	no	no
AGP cards	no	no	no	no	no	yes	no
USB devices	no	no	no	no	no	no	yes

*The front part can plug into an ISA slot, but the cards won't function properly unless plugged into the 32-bit VL-bus slot.

Support for Mass Storage Devices

All current motherboards have built-in connectors and support for mass storage devices such as EIDE hard drives (ATA and Ultra DMA) and ATAPI CD-ROM drives. In the old days before integrated motherboards, you had to install a controller card into an expansion slot to support mass storage drives. For more information regarding hard drive technologies, please refer to Chapter 7.

SCSI Support

Although some high-end motherboards come with built-in support for SCSI drives and devices, for the most part you need to install a SCSI controller card to get SCSI support. SCSI controller cards come in every format, although PCI dominates here as it does in every other type of expansion card. For more information regarding SCSI, please refer to Chapter 8.

Objective 3.03   AT and ATX Power Supplies

The PC can't do much without power, so PC techs need to know about the different types of power supplies and all the connections. This section looks at AT and ATX power supplies and the connections for motherboards and peripherals.

Motherboard Power

CPUs, RAM, chipsets—everything on your motherboard—need electrical power to run. Every power supply provides specialized connections to the motherboard to provide DC electricity in several voltages to feed the needs of the many devices. As mentioned earlier, different motherboard form factors require different connectors.

AT Power Connectors

A pair of connectors—called P8 and P9—link the AT power supply to the AT motherboard. Each of these connectors has a row of teeth along one side and a small guide on the opposite side that help hold the connection in place (see Figure 3-8). Figure 3-9 shows the plug on the motherboard.

| **FIGURE 3-8** | P8 and P9 connectors |

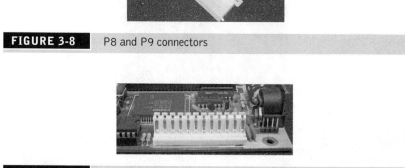

| **FIGURE 3-9** | A standard P8 and P9 connection |

You might find that installing P8 and P9 requires a little bit of work, because of facing, keying, and figuring out which one goes where. P8 and P9 are *faced* (that is, they have a front and a back), so you cannot install them backwards. Sometimes the small keys on P8 and P9 require that you angle the connectors in before snapping them down all the way. Figure 3-10 shows a technician angling in the P8 and P9 connectors.

Although you cannot plug P8 and P9 in backwards, you certainly can reverse them by putting P8 where P9 should go, and vice versa. When connecting P8 and P9 to the motherboard, keep the black ground wires next to each other. All AT motherboards and power supplies follow this rule. Be careful—incorrectly inserting P8 and P9 can damage both the power supply and other components in the PC. Figure 3-11 shows properly inserted P8 and P9 connectors.

FIGURE 3-10   Technician installing P8 and P9 connections

FIGURE 3-11   Installed P8 and P9; note that the black ground wires on the connectors are together

ATX Power Connector

ATX uses a single P1 power connector instead of the P8 and P9 commonly found on AT systems. The P1 connector requires its own special socket on the motherboard. P1 connectors include a 3.3-volt wire along with the standard 5-volt and 12-volt wires (Figure 3-12). The invariably white P1 socket stands out clearly on the motherboard (Figure 3-13). The P1 has a notched connector that allows you to insert it one way only—you cannot install the P1 connector incorrectly. Figure 3-14 shows a properly inserted P1 connection.

FIGURE 3-12   P1 connector

FIGURE 3-13   P1 socket

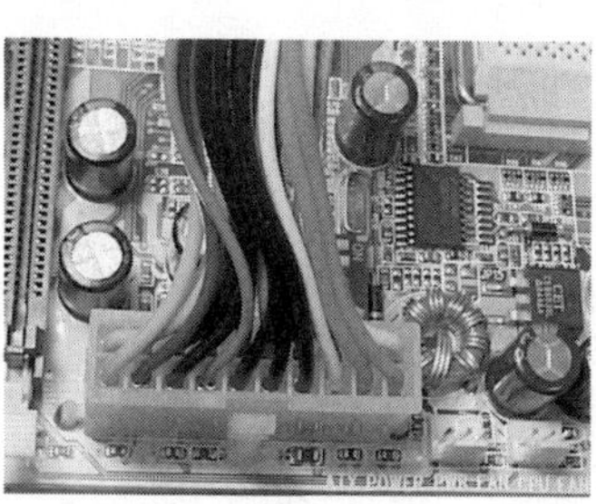

FIGURE 3-14   Properly installed P1 connector

Connections to Peripherals

A power supply has two or three types of connectors that plug into components such as hard drives, floppy drives, CD-ROM drives, Zip drives, and fans. Let's take a look at each of these power connections. Both AT and ATX share these same types of connectors.

Molex Connectors

The most common type of connection is called the *Molex*. The Molex connector is used primarily for devices that need both 12 volts and 5 volts of power (Figure 3-15), such as hard drives and CD media drives.

The Molex connector (Figure 3-16) has *chamfers* (notches), which make for easy installation. These chamfers can be defeated if you push hard enough, so always inspect the Molex connection to ensure proper orientation before you install. Installing a Molex backward will almost certainly destroy the device into which the Molex is connected.

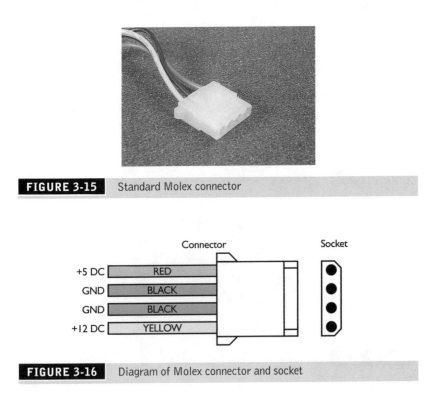

FIGURE 3-15   Standard Molex connector

FIGURE 3-16   Diagram of Molex connector and socket

Mini Connectors

Most systems also provide a *mini* connector (Figure 3-17). The mini is used primarily on 3.5-inch floppy drives, because floppy drive makers have adopted the mini connector for that use. It's very easy to install a mini connector incorrectly, which inevitably results in a smoked floppy drive. Note in Figure 3-18 that the exposed wires are the *top* of the socket. The mini connector installs with the 12-volt yellow wire on the left.

Wattage

Power supplies are rated in watts. A PC requires sufficient wattage for the machine to run properly. The average desktop PC with two hard drives and a CD-ROM will need about 115 to 130 watts while running and up to 200 watts when booting up.

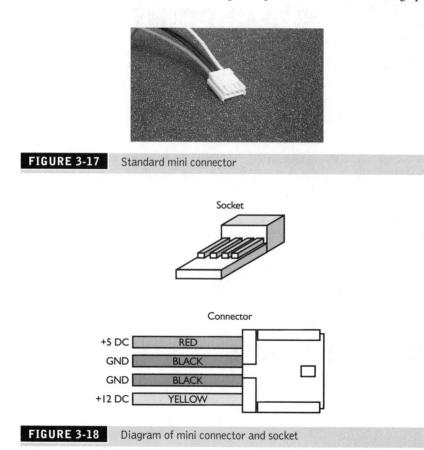

FIGURE 3-17   Standard mini connector

Socket

Connector

+5 DC — RED
GND — BLACK
GND — BLACK
+12 DC — YELLOW

FIGURE 3-18   Diagram of mini connector and socket

Play it safe and buy 230- to 250-watt power supplies. They are by far the most common wattages of power supplies and will give you plenty of extra power for bootup as well as for whatever you add to the system in the future.

Sizes

Power supplies are available in a modest variety of shapes and sizes, usually tied to the form factor. Most desktop and mini-tower PCs use the standard ATX power supply. When replacing a power supply, save time and repeat visits to your friendly neighborhood electronics parts shop—remove the suspect power supply and take it in with you to guarantee that you select the correct replacement.

CHECKPOINT

 Objective 3.01: Common Motherboards: Components and Architecture The two most common types of motherboards are Baby AT and ATX, although the former is on its way out of use. ATX motherboards offer notable advantages, not least being the integrated serial, parallel, and USB ports.

 Objective 3.02: Common PC Expansion Buses   Most current systems offer three expansion buses: PCI for general expansion cards, AGP for video, and USB for external devices. The 32-bit PCI bus enables plug and play expandability and data throughput of 33 MBps.

 Objective 3.03: AT and ATX Power Supplies   AT motherboards require P8 and P9 power connectors, oriented properly with the ground wires next to each other. ATX motherboards use the P1 connector. Hard drives and CD media drives use Molex power connectors; floppy drives use the mini connector.

REVIEW QUESTIONS

1. What could be labeled as the cornerstone of the PC?

    A. I/O buses

    B. Expansion slots

    C. The processor

    D. The motherboard

2. Which of the following motherboards are you most likely to see in modern PCs? (Select all that apply.)

    A. AT

    B. ATX

    C. Baby AT

    D. All of the above

3. If you have a PC with an AT motherboard and case and you decide you would like to upgrade the motherboard, can you replace it with an ATX motherboard?

    A. No

    B. Yes, if you reset the jumpers

    C. Yes, if you add more screw holes

    D. Yes, if you remove the integrated ports

4. What ports were integrated into the AT motherboard?

    A. Serial ports, parallel ports, USB ports, and mini-DIN ports

    B. A keyboard port

    C. Serial ports

    D. A mouse port

5. What type of connector attaches the AT power supply to the AT motherboard? (Select all that apply.)

    A. P1

    B. P2

    C. P8

    D. P9

6. What do you need to remember when connecting the AT power connectors to the motherboard?

    A. Keep the red wires together

    B. Keep the black wires together

    C. Keep the brown wires together

    D. It is impossible to put these connectors in wrong

7. The ATX motherboard was the same size as the Baby AT motherboard, but it was rotated _____ degrees.

   A. 45
   B. 180
   C. 60
   D. 90

8. What type of connector attaches the ATX power supply to the ATX motherboard?

   A. P1
   B. P2
   C. P8
   D. P9

9. What IRQs could an 8-bit ISA card theoretically use?

   A. 0–4
   B. 0–7
   C. 0–15
   D. 2–15

10. What IRQs could a 16-bit ISA card theoretically use?

   A. 0–4
   B. 0–7
   C. 0–15
   D. 2–15

11. What do PCI slots look like?

   A. Small and white
   B. Small and brown
   C. Small and green
   D. Large and black

12. What types of cards can you place in an AGP slot?

   A. Modem
   B. Video
   C. NIC
   D. PCI

13. Which of the following statements is true of USB?

   A. USB enables 12 Mbps data transfers
   B. USB is 16-bits wide
   C. USB slots are small and white
   D. USB slots are backward compatible and can support 8-bit or 16-bit ISA cards

14. Molex connectors supply which two voltages?

   A. 3.3 V and 5 V
   B. 5 V and 7.5 V
   C. 5 V and 12 V
   D. 7.5 V and 12 V

15. Which device typically uses a mini connector?

   A. Floppy drive
   B. Hard drive
   C. CD media drive
   D. Motherboards

REVIEW ANSWERS

1. **D** The motherboard can be considered the cornerstone of the PC. All your systems devices are either directly or indirectly attached to the motherboard, making it the most important part of your PC.

2. **B** **C** Baby AT and ATX motherboards are still used in PCs today. The full AT motherboard has become obsolete.

3. **A** You cannot replace an AT motherboard with an ATX motherboard using the same case. AT motherboards go into AT cases, and ATX motherboards go into ATX cases.

4. **B** The only port integrated into an AT motherboard is the keyboard (five-pin DIN) port. ATX motherboards provided us with more integrated ports.

5. **C** **D** P8 and P9 connectors attach the AT power supply to the AT motherboard. It is important to remember to keep the black ground wires together.

6. **B** You need to keep the black ground wires of the P8 and P9 connectors together, or you could destroy your motherboard.

7. **D** ATX motherboards were roughly the same size as the Baby AT, but rotated 90 degrees. The processor is located near the rear of an ATX motherboard.

8. **A** ATX power supplies connect to AT motherboards with a single P1 connector.

9. **B** 8-bit ISA cards theoretically could use IRQs 0–7, although in practice most cards could use only a couple of IRQs.

10. **C** 16-bit ISA cards theoretically could use IRQs 0–15, although in practice most cards could use only a couple of IRQs.

11. **A** PCI slots are easily recognizable because they are small and white.

12. **B** AGP was developed solely for video; therefore you can place video cards only into AGP slots. AGP ties the video card in with the processor for enhanced graphics.

13. **A** USB enables data transfers of up to 12 Mbps. USB is totally hot-swappable, which means that you can add new devices without opening up your computer.

14. **C** Molex connectors supply 5 V and 12 V DC to peripherals.

15. **A** Floppy disk drives use mini connectors.

CMOS Setup Utility

ETA	NEWBIE	SOME EXPERIENCE	EXPERT
	2 hours	1.5 hours	1 hour

The System BIOS and CMOS setup utility found in some form in every PC provide support for all the essential hardware in the system. As an A+ certified technician, you need to understand BIOS, CMOS, the boot sequence, and more, to be able to troubleshoot any system-level problem that comes your way. This chapter covers BIOS and CMOS in detail. Let's start at the beginning.

BIOS, Hardware, and the Boot Process

Objective 4.01

When you power on your PC, electricity flows into the PC and it wakes up. The system loads a ton of programs to establish communication between all the bits and pieces of metal, plastic, and silicon, and, eventually, the operating system loads and you get to click with your mouse.

This waking up, or to give it a real name, this *boot process*, follows set patterns. First, the *power good* wire wakes up the CPU. The CPU then starts a set of essential programs called the *Basic Input/Output Services* (BIOS). Every modern PC has a special read-only memory (ROM) chip on the motherboard that stores the System BIOS. Many techs (and exams) refer to the System BIOS as the *ROM BIOS* for this reason.

Travel Advisory

Current motherboards use *writable* ROM chips of various styles (EEPROM and Flash ROM being the most common) to store the System BIOS. This might sound like a contradiction in terms, but writable ROM chips enable you to install updated BIOS information without physically replacing the chip. Motherboard manufacturers make new BIOS programs available to make systems more stable and to enhance capabilities.

The System BIOS must load to provide that essential communication among all the internal devices. Unlike a person who wakes up knowing who they are and how many fingers they have, a computer literally rediscovers itself at first power up. Imagine if your body had to grow a new nervous system every morning!

POST

The System BIOS first runs a series of tests on the essential hardware, called the *Power On Self Test* (POST). During this process, the PC communicates what's going on—especially if it discovers problems—through a series of beeps initially or text messages that appear on the monitor if the video card functions properly.

Beep Codes and Error Codes

The beep codes for each PC vary according to the BIOS manufacturer, although you'll find certain codes on most PCs. A single happy chirp at boot up signals all is well and the system is ready to load the operating system. A long, repeating beep often signals a problem with RAM. A series of beeps—one long and three short— usually point to a problem with the video card or connection. The blank screen in the latter moments often helps provide a clue! So many beep codes exist per manufacturer that books have been released to deal primarily with them.

You'll find error codes a little easier to interpret because most BIOS manufacturers use the same codes. As you can see from Table 4-1, once the error number is displayed on your screen, it's easy to determine the offending device.

TABLE 4-1	Series Code Errors You Might Encounter During the POST	

Error Code	Device
100 Series Error (Any error from 100–199)	System Board or Motherboard
200 Series Error (Any error from 200–299)	Memory or RAM
300 Series Error (Any error from 300–399)	Keyboard
400 Series Error (Any error from 400–499)	Monochrome Video
500 Series Error (Any error from 500–599)	Color Video
600 Series Error (Any error from 600–699)	Floppy Drive
1700 Series Error (Any error from 1700–1799)	Hard Drive

> **Exam Tip**
>
> Learn the series errors. On the exam if asked what a 301 error code is, you should remember that everything in the 300 series of error codes would relate to the keyboard.

Once the POST completes successfully, the System BIOS finishes loading to provide basic support for key hardware. Certain aspects of that support need flexibility (for different size hard drives or different RAM speeds, for example). Every PC comes with some form of setup utility that enables you to set up changeable hardware, such as the hard drive. Although many chips and styles of utility programs have appeared on PCs over the years to perform this function, the name of the early chip—and it's a mouthful—has stuck: Complimentary Metal-Oxide Semiconductor. Most techs simply call it the CMOS (*see-moss*) chip.

Objective 4.02   CMOS Setup Utility

The CMOS chip enables you to make changes in a small data file. The BIOS routines access the data file to get a few parameters set properly for the specific hardware presumably in the system at that moment. I say "presumably" because, for the most part, the data file doesn't change automatically. It retains the settings given by a tech. This is important! If you change a piece of hardware supported by the System BIOS, but you forget to make the change in CMOS, the data file provides the BIOS routine concerned with *incorrect information*. This is, as techs like to say, a *bad thing*!

> **Travel Advisory**
>
> When changing hardware in a PC, remember to check the CMOS settings if necessary!

Although the programs that make up the System BIOS do all the heavy lifting in the early stages of the boot process, techs generally focus on the one aspect of that process they can control: setting up the CMOS properly. Let's take a tour of the typical CMOS now.

CMOS Settings

The CMOS chip retains configuration information such as the date and time, and specifics about components common to all PCs, such as serial and parallel ports, keyboard settings, and more. Barring some catastrophic problems, such as a zap of static electricity hitting the motherboard, the CMOS chip retains this information even when no power is running to your PC.

You can access the CMOS by entering a key combination at start up. For key combination instructions, you need to restart your computer and watch the screen at start up. Writing down your current configurations before you make any changes to the CMOS makes it easier to revert back later if you make an error and turn your PC into a giant, ugly paperweight.

Parallel Ports　The CMOS automatically configures the built-in parallel ports in newer systems for the broadest compatibility with parallel devices (such as printers, scanners, Zip drives, and so on), but you can, and often should, make changes. You can change the IRQ and I/O address for a parallel port in the CMOS settings, in case the port isn't working properly or a conflict is present.

The Standard Parallel Port setting works fine for older printers and such, but provides only unidirectional data flow. New, high-speed parallel devices definitely prefer the full-duplex (bi-directional), spanking-fast options of either ECP or EPP mode, which are ten times faster than the traditional bi-directional mode.

Extended Capabilities Port (ECP) enables parallel devices, such as printers and scanners, to access DMA channels. Enhanced Parallel Port (EPP) enables devices to access the DMA channels for devices other than printers and scanners such as LAN adapters or disk drives.

Exam Tip

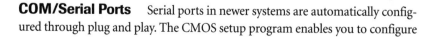
ECP and EPP are both ten times faster than regular bi-directional mode.

COM/Serial Ports　Serial ports in newer systems are automatically configured through plug and play. The CMOS setup program enables you to configure the IRQ and I/O addresses of serial ports if need be. You can also enable or disable serial ports in the CMOS to troubleshoot a device conflict.

Floppy Drive   CMOS enables you to set floppy drive configurations, such as the size and capacity of the floppy drive. You can also configure your computer to boot from the floppy disk first, or to enable or disable the floppy drive controller.

Hard Drive   Newer systems automatically detect your hard drive settings. In older systems, you need to specify heads, cylinders, and sector values in the CMOS.

Memory   Modern PCs detect and configure most RAM settings automatically and you need to do little in CMOS. RAM capacity, for example, isn't a CMOS settings program. The system counts the RAM at startup.

You can enable or disable parity error checking in the CMOS, and set specific RAM timings and other features. Leave most of the RAM settings to people who like to tinker on the PC, to eek out that last little bit of speed. Messing with RAM features in CMOS could cause your system to boot incorrectly or become unstable.

Boot Sequence   After loading and providing support for essential hardware, the BIOS searches for boot devices. By default, on current motherboards, the BIOS searches for the floppy drive first, and then the hard drive, and, finally, the CD-ROM drive. You can configure the search order in the CMOS settings program.

Date and Time   The computer's real-time clock is configured in the CMOS. The *real-time clock* is used by operating systems, as well as date- and time-oriented applications. If this clock starts losing time, you need to replace your CMOS battery.

Exam Tip

When the real-time clock starts losing time, its time to replace the CMOS battery!

Passwords   Setting passwords in the CMOS enables you to control who has access to the computer itself. When a user password is set, the computer won't fully boot for unauthorized persons.

In some CMOS programs, you can also set supervisor passwords that prevent unauthorized persons from accessing the CMOS. If you forget or lose the supervisor password, you'll be unable to access the CMOS. You can clear the supervisor password by setting a jumper on the motherboard or by removing and replacing the CMOS battery. Removing the CMOS battery will also clear any CMOS configurations you set and return you to the default settings, so this should be used as a last resort.

Exam Tip
Setting a jumper on the motherboard or removing and replacing the CMOS battery can clear CMOS supervisor passwords.

Plug and Play BIOS   Plug and Play BIOS settings can be set in the CMOS. You can configure this setting to tell the BIOS to configure the plug and play devices. This setting can also be configured to tell the BIOS the operating system will configure plug and play devices. If you're using a plug-and-play operating system such as Windows, the operating system will always override this setting.

CHECKPOINT

✔ **Objective 4.01: BIOS, Hardware, and the Boot Process**   After powering up, the System BIOS loads and runs the POST to test all the built-in and common devices in the PC. The POST gives you a beep code or text error message in the event of some failure.

✔ **Objective 4.02: CMOS Setup Utility**   The CMOS setup program enables you to modify settings for built-in and common devices, such as serial and parallel ports, floppy and hard drives, and so on. You access CMOS by entering a key combination that's specific to your brand of BIOS. You should write down your CMOS settings before making any changes, as well as update your CMOS settings after adding or replacing any devices in your system.

REVIEW QUESTIONS

1. Which of the following can you configure in the CMOS? (Select all that apply.)

   A. Parallel ports
   B. Serial ports
   C. Hard drive
   D. RAM count

2. When should you update your CMOS settings?

   A. When you boot into Windows
   B. Every time you boot your computer
   C. Every time you defragment your computer
   D. Whenever you replace a device supported by System BIOS

3. What should you do before making any changes to your CMOS settings?

   A. Reboot your computer
   B. Write down the current settings
   C. Remove all the cables from your PC
   D. Replace the BIOS

4. Why might you want to reconfigure the automatically set IRQ or I/O address of a port on your PC? (Select all that apply.)

   A. Device conflict
   B. Troubleshooting
   C. Replacement of the port
   D. There's no way to reconfigure these settings

5. Which of the following devices can take advantage of ECP mode? (Select all that apply.)

   A. Scanners
   B. LAN adapters

   C. Disk Drives
   D. Printers

6. Which of the following devices can take advantage of EPP mode? (Select all that apply.)

   A. Scanners
   B. LAN adapters
   C. Disk drives
   D. Printers

7. If your CMOS isn't capable of auto detecting your hard drive, which of the following values do you need to specify? (Select all that apply.)

   A. Heads
   B. Cylinders
   C. Clusters
   D. Sectors

8. If your RAM doesn't support parity, how should the Parity Error Checking option in the CMOS be set?

   A. Enabled
   B. Disabled

9. By default, which of the following is the first device the BIOS searches for a boot sector at start up?

   A. Hard drive
   B. CD-ROM drive
   C. Floppy drive
   D. All of the above

10. What do you need to do if the clock on your PC starts losing time?

   A. Replace your BIOS
   B. Replace the CMOS battery
   C. Replace your hard drive
   D. Reinstall Windows

11. If a user password has been set in the CMOS, what will happen?

   A. An unauthorized person will be unable to enter the CMOS settings program

B. The computer will not fully boot for unauthorized persons

C. Nothing will happen

D. Only certain settings in the CMOS will be available to unauthorized users

12. If you've set and forgotten a supervisor password for your CMOS, how can you get into the CMOS settings program? (Select all that apply.)

A. Reboot the PC and press F1

B. Set a jumper on your motherboard to clear the password

C. Reinstall Windows

D. Remove and reinstall the CMOS battery

13. At startup, where does your PC receive its first set of instructions?

A. Operating system

B. RAM BIOS

C. ROM BIOS

D. CMOS

14. If you're using Windows and set your Plug and Play BIOS so the BIOS configures your plug and play devices, what will happen?

A. Your BIOS will configure the devices

B. Windows will configure the devices

C. The devices will need to be configured manually

D. None of the above

15. If you boot your computer and receive a 301 error code, which of the following devices has a problem?

A. Floppy drive

B. Hard drive

C. Video

D. Keyboard

REVIEW ANSWERS

1. **A** **B** **C** Parallel ports, serial ports, and your hard drive are all configurable in the CMOS settings program. Your RAM is counted at start up and isn't set in the CMOS settings program.

2. **D** You need to update your CMOS settings whenever you add or replace a hardware device on your system that gets BIOS from the System BIOS.

3. **B** Before making any changes in the CMOS, you should write down the current CMOS settings. Taking the time to do this can save you from having to retrace your steps later.

4. **A** **B** **C** You might want to reconfigure the automatically set IRQ and I/O address settings of your ports if you're experiencing a device conflict, for troubleshooting purposes, or if you need to replace a port.

5. **A** **D** Scanners and printers can take advantage of ECP mode. ECP mode runs at ten times the normal bi-directional mode and allows access to DMA channels.

6. **B** **C** LAN adapters and disk drives take the best advantage of EPP mode. EPP mode runs at ten times the normal bi-directional mode and allows access to DMA channels.

7. **A** **B** **D** If your CMOS cannot auto detect your hard drive, you need to specify the number of cylinders, sectors, and heads.

8. **B** If RAM doesn't support parity, the Parity Error Checking option in the CMOS settings program should always be disabled. If you enable this feature and your RAM doesn't support parity, your computer might not boot properly.

9. **C** By default, at start up, your BIOS searches for your floppy drive first to boot. You can change the boot order in the CMOS, if necessary.

10. **B** If the clock on your PC starts losing time, this is a good indication it's time to change the CMOS battery.

11. **B** If a user password is set in the CMOS, the computer won't fully boot for unauthorized persons.

12. **B** **D** If you've set and forgotten a supervisor password in the CMOS, you can still enter the CMOS by setting a jumper on the motherboard to clear the password or by removing and reinstalling the CMOS battery.

13. **C** At startup, your PC receives its first set of instructions from the ROM BIOS. There's no such thing as the RAM BIOS, which you should remember for the exam.

14. **B** If you're using a plug and play operating system, regardless of the settings made for the Plug and Play BIOS, the operating system will override the settings.

15. **D** All 300 series error codes refer to the keyboard and, therefore, if you receive a 301 error code, this means you're experiencing a keyboard problem.

Processors

ETA	NEWBIE	SOME EXPERIENCE	EXPERT
	2 hours	1 hour	30 minutes

The Central Processing Unit (CPU)—sometimes referred to as the microprocessor or just processor—both directly and indirectly controls all your computer's functions and can be thought of as the brain of the PC. This all sounds well and good, but what exactly does the processor do?

In the human body, the brain transmits information to your different body parts, telling them what you want them to do. The processor in a computer works in much the same manner. The processor communicates information between your devices and tells your computer what you want it to do.

Much like people, processors come in many different sizes, shapes, and speeds. How quickly a person can complete his or her work depends on a combination of energy and skill in the subject matter. The main determining factors for the performance of your computer are the speed and skill of your processor. An older, slower CPU processes information more slowly than the latest generation red-hot screamer of a CPU.

Although many processors exist in the marketplace, CompTIA wants you to know about the processors created by the three main processor manufacturing companies today: Intel, AMD, and Cyrix.

Intel formerly used an x86 naming convention for its processors but, in 1993, because of an increased number of clones, the company began using the Pentium naming convention so it could copyright its processors. AMD followed suit, dropping the x86 system in favor of, first, a *K* naming convention and, subsequently, names (Duron and Athlon). Cyrix continues to use the *M* naming convention to date.

Objective 5.01   Intel Processors

Intel's first processor to break away from the x86 naming convention was the *Pentium* (586) released in 1993. Figure 5-1 shows an early Pentium. Pentium processors had a Dual Independent Bus Architecture and, as a result, were capable of *parallel processing* (using two sets of instructions at the same time). Pentium processors came in such speeds as 60, 66, 75, 90, 100, 120, 133, 150, and 166 MHz.

Pentium processors transmitted data 64-bits at a time, via the 64-bit data bus, located within the processor. The 32-bit address bus of the Pentium processor enabled it to address up to 4GB of memory.

Exam Tip

The Pentium processor was the first PC processor to have a 64-bit data bus.

FIGURE 5-1   An early Pentium

Pentium processors have 16K Level 1 (L1) cache memory, and can also access between 256K and 512K of Level 2 (L2) cache.

Pentium 60 and 66 MHz

Pentium 60 and 66 MHz processors connected to the motherboard via Socket 4. This processor had a 273-pin Pin Grid Array (PGA) and used 5 volts DC. (The term *PGA* is used to explain the pin orientation of a processor.)

Pentium 75–200 MHz

Pentium 75–200 MHz processors came in a 296-pin PGA format and connected the processor to the motherboard via Socket 7. These processors used 3.3 volts DC and could use an active or a passive heat sink.

Intel Pentium Pro Processors

Intel created the *Pentium Pro* in 1995 to compete in the high-end server market. The Pentium Pro wasn't meant to replace the Pentium in the company's mainstream market. This processor had a 387-pin SPGA format and connected to the motherboard via Socket 8. The extra pins on this processor generated a lot of heat and an onboard fan was necessary. Figure 5-2 shows a Pentium Pro.

The Pentium Pro had a 64-bit data bus and a 36-bit address bus. Intel released the Pentium Pro in speeds of 150, 166, 180, and 200 MHz. All speeds used 3.3 volts DC, except the 150 MHz version of the processor, which used 3.1 volts DC. Pentium Pro processors could handle four pipelines simultaneously and, as a result, were capable of performing the equivalent of three simultaneous processes.

FIGURE 5-2   Intel Pentium Pro

Exam Tip

With the Pentium Pro, Intel introduced a 36-bit, rather than a 32-bit address bus into this and future lines of processors—but nobody used the extra wires for addressing memory. For the A+ exams, think in terms of 32-bit RAM support for all Pentium or later Intel processors (up to 4GB) and you'll be safe.

In addition to a 16K L1 cache, the Pentium Pro processor also had an onboard L2 cache of 256K, 512K, or 1MB. This new onboard L2 cache ran at the same speed as the processor and, thus, provided an excellent boost in processing efficiency.

Intel Pentium MMX Processors

Intel created the *Pentium MMX*, which provided 57 more instructions for multimedia and communication capabilities. This processor had a 321-pin SPGA format and connected to the motherboard using Socket 7. Aside from markings on the chip, the MMX version looks the same as the earlier Pentiums.

Exam Tip

MMX (Multimedia Extensions) technology provided 57 more multimedia instructions. All subsequent Intel processors have MMX technology.

This processor was available in speeds of 166, 200, and 233 MHz and ran under two voltages. One voltage drove the processor and the other voltage provided the pins with power.

Additionally, a 32K L1 cache was available onboard and this processor could support 256–512K L2 cache.

Intel Pentium II Processors

Intel first introduced the Pentium II processor in 1997. This processor, as shown in Figure 5-3, had a new package layout or form factor called Single Edge Contact (SEC) and used Slot 1 to connect to the motherboard.

Exam Tip

The first processor to break away from the PGA form factor and use the SEC (Single Edge Contact) form factor was the Pentium II processor.

The Pentium II processor has a 64-bit wide data bus and a 36-bit wide address bus (effectively 32-bit RAM support). Intel shipped the Pentium II in speeds of 233, 266, 300, and 333 with a system bus speed of 66 MHz; and later shipped Pentium II processors that ran on a 100 MHz bus at core speeds of 350, 400, and 450 MHz. Regardless of the speed, and even running on only 3.3 volts DC, all Pentium II processors require special cooling fans. In addition, the Pentium II contains 32K of L1 cache and 512K L2 cache that runs at half the speed of the processor core.

FIGURE 5-3   Intel Pentium II (Photo courtesy of Intel)

Intel Celeron Processors

The Intel *Celeron* was designed to cash in on the popularity of the Pentium II chip. The Pentium II processor was a technological breakthrough at the time, but not everyone could afford it. Intel undoubtedly wanted to dominate the market and introduced a lower-end processor called the Celeron.

Intel released the relatively inexpensive Celeron in speeds of 266 and 300 MHz. The Celeron had a form factor design similar to that of the Pentium II, but without a protective casing, so it's referred to as a Single Edge Processor (SEP) package. Later Celerons come in a PGA package and plug into Socket 370 motherboards. Figure 5-4 shows an SEP Celeron and Figure 5-5 shows the underside of a PGA version.

The original Celeron contained no onboard L2 cache and consumers avoided it like the plague. Intel quickly released a redesigned 300 MHz model with 128MB L2 cache that ran at the same speed as the processor core, called the *Celeron 300A*. The improved Celeron has proved remarkably popular, so Intel has kept the model in production since then, increasing the clock speed to keep up with competing CPUs.

FIGURE 5-4   Intel Celeron (SEP)

FIGURE 5-5   Intel Celeron (PGA)

Intel Pentium III Processors

Intel released the Pentium III processor in 1999 to replace the aging Pentium II. The Pentium III initially came out in a 242-pin SEC package, but Intel eventually released the 370-pin PGA form factor. The 242-pin SEC connected to the motherboard using Slot 1 and used 2 volts DC. The 370-pin PGA connected to the motherboard using the PG370 ZIF socket, often referred to as simply *Socket 370*. Figure 5-6 shows an SEC Pentium III.

Pentium III processors came out in a wide variety of core speeds and motherboard system speeds. Initially released at 450 MHz with a 100 MHz system speed, Intel kept cranking up the speeds until the P-III topped out at 1.3 GHz and a 133 MHz system speed. Other variations exist as well. The Pentium IIIB techz introduced onboard Advanced Transfer Cache (ATC). Usually both technologies were desired to greatly improve speed and performance. Note that, content with mere speed and performance increases, Intel also equipped the Pentium III with an enhanced version of MMX, called SSE (Streaming SIMD Extensions), to handle the many multimedia chores required by the important applications—games!

Pentium III processors have a 64-bit data bus and a 36-bit address bus, like the Pentium II. And, like the Pentium II, the Pentium III can handle up to 4GB of memory. These processors have 32K of L1 cache and 512K of L2 cache.

Travel Advisory

Intel also included a serial number on the Pentium III processors that can be used to track the CPU down to the system it is installed in. Nevertheless, this serial number can be disabled in the BIOS, so it has not posed much of a problem to the consumer.

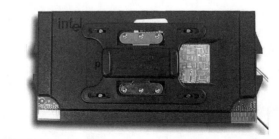

FIGURE 5-6   Intel Pentium III

Objective 5.02 | AMD Processors

Since the days of the Intel 486, Advanced Micro Devices (AMD) has released CPUs to compete with Intel products. In more recent days, AMD has arguably caught up and, in some cases, surpassed Intel in the capability of its products, a feat no one (outside of AMD) would have thought possible even a year or two ago. Let's check out AMD's A+ offerings.

AMD K5 Processors

The AMD K5 processor was released by AMD in 1995 to compete with the Pentium processor. The K5 processor had a 296-pin PGA and used Socket 7 to connect to the motherboard. This processor was available in 75, 90, 100, and 116 MHz and required you to use an active heat sink.

The AMD K5 processor had a 64-bit wide data bus and the 32-bit address bus allowed this processor to address up to 4GB of RAM. This processor used 3.52 volts DC and only supported 8K of L1 cache. Aside from markings on the chip, the K5 looked identical to a Pentium.

AMD K6 Series of Processors

AMD K6 series of processors had a 296-pin PGA form factor and connected to the motherboard using an enhanced socket 7 ZIF socket, called a Super Socket 7. All of the series—K6, K6-2, K6-2+, and K6-III—shared the same physical features of a 64-bit data bus and a 32-bit address bus. Initially available in speeds of 166–266 MHz, these processors used 3.3 Volts DC. By the end of production, the K6 series processors had reached core speeds of 550 MHz with 1MB of onboard L1 cache, and ran off only 2.2 volts DC. Figure 5-7 shows one of the last K6 models, the K6-2+ processor.

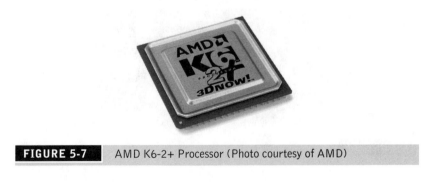

FIGURE 5-7   AMD K6-2+ Processor (Photo courtesy of AMD)

AMD Athlon Processors

AMD didn't sit still while Intel unveiled the Pentium II and Pentium III. Aside from developing the K6 series, in 1999, AMD released the Athlon processor in an SEC form factor—called *Slot A*—to compete directly with Intel's offerings. AMD later released the Athlon in a PGA form factor using Socket A. Slot A and Intel's Slot 1 resemble each other, but are *not* pin compatible. The same is true of Socket A and Socket 370. You cannot swap processors between the current AMD and Intel-specific motherboards. Figure 5-8 shows an early Slot A Athlon and Figure 5-9 shows a Socket A version.

Originally released at speeds of 550, 600, and 650 MHz, the Athlon was the first x86 processor to break the 1 GHz mark and has continued to develop since then. Athlons have 128K of L1 cache and either 256 MB or 512K L2 cache on *die* (that is, integrated into the CPU package).

AMD Duron Processors

AMD released the Duron processor, shown in Figure 5-10, to compete on the lower end of the CPU spectrum with Intel's Celeron CPU. Basically a cut-down Athlon, the Duron has the same 128K of L1 cache, but has only 64K of L2 cache. Other

FIGURE 5-8 Athlon Slot A

FIGURE 5-9 Athlon Socket A

FIGURE 5-10 AMD Duron

improvements (such as a 200 MHz frontside bus) make the Duron slightly faster than a comparative Celeron. The Duron debuted at 600 MHz and has continued to climb in clock speed ever since. Durons come in a Socket A PGA form factor.

Objective 5.03 Cyrix Processors

Cyrix has produced competitive CPUs since the days of the 486 (the predecessor to the Pentium), but concentrates on the lower end of the CPU spectrum. Cyrix had a worthy, pin-compatible alternative to the Pentium, called the 6x86 line, that ranged in P-Rating (that is, effective clock speed) from 166 MHz to 233 MHz.

The chipset giant VIA Technologies bought Cyrix a few years ago and has continued to release lower-end CPUs under the Cyrix label, such as the Cyrix M-II and VIA C3. Both CPUs are pin-compatible with Intel CPUs. The M-II plugs into later Socket 7 motherboards and the C3 plugs into Socket 370 motherboards.

Travel Assistance

For more information about processors, go to http://www.ts.nu/ Components/CPU/processors.html.

CHECKPOINT

✔ **Objective 5.01: Intel Processors**   Early Pentium processors had a Dual Pipeline Architecture and could handle two sets of instructions at once. These processors were the first x86 processors to have a 64-bit data bus, and used 5 volts DC. Pentium Pro processors had Quad Pipeline Architecture and a 64-bit data bus. These were the first PC processors to have an onboard L2 cache.

✔ **Objective 5.02: AMD Processors**   AMD Athlon and Duron processors compete for the high and low end of the current CPU market against the Pentium III (and Pentium 4) and the Celeron CPUs. Athlons come in both Slot A and Socket A configurations; Durons use only Socket A. Slot A looks like Slot 1, and Socket A looks like Socket 370, but neither is pin-compatible with the Intel-based connections.

✔ **Objective 5.03: Cyrix Processors**   Because of cross-licensing, many of VIA Cyrix products fit into Intel-compatible motherboards, a fact that undoubtedly infuriates Intel. From a tech's standpoint, you need to be familiar with the VIA Cyrix processors.

REVIEW QUESTIONS

1. Which of the following CPUs will fit into a Socket 7 ZIF socket?

    A. Pentium Pro
    B. Pentium MMX
    C. AMD K6
    D. Duron

2. Which processor was the first to have a 64-bit data bus?

    A. Pentium
    B. Pentium II

   C. Pentium Pro

   D. Athlon

3. What socket do Pentium Pro processors fit into?

   A. Socket 7

   B. Socket 4

   C. Socket 9

   D. Socket 8

4. Which processor was the first to integrate L2 cache into the processor casing?

   A. Intel Pentium II

   B. Intel Pentium Pro

   C. AMD Duron

   D. Cyrix MII

5. How many additional sets of multimedia instructions does the MMX technology provide us with?

   A. 64 more instructions

   B. 57 more instructions

   C. 32 more instructions

   D. 58 more instructions

6. How do Pentium II processors connect to the motherboard?

   A. Socket 7

   B. Socket 8

   C. Slot 1

   D. Slot A

7. What form factor did the Pentium II processor use?

   A. PGA

   B. SEC

   C. SPGA

   D. All of the above

8. What was the Pentium Celeron Processor created to be?

   A. A low-end AMD Athlon

   B. A low-end Pentium II

   C. A high-end Pentium II

   D. A high-end Pentium Pro

9. Which processor connected to the motherboard using the Socket 370 ZIF Socket?

    A. Pentium Pro
    B. AMD Duron
    C. Pentium II
    D. Pentium III

10. Which processor connects to the motherboard using Slot A?

    A. Pentium II
    B. AMD Duron
    C. Pentium III
    D. AMD Athlon

11. Why did manufacturers begin to integrate L2 cache into the processor casing?

    A. To increase performance and speed
    B. Because the motherboard needed room for other components
    C. L2 cache has always been integrated into processors
    D. To increase prices

12. What was the maximum possible speed of L2 cache on the motherboard?

    A. The processor speed
    B. The system bus speed
    C. The RAM speed
    D. Half the processor speed

13. The Pentium III commonly comes in which of the following technologies? (Choose two.)

    A. IIIA
    B. IIIB
    C. IIIC
    D. IIIE

14. When Intel rereleased the Celeron with onboard L2 cache, what was the new CPU called?

    A. Celeron B
    B. Celeron 300 A
    C. Celeron II
    D. Celeron L2

REVIEW ANSWERS

1. **B** **C** The Pentium MMX and AMD K6 CPUs both fit into Socket 7 ZIF sockets, as do most of the earlier Pentiums, the K5, and the Cyrix 6x86 and M-II processors.

2. **A** The Pentium was the first x86 processor to have a 64-bit wide data bus.

3. **D** Pentium Pro processors connect to the motherboard using Socket 8.

4. **B** The first processor to have an integrated L2 cache was the Pentium Pro. Before this, all L2 cache was located on the motherboard.

5. **B** The MMX technology provides us with 57 more multimedia instructions. MMX was created for multimedia and communications.

6. **C** Pentium II processors connect to the motherboard using Slot 1.

7. **B** The Pentium II Processor had an SEC form factor. This Single Edge Contact design fit into Slot 1.

8. **B** The Intel Celeron Processor was designed to help Intel gain control of the market after the release of the Pentium II. The Pentium II was high end and wasn't affordable. The Celeron was created both to be affordable and to perform well.

9. **D** Pentium III processors connected to the motherboard using the PG 370 ZIF socket. The later Celeron processors also use the Socket 370.

10. **D** The AMD Athlon processor connects to the motherboard using Slot A. Slot A looks similar to Slot 1, but it isn't pin-compatible with Slot 1.

11. **A** Manufacturers began integrating L2 cache into the processor casing to increase speed and performance.

12. **B** L2 cache on the motherboard was limited to the system bus speed.

13. **B** **D** The Pentium III processor could use either or both of the IIIB and IIIE technologies. The IIIB used a 133 MHz system bus and the IIIE had onboard advanced transfer cache.

14. **B** The Celeron processor had no onboard L2 cache when it was first released. When Intel added L2 cache to the Celeron, the new processor debuted as the Celeron 300A.

RAM

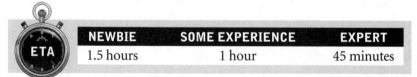

	NEWBIE	SOME EXPERIENCE	EXPERT
ETA	1.5 hours	1 hour	45 minutes

Whenever you run a program on your computer, that program loads into random access memory (RAM) before anything else happens. Double-click the Solitaire icon, for example, and before you can deal the cards, the application must load first into RAM. *RAM* functions for the CPU like short-term or working memory, much the way your own short-term memory enables you to solve problems. A critical piece of information in a book sitting across the room doesn't help you to solve a problem until after you pick up the book and read the information, right? Similarly, until the CPU retrieves the application from the hard drive and puts it into RAM, that application doesn't do anything for you.

The CPU needs RAM, therefore, and the more the merrier (for the most part). With insufficient or minimal RAM, the PC will run poorly and crash more often. A system running Windows 2000 Professional on a Pentium III with only 32MB of RAM, for example, will chug along at a crawl, not because of the CPU, but because of the minimal RAM. Slap 512MB of RAM in that same system and it'll seem so sprightly, you'll need to bolt it to the desk to stop it from dancing away!

Exam Tip

RAM holds running programs.

Objective 6.01   **Common Types of RAM**

Manufacturers originally placed RAM directly onto the motherboard, as shown in Figure 6-1, but this took up too much room and made upgrading difficult. Manufacturers soon discovered that soldering RAM on small cards that sat in special slots on the motherboard took up much less room, and made replacement and upgrading much easier.

RAM comes in a wide variety, defined by physical size, access speed, electrical setup, and width of the bus, measured in bits. The bit width of RAM determines the amount of information your CPU can access from or write to your RAM within one cycle. Let's look at the many types of RAM now.

SRAM (Static RAM)

Static RAM (SRAM) uses several transistors to hold each bit of data in memory. This technology has both advantages and disadvantages. Once you had data in SRAM, the system didn't need to do anything special to keep it there. In technical

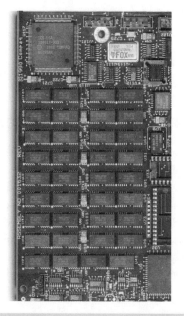

FIGURE 6-1   RAM soldered onto an ancient motherboard, now part of the
Total Seminars Tech Museum

terms, the SRAM memory *registers* needn't be refreshed. Plus, access time was low
and never interrupted by wait states. Because it used so many transistors to keep
each bit of data in place, however, SRAM cost much more than other RAM solutions. Computer manufacturers used SRAM in small quantities, primarily for
cache rather than for main system RAM. Figure 6-2 shows cache modules on a
motherboard.

FIGURE 6-2   SRAM on a motherboard

> **Exam Tip**
>
> The speedy SRAM didn't need to be refreshed, but it cost more than other RAM solutions so was used primarily for cache.

DRAM (Dynamic Random Access Memory)

Dynamic Random Access Memory (DRAM) used only a single capacitor per bit of data and, thus, cost substantially less than SRAM, but had many disadvantages. The DRAM memory registers (that is, the transistors) required periodic refreshing (every few milliseconds) during which the processor couldn't access the RAM (called a *wait state*). Refreshing caused DRAM to be slower than SRAM. Additionally, DRAM used more power than SRAM. Cost drives many things, however, so DRAM became the primary system RAM in all computers for many years. DRAM came in two varieties, such as Fast Page Mode (FPM) and Extended Data Out (EDO). FPM was the standard DRAM until edged out by the better technology of EDO.

> **Exam Tip**
>
> DRAM requires periodic refreshing.

EDO RAM

Extended Data Out RAM (EDO RAM) is a special type of FPM DRAM that works faster by grabbing larger chunks of data to feed to the CPU. Like regular FPM DRAM, EDO is asynchronous and doesn't use the system clock for timing. EDO RAM is sold in 72-pin SIMMs and 168-pin DIMMs, and it has access times of 50–60 nanoseconds.

SDRAM (Synchronous Dynamic RAM)

Synchronous Dynamic RAM (SDRAM)—the current RAM of choice in most systems—offers a great improvement over FPM and EDO RAM, delivering data in high-speed bursts. Plus, SDRAM runs at the speed of the system bus (thus, *synchronously*) and has access times in the 8–10 ns range.

Manufacturers rate SDRAM according to the highest speed data bus it runs on, such as 66, 100, and 133 MHz, and name the RAM accordingly: PC66, PC100, and PC133. This measurement of speed for SDRAM causes some confusion in older techs because until SDRAM, RAM was measured in nanoseconds. Manufacturers now label SDRAM with both a nanosecond and a megahertz rating to avoid any confusion.

Exam Tip

SDRAM transfers data in high-speed bursts and is measured in megahertz, not in nanoseconds.

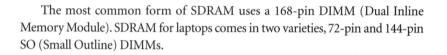

The most common form of SDRAM uses a 168-pin DIMM (Dual Inline Memory Module). SDRAM for laptops comes in two varieties, 72-pin and 144-pin SO (Small Outline) DIMMs.

Local Lingo

Double Data Rate (DDR)   Some current motherboards also support Double Data Rate (DDR) SDRAM, which runs at double the speed of the motherboard system speed (hence, the truth in naming). You'll see DDR SDRAM listed variously as 200 or 266 MHz, or as PC1600 or PC2100.

RDRAM

Rambus Inc. developed Rambus Dynamic RAM (RDRAM). RDRAM uses Rambus channels that have data transfer rates of 800 MHz. If that's not fast enough for you, you can also double the channel width for faster speeds. When the channel rates are doubled, RDRAM can reach data transfer speeds of up to 1.6 GHz. Naturally, RDRAM can only be used in systems that support it.

VRAM (Video RAM)

Video RAM (VRAM) can be found on video cards. VRAM provides faster access than EDO RAM because it can be both read from and written to at the same time, that is, VRAM is *dual ported*. The speed of VRAM makes it perfect for video.

WRAM (Windows Accelerator Card RAM)

Windows Accelerator Card RAM (WRAM) was developed for two reasons: for faster video and to speed up the Windows operating system.

WRAM had all the same features of SRAM. It could read and be written to at the same time, and it was dual ported. In addition, WRAM was faster than VRAM. As video technology became more advanced, it was harder for VRAM to produce high-quality video. WRAM's increased speeds provided excellent video.

WRAM was also created to speed up the Windows operating system. WRAM enabled users to run at faster speeds without replacing motherboards and processors. WRAM speeds up Windows by using the RAM on the card to perform functions specific to Windows.

Travel Advisory

Most video cards now use SDRAM (either single or double data rate) for video RAM.

Objective 6.02 Installing RAM Modules

You need to install RAM properly to have a happily functional PC. Otherwise, when you power on the PC, the monitor will stare blankly at you and the tiny speaker inside the case will wail mournfully—beeeeep-beeeeep-beeeeep-beeeeep-beeeeep—and incessantly until you kill the power. Installing RAM can sometimes be tricky, so here's the scoop on the different RAM modules and what you need to know.

SIMMs (Single Inline Memory Module)

Single Inline Memory Modules (SIMMs) were originally created to free up room on the motherboard. These RAM modules are available in either 30-pin or 72-pin layouts. 30-pin SIMMs put out 8 bits of data on the data bus at one time, which makes them 8-bits wide. They come in 1–16MB sticks. 72-pin SIMMs are 32-bits wide and are available in MB to 64MB sticks. Figure 6-3 shows two SIMMs.

Installing SIMMs is straightforward. You need to insert the SIMM into the memory slot on the motherboard at about a 45-degree angle, as shown in

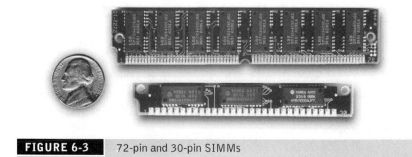

FIGURE 6-3   72-pin and 30-pin SIMMs

Figure 6-4. After you place the RAM in the correct location, you need to snap it into place, so it's upright or perpendicular to the motherboard. The keyed notches on the SIMMs help to ensure a proper insertion.

To remove SIMMs from the memory slots, you need to push the tab on either side out of the way. After moving the tabs, simply pull the SIMM out of the memory slot.

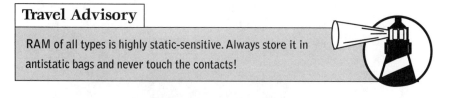

Travel Advisory

RAM of all types is highly static-sensitive. Always store it in antistatic bags and never touch the contacts!

FIGURE 6-4   Installing a 72-pin SIMM

DIMMs (Dual Inline Memory Module)

Dual Inline Memory Modules (DIMMs) for regular desktop PCs look similar to SIMMs, but are wider and longer. DIMMs have 168-pins, are 64-bits wide, and range in capacity from 8MB to 256MB sticks. Figure 6-5 shows a pair of 168-pin DIMMs. The 144-pin SO DIMMs are also 64-bits wide and come in roughly the same capacities as regular DIMMs. The 72-pin SO DIMMs for laptop PCs, in contrast, are only 32-bits wide.

To install a DIMM into the motherboard, you need to drop it into a blank memory slot and press down firmly. When you've pressed the RAM down into the slot firmly enough, the white locking pins snap into place, as you can see in Figure 6-6. DIMMs always have a notch on the pin-edge, so you cannot install them backwards. If a DIMM seems overly resistant to installation, check the orientation of the board!

To remove a DIMM, simply pull back the white locking pins and lift the DIMM right out of the memory slot.

FIGURE 6-5   168-pin DIMMs

FIGURE 6-6   Installing a DIMM

Travel Advisory

Remember to disconnect the AC power when you work with DIMMs or RIMMs (see the following section) on ATX motherboards. ATX motherboards always retain a small voltage when plugged in and plugging in RAM to a *hot* system is a *bad* idea!

RIMM (Rambus Inline Memory Module)

RDRAM comes on Rambus Inline Memory Modules (RIMM). RIMM sticks look like DIMMs, but have 184 pins and are 16–18-bits wide. Figure 6-7 shows a typical RIMM stick. Rambus memory modules can be purchased in 32, 48, 64, 96, 128, and 256MB sizes, and have 600, 700, and 800 MHz data transfer rates.

Installing RIMMs is a straightforward affair, similar to installing a DIMM, but you have to jump through a hoop or two. Some motherboards require you to place the RIMMs in every other slot, for example, if you install only two RIMMs. Further, each unpopulated slot must have a special CRIMM stick installed. A CRIMM is not RAM, but rather a terminator for open slots. Figure 6-8 shows a CRIMM installed next to a pair of RIMM sticks. (Of course, you'd need to add one more CRIMM to make this system work.)

FIGURE 6-7   RIMM

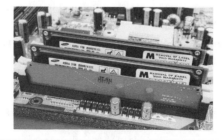

FIGURE 6-8   CRIMM (front) and RIMM

Objective 6.03   Memory Banks

Manufacturers arrange memory slots on motherboards in electronic groups of one, two, or four RAM slots, according to the type of RAM and type of processor. These groupings, called *memory banks,* match the width of the processor's data bus. On a Pentium or later motherboard, for example, each bank is 64-bits wide. So, a single 168-pin DIMM slot makes up a single bank, but you'd need two 72-pin SIMM slots to make a bank. Banking RAM enables the processor to access as much RAM as it can handle at one chunk, thus, making data access as efficient as possible.

The basic rule on *banking* is you need to fill a bank completely with identical (type and speed) RAM modules. Although some manufacturers created motherboards that could run with half banks filled (for example, a Pentium running on a single 72-pin SIMM), most motherboards follow the banking rule closely. Many motherboards won't work properly with two different speed SDRAM DIMMs installed, even though each DIMM makes up its own bank! Don't mix your RAM. You may receive memory errors (the infamous *blue screen of death*) or your PC won't boot properly.

Exam Tip

To determine the number of RAM modules needed to complete a bank, you need to divide the width of the external data bus by the bit width of the RAM. And remember that you should either fill a bank completely or leave the bank completely empty.

Memory banks should be either completely filled or completely empty. But this doesn't mean if you don't have enough RAM to fill even one bank that you can leave it empty. You need to have at least one bank of RAM in your PC for it to boot properly. Trying to boot your PC with absolutely no RAM results in beep codes and error codes.

Objective 6.04   Error-Checking RAM: Parity and ECC

Most RAM does a pretty good, error-free job (unless the chip has been popped with electrostatic discharge, of course) and that suffices for most users. On higher-end, mission-critical PCs such as some servers, however, you often want to build in a little more protection from errors. Some motherboards enable you to install specific error-checking RAM. The two most common styles of error-checking RAM are the old-style parity SIMMs and the newer error-correcting code (ECC) DIMMs.

Parity SIMMs had an extra bit per byte of data that functioned as a low-level error-checking feature. The data that went out was checked against the data that came back and the PC gave you an error message if a parity error occurred. A parity error message on a current system always indicates a problem exists with your RAM or with the CMOS settings for RAM. If you receive a parity message, check your RAM and CMOS.

Parity chips aren't as popular today as they have been in the past. When purchasing RAM, always refer to your motherboard book to determine whether your system requires parity or nonparity RAM chips.

Today's systems either use nonparity RAM or ECC RAM. Think of ECC RAM as a better type of parity RAM. ECC uses much more sophisticated error-checking electronics than parity and it can even correct small data errors on-the-fly without the system even knowing something was wrong! You'll find ECC RAM on some better workstation and server systems.

Objective 6.05 RAM and CMOS

As mentioned in Chapter 4, for the most part the System BIOS autodetects the RAM installed and loads the proper settings. Techs rarely need to mess with any RAM settings in CMOS. As an accomplished A+ tech, on the other hand, you should understand about RAM timings and shadowing.

Many current CMOS setup utilities enable you to alter the speed at which the system accesses RAM, by changing such cryptically sounding settings as the *SDRAM CAS Latency* and the *SDRAM RAS to CAS Delay*. All RAM is designed to function at specific settings, which is why mixing RAM in a system can cause crashes. In the very rare instance where you're stuck in the middle of Antarctica with no hope of getting a RAM replacement and need to make two differently timed RAM sticks play well together, try altering these settings. Increasing the numbers generally slows down access time, which might help.

More commonly, you'll run into the setting to *shadow* the System BIOS and Video BIOS into RAM. Applying this to a system (it's usually applied by default) means to copy the contents of the BIOS (that is, the programs) to system RAM for quicker access. You might also hear a related term, *memory mapped I/O*, in which the CPU uses the same address space to communicate with both main system RAM and to the video card RAM. Occasionally you'll run into a video card that does not like shadowing and thus wreaks all sorts of havoc with system stability, but this is increasingly rare. For the most part, leave the settings to their defaults.

CHECKPOINT

 Objective 6.01: Common Types of RAM   DRAM requires periodic refreshing, unlike SRAM, but costs substantially less than the alternatives. SDRAM improves on EDO or FPM DRAM by running at the speed of the data bus and moving data in high-speed bursts.

 Objective 6.02: Installing RAM Modules   To install SIMMs, DIMMs, and RIMMs successfully, you need to orient the RAM boards properly (remember the notches) and make certain they click into place. A long, repeating beep at startup and a blank screen are signs of a typical oops! moment where you didn't quite get the RAM in place. Disengage the power on ATX systems before working on RAM.

 Objective 6.03: Memory Banks   The basic rule on banking is you usually need to fill a bank completely with identical (type and speed) RAM modules.

 Objective 6.04: Error-Checking RAM: Parity and ECC   The two most common styles of error-checking RAM are the old-style parity SIMMs and the newer error-correcting code (ECC) DIMMs. Parity SIMMs had an extra bit per byte of data that functioned as a low-level error-checking feature. ECC uses much more sophisticated error-checking electronics than parity and can even correct small data errors on-the-fly.

 Objective 6.05: RAM and CMOS   Shadowing means to copy the programs from ROM to RAM for faster access. For the most part, leave the CMOS settings at their defaults.

REVIEW QUESTIONS

1. Which type of RAM never needs periodic refreshing?

    A. SRAM

    B. DRAM

C. FPM RAM

D. EDO RAM

2. Which type of RAM module has 168 pins?

A. SIMMs

B. DIMMs

C. RIMMs

D. None

3. Which RAM module is available with two different numbers of pins?

A. SIMMs

B. DIMMs

C. RIMMs

D. SRAM

4. What RAM module was created to work specifically with RDRAM?

A. SIMMs

B. DIMMs

C. RIMMs

D. EDO RAM

5. Which type of RAM is used mainly for cache memory?

A. SRAM

B. DRAM

C. EDO RAM

D. SDRAM

6. What is stored in RAM?

A. Currently running programs

B. Programs that aren't running

C. Nothing is stored in RAM

D. Hardware information

7. Which type of RAM requires the use of Rambus channels?

A. SRAM

B. DRAM

C. SDRAM

D. RDRAM

8. Which type of RAM is measured in megahertz?

    A. SRAM
    B. SDRAM
    C. DRAM
    D. VRAM

9. Which types of RAM can be both read from and written to at the same time?

    A. DRAM
    B. VRAM
    C. SRAM
    D. WRAM

10. How do you determine how much RAM you need to fill a memory bank?

    A. The width of the external data bus divided by the bit width of the RAM
    B. The width of the external data bus multiplied by the bit width of the RAM
    C. The width of the external data bus plus the bit width of the RAM
    D. The width of the external data bus subtracted from the bit width of the RAM

11. Which of the following statements about memory banks is true?

    A. You should use different sizes of RAM in a memory bank
    B. You should use different speeds of RAM in a memory bank
    C. All RAM in a memory bank should be the same speed
    D. You don't need to fill an entire memory bank

12. What were parity chips used for?

    A. Error checking for RAM
    B. To increase the speed of RAM
    C. To increase the capacity of RAM
    D. To speed up Windows

13. What component determines whether you need to use parity or nonparity RAM?

    A. Processor
    B. Hard Drive
    C. BIOS
    D. Motherboard

REVIEW ANSWERS

1. **A** SRAM requires no refreshing and, thus, incurs no CPU wait states.

2. **B** Dual Inline Memory Modules (DIMMs) have 168 pins. SIMMs have 30 or 72 pins and RIMMs have 184 pins.

3. **A** SIMMs are available in two different pin numbers. SIMMs are available in both 30-pin and 72-pin sizes.

4. **C** RIMMS were created for the insertion of RDRAM. RDRAM requires the use of Rambus channels and RIMM slots on the motherboard.

5. **A** SRAM is used mainly for cache memory because it's extremely expensive, but it doesn't need to be refreshed.

6. **A** Currently running programs are stored in RAM. When you start a program, part of the program is taken from the hard drive and placed into RAM to make your access speeds quicker.

7. **D** RDRAM requires the use of Rambus channels. RDRAM also requires you to have RIMM slots on your motherboard.

8. **B** SDRAM is measured in megahertz. Manufactures started including a nanosecond access speed setting after confusion occurred regarding the speed of the SDRAM.

9. **B** **D** WRAM and VRAM can be both read from and written to at the same time. The increased speed makes these types of RAM excellent for video.

10. **A** The amount of RAM needed to fill a memory bank is determined by the width of the external data bus divided by the bit width of the RAM.

11. **C** All RAM in a memory bank should be the same speed. If it isn't, the PC might not boot properly and it might have memory error messages.

12. **A** Parity chips were used to check RAM for errors.

13. **D** Your motherboard determines whether you need parity or nonparity RAM. If you're unsure, consult your motherboard book.

IDE
Devices

	NEWBIE	SOME EXPERIENCE	EXPERT
ETA	3 hours	2 hours	1 hour

Hard drives and other mass storage devices have used a variety of standards and interfaces over the years, such as IDE, ATA, EIDE, ATAPI, and Ultra DMA. All of them enable you to save programs and data for future use. This chapter reviews the common standards for mass storage devices and gives you details about cabling, interfaces, and setup procedures.

Objective 7.01   IDE Drives

Hard drives used Integrated Drive Electronics (IDE) or AT Attachment (ATA) technology for many years and most current systems offer backward compatibility for IDE drives. IDE and ATA use the same technology standards and the terms are used interchangeably.

Most of the controller electronics on an IDE drive resided right on the drive itself, enabling parallel data transfer between the system and the drive. This was referred to as a *system level interface*. The controller used I/O addresses starting at 1F0 and IRQ 14.

When working on early drives and motherboards, techs had to input the characteristics of the specific drive, such as the number of cylinders, heads, and sectors per track, into CMOS by hand. These characteristics—collectively referred to as the *CHS*—defined the physical geometry of the hard drive. Later motherboard BIOS chips could recognize IDE drives because of the standardized drive technology and set them up in CMOS through a process called *Autodetect*. The largest and last of the IDE drives had the following CHS values: 1,024 cylinders, 16 heads, and 63 sectors per track. Each sector could store up to 512 bytes of data. This put the upper-capacity limit for IDE drives at 528 million bytes, a value more precisely described as 504 megabytes.

Exam Tip

The original IDE specification supported a maximum drive size of 504MB.

Although this was a huge number for its day, computer programmers quickly wrote applications and operating systems to fill that space. Manufacturers responded by developing Enhanced IDE (EIDE) technology for drives and motherboards. (See more about EIDE in Objective 7.02, later in this chapter.)

Connections

IDE devices connected to the motherboard or to a special controller card via a sin-gle 40-pin ribbon cable. A colored stripe down one wire (pin 1) enabled you to orient the cable properly, pin 1 on the drive to pin 1 on the controller. In a rare dis-play of standardization, pin 1 on a hard drive always rested closest to the power connector. A maximum of two IDE devices could be connected in a single com-puter. Figure 7-1 shows the business end of an IDE device.

Jumpers

An IDE controller used jumper settings to distinguish between two drives on the same ribbon cable. Hard drives had two or three standard jumper settings, usually *Standalone*, *Master*, and *Slave*. Some drives had less obvious labels for the settings, such as C/D, which meant you added a shunt on that jumper to make the drive the master and removed the shunt to make it a slave. The only important rule was the same controller couldn't have two master drives or two slave drives.

FIGURE 7-1   40-pin connector of an IDE device connected

Objective 7.02   **EIDE Devices**

Dissatisfaction with the limitations of the IDE standard (two drives, only hard drives, and the 504MB limit) caused manufacturers to create the Enhanced IDE (EIDE) or ATA-2 standard. The new standard could support up to four IDE and/or EIDE drives in one computer. Additionally, EIDE supported AT Advanced Packet Interface (ATAPI) devices, such as CD-ROM drives. Finally, EIDE broke the IDE capacity barrier of 504MB using one of two methods of *sector translation*— logical block addressing (LBA) or enhanced CHS (ECHS or, simply, Large). The ATA-2 standard supports hard drives up to 8.4GB.

While ATA-2 certainly improved IDE dramatically, the amazing growth of hard drive sizes required, yet again, another need to improve the IDE standard. In the mid 1990s, an extension to the ATA-2 standard—called INT13 Extensions— was created. INT13 extensions allow for a maximum hard-drive size of up to 137GB—and we hope this will keep us for a while!

Exam Tip

If you put a drive bigger than 8.4GB into a system and it shows up as 8.4GB, you can still partition and format the drive, making it useful. Without INT13 extension support, however, you won't get to use the full capacity of the drive.

Current EIDE technologies, such as ATA/66 and ATA/100 drives, use DMA to achieve amazing data transfer speeds, in theory up to 100 MB/s (although real performance falls well below that goal). To achieve these high speeds, the drives need both a motherboard or controller card designed for them, and a special, 80-pin ribbon cable. (More on cabling in the following section.)

Travel Advisory

Today's blazingly fast drives run blazingly hot! If you set up a system with more than one hard drive, you will probably need to add an extra case or bay fan to change the air flow within the case to get the drives and cool them down.

Connections and Jumpers

Regular EIDE devices connect to the motherboard or controller card with a 40-pin ribbon cable. All modern motherboards provide two connections, allowing up to four total EIDE devices. Each cable enables you to connect up to two hard drives or ATAPI devices in any combination. Like the IDE standard, EIDE uses jumpers to distinguish between two drives/devices on a cable. You can set the jumpers Standalone (sometimes referred to as 1 Drive), Master, or Slave.

EIDE also follows the same rules as IDE regarding cabling. The red stripe on the cable should go to pin 1 on both the motherboard or controller card and the drive. Further, you cannot place two masters or two slaves *on the same cable*, although having two masters or slaves on *separate* cables is perfectly fine. Figure 7-2 shows master/slave jumper settings on a drive.

You can connect the variously named later EIDE drives (Ultra DMA, ATA 4/Ultra ATA 66, ATA/66, and ATA/100) using a typical 40-pin ribbon cable, but to achieve speeds beyond 33 MB/s these drives require a special EIDE cable with 80 conductors, instead of 40. The 80-conductor cable, as shown in Figure 7-3, still has only 40 pins for data transfer, just like the 40-conductor IDE cable. The difference between the 80-conductor cable and the 40-conductor cable is that every pin in the 80-conductor cable has its own ground conductor.

FIGURE 7-2   Master/slave jumpers on a hard drive

FIGURE 7-3   Two EIDE cables

When you have two EIDE controllers on a motherboard or controller card, the system distinguishes between them as *primary* and *secondary*. The resources for each controller (I/O addresses, IRQ) must be individually configured in CMOS. Each controller can handle up to two devices, jumpered as master, slave, or standalone. Figure 7-4 shows typical EIDE controllers on a motherboard.

In the early days of EIDE, controllers wouldn't handle devices configured as slave if the cable didn't also have a master, and you never set a CD-ROM drive as master and a hard drive as slave. Current motherboards are more forgiving, however. Nearly any configuration other than two masters or two slaves on a cable works fine. For practical purposes, if you have a single hard drive and a single CD-ROM drive in a system with two controllers, make the hard drive master/ standalone on the primary controller and the CD-ROM drive master on the secondary controller.

The Return of Cable Select

Presumably to make the installation of drives simpler for techs, a lot of manufacturers have returned to the old concept of *cable select*. For standard installations of two EIDE devices on a single cable, the placement of the drives doesn't matter as long as you configure the master/slave settings properly. With cable select, in contrast, you must place the slave device in the middle and the master at the end of the cable. Plus, you need to jumper the drives cable select (sometimes abbreviated as *c/sel* or *cs*), rather than master/slave. You'll notice the cable select cables by the tiny hole through one pin.

FIGURE 7-4   Primary and secondary EIDE controllers

Objective 7.03 CMOS AND EIDE

After physically installing the hard drive, its geometry must be entered into the CMOS through the CMOS setup program. Without this information, the hard drive won't work. Before IDE drives, you used to have to take the numbers from the drive and type in each value for the cylinders, heads, sectors/track, landing zone, and write precomp. IDE/EIDE drives can be queried through software and they simply tell the CMOS the correct settings.

Before roughly 1994, you had to use the hard-drive type to install a hard drive. This manual installation process was always a bit of a problem. You had to have the proper CHS values, you had to be sure to type them in correctly, and you had to store these values in case your CMOS was accidentally erased. Today, all PCs can set the CMOS properly by using autodetection. All IDE/EIDE drives have their CHS values stored inside them. Autodetection simply means the CMOS asks the drive for those stored values and automatically updates the CMOS. Two common ways exist to perform autodetection. First, most CMOS setup utilities have a hard-drive type called Auto. By setting the hard-drive type to Auto, the CMOS automatically updates itself every time the computer is started.

Second, most CMOS setup utilities enable you to actively query the drive(s)—to autodetect—which then writes the drive geometry information into CMOS. This avoids the drive query step at boot up, speeding up the boot process a little.

To have drives larger than 504MB, you must have a hard drive that has LBA/ECHS and a BIOS that supports LBA/ECHS. Similarly, to use the full capacity of drives larger than 8.4GB requires BIOS that supports INT13 extensions. If you have an EIDE drive larger than 504MB, you can be sure the drive supports LBA and ECHS. All current BIOS support LBA or ECHS. Just run the autodetection utility.

Modern CMOS setup utilities have numerous settings that affect EIDE drives, especially hard drives. You can enable or disable the primary and secondary controllers, for example, and specify the type of drive (LBA, Normal, or Large). You can use the autodetect feature to set up hard drives. Running autodetect causes the System BIOS to query the hard drive electronics and use optimal settings. Many CMOS setup utilities enable you to toggle Block mode on or off (on by default for newer systems and drives) and even manually configure Ultra DMA modes. For the most part, techs can safely use all the automatic settings with newer systems and drives.

Autodetect provides one other great service for techs, enabling you to learn quickly if you have physical configurations correct. If you install and configure a drive, but it fails to show up in autodetect, the vast majority of the time this means something's wrong with the physical setup. You might have the cable backward, for example, or the drive jumpered incorrectly. You might have forgotten to plug in the Molex connector (not that I've ever done that!). It could mean your drive is truly dead, but always check your connectivity first when autodetect fails.

Objective 7.04 Preparing Hard Drives to Hold Data

Once you install a hard drive with the proper jumpers, cabling, and CMOS settings, you must complete two more tasks before the drive can hold data: partitioning and formatting. Part II of this book covers in detail the specifics of partitioning and formatting in Windows 9*x* and Windows 2000, but here's a quick overview of the process.

Partitioning

To partition a hard drive, technicians use the FDISK command at the command prompt (Windows 9*x*) or the Disk Management tool (Windows 2000). Both enable you to create up to two partitions on a drive—*primary* and *extended*—and then to create *logical drives* in the extended partition. Figure 7-5 shows a screen shot of FDISK. Figure 7-6 shows the Disk Management tool in operation. Both tools enable you to add and delete partitions, and to make *active* partitions (required if you want to boot to a drive).

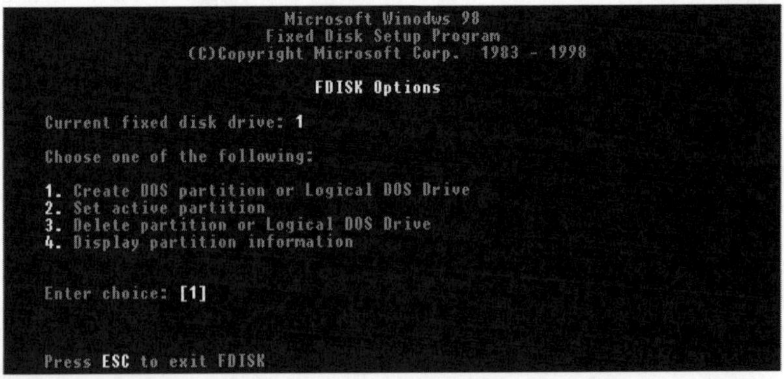

```
                     Microsoft Winodws 98
                   Fixed Disk Setup Program
           (C)Copyright Microsoft Corp.  1983 - 1998

                        FDISK Options

Current fixed disk drive: 1

Choose one of the following:

1. Create DOS partition or Logical DOS Drive
2. Set active partition
3. Delete partition or Logical DOS Drive
4. Display partition information

Enter choice: [1]


Press ESC to exit FDISK
```

FIGURE 7-5   FDISK

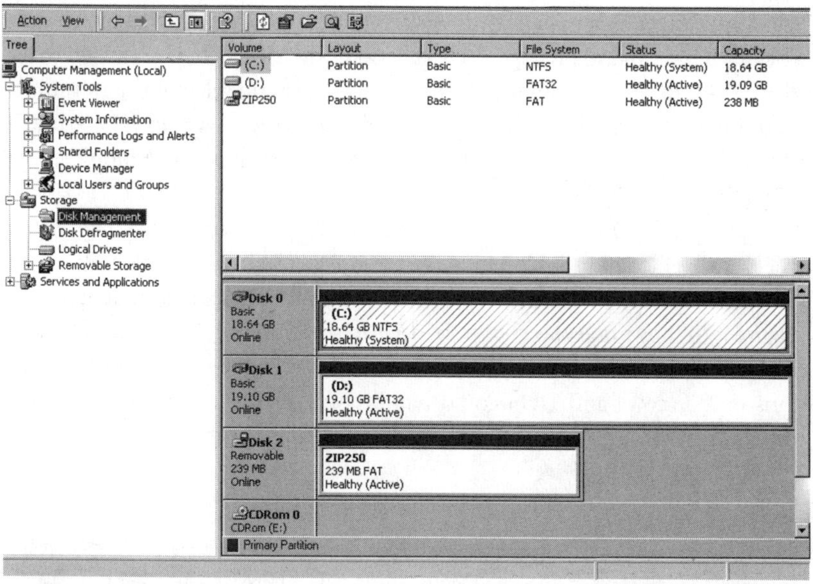

FIGURE 7-6   Disk Management

You can have anywhere from 0–24 logical drives in your system. Drive letters A: and B: are reserved for floppy drives, so hard drive partitions usually begin drive lettering with the C: drive. CD-ROM drives and other EIDE devices need drive letters as well, so you rarely see hard drives taking up all the letters.

Drive letters are assigned automatically at boot up to each hard drive that has a primary partition or a logical drive in an extended partition. Blank drives don't get a letter. Part II of this book goes into much more detail on partitioning.

Travel Advisory

Usually drive letters are assigned sequentially (that is, the first drive gets C:, the next D:, and so on), but Disk Management enables you to assign any available letter to any EIDE device. This can lead to some funky drive settings in Windows 2000!

Formatting

Even after you partition your hard drive into volumes, those volumes cannot store information until you format the drive(s). Formatting creates a filing system for the drive—essentially a big spreadsheet that tracks what piece of data is stored in which location. Each operating system offers several ways to format a drive.

Windows 9x technicians can use the FORMAT command followed by the drive letter at the command prompt, such as C:\>FORMAT D:. Or, you can alternate-click a drive in My Computer or Windows Explorer and select Format from the drop-down menu. Both methods function the same way in Windows 2000 but, in addition, you can select a drive in Disk Management and use the Action menu to format it.

Windows 2000 supports three drive formats, New Technology File System (NTFS), File Allocation Table 32 (FAT32), and FAT. (FAT without a number is the same thing as FAT16.) The previous screen shot of the Disk Management console (Figure 7-6) shows one of each type of drive in a Windows 2000 system. Windows 95B/98/ME support two drive formats—FAT32 and FAT16—while previous versions of Windows and DOS could handle only FAT16. Formatting and File Allocation Tables are discussed in more detail in Part II of this book.

Travel Advisory

Windows 9x systems cannot read anything stored on hard drives formatted as NTFS!

CHECKPOINT

✔ **Objective 7.01: IDE Drives**   IDE hard drives connect to the controller via a 40-pin ribbon cable, pin one of the drive aligned to pin one on the controller. The IDE standard allowed two drives—jumpered master and slave—limited to 504MB capacity each.

✔ **Objective 7.02: EIDE Devices**   EIDE drive connectivity and jumpers mirrors that of IDE, but enabled up to four drives or other EIDE devices to connect to the two drive controllers. LBA and ECHS broke the 504MB limit, and INT13 Extensions broke the 8.4GB limit.

✔ **Objective 7.03: CMOS and EIDE**   Use autodetect to enter CHS data for drives into CMOS, if possible. Autodetect gives you the added bonus of testing your connectivity and jumper settings. If you set things up incorrectly, the drive won't autodetect.

✔ **Objective 7.04: Preparing Hard Drives to Hold Data**   FDISK in Windows 9x and Disk Management in Windows 2000 enable you to create up to two partitions on a drive—*primary* and *extended*—and then to create *logical drives* in the extended partition. A hard drive must have an *active* partition to be bootable. Windows 2000 supports three drive formats: NTFS, FAT32, and FAT. Windows 95B/98/ME support two drive formats: FAT32 and FAT16. Previous versions of Windows and DOS could handle only FAT16.

REVIEW QUESTIONS

1. Which of the following statements regarding master/slave configurations is true?

   A. You need a slave device to have a master device
   B. You need a master device to have a slave device
   C. EIDE systems can have two slaves, but only one master on a single cable
   D. EIDE systems cannot have two masters or two slaves on a single cable

2. What does the FDISK utility do?

   A. Sets up the file allocation tables
   B. Sets up the master/slave configuration
   C. Partitions a hard drive
   D. Separates a hard drive into clusters

3. How many pins on the ribbon cable are used to connect an IDE drive?

   A. 36
   B. 40
   C. 60
   D. 80

4. How many pins does an 80-conductor EIDE cable use for data transfer?

   A. 36
   B. 40
   C. 60
   D. 80

5. If autodetect doesn't see your newly installed hard drive, what can you suspect as the most probable reason?

   A. There's some problem with connectivity or jumper settings
   B. There's some problem with your System BIOS
   C. The hard drive is dead
   D. There's no problem

6. How many IDE drives can you install in a system that uses IDE technology?

   A. 1
   B. 2
   C. 3
   D. 4

7. How many EIDE drives can you install in a system that uses EIDE technology?

   A. 1
   B. 2
   C. 3
   D. 4

8. Where do you place the master hard drive on a standard, non-cable select EIDE cable?

   A. At the end of the cable
   B. In the middle of the cable
   C. It doesn't matter
   D. EIDE cables are for floppy drives

9. Where do you place a slave device on a cable select EIDE cable?

   A. At the end of the cable
   B. In the middle of the cable
   C. It doesn't matter
   D. Slave devices aren't attached to the EIDE cable

10. What was the capacity limitation of the original IDE standard?

   A. 504MB
   B. 512MB
   C. 528MB
   D. 8.4GB

11. The red stripe on the IDE cable corresponds to which pin?

   A. Pin 0
   B. Pin 1
   C. Pin 40
   D. Pin 80

12. How should you configure a new CD-ROM drive on a system using modern EIDE technology?

    A. As master
    B. As slave
    C. As either master or slave; it doesn't matter
    D. A CD-ROM drive can only be set to standalone

13. Which of the following terms is *not* a common EIDE drive jumper setting?

    A. Master
    B. Standalone
    C. Slave
    D. Secondary

14. How many logical drives can you configure using FDISK?

    A. 1
    B. 2
    C. 4
    D. 24

15. What does formatting a hard drive in Windows 9x do?

    A. Sets up the File Allocation Tables
    B. Partitions the hard drive
    C. Sets the master/slave configuration of the hard drive
    D. Partitions the hard drive and creates a logical drive for the boot sector

REVIEW ANSWERS

1. **D** EIDE systems cannot have two masters or two slaves on a single cable.

2. **C** FDISK partitions a hard drive. You can create up to four partitions on a hard drive. You can also create an extended partition with logical drives on it.

3. **B** An IDE ribbon cable has 40 pins.

4. **B** 80-conductor EIDE cables use only 40-pins for data transfers. The difference between the 40-conductor and the 80-conductor cable is each pin in the 80-conductor cable has its own ground wire.

5. **A** Some problem exists with connectivity or jumper settings.

6. **B** You can connect up to two IDE devices in a system that uses IDE technology.

7. **D** You can connect up to four IDE/EIDE devices in a system that uses EIDE technology.

8. **C** With non-cable select cables, the jumper settings on the drives determine whether the drivers are master or slave. Position on the cable doesn't matter.

9. **B** You place a slave drive at the middle of the cable select EIDE cable.

10. **A** IDE had a capacity limitation of 504MB. EIDE technology broke this limitation.

11. **B** The red stripe on the IDE connector corresponds to pin 1.

12. **C** Early EIDE technology required CD-ROM drives to be configured as slave. Modern EIDE controllers can handle CD-ROM drives as master or slave drives.

13. **D** Secondary is a term used for EIDE controllers on the motherboard.

14. **D** You can configure up to 24 logical drives on an extended partition using FDISK. Drives A: and B: are reserved for floppy drives.

15. **A** Formatting a hard drive in Windows 9x sets up the File Allocation Tables. A hard drive must be formatted before information can be stored on it.

SCSI

CHAPTER 8

	NEWBIE	SOME EXPERIENCE	EXPERT
ETA	3 hours	2 hours	1 hour

117

A company called Shugart Systems introduced Small Computer Systems Interface (SCSI) in 1979 as a system-independent means of mass storage. SCSI can best be described as a miniature network inside your PC. While SCSI theoretically supports any type of peripheral device, for the most part, SCSI makes the most sense for mass storage devices, such as hard drives, tape drives, removable drives, and CD-Media.

Objective 8.01   Fundamentals of SCSI

SCSI manifests itself through a SCSI chain, which is a series of SCSI devices working together through a host adapter. The *host adapter* is the device that attaches the SCSI chain to the PC. Figure 8-1 shows a typical SCSI host adapter.

The typical host adapter card has two connections (although one or three connections is not uncommon). The first connector, at the left of the figure, is for devices on the outside (external) of the PC. The second connector is at the top of the figure. This connector is for inside (internal) SCSI connections. All SCSI chains connect to the PC through a host adapter. The SCSI chain extends from the host adapter to all the SCSI devices via special types of cabling (Figure 8-2).

When installing SCSI devices, you need to watch out for the two most important configuration issues: SCSI ID and termination. In most SCSI installations, these two configurations are the only ones you need to consider—failing to do so can virtually insure your SCSI installation will fail—so let's look at each of them.

FIGURE 8-1   SCSI host adapter

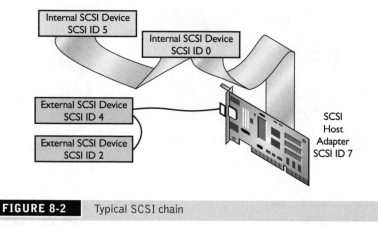

FIGURE 8-2   Typical SCSI chain

SCSI IDs

As mentioned earlier, you can view the SCSI interface as a miniature network within a desktop computer, and the individual components of this network each require a unique identifier: the *ID number*. The values for ID numbers range from 0 to 7 (0 to 15 in some SCSI implementations). The SCSI standard sets the priority of the SCSI IDs at 0 for the highest, and then 1, 2, and so on. A device with a higher priority SCSI ID theoretically will run faster, although in the real world you'd probably never notice.

SCSI ID numbers are similar to many other hardware settings in a PC in that no two devices can share the same ID number. A SCSI device can have any SCSI ID, as long as no two devices connected to a single host adapter share the same ID.

Some conventions exist for SCSI IDs. Typically, most people set the host adapter to 7. You can usually change this, but nothing is gained by deviating from such a well-established tradition. No rules apply to the order of SCSI ID assignment. It doesn't matter which device gets which number—you can leave out numbers and any SCSI device can have any SCSI ID.

You can set a SCSI ID for a particular device by configuring jumpers or switches on that device. All internal SCSI hard drives, for example, use jumpers to set their SCSI IDs. Figure 8-3 shows a hard drive's jumper settings.

Most manufacturers of host adapters use SCSI ID 0 or 7, although a few older adapters often require SCSI ID 6. When in doubt, pick SCSI ID 7. Most modern SCSI host adapters come out of the box preset to 7 anyway.

It's important to note that, even though the SCSI *standard* allows SCSI IDs to run from 0 to 7 or even 0 to 15, not all SCSI *devices* are designed to use every

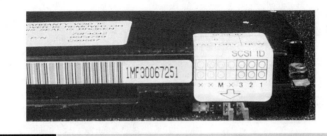

FIGURE 8-3   SCSI hard drive jumper settings

Exam Tip

The term **SCSI ID** is often used interchangeably with the term **SCSI Address**—you'll need to know them both.

Also, no two devices should ever share the same **SCSI ID**. It won't cause any damage, but they won't work!

possible SCSI ID. For example, the Zip drive shown in Figure 8-4 only has settings for SCSI ID 5 or 6.

I always laugh when a student asks, "How do you set SCSI IDs?" This depends on the device you happen to have in your hands at the moment. While most SCSI devices use jumpers, it's not at all uncommon to find devices that use switches, wheels, or even software to set their IDs. The moral of this story: read the instructions that come with each device!

Termination

Whenever you send a signal down a wire, some of that signal reflects back up the wire, creating an echo and causing electronic chaos. SCSI chains use termination

FIGURE 8-4   SCSI Zip drive

to prevent this problem. *Termination* simply means putting something on the ends of the wire to prevent this echo. Terminators are usually pull-down resistors and can manifest themselves in many different ways. Most of the SCSI devices inside a PC have the appropriate termination built in, but you can purchase a special plug that you snap on to the end of the SCSI chain.

The rule with SCSI is you *must* terminate *only* the ends of the SCSI chain. A SCSI chain refers to a number of devices—including the host adapter—linked by a cable. You must terminate the ends of the cable, which usually means you need to terminate the two devices into which the ends of the cable plug. Do not terminate devices that aren't on the ends of the cable. Because any SCSI device might be on the end of a chain, most manufacturers build SCSI devices that can self-terminate (See Figure 8-5).

Exam Tip

Always terminate the ends of a SCSI chain and nothing but the ends of a SCSI chain!

SCSI devices employ a variety of technologies to set termination. Figure 8-6 shows a hard drive that's terminated using a jumper setting.

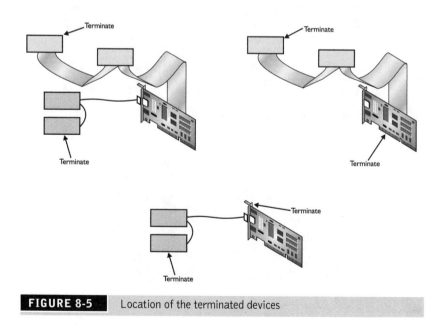

FIGURE 8-5   Location of the terminated devices

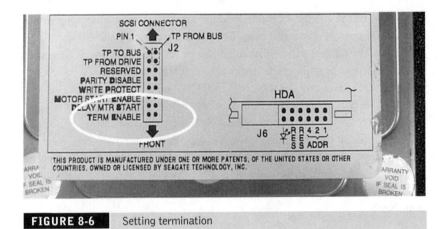

FIGURE 8-6   Setting termination

The hard drive in Figure 8-7 has terminating resistors inserted. They must be removed to unterminate the drive.

The Zip drive in Figure 8-8 uses a slide for termination.

Some host adapters set termination using software. Figure 8-9 shows a typical host-adapter configuration program.

FIGURE 8-7   Hard drive with removable terminating resistors

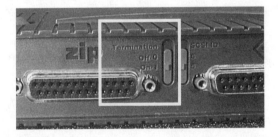

FIGURE 8-8   Zip drive termination

```
════════ Array1000 Family at Bus:Channel 02:A ════════
┌─Configuration ─────────────────────────────────────────────┐
│                                                             │
│  SCSI Bus Interface Definition                              │
│    Host Adapter SCSI ID.............................. 7      │
│    SCSI Parity Checking.............................. Enabled│
│    Host Adapter SCSI Termination..................... Press <Enter>│
│                                                             │
│                                                             │
│  Additional Options                                         │
│                                                             │
│    SCSI Device Configuration......................... Press <Enter>│
│    Array1000 BIOS.................................... Enabled│
│    BIOS Support for Bootable  C-ROM.................. Enabled│
│                                                             │
│                                                             │
│          <F6> - Reset to Host Adpater Defaults              │
└─────────────────────────────────────────────────────────────┘
```

FIGURE 8-9   Software termination setting

Be careful when you terminate a device, because improper termination can, in a few rare situations, cause damage to SCSI devices. (Messing up termination may destroy SCSI equipment! Be sure to read "SE, HVD, and LVD SCSI" later in the chapter.) Unlike setting SCSI IDs, termination can be a little tricky. But before we can discuss the different types of termination options, you must understand the different types of SCSI.

Objective 8.02   SCSI Types

SCSI has been around for quite a while and has seen a number of standards over the years. These different standards are usually called *SCSI types* and sometimes called *SCSI flavors*—the terms are interchangeable. The American National Standards Institute (ANSI) governs the creation and adoption of SCSI types. To date, three SCSI types have been recognized, all of which enjoy large support. Each improved version invariably provides some degree of support for earlier versions.

SCSI-1

The *SCSI-1 standard* defined an 8-bit, 5-MHz bus capable of supporting up to eight SCSI devices, but it was fuzzy in describing many aspects of SCSI. As a result, many manufacturers of SCSI devices had different opinions as to how to implement those standards. So, SCSI-1 was more of an opinion than a standard.

In 1986, SCSI began to appear on IBM-compatible PC machines and everyone seemed to have a proprietary SCSI device. The key word here is "proprietary" (meaning that only the company that produced, designed, manufactured, and sold the device supported it). SCSI was being used in PCs for stand-alone devices, such as hard drives, and each device came with its own host adapter. Makers of SCSI devices had no interest in chaining their particular device with anyone else's—primarily because they assumed (for the most part correctly) their device was the only SCSI device in the PC. Each SCSI device had its own command set and no two command sets were the same. It was often impossible to get one vendor's SCSI hard drive to work with another vendor's SCSI adapter card.

SCSI-1 supported up to eight devices (including the host adapter) on the SCSI chain, but they transferred data through a parallel path only 8-bits wide. For most PCs using SCSI-1 devices, an 8-bit pathway wasn't much of a bottleneck. Although the devices themselves weren't capable of high-speed data transfers, neither were the 80286-based machines of the time. SCSI-1 devices seemed fast by comparison. Plus, the only common hard-drive interface competition was the ST-506 controller, and 8-bit SCSI was far faster!

SCSI-2

In contrast with its predecessor, the *SCSI-2 standard* is quite detailed and applies common rules on command sets and cabling. One of the more important parts is the definition of 18 commands that must be supported by SCSI-2-compliant devices. This set of commands, called the common command set (CCS), made the job of hooking up devices from various manufacturers less of a nightmare. The CCS also introduced new commands for addressing devices besides hard drives, including CD-ROM drives, tape drives, and scanners. Finally, SCSI-2 incorporated a new feature called *command queuing*, which enabled a SCSI device to accept multiple commands at once.

Travel Assistance	
Check out http://www.paralan.com for some great details on the SCSI-2 standard, as well as SCSI in general!	

SCSI-2 also defined permitted types of connectors. Before SCSI-2, no true standard existed for SCSI connectors, although a few types became de facto standards. The new SCSI-2 connector standard ensured that any two SCSI-2-compliant devices could be physically connected. SCSI-2 also provided a more detailed specification for terminations.

The plethora of data bus widths and data transfer speeds is the most confusing part of the SCSI-2 standard. SCSI-2 defined two optional 16-bit and 32-bit busses called *wide SCSI*, and a new, optional 10-MHz speed called *fast SCSI*. SCSI-2 devices could now be 8-bit (narrow), 16-bit (wide), or 32-bit (also called *wide*), and they could be 5 MHz (slow, the standard) or 10 MHz (fast). This adds up to six subflavors of SCSI-2. Table 8-1 shows the various combinations, plus the SCSI-1 standard for comparison.

TABLE 8-1 SCSI Bus Widths and Speeds		
SCSI Type/Bit Width	**5MHz (Standard)**	**10 MHz (Fast)**
SCSI-1: 8-bit	5 MB/s	NA
SCSI-2: 8-bit	5 MB/s	10 MB/s
SCSI-2: 16-bit (wide)	10 MB/s	20 MB/s
SCSI-2: 32-bit (wide)	20 MB/s	40 MB/s

Even though SCSI-2 defined a 32-bit SCSI bus, it was almost completely ignored by the industry because of its high cost and a lack of demand. In the real world, wide SCSI means 16 bits wide.

Fast SCSI-2 transfers data in fast synchronous mode, meaning the SCSI device being talked to (the target) doesn't have to acknowledge (ack) every individual request (req) for data from the host adapter (initiator). Using this mode doubles the transfer speed, from approximately 5–10 MB/s for narrow; 10–20 MB/s for wide. However, experience has shown that external fast SCSI devices rarely provide this "fast" performance unless the SCSI cable provides proper shielding and electrical impedance or "load." Cables that do provide proper shielding and load are generally a bit more expensive, but you need them to achieve true "fast" performance.

SE, HVD, and LVD SCSI

SCSI-1 devices were all single-ended (SE), meaning they communicated each bit of information through only one wire. This one wire was measured or referenced against the common ground provided by the metal chassis and, in turn, by the power supply of the system. The big problem with SE SCSI is line noise, called *common-mode noise*, usually spread through either the electrical power cables or the data cable. An SE SCSI device is vulnerable to common-mode noise because it can't tell the difference between valid data and noise. When noise invades the data stream, the devices must resend the data. The amount of noise generated grows dramatically with the length of a SCSI cable, limiting the total length of an SE SCSI chain to about six meters, depending on the type of SCSI.

To achieve much longer SCSI chains, SCSI-2 offered an optional solution called High Voltage Differential (HVD) SCSI (formerly called differential SCSI). HVD devices employ two wires per bit of data: one wire for the data bit and one for the inverse of the data bit. The inverse signal takes the place of the ground wire in the single-ended cable. By taking the difference of the two signals, the device can reject the common-mode noise in the data stream. This allows for much longer SCSI chains, up to 25 meters.

Unfortunately for techs, there are few apparent differences between SE and HVD SCSI devices. The connectors and cabling seem identical. This is a bit of a problem because under no circumstances should you try to connect SE and HVD devices on the same SCSI chain. At the very least, you'll probably fry the SE device and, if the HVD device lacks a security circuit to detect your mistake, you'll probably smoke it as well.

Don't panic! Although HVD SCSI devices exist, they are rare and usually found only in aging high-end servers. SE SCSI devices and controllers still reign. The makers of HVD SCSI know the danger and will clearly label their devices.

The problems of cable length versus cost led manufacturers to come up with a second type of differential SCSI called Low Voltage Differential (LVD). LVD SCSI requires less power than HVD and is compatible with existing SE SCSI controllers and devices. LVD devices can sense the type of SCSI, and then work accordingly. If you plug an LVD device into a single-ended chain, it acts as a single-ended device. If you plug an LVD device into LVD, it runs as LVD. LVD SCSI chains can be up to 12 meters in length. The safety, ease of use, and low cost of LVD has made it quite popular in higher-end PCs and servers.

SCSI-3

SCSI technology didn't stand still with the adoption of SCSI-2. Manufacturers have developed significant improvements in SCSI-2, particularly in increased speeds and easier configuration. The T-10 SCSI committee collected these improvements and created a working set of standards collectively called *SCSI-3*. SCSI-3 devices have many names and technologies, such as *Ultra2 or Wide Ultra*.

SCSI-3 also includes interfaces for various types of serial SCSI, including the popular FireWire. Let's take a minute to look at these.

One of the more popular and widely adopted features of SCSI-3 is that wide SCSI can control up to 16 devices on one chain. Each device gets a number from 0 through 15, instead of 0 through 7. Many people think this feature is part of SCSI-2 because wide, 16-device control came out quickly after the SCSI-2 standard was adopted.

The terms Ultra and Fast-20 are used by many SCSI component manufacturers to define a high-speed 20-MHz bus speed. Ultra2 and Fast-40 define a 40-MHz bus speed, and Ultra3 and Fast-80 define an 80-MHz bus speed. The narrow and wide SCSI types still exist. Table 8-2 compares the possible speeds for these two widths.

TABLE 8-2 Narrow SCSI vs. Wide SCSI		
SCSI Type/Bit Width	**8-bit (Narrow)**	**16-bit (Wide)**
Ultra SCSI (FAST20)	20 MB/s	40 MB/s
Ultra2 SCSI (FAST40)	40 MB/s	80 MB/s
Ultra3 SCSI (FAST80)	80 MB/s	160 MB/s

The SCSI-3 standard also includes optional hot swap capabilities. To hot swap means to be able to unplug a drive from the SCSI chain without rebooting or resetting the chain. Hot swapping is extremely useful in laptops and servers, and is already popular for high-end SCSI drives.

With the development of SCSI-3 standards and devices, you might assume older SCSI-2 devices would go away, but this hasn't been the case. Manufacturers continue to produce SCSI-2 devices and controllers, and put them into the marketplace right alongside the higher-end SCSI-3 devices and controllers. The SCSI picture is, therefore, somewhat complex from a tech's perspective. Table 8-3 shows the current SCSI picture, including the latest and greatest Ultra320 standard and the cabling length considerations for the many flavors.

The following notes apply to Table 8-3:

1. The listed maximum bus lengths may be exceeded in point-to-point and engineered applications.

TABLE 8-3	Current SCSI Picture

SCSI Trade Assoc. Terms	Bus Speed (MB/s)	Bus Width (bits)	Max. Bus Lengths Meters[1]			Max. Device Support
			SE	LVD	HVD	
SCSI-1[2]	5	8	6 [3]		25	8
Fast SCSI-1[2]	10	8	3 [3]		25	8
Fast Wide SCSI	20	16	3 [3]		25	16
Ultra SCSI[2]	20	8	1.5 [3]		25	8
Ultra SCSI[2]	20	8	3	–	–	4
Wide Ultra SCSI	40	16	– [3]		25	16
Wide Ultra SCSI	40	16	1.5	–	–	8
Wide Ultra SCSI	40	16	3	–	–	4
Ultra2 SCSI[2,4]	40	8	[4]	12	25	8
Wide Ultra2 SCSI[4]	80	16	[4]	12	25	16
Ultra3 SCSI or Ultra160[6]	160	16	[4]	12	[5]	16
Ultra320	320	16	[4]	12	[5]	16

(Table courtesy of the SCSI Trade Association—http://www.scsita.org)

2. Use of the word "Narrow," preceding SCSI, Ultra SCSI, or Ultra2 SCSI, is optional.
3. LVD wasn't defined in the original SCSI standards for this speed. If all devices on the bus support LVD, then 12-meters operation is possible at this speed. However, if any device on the bus is singled-ended only, then the entire bus switches to Single-Ended mode and the distances in the single-ended column apply.
4. Single-ended isn't defined for speeds beyond Ultra.
5. HVD (Differential) isn't defined for speeds beyond Ultra2.
6. After Ultra2, all new speeds are wide only.

Internal vs. External
SCSI Devices

You read earlier that SCSI devices will reside either inside the PC (internal devices) or outside the PC (external devices). The SCSI chain can't tell the difference between internal and external devices but, of course, they look different to humans who can see the different styles of casing that substitute for the protection of the PC case. Regardless of whether it's internal or external, each device needs a SCSI ID and, if it sits on the end of the SCSI chain, it needs termination.

The one significant difference between the two types of SCSI devices lies in the cabling. Internal SCSI devices use ribbon cables, while external devices use an insulated cable. Because external devices cannot use ribbon cables, they often have two ports to allow for daisy chaining.

Objective 8.04 # SCSI Cabling

There's no such thing as official SCSI-1, SCSI-2, Ultra SCSI, or any other flavor of SCSI cable or connector, although manufacturers generally follow similar guidelines today. Which cable you need depends on whether the device is internal or external, what types of connectors are available, and the type of SCSI you use.

Types of SCSI Cables

The most common kind of SCSI cable is type A (Figure 8-10), which has 50 wires and is used for 8-bit data transfers under both the SCSI-1 and SCSI-2 standards. Type A is also used for 8-bit Fast SCSI-2.

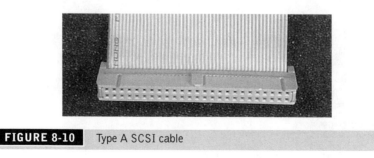

FIGURE 8-10   Type A SCSI cable

In the earliest days of SCSI-2, 16-bit data transfers required a different type of cable, known inventively as type B. It had 68 wires and was used in parallel with the 50-wire type A cable. Because the industry was so underwhelmed by this dual-cable concept, the B cable quietly and quickly disappeared, to be replaced by the type P cable (Figure 8-11). Like its predecessor, this cable had 68 wires. Unlike type B cable, type P cable can be used alone.

Some of the higher-end SCSI-3 host adapters and drives use an 80-pin cable called an SCA 80. The extra wires enable you to hot swap the drives, but that's about it. The drives work fine either using 68-pin cables and an adapter, or their own 80-pin cable.

Types of External Connectors

All external connectors on SCSI devices are female. The types of external connectors are as follows:

- 50-pin Centronics, an obsolete SCSI-1 connector (Figure 8-12a).
- 50-pin HD (High Density) SCSI-2 (Figure 8-12b).
- 68-pin HD DB, used for wide SCSI-2 and SCSI-3 (Figure 8-12c).
- 25-pin standard D-type (looks like a parallel connector), used for SCSI-2, most commonly on Macintoshes and many removable drives (Figure 8-12d).

Exam Tip

Make sure you know what types of connectors are used for both narrow and wide SCSI, and make sure you know your cable lengths!

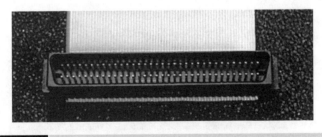

FIGURE 8-11   Type P SCSI cable

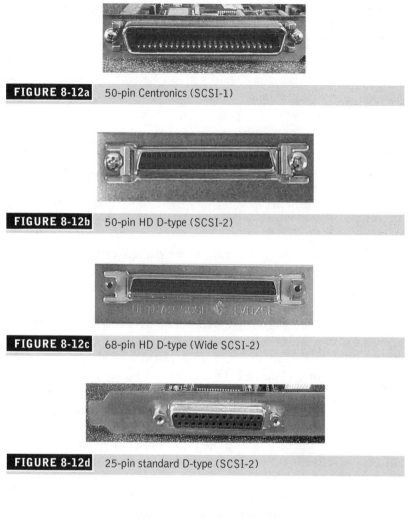

FIGURE 8-12a 50-pin Centronics (SCSI-1)

FIGURE 8-12b 50-pin HD D-type (SCSI-2)

FIGURE 8-12c 68-pin HD D-type (Wide SCSI-2)

FIGURE 8-12d 25-pin standard D-type (SCSI-2)

Objective 8.05

Proper Procedures for Installing and Configuring SCSI Devices

Today's world of plug and play makes installing SCSI devices almost trivial. All versions of Windows come with a special set of drivers that will recognize most SCSI devices. As long as you do the physical installation properly, you shouldn't encounter any problems with the installation of a SCSI device.

Let's say you want to install a SCSI CD-RW into a Windows 2000 PC. If the PC has no SCSI devices of any type, your first step is to get a SCSI host adapter. While many SCSI devices come with a cheap host adapter, you'll be a much happier camper if you yank a few extra dollars out of that wallet and buy a better host adapter. When it comes to good host adapters, I go with one name: Adaptec. Adaptec enjoys widespread and well-deserved popularity for its high-quality host adapters. I don't buy anything else.

Travel Assistance

Check out the Adaptec web site for great host adapters and great SCSI info! http://www.adaptec.com

Make sure you get the right host adapter for your needs. If you have wide SCSI devices, get a wide host adapter. If you have narrow SCSI devices, get a host adapter that supports narrow devices. If you have both wide and narrow types, you can get host adapters that support both. If you're installing a giant-sized tape drive, make sure you get a SCSI controller that has INT13 extensions built in, just as you would for a hard drive larger than 8.4GB. While you're shopping, don't forget that a given host adapter only supports certain speeds and terminations—if I only had a dollar for all the times I had to return a host adapter just because I failed to notice it didn't support the speed or termination my devices needed!

Personally, I like to get the host adapter installed and running before I start installing the SCSI devices. Many techs might disagree with this and just slap the entire chain together, and then restart the PC. I think it's too easy to mess up a termination or SCSI ID, so I do one step at a time. Once I see the host adapter in Device Manager, I know it's safe to start installing SCSI devices.

Even though most good host adapters have tools that enable you to scan the SCSI chain and see all the SCSI IDs, I still take a second or two while installing a SCSI device and jot them down on a piece of paper. It only takes one experience of ripping out a perfectly installed SCSI hard drive to redo its SCSI ID for writing them down to seem an obvious plan of action.

Also, don't forget your terminators! While most techs remember to terminate the SCSI devices, they often forget to terminate the host adapter when it's the end of the chain. Host adapters are as much a part of the SCSI chain as any other device and they also need termination. Fortunately, most good (Adaptec) host adapters now have an autotermination feature, so they can automatically terminate themselves when they detect they're at the end of the chain.

Objective 8.06 # Address/Termination Conflicts

You'll always know when you get a SCSI address or termination conflict because the SCSI device won't be visible to your system. When this happens, invariably during a new installation, you can pretty much bet you messed up either the termination or the SCSI ID. Fortunately, the diagnosis is fairly easy: you run a SCSI chain scanning utility. If you have a good host adapter (did I mention Adaptec?), this utility will be built right into it. You have to reboot the system to get to the scanning tool. If you have a cheap host adapter, you'll need to get a SCSI chain-scanner program. Most host adapter makers give these programs away free or you can often find one in a good PC diagnostic tool. Whatever the case, get one and use it. It usually tells you the problem instantly. If you forgot to terminate properly, the scanning software won't show any devices on the chain. If you only see a few devices, you probably put a terminator somewhere other than on the end of the chain. Turn the system off, reset the termination, and try again.

That same scanning program will usually tell you if two (or more—yikes!) devices share a SCSI ID. When you scan the chain, it'll look like you have only one device, but it has cloned itself. Literally every SCSI ID will show the same device, repeated over and over, as if there were only one! This is the classic symptom of messed up SCSI IDs. Unfortunately, the scanning software doesn't tell you which devices are actually using the same ID, so you must dismantle everything and recheck all the SCSI ID settings. Wheee! What fun! Too bad you didn't write them down like I told you to—but that's okay, you're young and will learn ... eventually.

CHECKPOINT

✔ **Objective 8.01: Fundamentals of SCSI** No two SCSI devices on the same SCSI chain can share the same ID number. The rule with SCSI is you must terminate only the ends of the SCSI chain. Do not terminate devices that aren't on the ends of the cable.

✔ **Objective 8.02: SCSI Types** SCSI-1 supported up to eight devices on a chain and transferred data in 8-bit parallel. SCSI-2 comes in narrow (8-bit), wide (16-bit or 32-bit), standard (5 MHz), and fast (10 MHz) varieties. SCSI-3 comes in a variety of flavors, usually called Ultra SCSI or some close variation.

✔ **Objective 8.03: Internal vs. External SCSI Devices**   Internal SCSI devices use ribbon cables, while external devices use an insulated cable. Regardless of whether a device is internal or external, each device needs a SCSI ID. If a device sits on the end of the SCSI chain, it needs termination.

✔ **Objective 8.04: SCSI Cabling**   SCSI-1 and SCSI-2 use 50-pin type A cables for internal connections. Fast SCSI-2 uses a 68-pin type P cable. External cables provide more variety. SCSI-1 used 50-pin Centronics or HD DB connectors. Normal SCSI-2 uses 50-pin HD DB or 25-pin DB. Fast SCSI uses 68-pin HD DB connectors. SCSI-3 uses 68-pin or 80-pin internal cables and 68-pin external cables.

✔ **Objective 8.05: Proper Procedures for Installing and Configuring SCSI Devices**   Set jumpers and termination properly for all devices. I suggest installing and configuring the host adapter first.

✔ **Objective 8.06: Address/Termination Conflicts**   Use the host adapter scanning utility to check improper addressing or termination settings. If the scan returns settings that seem odd, check the devices for proper settings.

REVIEW QUESTIONS

1. Which of the following statements are true about SCSI IDs? (Select all that apply.)

   A. They must follow the SCSI chain in sequence

   B. No physical order requirement exists for the use of SCSI IDs

   C. The device itself is where the SCSI IDs are set, either by jumpers and shunts, or DIP switches

   D. The host adapter dynamically assigns SCSI IDs for a device when its ROM is accessed at boot up

2. Judy is worried that her SCSI chain might be too long to work properly. What is the maximum length for narrow and normal (slow) SCSI-2 chains?

   A. 0.5 meters

   B. 1 meter

   C. 3 meters

   D. 6 meters

3. Which of the following connectors might be something other than a valid SCSI connector?

   A. 50-pin Centronics
   B. 50-pin HD D-type
   C. 68-pin HD D-type
   D. 28-pin parallel

4. How many devices can be connected on a fast/narrow SCSI-2 bus, including the host adapter?

   A. Six
   B. Seven
   C. Eight
   D. Nine

5. Serial SCSI is part of which SCSI standard?

   A. SCSI-1
   B. SCSI-2
   C. Ultra SCSI
   D. SCSI-3

6. SCSI devices can be classified into two groups. What are they?

   A. Stand-alone
   B. Internal
   C. External
   D. Variable

7. Which of the following is true about SCSI chains?

   A. SCSI chains must have at least three devices
   B. SCSI chains must have terminators at each end
   C. SCSI chains must have at least one SE and one HVD device
   D. SCSI chains must have terminators on each of the devices

8. Edwina wants to add a CD-ROM drive to her system. She plugs it in to the SCSI host adapter, sets the termination properly, and boots up the system. The host adapter doesn't recognize the CD-ROM. What did Edwina forget to do?

   A. Install ASPI drivers
   B. Turn off the host adapter's ROM
   C. Verify that the CD-ROM drive has a unique SCSI ID
   D. Nothing, she just needs to boot two more times for the CD-ROM drive to kick in

9. Dave wants to boot to his SCSI hard drive. What ID number must he use for the drive?

   A. He must set it to the highest possible ID
   B. He should set it to one ID number lower than any EIDE drives in the system
   C. He needs to set it to whatever ID number the host adapter requires
   D. It doesn't matter; the system looks for the active partition

10. One of the differences between SCSI and IDE is

   A. SCSI hard drives are much larger and faster
   B. The red stripe on the SCSI cable always goes toward the Molex power connector
   C. If a SCSI cable is on the device incorrectly, the device can be damaged; with IDE drives the device, if cabled incorrectly, won't be damaged
   D. The interface to the computer is the only difference

REVIEW ANSWERS

1. **B** **C** SCSI IDs can be used in any order and SCSI devices IDs are set on the device itself.

2. **D** Narrow, slow SCSI has a maximum chain length of six meters.

3. **D** Some SCSI devices use a 25-pin connector that looks exactly like a 25-pin parallel connector. Don't mix the two!

4. **C** Narrow SCSI-2 supports a maximum of eight devices.

5. **D** Serial SCSI is part of the SCSI-3 standard.

6. **B** **C** All SCSI devices are either internal or external.

7. **B** All SCSI chains must be terminated at each end.

8. **C** The CD-ROM and the host adapter are almost certainly using the same SCSI ID.

9. **C** Most SCSI host adapters reserve ID 0 for bootable devices, but this setting can usually be changed. IBM host adapters traditionally reserve ID 6 for bootable devices. The key factor, however, is to match the drive ID to your host adapter's setting for bootable devices.

10. **C** Improperly connecting a SCSI device may destroy that device. IDE devices are much more tolerant of poor connections.

Upgrading System Components

	NEWBIE	SOME EXPERIENCE	EXPERT
ETA	1.5 hours	1 hour	45 minutes

The PC market changes dramatically and rapidly, with bigger programs demanding more and faster hardware, and faster, more sophisticated hardware encouraging programmers to produce much more complex programs. A system upgrade at some point, therefore, is inevitable. Even if you purchase the most powerful system on the market today, you'll eventually need to upgrade certain components to avoid it becoming obsolete. As a technician, you need to know how to perform the most common upgrades to computer systems. Some of the most common upgrades include memory, hard drive, CPU, and System BIOS.

Objective 9.01   Upgrading System Memory

As you may recall from Chapter 6, RAM provides working memory for the CPU. Insufficient quantities of RAM can cause a system to bog down and run much more poorly than it otherwise could. Conversely, upgrading the quantity and quality of RAM can make a sluggish system into a snappy, robust machine. Further, applications and operating systems require varying quantities of free RAM in which to load, with the basic rule being that newer programs always need more RAM than older versions of the same program. Windows 2000 runs poorly on less than 128MB of RAM, for example, whereas Windows 95 runs fine with that amount.

Upgrading RAM modules is one of the most common system upgrades you can perform, but requires you to resolve quite a few issues. You can't just slap any old RAM into any old system. That would be far too easy! Here are the issues and some guidelines for finding answers.

- *How much RAM does the system currently have?* Hint: You need to look inside or watch the RAM count at startup.
- *How much RAM can the system use?* Your best bet to finding this information lies in the motherboard manual. If you don't have one handy, you need to go to the web site of the motherboard manufacturer.
- *Which type(s) and speed(s) of RAM does the system have?* The common types of RAM are FPM and EDO SIMMs, and EDO and SDRAM DIMMs. FPM and EDO RAM comes in several speeds, such as 60, 70, and 80 ns. SDRAM is measured by the fastest speed it can synchronize to the motherboard speed, such as 66, 100, and 133 MHz.
- *Which type(s) and speed(s) of RAM can you put in the system?* As with the amount, the motherboard manual—or the manufacturer's web site— provides your best option for discovering this information. You can also

look at the motherboard for slot types, which will give you a clue. New motherboards have as many problems with this as did old motherboards. Most PCs with a 133 MHz system bus, for example, can't use PC100 SDRAM. They'll lock up like a stone or quickly display memory errors. Check the manual and get it right!

- *Can you mix types in different banks?* Many Pentium motherboards with two banks of 72-pin SIMM slots, for example, could handle FPM SIMMs in one bank and EDO SIMMs in the other. Some Pentium and Pentium II systems came with both SIMM and 168-pin DIMM slots, as a further example, and it was up to the manufacturer to determine whether the motherboard could handle both at the same time. Check the motherboard manual or the manufacturer's web site. Sometimes you simply need a BIOS upgrade to support both SIMMs and DIMMs at the same time. See Objective 9.04 later in this chapter for more information about upgrading the System BIOS.

Finally, you need to remember the General Rules of RAM Installation:

- You should always fill a bank of RAM.
- You should never mix types or speeds, especially within a bank.

Steps in the Upgrade Process

To upgrade the RAM in your system by adding RAM modules, follow these steps.

1. Open the computer case and locate the SIMM or DIMM slots on the system board.
2. Determine how many RAM modules you'll need to fill a bank. Remember, you should fill an entire bank or memory errors may occur.
3. Remove the RAM from the antistatic bag.

Exam Tip

You should either fill a memory bank completely or leave it entirely empty.

---

4. SIMM modules must be inserted into SIMM slots on an angle and snapped upright into position so they're perpendicular to the motherboard.
5. DIMM modules must be inserted into the slot and pressed down firmly.

Travel Advisory

Make certain that on ATX motherboards with soft power, you *unplug* the AC cable from the power supply (or from the wall socket) and wait for a few seconds. ATX motherboards always have a trickle of electricity running through the motherboard when plugged in. You can destroy RAM or socket if you install RAM when the motherboard is hot.

To perform a complete RAM upgrade by removing the existing RAM modules and inserting new RAM modules, follow these steps:

1. Open the computer case and locate the RAM modules inserted into the SIMM or DIMM slots on your motherboard.
2. Determine the amount of RAM needed to fill a memory bank completely.
3. Carefully move the white plastic pins or small metal clips, and lift the existing RAM out of the sockets.
4. Remove the RAM from the antistatic bag.
5. SIMM modules must be inserted into SIMM slots on an angle and snapped upright into position so they're perpendicular to the motherboard.
6. DIMM modules must be inserted into the slot and pressed down firmly.

Objective 9.02

Adding or Replacing Hard Drives

Upgrading a hard drive can give a PC needed storage capacity and, sometimes, a nice performance boost. Insufficient file space causes major headaches, leaving you scrounging around trying to find temporary files or other unnecessary files to delete, just to load a new program. Worse, because Windows needs hard drive space for a swap file (see "Virtual Memory" in Chapter 18 of this book), running low on free hard drive space can cause dramatic system instability and slowdown. As you know from Chapter 7, installing hard drives properly requires you to consider a lot of little details, such as physical connectivity, CMOS settings, BIOS and drive technology. Plus, you need to think about operating system issues, such as partitioning, formatting, drive lettering, and so on. All these issues combine into two different questions when it comes to upgrading hard drives: Do you want to add another drive? Or, do you want to replace a drive that's already in the system?

Add or Replace?

First, here's the cold, hard fact. Adding another hard drive to a system is much easier than replacing an existing hard drive. You get a nice new drive letter and lots of space with relatively little effort. So why even discuss replacing an existing drive? Well, most folks like to install programs in the default \Program Files folder in Windows and they also like to store all their files in the default \My Documents folder. Given that preference, adding another hard drive doesn't do too much good. Folks like the convenience of using their tried and true default folders and many users, especially newbies, have a problem when you tell them they have to start sorting all their MP3 files on the new E: drive you just installed. So, it's more a matter of convenience of installation versus convenience of use. Let's look at the issues involved with both.

Adding a New Drive

Adding an additional drive usually just means installing the new drive as slave to the existing drive or as a master on the secondary—either way works equally well. Run the CMOS to ensure your system sees the drive, and then partition and format to get the new drive. You might have to install a new drive bay or a bay adapter to secure a 3.5" drive in an empty 5.25" bay. You can find adapter kits at almost any computer store. And if you've already used up both primary and secondary controllers, you'll need an add-on hard drive controller.

Travel Assistance
Check out Promise Technologies, makers of excellent PCI hard drive controller cards at http://www.promise.com.

The one downside to adding a drive comes from the CD-ROM. In Windows 9x, the CD-ROM's drive letter changes, so it always gets a letter after the hard drives. So, if your CD-ROM was drive D:, it changes to drive E: after you install the new drive. No big deal except for the many programs that remember they were installed from the D: drive, so be ready to tell installation programs to look to the new drive letter for the CD-ROM disc.

The operating system, to a more or less degree, enables you to change the drive numbering of CD-ROMs and hard drives. You can move the CD-ROM drive to a letter farther down the alphabet easily with either a command line switch (MSCDEX /L:*x*, where *x* is the preferred drive letter) or in Device Manager (a simpler solution).

The Disk Management tool in Windows 2000 goes one better and enables you to change the drive letter for a CD-ROM drive *or a hard drive* with ease. Chapter 20 covers the Disk Management utility in more detail.

Exam Tip
Windows 2000 enables you to modify drive lettering.

Replacing a Drive

Replacing a drive takes time, tools, and a bit of effort. You might want a new drive, but you also want all your old programs and data, correct? To do this, you need to take a few steps. First, install the new drive just as previously described. You then need to transfer everything from the old drive to the new drive. Fortunately, many handy programs exist that make this step fairly easy. Third, remove the old drive and reconfigure the new drive as the primary master. If you've done everything right, the new drive magically boots up and looks exactly like the old drive with one exception: you have a lot of free drive space that didn't exist before. Be sure to back up all critical data first—this is serious surgery and things can go wrong! My two favorite utilities for copying hard drives are Symantec's Ghost and PowerQuest's DriveCopy.

Remember, you don't have to copy the data from one drive to another! Many techs use the excuse of a new drive as an opportunity to do a clean installation. They install the new drive as primary master and just reinstall everything. Be sure to install the old drive as a slave, so you can copy your favorite files to the new installation.

Objective 9.03   # Replacing the CPU

New programs and operating systems can bring Old Faithful to its digital knees, demanding more and more processing power just to accomplish seemingly simple tasks. When your system runs slowly, your CPU could be the culprit. The great part about current motherboards is that they support more than one model or speed of CPU. You need to consult your motherboard book to verify which processors the motherboard supports. Upgrading the CPU isn't as difficult as you may think. To upgrade your CPU follow these steps:

1. Disconnect the AC power on ATX systems.
2. Remove the old CPU from the socket or slot.
3. Remove the new CPU from its packaging. Be careful not to touch the pins on PGA-packaged CPUs because they can be easily bent. Don't touch the pins or contacts of the CPU.
4. Align Pin 1 of the processor with Pin 1 of the processor socket, or line up the notches on Slot 1 and Slot A processors.
5. Configure the jumpers on your motherboard (if any) to reflect the new processor model, speed, and voltage.
6. If you don't have motherboard jumpers, reconfigure the CMOS settings to reflect the new CPU.

Objective 9.04 # Upgrading the System BIOS

The PC hardware industry changes so rapidly that no BIOS programmer can possibly get every detail perfect the first time. From a practical stance, this means a specific PC might or might not support every latest and greatest offering from the hardware folks. Worse, some systems might not quite run stably using the latest motherboard chipset offerings, occasionally rushed out the door to support the newest $X+$ GHz CPU. Shocking, but true!

In the old days, you had one option when your motherboard simply couldn't handle the game—rip out the old System ROM and put in a new one purchased from the manufacturer. Current motherboards have EEPROM or Flash ROM chips holding the System BIOS and CMOS setup utility and thus enable you to upgrade or *flash* the BIOS chip.

> **Exam Tip**
>
> If a device is too new to be found in the CMOS settings program, you need to upgrade your BIOS.

You can upgrade the BIOS in two ways. You can either flash the BIOS or replace the BIOS entirely. You need to record your CMOS settings before doing any kind of BIOS upgrade, so you can reset your settings on the new BIOS after the upgrade.

Replacing the BIOS

Not all System BIOS chips are Flash ROM or EEPROM. If your BIOS cannot be flashed, you need to replace the entire BIOS. To replace the BIOS, follow these steps:

1. Unplug your AC power on ATX systems.
2. Locate the BIOS on your system board.
3. Remove expansion cards that are in your way.
4. Use chip pullers to remove the old BIOS. Chip pullers resemble big tweezers.
5. Align the new BIOS over the BIOS socket.
6. Insert the new BIOS into the BIOS socket.
7. Press down firmly on the new BIOS until it's properly seated into position.

Flashing the BIOS

Flashing the BIOS requires your system to have a Flash BIOS or EEPROM chip. Flash BIOS chips can be upgraded electronically with a special disk provided by the manufacturer of the BIOS. To flash your BIOS, follow these steps:

1. Obtain the flashing program from the manufacturer's web site.
2. Turn your system off.
3. Insert a valid boot disk of some sort and boot to the A: prompt.
4. Insert the disk containing the flashing program and new BIOS into the floppy drive.
5. Run the flashing program. Make sure to back up the old BIOS! Most flashing programs automatically prompt you to back up this file. Do it!
6. Restart your system.

That's all there is to it. Your BIOS update will communicate with newer devices. (And Windows will refind all your current hardware, so have a copy of your Windows CD-ROM disc handy.) It's that simple.

CHECKPOINT

✔ **Objective 9.01: Upgrading System Memory** Upgrading memory can increase system performance and stability. Upgrading RAM enables your processor to access information faster. Refer to the motherboard manual to determine what type and amount of RAM a particular motherboard can handle. Remember the basic rule of RAM: *don't mix!*

✔ **Objective 9.02: Adding or Replacing Hard Drives**   Upgrading or adding a new hard drive can give you valuable disk space. Adding means you need to think about physical connectivity and CMOS issues. Replacing requires you to back up essential files. Don't forget that last bit!

✔ **Objective 9.03: Replacing the CPU**   Upgrading your CPU can increase system performance. Some motherboards can support more than one model or speed of processor. You need to consult your motherboard book to verify which processors your motherboard can support.

✔ **Objective 9.04: Upgrading the System BIOS**   Information is transferred between your devices and your system via the BIOS. If a device is too new for your BIOS to have an instruction set for it, you'll need to upgrade your BIOS. Flashing the BIOS requires you to have a Flash BIOS. Flash BIOS chips can be upgraded electronically with a program provided by the BIOS manufacturer. If you don't have a Flash BIOS, you'll need to replace the BIOS.

REVIEW QUESTIONS

1. You perform a RAM upgrade on a computer system with a soft power function. You keep the system plugged into the wall to ground the computer case. You install the RAM in the machine and reboot. After you reboot, you receive a POST error. What most likely happened?

   A. You need to configure the new RAM in the system CMOS
   B. You need to unplug a machine with soft power before you install RAM
   C. You placed the RAM in the wrong slot
   D. The RAM you selected isn't compatible with you motherboard

2. You just installed another EIDE hard drive on your system to serve as an archive for documents. You match up the cables correctly, installing the new hard drive on the same cable as the original boot drive. You cannot reboot your system to your operating system. What is the problem?

   A. You cannot add a new drive to your system
   B. EIDE cannot handle more than one drive per cable
   C. Your new drive isn't jumpered correctly
   D. You need to make the old drive the slave to the new drive

3. You install a 1GB EIDE hard drive on to an old 386SX system to serve as a Linux lab machine. When you reboot, you find the system is unable to recognize the new hard drive. What is most likely the problem?

   A. The 386SX chipset doesn't support EIDE hard drives
   B. The hard drive is too large for the BIOS
   C. Your new drive isn't jumpered correctly
   D. Older motherboards don't support EIDE hard drives

4. What do you need to flash your BIOS? (Select all that apply.)

   A. A special program provided by the BIOS manufacturer
   B. A new BIOS
   C. A removable BIOS
   D. A special probe

5. How can upgrading the RAM in your system increase your system performance? (Select all that apply.)

   A. Upgrading RAM doesn't increase system performance
   B. Upgrading RAM enables the processor to access information faster
   C. Upgrading RAM automatically upgrades the BIOS
   D. Upgrading RAM enables your system to access more information from expanded and extended memory without accessing the hard drive.

6. How can you find out which types of processors a motherboard supports?

   A. The information is contained in the CMOS settings program
   B. Consult your motherboard book
   C. Consult the CPU packaging
   D. The information will be written directly on the motherboard

7. Joe wants to add a new 40GB EIDE hard drive to his system, which currently contains an 8.4GB primary master, a 6.2GB primary slave, a 52X CD-ROM drive as secondary master, and a new CD-RW drive as secondary slave. What does he need to do?

   A. Reconfigure the CD-media drives on the secondary controller to be slaves, and add the new hard drive as secondary master
   B. Install a SCSI host adapter to support the new drive
   C. Install an EIDE add-on card to support the new drive
   D. This can't be done; he needs a new system

8. When you install a 128MB SDRAM DIMM into a Pentium motherboard that already has installed a pair of 32MB EDO SIMMs, the system does not recognize the new RAM. What could be the problem?

   A. The motherboard does not support DIMMs
   B. You need to upgrade the BIOS to support both SIMMs and DIMMs at the same time
   C. You need to reload the operating system to support both SIMMs and DIMMs at the same time
   D. You need to upgrade the SIMMs to match the capacity of the DIMM

REVIEW ANSWERS

1. **B** You always want to unplug a soft power system before you install RAM because a constant charge runs through the system board.

2. **C** When installing two EIDE hard drives on one cable, you must be sure you have the master/slave jumpers correct.

3. **B** With older motherboards, to have drives larger than 504MB, you must have a hard drive that has LBA/ECHS and a BIOS that supports LBA/ECHS.

4. **A** To flash your BIOS, you need to have a Flash BIOS. You also need a special program provided by the BIOS manufacturer. When you flash the BIOS, the BIOS is upgraded electronically.

5. **B** **D** Upgrading RAM increases system performance by enabling your processor to access information faster. Upgrading your RAM also enables your system to access more information from expanded and extended memory, without accessing the hard drive.

6. **B** To determine which types and speeds of processors your motherboard can support, you need to consult the motherboard book.

7. **C** Joe needs to install an EIDE add-on card to support the new drive; a SCSI adapter would work with a SCSI drive, but not EIDE.

8. **B** You need to upgrade the BIOS to support both SIMMs and DIMMs at the same time if possible. It could be that the motherboard simply will not support both at the same time.

System Resources

	NEWBIE	SOME EXPERIENCE	EXPERT
ETA	3 hours	2 hours	1 hour

Every device in your PC, from the hard drive to the mouse, needs a method to talk to the CPU to function properly. If the mouse moves, it needs a way to tell the CPU that it has moved so the CPU can, in turn, talk to the video card to show the new mouse position. If the hard drive wants to send a file to RAM, it needs a way to tell the CPU that the data is ready so the CPU can move the file off the hard drive and into RAM. Equally, the CPU needs a way to talk to the devices to get them to do whatever they should do, such as the video card updating the location of the mouse pointer on the monitor.

To do this, the inventors of the PC created a group of wonderful little functions known collectively as system resources. *System resources* break down into three types: I/O addresses, Interrupt Requests (IRQs), and Direct Memory Access channels (DMAs). Let's look at each of these in detail to appreciate how they work.

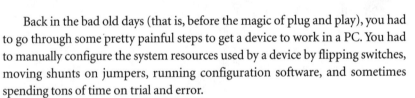

Local Lingo

System Resources   Collective name for I/O addresses, IRQs, and DMA channels used by devices in a PC.

Back in the bad old days (that is, before the magic of plug and play), you had to go through some pretty painful steps to get a device to work in a PC. You had to manually configure the system resources used by a device by flipping switches, moving shunts on jumpers, running configuration software, and sometimes spending tons of time on trial and error.

In today's world of plug and play (PnP) devices, many might argue that this topic isn't important, but that analysis misses a key point. Granted, the ability to snap in a new device and have it work automatically is wonderful, but it also doesn't work every time! As you'll see, many PnP devices today have some rather nasty habits and don't work properly. Understanding how system resources work together to enable a sound card or modem to run properly is absolutely vital for an accomplished PC tech. You need to understand the expansion bus and motherboard, so let's start with something you already know—the external data bus and address bus.

Objective 10.01 I/O Addresses

Previous chapters explained that the CPU uses the external data bus to transfer lines of programs between memory (RAM and ROM) and the CPU. The external data bus also enables data to travel back and forth from peripherals, such as the keyboard, hard drives, and CD-ROM drives, to the CPU. The CPU uses the address bus to access programs both in RAM and ROM. The CPU uses BIOS routines stored in ROM and RAM to tell peripherals to do whatever it is they're supposed to do. That leaves two related questions: "If everything in the computer connects to both the external data bus and the address bus, how does the CPU know how to talk to a particular device? Second, how do particular devices know the CPU is talking to them?"

The *expansion* bus consists of two separate buses: the external data bus and the address bus. The address bus holds the answers to the questions posed above. Every device on the PC connects to both buses. When IBM first designed the PC, it assigned groups of unique patterns of 1's and 0's on the *address bus* for each device in the computer. But the address bus only enables the CPU to tell the chipset what line of program to get, correct? Not anymore.

The address bus has a second, very different function. The 8086 CPU used an extra wire, called the IO/MEM (input/output or memory) wire to notify devices the CPU was *not* using the address bus to specify an address in memory. Instead, the CPU used the address bus to communicate with a particular device. The 8086 address bus had 20 wires, but when the IO/MEM wire had voltage, only the first 16 wires were monitored by the devices. This is still true today. You might have a Pentium 4 with a 36-bit address bus, but the moment the CPU places a voltage on the IO/MEM wire, the RAM takes a nap and every device watches the first 16 wires on the address bus, waiting to see if one of their patterns of 1's and 0's comes up.

All devices, both those embedded on the motherboard (like the keyboard controller) and those inserted into expansion slots (like a video card), respond to special, unique patterns built into them. Every device gets a number of patterns, not just one pattern! Each different pattern of 16 ones and zeros is a unique command for that device. For example, the keyboard controller has four unique patterns. The hard-drive controller responds to 16 unique commands, each telling the hard drive to perform a certain function. If the CPU lights up the IO/MEM wire and puts the pattern 0000000111110000 onto the address bus, the hard-drive controller sends back a message describing its error status. All the different patterns used by the CPU to talk to the devices inside your computer are known as the *I/O addresses*. See Figure 10-1.

I/O addresses function inside the PC as long strings of 1's and 0's, but tech people use hexadecimal notation to display specific addresses. The starting I/O address for the floppy drive controller is 0000 0011 1111 0000, for example, but appears in print as 03F0 (because no one wants to remember all those 1's and 0's!). Each hexadecimal character takes the place of four binary characters. Even I/O addresses that appear to be regular decimal numbers—the secondary hard drive controller, for example, uses I/O address 0170—are hexadecimal representations of a binary number.

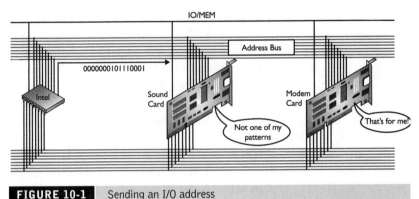

FIGURE 10-1   Sending an I/O address

Travel Assistance

For those of you new to hexadecimal, surf on over to "The
Dreaded Hex" Tech File at Total Seminars,
http://www.totalsem.com/techfiles.htm.

The Rules of I/O Addresses

Three basic rules apply to I/O addresses: all devices have I/O addresses, all devices
use more than one address, and two devices cannot have the same I/O address in
a single system. What's amazing for the PC industry is these three rules apply universally.

All Devices Must Have I/O Addresses   The CPU uses I/O addresses to
talk to everything in your computer. Every device in your computer either has a
preset I/O address or you must give it one. Basic devices in the computer have preset I/O addresses. The primary hard-drive controller on a motherboard, for example, always gets the preset I/O addresses of 01F0-01FF. A sound card, in contrast,
has to have I/O addresses configured when you install it into a system.

All Devices Use More Than One I/O Address   All devices respond to
more than one pattern of 1's and 0's. The CPU uses the different I/O addresses to
give various commands to each device, and each device must also have one or
more I/O addresses to respond to the CPU. For example, the hard drive's I/O
address range is 01F0-01FF. If the CPU sends a 01F0 pattern, it asks the hard-drive

controller if an error exists anywhere. The command 01F1 is a totally separate command. No device has only one I/O address.

Once a Device Has an I/O Address, No Other Device Can Use That Address
When you install an expansion card—such as a new sound card—in your system, you must know the I/O addresses currently taken. You then must make certain the sound card uses I/O addresses that no other device uses. Every device in your computer has an I/O address. No two devices can share any I/O addresses or the device(s) won't work.

Travel Advisory

If two devices share an I/O address, the PC will lock up!

You need to determine, therefore, the I/O addresses in use in a particular PC. Fortunately, most of the I/O addresses were set up by IBM a long time ago, so this isn't a tough call. When IBM released the PC to the public domain, they provided a list of I/O addresses that manufacturers must use to make components and systems IBM-compatible. This list, shown in Table 10-1, is still followed by every PC in the world today.

TABLE 10-1   The Original IBM I/O Address List

I/O Address Range	Usage
0000–000F	DMA controller
0020–002F	Master IRQ controller
0030–003F	Master IRQ controller
0040–0043	System timer
0060–0063	Keyboard
0070–0071	CMOS clock
0080–008F	DMA page registers

(continued)

TABLE 10-1   The Original IBM I/O Address List (*continued*)

I/O Address Range	Usage
0090–009F	DMA page registers
00A0–00AF	Slave IRQ controller
00B0–00BF	Slave IRQ controller
00C0–00CF	DMA controller
00E0–00EF	Reserved
00F0–00FF	Math coprocessor
0170–0177	Secondary hard drive controller
01F0–01FF	Primary hard drive controller
0200–0207	Joystick
0210–0217	Reserved
0278–027F	LPT2
02B0–02DF	Secondary EGA
02E8–02EF	COM4
02F8–02FF	COM2
0378–037F	LPT1
03B0–03BF	Mono video
03C0–03CF	Primary EGA
03D0–03DF	CGA video
03E8–03EF	COM3
03F0–03F7	Floppy controller
03F8–03FF	COM1

Techs have a few quirks (go figure!) when discussing I/O addresses that you need to know to talk the talk. Sixteen-bit I/O addresses, as you know from the preceding discussion, are always represented by four hexadecimal numbers, such as 01F0. When discussing I/O addresses, however, most techs drop the leading zeros. Techs refer to address 01F0, for example, as 1F0. Also, almost no one talks about the entire range of I/O addresses. We usually discuss only the first I/O address, which we call the *I/O base address*. If the hard drive uses the I/O addresses of 1F0–1FF, for example, the I/O base address is 1F0. Finally, when discussing any hex value, many people put a lowercase h on the end to show you it's a hex value. For example, some people will show the I/O base address for the floppy controller as 3F0h. Glance at Table 10-1 one more time and list the base addresses for some of the devices in "tech speak"—mono video is 3B0h; primary EGA is 3C0h; and so on. I'll stick with the common usage in the next few paragraphs.

Take a close look at the I/O address map one more time. Notice there are neither I/O addresses for sound cards nor I/O addresses for network cards. In fact, IBM mapped out the I/O addresses for only the most common devices. So, if you want to install a sound card, what I/O addresses are available? Look at I/O base address 210h, and then look at the next I/O base address—it's 278h, isn't it? All the I/O addresses between these two are open for use, so plenty of unused addresses exist! By the way, you'll notice the last address is 3FFh, so couldn't you use all the addresses from 3F8 all the way to FFFF? PCI devices use the higher ranges today, but the traditional table stops at 3FFh.

Exam Tip

Don't bother memorizing all the I/O addresses! Just make sure you know the ones for common devices such as floppy drives, hard drives, and LPT and COM ports.

I/O addresses provide a two-way communication pathway between peripherals and the CPU. If the CPU wants to talk to a device, it can run BIOS routines or device drivers (little programs, remember?) that can use I/O addresses to initiate conversations over the external data bus.

Objective 10.02   IRQs

The CPU can now communicate with all the devices inside the computer using I/O addresses, but a small problem still exists. I/O addressing enables two-way communication, but the CPU must start all that communication. A device such as a mouse can't send its own message to the CPU to get the CPU's attention. It must wait for the CPU to speak to it first. So, how does a device initiate a conversation with the CPU? For example, how does the mouse tell the CPU it has moved? How does the keyboard tell the CPU somebody just pressed the J key? The PC needs some kind of mechanism to tell the CPU to stop doing whatever it's doing and talk to a particular device.

This mechanism is called *interruption*. Every CPU in the PC world has an INT (interrupt) wire. If this wire is charged, the CPU will stop what it's doing and deal with the device. Say you have a PC with only one peripheral, a keyboard. The CPU is running WordPerfect, and the user presses the J key. The keyboard is connected to the CPU's INT wire and charges the wire. The CPU temporarily stops running WordPerfect and runs the necessary BIOS routine to query the keyboard.

This would be fine if the computer had only one device. As we all know, however, PCs have many devices, and almost all of them will need to interrupt the CPU at some point. So, the PC needs some kind of traffic cop chip to act as an intermediary among all the devices and the CPU's INT wire. Today's PC uses a special chip called the *chipset* to act as the intermediary between the CPU's INT wire and all the devices.

The chipset connects to the INT wire of the CPU on one side and has another 15 wires called IRQs (interrupt requests) that extend out from the chip into the motherboard. Every device that needs to interrupt the CPU gets an IRQ. If a device needs to interrupt the CPU, it lights its IRQ and the chipset then lights the INT wire on the CPU. Whenever the INT wire lights up, the CPU talks to the chipset via its I/O addresses to determine which device has interrupted. The chipset tells the CPU which IRQ is lit and this enables the CPU to know which BIOS routine to run.

The Rules of IRQs

IRQ setup and use in a system follows a clear pair of rules: first, almost every device needs an IRQ. This includes devices built into the motherboard as well as devices that use the expansion bus slots. Second, under almost all circumstances, no two devices can share an IRQ. If one device uses IRQ3, for example, no other device can use that IRQ.

Travel Advisory

If two devices share an IRQ, the system will
invariably lockup.

Technicians need to determine current IRQ usage and to set up new devices
to use available IRQs, rather than to share them. For the most part, Plug and Play
BIOS routines and devices make IRQ assignment automatic, but A+ techs should
understand the settings in case something goes awry.

To prevent devices from sharing IRQs, IBM gave an IRQ map to card manufacturers so they knew which IRQs to use for certain types of devices, just like IBM did
for I/O addresses (refer to Table 10-1). Note the strange IRQ 2/9—this is a holdover
from the early PC days where two chips were needed to control all the IRQs. This is
called the *cascade* and it still exists for backward-compatibility. Don't worry about
why this takes places. Just know that IRQ 2 and IRQ 9 are really the same IRQ!

These settings are somewhat flexible. If a device that uses a certain IRQ isn't
present, then another device can use that IRQ. For example, if you don't have a
secondary hard-drive controller, you can use IRQ15 for another device. Table 10-2
shows the default IRQ map. I've added in parentheses the devices that commonly
grab particular IRQs, although they are not part of the default list.

Exam Tip

Memorize the IRQ chart!

TABLE 10-2 IBM Assignments for IRQs

IRQ	Default Function
IRQ 0	System timer
IRQ 1	Keyboard
IRQ 2/9	Open for use (PCI steering)

(continued)

TABLE 10-2	IBM Assignments for IRQs (*continued*)
IRQ	**Default Function**
IRQ 3	Default COM2, COM4
IRQ 4	Default COM1, COM3
IRQ 5	LPT2 (sound cards)
IRQ 6	Floppy drive
IRQ 7	LPT1
IRQ 8	Real-time clock
IRQ 10	Open for use
IRQ 11	Open for use (USB)
IRQ 12	Open for use (PS/2 mouse port)
IRQ 13	Math coprocessor
IRQ 14	Primary hard drive controller
IRQ 15	Secondary hard drive controller

A couple of things you should note about Table 10-2. First, USB controllers often take IRQ 11, a fascinating but irrelevant tidbit. More to the point, if you remember all the way back to Chapter 1, you'll recall that you can daisy chain up to 127 USB devices on a single controller. All those devices would still only use a *single IRQ*. Sweet!

Also, notice that some of these IRQs are assigned to COM and LPT ports. Odds are good you've seen these fellows occasionally—let's make sure you know what they do!

COM and LPT Ports

IRQs and I/O addresses weren't invented for the IBM PC. Mainframes, minis, and pre-PC microcomputers all used IRQs and I/O addresses. When IBM designed the PC, it wanted to simplify the installation, programming, and operation of devices.

Because virtually every peripheral needs both an IRQ and I/O address, IBM created standard preset combinations of IRQs and I/O addresses. For *serial* devices, the preset combinations are called *COM ports*. For *parallel* devices, they are called *LPT ports*. The word "port" is used to describe a "portal" or two-way access. Table 10-3 lists the preset combinations of I/O addresses and IRQs.

TABLE 10-3	COM and LPT Assignments	
Port	**I/O Address**	**IRQ**
COM1	3F8	4
COM2	2F8	3
LPT1	378	7
LPT2	278	5

Ports do make installation easier. Look at modems. Many don't have a setting for IRQs or I/O addresses. Instead, you set their COM port. Most people don't realize that when they select a COM port, they actually assign the IRQ and I/O address. If you set a modem to COM1, for example, you set that modem's IRQ to 4 and the modem's I/O address to 3F8 (see Table 10-3).

Local Lingo

COM and LPT ports   Preset combinations of IRQs and I/O addresses.

Physical vs. I/O Ports

I need to clarify something right away. A serial port is a physical item, a 9- or 25-pin male DB connector in the back of your PC, but a COM port is just the I/O address and IRQ assigned to it. A parallel port is a 25-pin female DB connector on the back of your PC, but an LPT is just the I/O address and IRQ assigned to it. Think of a telephone. If someone pointed to your phone and said, "that is a 324-5444," you would correct him or her: "No, that's a telephone. The number assigned to it is 324-5444." Same with serial and parallel ports. You wouldn't look at a serial port and say, "That's COM1."

COM3 and COM4

Back in the original PCs, IBM dedicated two IRQs to serial ports: IRQ4 for COM1 and IRQ3 for COM2. Many systems needed more than two serial devices, however, and manufacturers complained loudly about the lack of COM ports. IBM then established two more COM port standards—COM3 and COM4—and assigned two previously unused I/O addresses (3E8–3EF for COM3 and 2E8–2EF for COM4) to these ports. See Table 10-4.

Exam Tip

Memorize the I/O addresses and IRQs for the four COM ports!

TABLE 10-4 COM Port Assignments

COM Port	I/O Address	IRQ
COM1	3F8	4
COM2	2F8	3
COM3	3E8	4
COM4	2E8	3

Hey, wait a minute! One of the most important rules for setting IRQs is that two devices shouldn't share an IRQ, but an exception exists to that rule. Two (or more) devices can share the same IRQ as long as they never talk at the same time!

Back in the old days, many devices could share IRQs. For example, you could have a dedicated fax card and a modem on the same IRQ. Neither device had a device driver (they used the BIOS for the COM port), and the fax would never run at the same time as the modem (this was before Windows). So these two devices could be set to COM1 and COM3. In today's computers, you can no longer set one device as COM1 and another device as COM3, or one device as COM2 and another as COM4. If you do, the computer will lock up.

If you accidentally have two devices sharing the same IRQ, the computer will eventually lock up. You won't destroy anything—just set one device to another IRQ to correct the problem and try again.

LPT Ports

LPT port settings apply to parallel connections for devices such as printers. In the old days, in fact, only high-speed printers used parallel ports. When IBM standardized ports for parallel devices, they called them LPT ports, "LPT" being an abbreviation for line printer. Although IBM assigned both an I/O address and IRQ to the LPT ports, no devices at the time needed the IRQ. IBM, therefore, standardized the LPT ports so they wouldn't talk back, which meant IRQ7 for LPT1 and IRQ5 for LPT2 were never used by the LPT port, and other devices could "share" them.

This led to many techs' woes, however, because sound card manufacturers routinely set the cards to default to LPT7 or 5. This scheme worked well for a short while, but when new printers started using IRQs, PCs locked up by the millions.

Today, the picture is even more complicated. Many devices other than simple line printers plug into the parallel port in the back of your PC. These devices (for example, tape backups and Zip drives) use an interrupt. So, if you use IRQ7 for another device, don't plug anything other than your printer into LPT1. Even that might not work, however, because most new printers use the IRQ assigned to the port! If you need an extra parallel port, you can still purchase an LPT2 parallel port card.

COM and LPT Ports Today

There's still a lot of confusion about COM and LPT ports among techs today, but now that you understand what IBM originally set up, I can eliminate the confusion. First, even though IBM dictated a specific I/O address and IRQ for a particular COM or LPT port, you can change the IRQ as long as the device can handle it and the software that talks to that device knows about the change. So you can change, say, COM1's IRQ from 4 to 5 if the hardware and software enables it. Let's use my motherboard as an example. My computer, like most computers today, has two built-in serial ports. You can change the COM port settings by accessing the CMOS, as shown in Figure 10-2.

Note that serial port 1 is set to I/O address 3F8 and IRQ4. What COM port is that? It's COM1, but I could change that serial port to any of the following settings:

- 3F8/IRQ4: standard COM1
- 2F8/IRQ3: standard COM2
- 3F8/IRQ5: COM1 I/O address combined with the nonstandard IRQ5
- 2F8/IRQ5: COM2 I/O address combined with the nonstandard IRQ5

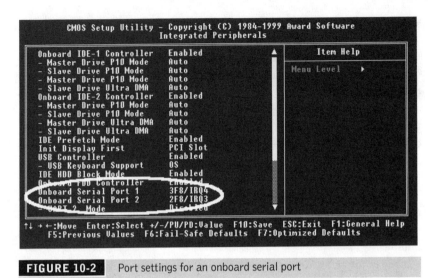

```
      CMOS Setup Utility - Copyright (C) 1984-1999 Award Software
                        Integrated Peripherals

   Onboard IDE-1 Controller      Enabled         ▲        Item Help
   - Master Drive PIO Mode        Auto
   - Slave Drive PIO Mode         Auto                Menu Level    ▶
   - Master Drive PIO Mode        Auto
   - Slave Drive Ultra DMA        Auto
   Onboard IDE-2 Controller      Enabled
   - Master Drive PIO Mode        Auto
   - Slave Drive PIO Mode         Auto
   - Master Drive Ultra DMA       Auto
   - Slave Drive Ultra DMA        Auto
   IDE Prefetch Mode             Enabled
   Init Display First            PCI Slot
   USB Controller                Enabled
   - USB Keyboard Support         OS
   IDE HDD Block Mode            Enabled
   Onboard FDD Controller        Enabled
   Onboard Serial Port 1         3F8/IRQ4
   Onboard Serial Port 2         2F8/IRQ3
   UART 2 Mode                   Disabled        ▼

   ↑↓ →←:Move  Enter:Select  +/-/PU/PD:Value  F10:Save  ESC:Exit  F1:General Help
      F5:Previous Values  F6:Fail-Safe Defaults  F7:Optimized Defaults
```

FIGURE 10-2   Port settings for an onboard serial port

In current usage, therefore, COM1, COM2, and so forth often refer specifically to the I/O address, but not necessarily to the IRQ. Many motherboards, for example, show the default serial port settings as COM1/IRQ4 or COM2/IRQ3. We know by definition that COM1 uses IRQ4 and COM2 uses IRQ3. Why do they do this? Why don't they simply show COM1 and COM2? Why add the IRQs if any decent A+ Certified tech already knows this? In this day of COM ports that easily change to nonstandard IRQs, the motherboard folks separate the COM port from the IRQ, ensuring that you won't accidentally create an unintentional conflict.

Exam Tip
Memorize the I/O addresses and IRQs for the LPT ports!

The combination of I/O address and IRQ is the cornerstone of CPU-device communication. But there's one more aspect of this communication I must discuss—the badly misunderstood concept of DMA.

Objective 10.03   # DMA

CPUs do a lot of work. They run the BIOS, operating system, and applications. CPUs handle interrupts and access I/O addresses. They are busy little chips.

CPUs also deal with one other item—data. CPUs constantly manipulate data. CPUs move data from one place in RAM to another. Peripherals send data to RAM (for example, a scanner) via the CPU, and the CPU sends data from RAM to peripherals (for example, a laser printer).

Moving all this data is obviously necessary, but it's also simple to do. Moving data wastes the CPU's power and time. Moreover, with all the caches and such on today's CPUs, most of the time the system does nothing, while the CPU handles some internal calculation.

So, why not make devices that access memory directly, without involving the CPU? The process of accessing memory without using the CPU is called Direct Memory Access (DMA).

DMA enables the system to run background applications without interfering with the CPU, as shown in Figure 10-3. This is excellent for creating background sounds in games, and for accessing floppy and hard drives.

The concept of DMA as described here, however, has a problem. What if more than one device wants to use DMA? What keeps these devices from stomping on the external data bus at the same time? Plus, what if the CPU suddenly needs the data bus? How can you stop the device using DMA so the CPU, which should have priority, can access the bus?

Knowing this, the PCs chipset also controls all DMA functions. This primitive CPU can handle all the data passing from peripherals to RAM and vice versa. This takes necessary, but simple, work away from the CPU, so the CPU can spend time doing more productive work.

The chipset sends data along the external data bus when the CPU is busy and not using the external data bus. This is perfectly acceptable because the CPU

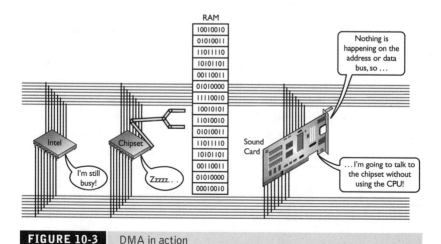

FIGURE 10-3   DMA in action

accesses the external data bus only a small percentage of the time, usually only 5 percent of the time on a Pentium or later CPU.

The chipset links to the CPU via the HRQ wire. The chipset uses the HRQ wire to inform the CPU when the external data bus is going to be busy. The chipset has eight wires, called DRQs (DMA requests), which lead to the DRAM refresh circuitry and ISA slots. DRQs were, and still are, more commonly known as *DMA channels*. If a device wants to perform a DMA data transfer, it must activate its assigned DMA channel.

In the early days, PCs used two cascaded DMA controller chips for a total of seven DRQs, and modern chipsets retain this structure for backward compatibility. The cascade made DRQ0 and DRQ4 the same wire, just like IRQ2/9. Oddly enough, however, techs never say DRQ 0/4—just DRQ0.

DRQs work exactly like IRQs, with all the same rules—such as no two devices being able to share the same DMA channel. DMA channel and DRQ are identical terms. No two devices can share DRQs.

> **Exam Tip**
>
> Don't bother memorizing DMA channels; just make sure you understand what DMA does!

DMA Limitations

DMA, as originally designed by IBM, has some serious limitations. First, DMA is designed to run from cards installed on the ISA bus. As a result, DMA is limited to a maximum speed of roughly 8 MHz. Second, the first DMA functions could handle only byte-wide (8-bit) data. Although this wasn't a problem in the first IBM PC, as PCs moved from 8088s through 286s, 386s, and 486s, it was often faster to skip 8-bit DMA and just wait for the CPU to move data.

The chipsets in later systems enabled 16-bit data transfers. If a device wants to use 8-bit transfers, it should use the lower DMA channel: 0 through 3. If a device wants to use 16-bit transfers, it should use a high DMA channel: 5 through 7. But even 16-bit data transfers ran at 8 MHz, which made them too slow for modern systems. This slowness relegated "Classic" DMA to low-speed, background jobs like floppy drive access, sound creation, and tape backup. A new process called bus mastering, however, has created a resurgence in the use of DMA in modern systems.

Bus Mastering

Most devices today that use DMA do so without accessing the chipset or the CPU. These devices are known as bus masters. *Bus-mastering* devices skip the chipset altogether—they have circuitry that enables them to watch for other devices accessing the external data bus and can get out of the way on their own. Bus mastering has become extremely popular in hard drives. All of today's EIDE hard drives take advantage of bus mastering. Hard-drive bus mastering is hidden under terms such as Ultra DMA and, for the most part, is totally automatic and invisible.

Who Uses Classic DMA?

Not many devices use classic DMA. On most systems, only sound cards and floppy drives still use classic DMA. However, you might still find virtually any type of device designed to use DMA. See Table 10-5.

TABLE 10-5	DMA Assignments	
DMA Channel	**Type**	**Function**
0	8-bit	None
1	8-bit	Open for use
2	8-bit	Floppy drive controller
3	8-bit	Open for use
5	16-bit	Open for use
6	16-bit	Open for use
7	16-bit	Open for use

Understand the "Big Three!"

Although it's important to understand the *whys* of I/O addresses, IRQs, and DMA, we need to discuss the *hows* of installation, configuration, and troubleshooting these big three. Today's PnP card installation makes problems more rare, but problems still occur often enough to warrant a good understanding of I/O addresses, IRQs, and DMA. The best way to do this is to give you a solid methodology to ensure that you can set up any device in any PC with a minimum of effort and a maximum of speed. Let's look at the more modern expansion buses available today and see how the big three fit into the picture of the modern PC.

Objective 10.04   Plug and Play

Plug and Play (PnP) consists of a series of standards designed to enable devices to self-configure. PnP is a broad standard, crossing over every type of expansion bus. PnP, in theory, makes device installation trivial. You simply install a device and it automatically configures its I/O address, IRQ, and DMA with no user intervention. Unfortunately, given the amazing variety of devices currently used in PCs all over the world, PnP has yet to reach this worthy goal—but it's getting close!

Identifying Plug and Play

For PnP to work properly, the PC needs three items. First, you need a PnP BIOS. If you have a Pentium or later computer, you have a PnP BIOS. You can verify this by watching the boot process and see if it's advertised. Figure 10-4 shows a typical PnP BIOS. A PnP BIOS will also have a reference in the CMOS, as shown in Figure 10-5.

Second, PnP also requires a PnP operating system, such as Windows 9x or Windows 2000. Older operating systems, such as DOS and Windows 3.x, could use PnP devices with the help of special device drivers and utility programs. Thankfully, the A+ exam isn't interested in these old operating systems.

Last, you need a PnP device. How do you know it's a PnP device? Easy! No one makes non-PnP devices anymore! Every modem, every network card, every sound card, every everything fully supports PnP. Non-PnP devices belong in a museum.

```
Award Modular BIOS v6.00PG, An Energy Star Ally
Copyright (C) 1984-2000, Award Software, Inc.

GREEN AGP/PCI/ISA SYSTEM

Main Processor : Pentium III 850MHz(100x8.5)
Memory Testing : 114688K

Award Plug and Play BIOS Extension v1.0A
Copyright (C) 2000 Award Software, Inc.

  Primary Master  : WDC WD1020AA, 80.10A80
  Primary Slave   : None
Secondary Master  : ATAPI CD-ROM DRIVE 40X
Secondary Slave   : None



Press DEL to enter SETUP
06/02/2000-694X-686A-XXXXXXXX-QW
```

FIGURE 10-4   PnP BIOS shown at boot

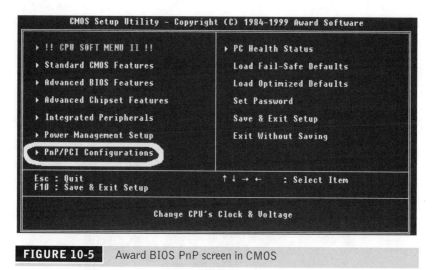

FIGURE 10-5 Award BIOS PnP screen in CMOS

Unfortunately, although no one makes non-PnP devices any longer, the large installed base of non-PnP devices (we call non-PnP devices *legacy* devices) motivates CompTIA to test your skills installing them.

Which leads us to the original question: How do you tell a PnP device from a legacy device? First of all, every PCI device is PnP—same for AGP devices. New ISA devices clearly advertise their PnP capabilities on the box, as well as in the device's documentation.

The word "legacy" works for any non-PnP aspect of the system. For example, if you have a non-PnP motherboard, we call it a *legacy motherboard*. If you have a non-PnP sound card, we call it a *legacy card*. If you use a non-PnP operating system, we say you use a *legacy operating system*. Get the idea? Good.

So, basically, the only legacy devices are old ISA cards. Let's assume you're holding an old ISA card and, because the card is old, it's probably safe to assume you don't have the box or documentation either. You have two options here. Drop the card into a system and see if the BIOS (Figure 10-6) recognizes the device as PnP.

If the BIOS fails to recognize the device, it still could be PnP, but you need to take a close look at the card itself. Look for jumpers on the card that set the I/O address and IRQ, as in Figure 10-7.

Once you see the I/O address and IRQ settings, you can probably assume it's legacy. Some cards have the capability to switch between PnP and legacy by moving a jumper or by running a special configuration program that came with the device. Figure 10-8 shows a modem that could switch between PnP and legacy.

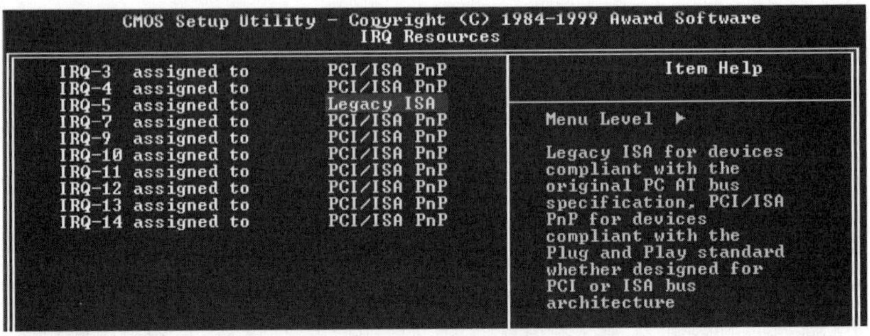

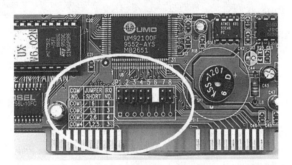

FIGURE 10-6   Legacy device recognized in BIOS

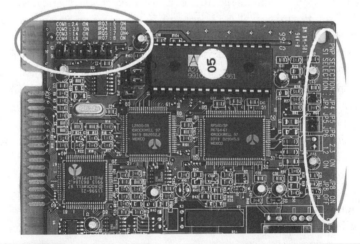

FIGURE 10-7   ISA device with jumper markings to set I/O addresses
and IRQs manually

FIGURE 10-8   Modem with legacy or PnP option (jumpers open for
PnP—jumpers closed for legacy)

How Plug and Play Works

Let's look at a hypothetical scenario to learn how PnP works. To do this, assume you have a machine with PnP BIOS, a PnP operating system (Windows 2000, for this example), and a mix of PnP and legacy devices. When you install a new PnP card, such as a fax/modem, PnP goes through a fairly standard process, the majority of which takes place during the boot process. Let's watch as the PnP boots, allocating system resources to devices in the system.

The PnP BIOS takes over immediately after the POST, first telling all PnP devices to "be quiet," so the BIOS can find any legacy ISA devices.

The PnP BIOS must then determine the resources used by legacy devices to see what's left over for the PnP devices. Basically, you can go two ways—the BIOS can try to find the ISA devices by querying a special list it keeps (more on this shortly), or you can tell the BIOS what system resources the legacy device uses and the BIOS will work around those resources. You can determine what BIOS will do by going into CMOS setup and changing the PnP settings.

Figure 10-9 shows the PnP/PCI Configurations screen from a typical Award BIOS. The left side of the screen contains the PnP settings. Two items enable you to direct how BIOS will perform its resource search: the Resources Controlled By setting and the Reset Configuration Data option.

The Resource Controlled By setting enables you to select between Auto and Manual. If you set this to Auto, the BIOS defers all system resource determination to the operating system. If you set it to Manual, you must manually set all the IRQ and DMA information to either PCI/ISA PnP or Legacy ISA.

Never use the manual setting unless your system contains legacy devices. If you do have legacy devices, I find the manual setting easier to use because I know what IRQs and DMAs the legacy devices use (because of jumper settings, and so on).

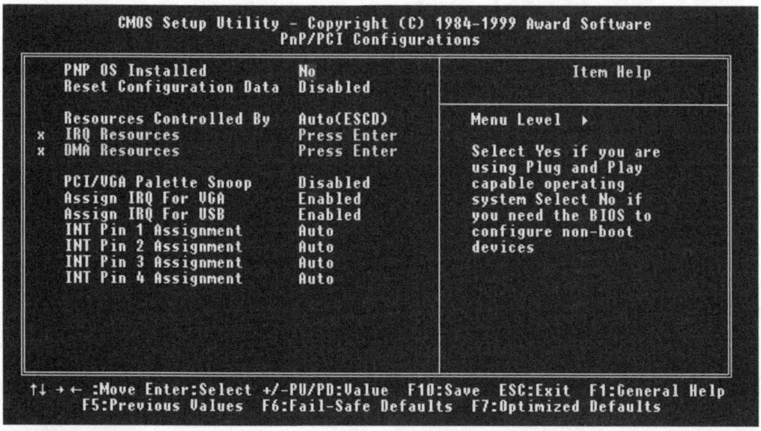

```
            CMOS Setup Utility - Copyright (C) 1984-1999 Award Software
                            PnP/PCI Configurations

      PNP OS Installed          No                         Item Help
      Reset Configuration Data  Disabled
                                                    Menu Level  ▶
      Resources Controlled By   Auto(ESCD)
    x IRQ Resources             Press Enter         Select Yes if you are
    x DMA Resources             Press Enter         using Plug and Play
                                                    capable operating
      PCI/VGA Palette Snoop     Disabled            system Select No if
      Assign IRQ For VGA        Enabled             you need the BIOS to
      Assign IRQ For USB        Enabled             configure non-boot
      INT Pin 1 Assignment      Auto                devices
      INT Pin 2 Assignment      Auto
      INT Pin 3 Assignment      Auto
      INT Pin 4 Assignment      Auto




    ↑↓ → ← :Move Enter:Select +/-PU/PD:Value  F10:Save  ESC:Exit  F1:General Help
          F5:Previous Values  F6:Fail-Safe Defaults  F7:Optimized Defaults
```

FIGURE 10-9   Award BIOS PnP/PCI Configurations screen

The second item in CMOS setup that concerns the BIOS search is the Reset Configuration Data option. To understand this option, you need to understand the function of what I call the device list.

Every PnP BIOS keeps a list of all system resources used, usually on the CMOS or Flash ROM. Interestingly, no official name exists for this storage area—although most folks call it the Extended System Configuration Data (ESCD) list. The PnP standard doesn't define the physical location of this data, but the standard strictly defines the PnP BIOS routines. In other words, the PnP standard doesn't care where the BIOS stores the information, just how the BIOS must respond when queried. I call this storage area simply the *device list*. In the example, assume the IRQ and DMA resources are manually configured in CMOS. The PnP BIOS then refers to this list to determine which resources are already used.

Now that the BIOS knows which resources are available, it can "wake up" each PnP device, asking the device which system resources it needs, as you can see in Figure 10-10. You can't give just any available system resource to a PnP device. Each PnP device has an internal list of acceptable system resources from which the BIOS must choose.

If a device can use only IRQs 3, 5, or 7, for example, then the BIOS can't allocate IRQ10 to the device; it must choose from the device's list. As each PnP device calls for certain resources, the BIOS allocates those resources to the PnP device. So, taking the example shown in Figure 10-10, PnP 1 might get I/O 310-31F, IRQ 2/9, and DMA 1; PnP 2 might get I/O 220-227 and IRQ11. The BIOS then adds them to the device list.

Sometimes adding another piece of equipment can confuse the PnP settings. For example, if you have a PnP device that needs a resource already taken by

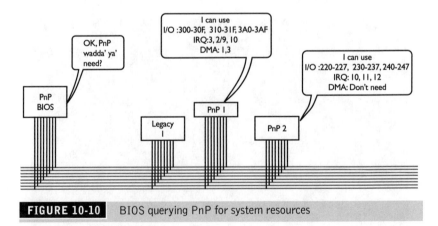

FIGURE 10-10   BIOS querying PnP for system resources

another device, you need to make the system reallocate the resources. That's where the Reset Configuration Data option comes into play, by making the PnP BIOS reconfigure all the devices. This is most often done when you install a device that the system refuses to recognize.

The operating system can also update and edit the device list. Unlike the BIOS, Windows makes a strong attempt to find the IRQs and DMAs for legacy devices through its own system information program. This program runs automatically at boot and when the Add New Hardware (or Add/Remove Hardware) Wizard is run from the Control Panel.

Once the operating system takes over, it queries the PnP BIOS to determine if you have installed a device. If it discovers a new device, the operating system then updates its own system resource information, makes changes to the resources if necessary, and, depending on the operating system, may prompt the user for the device driver.

Even with an occasional legacy device, PnP works magnificently, most of the time. On the more rare occasions when something goes wrong, a tech who lacks knowledge about system resources might find it difficult to fix the problem. The next chapter provides you with a methodology for device installation that gives you the tools you need to make every device installation successful.

CHECKPOINT

✔ **Objective 10.01: I/O Addresses**   Every device in a PC will have a set of I/O addresses. If two devices share I/O addresses, the system will crash. I/O addresses are written in hexadecimal, such as 3F8 or 2E8.

✔ **Objective 10.02: IRQs**   Almost all devices have an IRQ and no two devices can use the same IRQ. Know the standard I/O addresses and IRQs for all COM and LPT ports.

✔ **Objective 10.03: DMA**   A few devices use DMA—notably sound cards—and the rule against sharing resources applies. No two devices can share DMA channels.

✔ **Objective 10.04: Plug and Play**   PnP automatically configures system resources. Use the Add New Hardware Wizard (Windows 9x) or Add/Remove Hardware Wizard (Windows 2000) to install new devices into a Windows system.

REVIEW QUESTIONS

1. How does the CPU communicate with a device?

   A. The CPU uses the device's I/O addresses over the address bus
   B. The CPU uses the device's I/O addresses over the data bus
   C. The CPU uses the device's IRQ over the address bus
   D. The CPU uses the device's IRQ over the data bus

2. Steve adds two expansion cards to his system: a sound card and a network card. The sound card uses I/O addresses 300–330 and IRQ5. The network card uses I/O addresses 310–340 and IRQ2. When he boots the computer, it completely locks up. What's most likely the problem?

   A. The network card cannot use IRQ2; it's a reserved IRQ
   B. A buggy device driver
   C. IRQ conflict between the sound card and the network card
   D. I/O address conflict between the sound card and the network card

3. How does a device initiate a conversation with the CPU?

   A. By using I/O addresses
   B. By using polling
   C. By using an IRQ
   D. The device has to wait for the CPU to initiate all conversations

4. What is a COM port?

   A. A serial port
   B. A parallel port
   C. A preset combination of I/O addresses and IRQ for a serial device
   D. A preset combination of I/O addresses and IRQ for a parallel device

5. Of the following, which is most likely to be a legacy card?

   A. PCI card
   B. AGP card
   C. ISA card
   D. IDE card

6. What is the default IRQ for COM2?

  A. 2
  B. 3
  C. 4
  D. 5

7. What is the default IRQ for LPT1?

  A. 3
  B. 4
  C. 5
  D. 7

8. Which of the following are required for PnP to function properly?

  A. PnP-enabled BIOS
  B. PnP-enabled device
  C. PnP-enabled operating system
  D. All of the above

9. Which tool do we use in Windows 9x and Windows 2000 to install hardware?

  A. Add New Hardware Wizard
  B. Device Manager
  C. Task Manager
  D. CONFIG.INI

10. What CMOS function resets all the PnP information for the system?

  A. Legacy
  B. Reset Configuration Data
  C. Clear CMOS
  D. Advanced System

REVIEW ANSWERS

1. **A** The CPU uses the device's I/O addresses over the address bus to communicate with that device.

2. **D** The I/O addresses assigned to the cards clearly overlap, causing the problem.

3. **C** A device uses its IRQ to initiate a conversation with the CPU.

4. **C** A COM port is a preset combination of I/O addresses and IRQ for a serial device.

5. **C** The ISA card is most likely to be legacy. PCI and AGP cards are PnP by default, and drives, not cards, connect to the IDE controllers.

6. **B** The default IRQ for COM2 is 3.

7. **D** The default IRQ for LPT1 is 7.

8. **D** All three are required for PnP to work correctly.

9. **A** The Add New Hardware Wizard is the Primary tool for adding new devices to a Windows 9x or a Windows 2000 system.

10. **B** Most CMOS have a Reset Configuration Data option to reset all PnP information.

Installing and Configuring Peripherals

ETA	NEWBIE	SOME EXPERIENCE	EXPERT
	4 hours	3 hours	1.5 hours

Mastering the craft of the PC technician requires you to learn a lot of details about a zillion things. Even the most basic PC contains hundreds of discrete hardware components, each with its own set of characteristics, shapes, sizes, colors, connections, and so forth. This chapter should enable you to put together a typical PC.

Objective 11.01 **Assembling the PC**

Building a PC generally means starting with a case (called a *system unit* or an *enclosure*), power supply, and motherboard. From there, you can add the other essential ingredients, such as the CPU, RAM, video card, and keyboard. From this base, you can add a monitor, drives, and operating system to create a fully functional PC. Let's start with the essentials.

Power Supply and Wiring

The *power supply,* as its name implies, provides the necessary electrical power to make the PC operate. The power supply takes standard (in the United States) 110-volt AC power and converts it into 12-volt, 5-volt, and 3.3-volt DC power. Most power supplies are about the size of a shoebox cut in half and are usually gray or metallic colored.

A number of connectors lead out of the power supply. Every power supply provides special connectors for the motherboard and a number of other general-use connectors that provide power to any device that needs electricity.

You can see the power supply if you look at the back of your PC. It has a connection for a power plug that, in turn, runs to an electrical outlet and also has a big fan inside. Every PC uses a fan or two to keep the interior of the PC cool. The power plug connects to the motherboard and provides power. See Chapter 3 for the scoop on power supplies.

The Motherboard

When you put in a motherboard, don't be afraid to be a little tough here! Installing motherboards can be a wiggling, twisting, knuckle-scraping process. Chapter 3 covered the important details, so you should refer back to it for review. Just remember to use the proper form factor for the case (ATX for ATX case), plug in the motherboard power, and attach the wires for the LEDs and switches on the front of the case. Figure 11-1 shows a typical motherboard with connections nicely labeled.

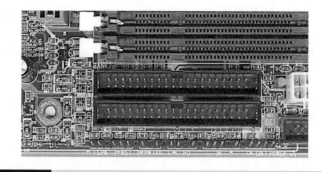

FIGURE 11-1 Motherboard wire connections labeled on the motherboard

CPU

Inserting and removing PGA-style CPUs is a relatively simple process. Figure 11-2 shows a technician installing a Celeron PPGA into a Socket 370. Note the notch and dot printed on the corners of the CPU. These *orientation markers* or *index corners* are designed to help you align the CPU correctly. It must line up with the notch (or notches) on the socket. Be careful! Although the orientation marks make it difficult to install a CPU improperly, incorrectly installing your CPU will almost certainly destroy the CPU or the motherboard, or both!

Chapter 9 covered the steps in the CPU install process, so refer back for details. But the following offers a few reminders and additional tips.

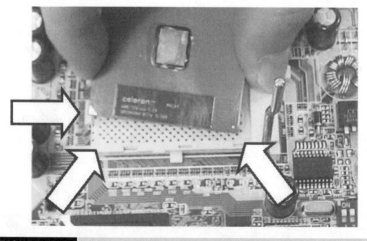

FIGURE 11-2 Close-up of CPU and socket showing orientation marks and notches

Installing a CPU into a ZIF socket is as simple as making sure the orientation notches line up on the CPU and the ZIF socket. Lift the ZIF arm, align the CPU, and it should drop right in. If it doesn't, verify your alignment and check for bent pins on the CPU. If you encounter a slightly bent pin, try a mechanical pencil that takes thick (0.9mm) lead. Take the lead out of the mechanical pencil, slide the pencil tip over the bent pin, and straighten it out. Be careful—a broken CPU pin ruins the CPU! Make sure the CPU is all the way in (no visible pins) and snap down the ZIF arm.

All modern CPUs need some form of heat dissipation, such as large heat sinks and powerful fans. Some PGA-type CPUs come with permanently attached fans, but most require you to install a fan after the CPU has been inserted into the socket. SEC-type CPUs commonly come packaged with an attached fan.

Before inserting a fan on a PGA-style CPU, you need to add a small amount of heat sink compound. This paste, usually white, helps transfer heat from the CPU to the heat sink/fan. Any electronics store sells heat sink compound. Many fans come with heat sink compound already on them; the heat sink compound on these pre-doped fans is covered by a small square of tape—be sure to take it off before you snap down the fan.

Securing PGA fans makes even the most jaded PC technician a little nervous. In most cases, you must apply a fairly strong amount of force to snap the fan into place—far more than you might think you should. Be extremely careful! Also, make certain that you use only a fan designed to work with your CPU package. Some Socket 370–specific fans, for example, will crack the ceramic casing on Socket A Duron CPUs, and *vice versa*.

To install an SEC-style CPU, slide it straight down into the slot. Special notches in the slot make it impossible to install them incorrectly, so remember—if it doesn't go in easily, it's probably not correct! All SEC CPUs must have a fan. Like CPU mounts, fans come in a bewildering variety of shapes and sizes. Be sure to add a *small* amount of heat sink compound before you mount the fan.

CPU fans require power. Look first for a 3-pin power connection on the motherboard and snap it into place. Most motherboards clearly mark this connector. If the CPU fan has a Molex connector, simply connect it to a corresponding Molex connector from the power supply.

Travel Advisory

Be sure to plug in the CPU fan's power. You can quickly toast a CPU if the fan does not run!

RAM

Chapter 9 covered installation of RAM SIMMs, DIMMs, and RIMMs (oh my!) in detail, so I won't rehash that information here. Just remember that all DRAM chips are extremely sensitive to static, so use extreme caution when installing DRAM. When I install DRAM, I always use an antistatic wrist pad, available at any electronics store. Always handle SIMMs and DIMMs like a piece of film, keeping your fingers on the edges. Few tech moments feel quite as awful as destroying a 512MB DIMM because of static discharge.

Video

Video cards enable the PC to display images on a monitor, as you know. All video cards have basic compatibility with all PCs (assuming expansion slot compatibility, of course) because they come with their own BIOS. You can generally just plug them in and get something on the screen, but a few issues crop up that you need to know about. Let's look at video memory and bandwidth issues, such as PCI vs. AGP, and then go into installation.

Video Memory

Video memory, which is crucial to the operation of a PC, is probably the hardest-working set of electronics on the PC. Video RAM constantly updates to reflect every change that takes place on the screen. The original video RAM was plain old DRAM, just like the DRAM on the motherboard. Unfortunately, DRAM has some significant limitations. As a result, manufacturers have developed a number of other types of RAM especially for video, as you'll recall from Chapter 6.

Memory produces two bottlenecks for data—access speed and data throughput. Typical low-cost video cards (usually $20 to $50 USD) commonly use DRAM for data storage. A few aspects of DRAM slow it down, making it a less-than-optimal choice for video RAM. One is the need to refresh DRAM memory approximately 18.5 times per second. During these refresh periods, neither the CPU nor graphics processor can read the memory bits in the video RAM. Another slowdown is the access/response time of DRAM. Even the fastest commonly available DRAM (50 ns) is too slow to handle the higher resolutions and color depths found on larger monitors. The final bottleneck for DRAM is physical. Its data lines are used both for writing data to the video port and receiving data from the CPU.

Manufacturers have overcome these bottlenecks in two ways—upping the width of the bus between the video RAM and video processor, and using specialized RAM that avoids the DRAM issues.

First, manufacturers reorganized the video display memory on cards from the typical 32-bit-wide structure to 64, 128, or even 256 bits wide. This wouldn't be of much benefit—because the system bus is limited to 32 or 64 bits—if it weren't for the fact that most video display cards are really coprocessor boards. Most of the graphics rendering and processing is handled on the card by the video processor chip rather than by the CPU. The main system simply provides the input data to the processor on the video card. By making the memory bus on the video card as much as eight times wider than the standard 32-bit pathway (256 bits), data can be manipulated, and then sent to the monitor much more quickly.

PCI

The standard PCI slots used in almost all systems are limited to 32-bit transfers at roughly 33 MHz, yielding a maximum bandwidth of 132 MB/s. It sounds like a lot until you start using higher resolutions, high-color depths, and higher refresh rates.

For example, take a typical display at 800×600—classic SVGA mode—with a fairly low refresh of 70 Hz. The 70 Hz means the display screen is being redrawn 70 times per second. If you use a low-color depth of 256 colors, which is eight bits ($2^8 = 256$), you can multiply all the values together to see how much data per second has to be sent to the display:

$$800 \times 600 \times 1 \text{ byte} \times 70 = 33.6 \text{ MB/s}$$

If you use the same example at 16 million (24-bit) colors, the figure jumps to 100.8 MB/s. You might say, "Well, if PCI runs at 132 MB/s, it can handle that! This statement would be true if the PCI bus had nothing else to do but tend to the video card—but almost every system has more than one PCI device, each requiring part of that throughput. The PCI bus simply cannot handle the needs of many current systems.

AGP

Simply leaving the Accelerated Graphics Port (AGP) as a faster and wider PCI would seriously misrepresent the power of AGP. AGP has several technological advantages over PCI, including the bus, internal operations, and capability to handle 3-D texturing.

First, AGP currently resides alone on its own personal data bus, connected directly to the North Bridge (see Figure 11-3). This is important because more advanced versions of AGP outperform every bus on the system except the frontside bus!

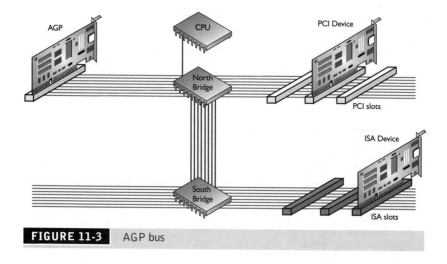

FIGURE 11-3   AGP bus

Second, AGP takes advantage of pipelining commands, similar to the way CPUs pipeline. Third, AGP has a feature called *sidebanding*—basically, a second data bus that enables the video card to send more commands to the North Bridge while receiving other commands at the same time. Further, the upcoming AGP 8*x* standard will allow for more than one AGP device—assuming the current specification remains unchanged in that regard.

Video Card Installation

The only great downside to AGP lies in the close connection tolerances required by the cards themselves. It's common to snap in a new AGP card and power up just to get a no video card beep or a system that doesn't boot. Always take the time to ensure that an AGP card is snapped down securely and screwed down before starting the system.

CMOS Options for Video

I'm always impressed by the number of video options provided in CMOS, especially in some of the more advanced CMOS options. I'm equally impressed by the amount of misinformation provided on these settings. In this section, I touch on some of the most common CMOS settings that deal with video.

Video Every standard CMOS setup shows an option for video support. The default setting is invariably EGA/VGA. Many years ago, this setting told the BIOS what type of card was installed on the system, enabling it to know how to talk to that card. Today, this setting has no meaning. No matter what you put there, it will be ignored and the system will boot normally.

Init Display First This CMOS setting usually resides in an advanced options or BIOS options screen. In multimonitor systems, Init Display First enables you to decide between AGP and PCI as to which monitor initializes at boot. This also determines the initial primary monitor for Windows 9x and Windows 2000.

Assign IRQ for VGA Many video cards don't need an IRQ. This option gives you the capability to choose whether your video card gets an IRQ. In general, lower-end cards that don't provide input to the system don't need an IRQ. Most advanced cards will need one. Try it both ways—if you need it, your system will freeze up if you don't assign an IRQ. If you don't need an IRQ, you get an extra IRQ.

VGA Palette Snoop True VGA devices only show 16 out of a possible 262,000 colors at a time. The 16 current colors are called the *palette*. VGA Palette Snoop opens a PCI video card's palette to other devices that may need to read or temporarily change the palette. I don't know of any device made today that still needs this option.

Video Shadowing Enabled As mentioned in previous chapters, this setting enables you to shadow the Video ROM. In most cases, this option is ignored because today's video cards perform their own automatic shadowing. A few cards require this setting to be off so, after years of leaving it on, I generally leave it off now.

Keyboard

You need a keyboard for most systems, or you won't get through POST. A missing keyboard or even a stuck key will create a text error and possibly a beep code as well. You'll recall from Chapter 1 that keyboards today come in three varieties: AT, PS/2, and USB. Get the one that works for your system or grab an adapter if necessary. All set? You have the system essentials installed.

Objective 11.02

Adding the Basic Ingredients

Once you have the system components in place and functional, it's time to add the rest of the basic ingredients of the PC—monitor, floppy drive, hard drive, mouse, CD-ROM, modem, NIC, and sound card. Whew! That's a lot to do in one small chapter, so let's get cracking!

Monitors

As far as A+ Certification is concerned, the standard VGA or SVGA CRT monitor rules the roost and the desktop. Aside from the fact that the monitor cable has a 3-row, 15-pin connector, the exams assume you know about display settings, refresh rate, dot pitch, and interlacing.

Display Settings

Monitor resolution is always shown as the number of horizontal pixels times the number of vertical pixels. A resolution of 640 × 480, therefore, indicates a horizontal resolution of 640 pixels and a vertical resolution of 480 pixels. If you multiply the values together, you can see how many pixels are on each screen: 640 × 480 = 307,200 pixels per screen. Lower resolution means fewer (and, therefore, larger pixels) on screen; higher resolution means more (and, therefore, smaller pixels) on screen.

Some common resolutions are 640 × 480, 800 × 600, 1,024 × 768, 1,280 × 1,024, and 1,600 × 1,200. Notice that these resolutions match a 4:3 ratio. We call this the *aspect ratio*. Most monitors are shaped like television screens, with a 4:3 aspect ratio, so most resolutions are designed to match—or at least to be close to—that shape.

The last important issue is to determine the maximum possible resolution for a monitor. In other words, how small can one pixel be? Well, the answer lies in the phosphors. A pixel must be made up of at least one red, one green, and one blue phosphor to make any color, so the smallest theoretical pixel would consist of one group of red, green, and blue phosphors, a *triad*. Various limitations in screens, controlling electronics, and electron gun technology make the maximum resolution much bigger than one triad.

Refresh Rate

Video data is displayed on the monitor as the electron guns make a series of horizontal sweeps across the display, energizing the appropriate areas of the phosphorous coating. The sweeps start at the upper-left corner of the monitor, and move across and down to the lower-right corner. The screen is "painted" only in one direction, and then the electron gun turns and retraces its path across the screen, to be ready for the next sweep. These sweeps are called *raster lines.*

The speed at which the electron beam moves across the screen is known as the horizontal refresh rate (HRR). The monitor draws a number of lines across the screen, eventually covering the screen with glowing phosphors. The number of lines isn't fixed, unlike television screens, which all have a fixed number of lines. After the guns reach the lower-right corner of the screen, they all turn off and point back to the upper-left corner. The amount of time it takes to draw the entire screen and get the electron guns back up to the upper-left corner is called the vertical refresh rate (VRR).

Set the VRR as high as the monitor and video card can handle. You should consider 85 Hz as a standard and go up from there. Running your monitor at 60 Hz or lower can damage your eyes, so don't do it! On the other hand, just because your video card can drive your monitor at 100 Hz, you shouldn't necessarily go there either. You'll damage your monitor if you run it too high. On some monitors, just changing from VGA (640×480) to SVGA (800×600) at the same color depth can exceed the ability of the monitor to refresh. You'll be looking at a blank or fuzzed-out screen on a very unhappy monitor! Check what your monitor can handle at the resolution you want to run and set it up accordingly in the Display Properties applet in the Control Panel.

Dot Pitch

The resolution of a monitor is defined by the maximum amount of detail the monitor can render. The dot pitch of the monitor ultimately limits this resolution. The *dot pitch* defines the diagonal distance between phosphorous dots of the same color and is measured in millimeters. Because a lower-dot pitch means more dots on the screen, it usually produces a sharper, more defined image. Dot pitch works in tandem with the maximum number of lines the monitor can support, to determine the greatest working resolution of the monitor. It might be possible to place an image at 1600×1200 on a 15-inch monitor with a dot pitch of .31 mm, but it wouldn't be readable.

The dot pitch can range from as high as .39 mm to as low as .18 mm. For most Windows-based applications on a 17-inch monitor, most folks find that .28 mm is the maximum usable dot pitch that still produces a clear picture.

Interlacing

To keep costs down, some low-end monitors produce *interlaced* images, which means the monitor sweeps or refreshes alternate lines of pixels on the display. In other words, it takes two sweeps through the screen to make one image. In its first pass, the monitor covers all the odd lines and, on the next pass, it covers the even lines. Interlacing enables a low-end monitor to support faster refresh rates by giving it twice as much time to make a screen. But interlacing depends on the ability of the eye and brain to combine the two separate sets of lines into one stable image. Interlacing is another way of creating eyestrain and headaches, so avoid it!

Video System

A monitor does not work in a vacuum, of course, but rather works hand-in-glove with the video card to produce the maximum resolution and refresh rate displayed. The amount and speed of the video RAM can seriously limit color depth. A monitor that can easily display 1024×768 with 24-bit color, will choke on an old video card with only 1MB of RAM. Do the math. $1024 \times 768 = 786,432$ pixels. Multiply that times 3 bytes per pixel for color information and suddenly you're looking at over 2MB of data to display the screen once, all of which needs to run through video RAM. Bottom line, if you run into a problem with "video," you need to check both the monitor *and* the video card!

Floppy Drives

The floppy drive enables you to access floppy disks (diskettes). The common 3.5-inch floppy drive accepts diskettes 3.5 inches in diameter, which makes a certain sense. You might also run into the rare and quite obsolete 5.25-inch drive, which accepts 5.25-inch floppy disks. Most 3.5-inch drives use a mini connector for power, whereas the 5.25-inch drives use a Molex.

The floppy drive connects to the computer via a 34-pin *ribbon cable,* which, in turn, connects to the motherboard. The connection on the motherboard is known as the floppy controller. In early PCs, the *floppy controller* was a special card that inserted into an expansion slot, but today's PCs all have the floppy controller built into the motherboard, as shown in Figure 11-4. Although the floppy connection is no longer the controller, the name has stuck.

Floppy drive ribbon cables differ from other types of ribbon cable in two ways. First, they're the narrowest ribbon cable, only slightly more than 1-inch wide. Second, the cable has a twist in the middle, usually close to where the floppy drive cable connects to the floppy drive. A PC can support up to two floppy drives. If it has two, both drives connect to the same ribbon cable. The A: drive connects to the end of the ribbon cable, whereas the B: drive connects in the middle.

FIGURE 11-4 On-board floppy drive controller

Inserting Ribbon Cables The ribbon connector plugs into the floppy controller on the motherboard. Make sure to orient the cable so the colored stripe points to pin 1. The motherboard usually has pin 1 clearly marked. Not all motherboards are so clear. Here are a few tips on finding pin 1. By the way, these rules work for all ribbon cables, not only floppy cables!

Ribbon cable connectors usually have a distinct orientation notch in the middle. If they have an orientation notch and the controller socket has a distinct slot in which the orientation notch will fit, you have pin 1. Unfortunately, not all connectors use the orientation notch, and many floppy drive controllers don't have slots.

Try looking in the motherboard book. All motherboard books provide a graphic of the motherboard, showing the proper orientation position. Look at other ribbon cables on the motherboard. In almost all motherboards, all plugs orient the same way.

Last of all, guess! You won't destroy anything by inserting the cable backwards. But when you boot up, the floppy drive won't work! Plus, if you reverse only one end of the cable, the floppy drive LED will light up and stay lit. No big deal. Turn off the system and try again!

After you insert the floppy ribbon cable into the floppy controller, you now need to insert the ribbon cable into the floppy drive. Watch out here! You still need to insert the cable into pin 1—all the rules of ribbon cable insertion work here, too.

Exam Tip

Reversing one end of a floppy drive ribbon cable causes the FDD LED to light up and stay lit.

Exam Tip

The A+ Exam test is *very* interested in the pins on cables! Know the number (34) and orientation (pin 1 to pin 1) for the pins.

By default, almost all PCs will first look on the A: floppy disk, and then to the C: drive at boot, looking for an operating system. How many of you have seen someone (maybe you) turn on a PC and get this famous error message?

```
Non-System disk or disk error
Replace and strike any key when ready
```

After a brief moment of panic, you then notice that someone (definitely *not* you) had left a floppy disk in the drive when he or she turned it off. The system started up, saw the floppy disk, and tried to read the operating system! This process enables technicians to insert a floppy disk into a sick computer to run programs when the hard drives fail. It also allows for silly errors like the one I just described, as well as enabling hackers to insert bootable floppy disks into servers and do bad things. You can change the boot sequence in CMOS. (For more information on troubleshooting floppy drives, see Chapter 13.)

Hard Drive

Although you could get by with only a floppy disk drive as your boot and mass storage device, most PCs require a hard drive installed, either EIDE or SCSI. Chapter 7 gave you all the details on EIDE drives, and Chapter 8 the scoop on SCSI, so I won't bother rehashing here. Just remember that cabling and jumper settings absolutely have to be correct for drives to work. Two masters on a single cable works as well as two drives set to ID 7 on a SCSI cable—not at all! And don't forget to plug in those Molex connectors.

Mouse

For many years, no such thing existed as a dedicated mouse port. Mice simply connected via either 9-pin or 25-pin serial ports. The acceptance of the mouse as an integral part of the PC, however, created a demand for the mouse to have its own connector, just as the keyboard had its own connector. In the mid-1980s, a new type of mouse connection debuted with the introduction of the IBM PS/2 personal computer. Although still a serial port, the new PS/2-style dedicated mouse port used a mini-DIN connector.

In older days, serial ports were on a card, usually called an *I/O card*. Modern motherboards now have built-in serial ports. The serial ports usually connect directly to the back of the motherboard, although a few modern systems connect the serial port to the motherboard via a small ribbon cable. This bit of cable is rather ingloriously referred to as a *dongle*.

Many PC systems now use a USB port for the mouse. USB's daisy-chain feature often enables you to connect a USB mouse to the front of the system or into the keyboard, significantly reducing the amount of cable lying around your PC!

CD-Media Drives

When CD-ROM drives were first developed, they had their own special controllers. Sound card makers then began to add those special controllers to their sound cards. These special controllers are now pretty much obsolete and have been replaced by CD-ROM drives that run on either EIDE or SCSI controllers, just like hard drives. Most PCs have an EIDE hard drive and an EIDE CD-ROM drive on one controller.

SCSI CD-ROM drives go on the same ribbon cable as the SCSI hard drives. One nice aspect to SCSI is because you can have up to seven devices on one ribbon cable, you can set up systems with a large number of CD-ROM drives. Of course, CD-ROM drives, like hard and floppy drives, also need power cables.

Many PCs now come with some type of recordable CD-ROM drive. For many years, the CD-R (Compact Disk-Recordable) was the only available form of recordable CD. CD-R drives enabled you to record on to special CD-R discs, but once the data was "burned" on to the CD-R, it couldn't be erased. Most regular CD-ROM drives, as well as CD-R drives, could read the CD-R discs.

Today, CD-RW (Compact Disk-Rewritable) drives have completely wiped out plain CD-R drives. As the name implies, CD-RW drives can write to special CD-RW discs, and then erase and rewrite a certain number of times to the same disc. Only CD-RW drives can read the CD-RW media, but CD-RW drives can write to CD-R discs as well. CD-RW drives read regular CD-ROM discs, CD-R discs, and CD-RW discs. The CD-RW drive's capability to read and write to such a variety of media has rendered the CD-R drive obsolete.

Objective 11.03   Installing Devices

Most technicians look at the concept of device installation from one of two extremes. On one side, we see the techs who simply drop a device in the PC and assume it will work. I call this Russian Roulette and, like the real Russian Roulette, it works great five out of six times! But, oh, when things go wrong—disaster! Don't play Russian Roulette with your system! The other extreme comes from the fraidy cat techs who, usually because of a bad past installation experience, insist on full system backups and about 20 other safeguards before they get anywhere near installing a device. Strive for somewhere between these two extremes with a quick, efficient methodology that minimizes risk to your system.

I use a three-step system of device installation. First, know the device! Second, install the thing. Third, get thee to Device Manager for some final tweaks and checks. Let's look at each step in detail.

Know the Device You're Installing

Learn about the device you want to install, preferably *before* you purchase it! Does the device work with your operating system? Does it have drivers for your operating system? If you use Windows 98 or Windows 2000, the answer to these questions is almost always "yes." If you use an old operating system like Windows 95 or an uncommon operating system such as Linux, these questions become critical. Check the device's documentation and check the web site for the device to see that you have the correct drivers. While you're checking, make sure you have the latest driver. Most devices get driver updates more often than the weather changes in Texas.

Install the Device

This step varies depending on whether you install a PnP or legacy device. For PnP, turn off the system, drop in the card, and reboot. The system will recognize the card and prompt for drivers. Legacy devices create a bit more hassle as you'll see but, before we go any further, you need to know the proper way to handle cards in general.

Handling Cards

Optimally, a card should be in one of two places: in a computer or in an antistatic bag. When inserting or removing a card, be careful to hold the card *only on its edges—don't hold the card by the slot connectors or touch any components on the board!*

Never insert or remove a card at an extreme angle. This might damage the card or wipe out the CMOS data. A slight angle is acceptable and even necessary for removing a card. Always screw the cards to the box with their connection screw. This keeps the cards from slipping out and potentially shorting against other cards. Also, many cards use the screw connection to ground the card to the box.

Many technicians have been told to clean the slot connectors if a particular card isn't working. This is almost never necessary and, if done improperly, can cause damage. An installed card should never need the slots cleaned. You should only clean slot connectors if you have a card that's been on the shelf for a while and the slot connectors are obviously dull. *Never use a pencil eraser!* Pencil erasers leave behind bits of residue that wedge between the card and the slot connector, preventing contact and causing the card to fail. Use a Bright Boy cleaning block. *Bright Boy cleaning blocks* look like large, gray pencil erasers and are perfect for polishing contacts. Be sure to rub lightly or you'll rub the contact completely away! Look for a Bright Boy cleaning block at your local hobby shop.

Installing Legacy Devices

Legacy devices add complexity to the installation process, requiring you to locate available resources, assign those resources, and then install the device! First, run Device Manager to determine the available resources for the system. All versions of Device Manager enable you to view the devices by resource. Once you determine the available resources, you must configure the device to use those resources. You might have to set jumpers, flip switches, or run a special setup program to do this. After you configure the legacy device's system resources, you need to inform Windows of the legacy device by running the Add/Remove Hardware Wizard.

Inspect and Verify

Go into Device Manager and verify the device is working properly. Assuming Device Manager shows the device working properly, put the device to work by making it do whatever it's supposed to do. If you installed a printer, print something. If you installed a scanner, scan something. If it works, you're done!

Ah, if only it always worked this easily. Many times the Device Manager shows us a problem. First, it might not even show the new device. In that case, verify you inserted the device properly and the device has power, if necessary. Run the Add/Remove Hardware Wizard and see if Windows recognizes the device. If the Device Manager doesn't recognize the device at this point, you have one of two problems: (a) The device is physically damaged and you must replace it or (b) the device is legacy and you failed to configure its system resources properly.

Objective 11.04   Installing Other Common Peripherals

Few self-respecting PCs would run around without a modem, network card, and sound card, so you need to know how to install each one. Let's check out the quirks for each expansion card.

Modems

A *modem* works with your telephone line to translate analog telephone signals into digital serial data. Modems can also translate digital serial data into analog telephone signals. An *external* modem sits outside the PC and plugs into a serial port. An *internal* modem is a card that snaps into an expansion slot. Internal modems carry their own onboard serial port. All modems, internal or external, have two RJ-11 sockets. One connects the modem to the telephone jack on the wall, and the other is for an optional telephone, so you can use the phone line when the modem is not in use.

Installation

Modems are extremely robust devices. The chance of a modem failing at the hardware level is quite small. The majority of the time, modem problems are actually problems with COM ports or with the way the communication software talks to the modem.

Set Up and Verify the COM Ports   Even in today's plug and play world, the number one reason modems don't work is COM port and IRQ conflicts. Make sure you install non-conflicting I/O addresses and interrupts.

If, by any chance, you're stuck with a legacy modem, don't forget COM3 and COM4 on most older modems were preset to IRQ4 and IRQ3, respectively. If COM1 and COM2 are already in use, then they're almost certainly using IRQ3 and IRQ4. Be sure to set the modem's IRQ to something other than IRQ3 or 4. Use IRQ5, 7, or whatever the legacy modem lets you use.

The capability of Windows 9x and Windows 2000 to handle plug and play modems makes most installations a true no-brainer—as long as the modem is configured for PnP. Most PnP modems have a jumper that turns the PnP option on or off. If the modem isn't PnP, the Add New Hardware Wizard will usually do an excellent job finding your modem.

Unfortunately, the Add New Hardware Wizard in Windows 9x will sometimes have trouble with uncommon IRQs. After running the Install Wizard, verify the port settings through the Device Manager. If the settings are incorrect, manually change them and reboot.

Verify the Modem's BIOS   Modern modems all have onboard BIOS. The term "BIOS" is actually a bit of a misnomer. A better term might be "command set"—the capability to handle different commands from modem drivers or from other modems. This BIOS does not occupy any DOS memory addresses, thus avoiding memory-management problems. It usually manifests as a flash ROM on the modem, making it upgradeable through software.

Upgradability is convenient because as anticipated new technologies arise— the latest one being the 56K V.90 standard—modem makers can easily upgrade modems, giving customers confidence to purchase modems in the face of ongoing improvements. Upgrading is quite simple: you download a program from the Internet, AOL, or whatever, and then run the program from a command prompt (the actual upgrade process depends on the maker of the modem). The downside is the BIOS can be corrupted quite easily, usually by something as simple as removing and reinserting the modem.

The BIOS can also have many upgrades, so making sure you have the right version is important. Contact the modem's manufacturer to verify the current version.

Communication Programs

Now that the modem's COM port is correct, you must make sure the communication software knows the type of modem you have, so it will know how to give the correct AT commands.

Windows communication programs don't need to know what type of modem you have installed—this information is handled by the Windows operating system. Just make sure you have the latest INF file for your modem and version of Windows to ensure seamless operation. The INF files that come with Windows 9x are almost certainly unacceptable. As a rule, always take a quick trip to the manufacturer's web site to grab the latest INF file before you install.

Given the low level of changes in modem technology, the modem drivers that come with Windows 2000 are often superb. The biggest problem with Windows 2000 is finding drivers for older modems, not worrying if the built-in Windows 2000 driver is the latest version.

On the rare occasions where Windows has difficulty recognizing your modem, try installing another brand of driver instead. Try Hayes Compatible or Standard settings, if available. Try modems that sound like your modem. Look at your modem and see if it has a chipset name, and then look for an option based on the chipset, rather than the modem type. If you can't determine a chipset, try Rockwell, which is a common and fairly generic type. You *can* find one that will work—just keep trying!

Windows 2000   To configure dialing rules and settings for a modem in Windows 2000, use the Phone and Modem Options tool in the Control Panel. As with many tech features of Windows 2000, you need to be logged on as an administrator or a member of the Administrators group to change some settings in the Phone and Modem Options applet. Windows 2000 will do a lot of work for you, but it will not detect certain internal modems, requiring you to do a manual installation through the Control Panel. Also, you might have to adjust the mode settings of modems supported by Network and Dial-up Connections to make them work with other modems on the Microsoft Windows Hardware Compatibility List. You might have to experiment with the settings a little bit, but in general, Windows 2000 is great at installing and configuring modems.

Travel Assistance

It might be useful to check the Microsoft web site for service packs and updates that might include additional modem support and fixes—http://www.microsoft.com/

NICs

Installing a network information center (NIC) into any version of Windows is usually a no-brainer, as most NICs today are completely plug and play. For the most part, this is simply a matter of turning off the PC, installing the card, and turning the system back on. The only trick is remembering to use the disk that comes with the NIC, even if Windows offers to use its own drivers. All the issues discussed with respect to installing devices also hold true for NICs—just because they're network cards doesn't mean anything else special needs to happen. If the NIC shows up in the Device Manager, you're done with this step. If it doesn't, well, go back to any of the previous chapters and review what it takes to install a device! Figure 11-5 shows a typical NIC, nicely installed in Windows 2000 Device Manager.

A few legacy NICs survive out there, so you still might need to install a NIC manually. As with all cards in the PC, NICs will use an I/O address and IRQ. Some will even use memory locations or DMA channels. It's important to remember that with legacy NICs, the card first needs to be configured using its setup program, which usually means first booting to Safe Mode Command Prompt Only (in Windows 9x) to run the configuration program that came with the NIC. After setting up the NIC's I/O address, IRQ, and so on you restart Windows, install the NIC's driver, and manually set the system resources for the NIC in the Device Manager. Although some cards still use jumpers, most NICs use software-based resource setting manifested by a setup/install program on an accompanying floppy disk.

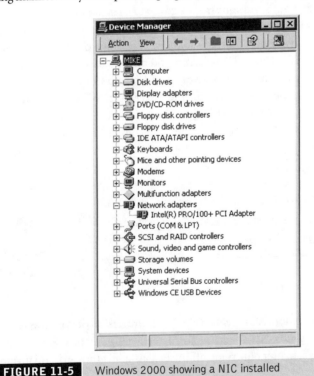

FIGURE 11-5 Windows 2000 showing a NIC installed

These programs should only be run from Safe Mode Command Prompt Only or from a bootable floppy. This is because Windows 9x will invariably interfere with them if you try to install them in the GUI. (Windows 2000 probably won't support the old NICs at all.) After you set up the NIC, be sure to save the information on the card (some do this automatically), and then *write down* the information, so you don't have to try to remember it when you need to set up the system resources manually. If you forget, you'll get to run that setup program again. After the card has been installed, you can then install the drivers manually. Click the Install New Hardware icon in the Control Panel. Although Windows will often find a legacy card automatically, it's usually faster to do the install manually. Select Network Adapters, and then click the Have Disk button to tell Windows where to locate the driver.

If the NIC didn't come with a diskette, check to see if Windows has a driver. If Windows doesn't have the driver, contact the company from which you purchased the card or try the manufacturer's web site. Many of the no-name Ethernet cards will use a driver called NE2000 compatible. Most of the time, the card will then install itself with a series of preset, and always incorrect, resources you'll have to correct manually.

Sound Cards

To play and record sounds, a sound card needs to connect to at least a set of speakers and a microphone. Virtually all sound cards have two miniature audio jacks for a microphone and a speaker. Many also provide miniature audio jacks for *line in* and *line out*. Most sound cards also provide a female 15-pin DB socket that enables you to attach an electronic musical instrument or to add a joystick to your PC.

The microphone and speaker sockets, as their names imply, connect a microphone and a set of speakers to the sound card. Line in enables a sound card to record from a stereo, tape recorder, or other audio source. Line out enables the sound card to output to those same types of devices. Most systems use only the speaker and microphone sockets. And, most PCs also have a small cable inside the case that runs between the sound card and the CD-ROM drive. This cable enables the CD-ROM drive to play audio CD-ROMs through the sound card, which, in essence, turns your PC into a stereo system.

Installation

Sound cards are notorious for having complicated device drivers, mainly because of their multiple functions of waveform, MIDI, and possibly CD-ROM. The trick to understanding sound card device drivers is to remember this multiple-function aspect and to treat each function as though it were a separate device requiring its own device drivers. Instead of thinking *sound card* driver, think *waveform* driver, *MIDI* driver, *CD-ROM controller* driver, and so on based on what features are contained in the individual sound card. Windows 9*x* and Windows 2000 PnP will find nearly every sound card ever made, although problems might occur with extra devices, such as onboard ATAPI controllers.

Some legacy cards, in fact, might not appear in Device Manager, even though they seem to be working fine. This is particularly true of older cards with Windows 3.*x* drivers. Windows 95 supports some of those drivers, as well as some older DOS drivers. In that case, the drivers are run through the SYSTEM.INI or CONFIG.SYS.

Installing a sound card using Windows 9*x* drivers normally generates multiple New Hardware Found screens from Windows 9*x* systems. Watch out for sound cards that add a bunch of applications you might not want. This is often difficult to determine ahead of time, so be ready to do some uninstalling—unless you want programs like talking parrots that repeat everything you say!

Windows 9x/2000   PnP in Windows 9*x* and Windows 2000 has made non-PnP sound cards completely obsolete. Device driver installation has been reduced to inserting a floppy or CD-ROM with the proper INF file—on the rare chance that Windows doesn't already have the necessary sound card. Windows now includes a basic, but complete, set of applications for playing and recording WAV files, and for playing MIDI files and CD-ROMs, plus a handy volume control applet that sits on the taskbar. Still, with all the conveniences Windows 9*x* and Windows 2000 provide, a good tech should be aware of a few nuances.

Device Manager

The first stop in understanding sound cards is the Device Manager. It can find any device recognized by Windows 9*x*/2000. Device Manager demonstrates quite clearly how Windows sees the several functions of the sound card as separate devices.

System resources rarely need to be changed, especially if the sound card is PnP. But, as we know from earlier chapters, even PnP devices sometimes create unanticipated resource conflicts. You can change the resources for each device simply by selecting properties for that particular device.

Once Windows recognizes the sound card and displays the separate devices in the Device Manager without errors, the sound card is ready to go! This assumes the speaker cables are properly inserted, the speakers are on, if necessary, and the volume is set loud enough to be heard.

Control Panel

The next stop on a new sound card install takes us to the Control Panel. I use the Sounds applet in Windows 9x (Sounds and Multimedia in Windows 2000) in the Control Panel to test the speakers by playing some test sounds.

There's no magic in using this applet to test. Use anything you want—just make those speakers make some noise! If the Play button in the Sounds applet is grayed out, you better head back over to the Device Manager—something is wrong! While you're testing, you might want to adjust the sound volume to a level comfortable for you—and for your neighbors.

The Volume Control handles volume for both incoming and outgoing sound. Open the Volume Control from the System Tray. One click brings up only the speaker volume—a great way to turn down the volume or mute the sound quickly. Alternate-click and select Adjust Audio Properties for a quick trip to the Sounds applet.

Double-clicking the Volume Control icon on the System Tray brings up the main Volume Control settings. These settings differ by sound card, so be sure to select the Options | Advanced Controls or Options | Properties menu to see all the devices, as Figure 11-6 shows.

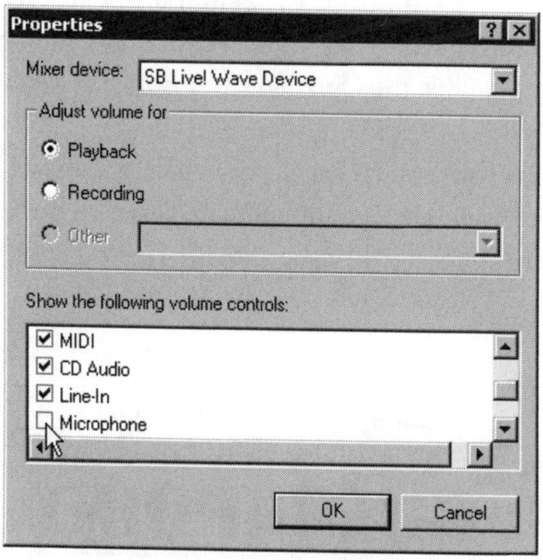

FIGURE 11-6   Selecting which sound devices to display

Using the Device Manager as a Troubleshooting Tool

Objective 11.05

The Device Manager rarely fails to see a device. More commonly, device problems manifest themselves in Device Manager via error symbols—a black !, a red *X*, a blue *I*, or a green ?.

- A black ! on a yellow circle indicates a missing device, one Windows does not recognize, or a device driver problem. The device might still work with this error.
- A red *X* indicates a disabled device. This usually points to a system resource conflict or a damaged device. The device won't work with this error.
- A blue *I* on a white field indicates a PnP device on which someone has configured the system resources manually. This merely provides information and doesn't indicate an error with this device.
- A green ? indicates Windows doesn't have the correct driver, but has successfully installed a compatible driver. The device works, but may lack certain functions. This error symbol only appears with Windows ME.

The ! symbol is the most common error symbol and it's usually the easiest to fix. First, double-check the device's connections. Second, try reinstalling the driver with the Update Driver button. To get to the Update Driver button, click the desired device and select Properties. In the Properties dialog box, select the Driver tab. On the Driver tab, click the Update Driver button. (For more information on Device Manager, see Chapter 18.)

Think of PnP as you would one of your children: love it, trust it, and let it do what it wants—but watch it carefully in case it tries to do something irrational. PnP makes installations easier, but shouldn't make you complacent.

CHECKPOINT

✔ **Objective 11.01: Assembling the PC**   Snap SEC-style CPUs into their slot firmly. Make sure the AC power is disconnected from the PC. Don't forget to plug in the power for the fan before you turn on the PC.

✔ **Objective 11.02: Adding the Basic Ingredients**   Floppy drive installation requires you to supply power—usually a mini-connector—and insert a 34-pin ribbon cable properly, with pin one going to pin one on both the drive and the motherboard. The red stripe down one side indicates pin one. If you see the FDD LED light up and stay lit, you know the cable is reversed on one end or the other. Hard drives and CD-media drives require you to jumper them properly—master, slave, or standalone—and orient the ribbon cable pin one to pin one on the motherboard. Plus, they need power.

✔ **Objective 11.03: Installing Devices**   When installing expansion cards, be careful to handle them only on the edges and don't touch the contacts. Also, always insert them at a 90-degree angle to the motherboard with the AC power disconnected.

✔ **Objective 11.04: Installing Other Common Peripherals**   Verify the COM ports specified for a modem and check Device Manager to avoid conflicts with other devices. Also, if you have a 56K modem that doesn't like your ISP, check with the manufacturer for a BIOS update to the V.90 standard.

✔ **Objective 11.05: Using the Device Manager as a Troubleshooting Tool**   Rely on Device Manager to assist you in troubleshooting, and diagnosing installation and driver problems. Pay attention to the errors or warnings marked next to any device.

REVIEW QUESTIONS

1. A sound card is working in Windows 95, but no sound card is installed in the Device Manager. How can this happen?

    A. Windows 95 protected mode drivers don't show up in the Device Manager

    B. The Registry is corrupt

    C. Windows 95 is using drivers from CONFIG.SYS or SYSTEM.INI

    D. This can't happen

2. When installing a NIC card, the only trick to remember is to:

    A. Use the driver Windows offers to run the NIC

    B. Use the disk containing the driver that came with the NIC

    C. Have the PC turned on when placing the NIC card in it

    D. If the NIC shows up in the Device Manager, you're done with the installation

3. A new device has been installed in a Windows 95 system. On reboot, the device isn't functioning. When inspecting the device in the Device Manager, you notice a yellow exclamation point. This tells you:

   A. The device isn't working properly
   B. The device driver is corrupted
   C. The device isn't getting power
   D. The device is destroyed

4. You just purchased a new PnP device for your PC and, after you install the support software, the device fails to work. What needs to be upgraded in the PC?

   A. Virtual memory
   B. File System
   C. System BIOS
   D. Driver Database

5. You need to install a legacy ISA modem that only supports COM1 and COM2 using the standard I/O addresses and IRQs into a modern ATX system. Which of the following would be the best action to insure no IRQ conflicts?

   A. Configure the PC to use IRQ 2/9
   B. Use IRQ 12 for the modem
   C. Disable one of the two onboard serial ports in CMOS
   D. Disable the modem's IRQ

6. A yellow circle with an exclamation point on an icon in the Device Manager means the item:

   A. Is disabled
   B. Has problems
   C. Is defective
   D. Is removed

7. If a device doesn't plug and play in Windows 95, where can you assign system resources?

   A. In the Print folder
   B. In the Device Manager
   C. At the command prompt
   D. From the Start menu

8. You install a P35U Camera device in the graphic. You view your device in the Device Manager and notice that next to the device is a red *X*. What does the red *X* signify?

   A. This device is disabled

   B. This device isn't recognized by Windows

   C. This device isn't installed

   D. This device is enabled with restrictions

9. You can add new device drivers in all the following ways, except:

   A. By using the Hardware Wizard

   B. In the System applet in the Control Panel

   C. By using the manufacturer's setup disk

   D. By using plug and play

10. What must be installed to enable Windows 9*x* and Windows 2000 to play audio CD-ROMs?

   A. Windows 9*x* and Windows 2000 cannot play audio CD-ROMs

   B. Nothing has to be installed—just insert the audio CD-ROM and it will play

   C. The CD-Audio connector that links the sound card directly to the CD-ROM drive

   D. A special set of speakers must be installed for audio CD-ROMs to play

REVIEW ANSWERS

1. **C** Windows 95 will support older DOS or Windows 3.*x* drivers. When this happens, the device won't appear in Device Manager, yet it will work.

2. **B** The only trick to remember is you should use the disk that came with the NIC as the driver source, rather than to accept the driver suggested by Windows.

3. **A** The exclamation point only tells you the device isn't working properly. It can't tell you *why* the device isn't working properly.

4. **C** PnP standard has evolved at such a fast pace over the past several years and some system BIOS have grown too dated to support newer PnP devices. If a new PnP device fails to work on a PC, check the web site of the motherboard's maker for the latest update for your BIOS.

5. **C** Disabling one of the onboard serial ports will make COM1 or COM2 available to the modem.

6. **B** If you ever see an exclamation point in a yellow circle on an icon, the device indicated isn't working correctly. This doesn't mean it's defective, but it's probably not set up correctly.

7. **B** Device Manager is the tool for configuring devices and assigning resources, even for non-PnP devices.

8. **A** A red *X* on a device in Device Manager shows the device is disabled.

9. **B** The System applet in the Control Panel enables the user to view items already on the system and setup, but not add new devices. You can update existing drivers here.

10. **C** Although you could connect a pair of speakers to the CD-ROM drive's headphone jack, that might lead to tittering and office gossip behind your back! Connect the CD-ROM drive inside the case directly to the sound card via the special CD-audio cable.

Printers

ETA	NEWBIE	SOME EXPERIENCE	EXPERT
	6 hours	4 hours	2 hours

Despite the glorious promise of the paper-free office, printing continues to be a necessary function in homes and businesses worldwide. A good tech understands the various types of printers and printer connections, and can diagnose and troubleshoot printing problems to keep users up and running with all those paper documents.

Objective 12.01 Printers

Printers are one of the most common types of PC peripherals. The A+ exam has traditionally stressed this area. This chapter can help you to identify the different printer types, connections, configurations, and common troubleshooting issues.

Dot Matrix Printers

Dot matrix technology uses a series or matrix of pins to create dots on a piece of paper arranged to form characters. The speed at which a dot matrix printer prints is measured in the number of characters it can produce per second. The printhead mechanism pushes each pin into the ribbon, which then strikes the paper. The original dot matrix printheads had 7 pins, while newer, letter-quality printheads have 24 pins.

Dot matrix printers are called *impact* printers because the printing mechanism physically strikes the page. Paper moves through a dot matrix printer using a *tractor feed* mechanism, as shown in Figure 12-1. Spoked wheels located on each side of the paper feed mechanism move the paper. The spokes on the outer edges of the wheels fit into holes on the sides of specially designed *continuous form* paper. As the wheels turn, they pull the paper through the printer.

Inkjet Printers

Inkjet printers create printouts by squirting ink out of special inkjet cartridges. They use both black and colored ink cartridges, and they can combine ink colors to create a wide range of hues. Inkjet printers are *nonimpact* printers because their print mechanism never actually touches the paper. Because they process an entire page at a time before starting to print it, they are referred to as *page* printers. Inkjet printers use a *friction feed* mechanism to feed paper through the printer. Sheets of paper are stacked in the paper tray, where small rollers press down to create friction and pull a sheet of paper through the printer.

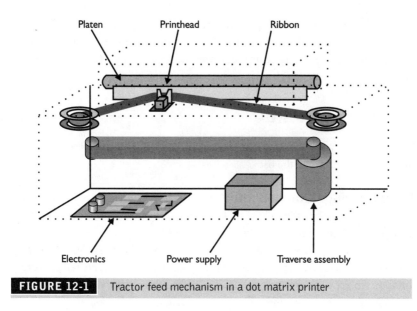

Platen   Printhead   Ribbon

Electronics   Power supply   Traverse assembly

FIGURE 12-1   Tractor feed mechanism in a dot matrix printer

Most inkjet printers use a thermal process to eject ink onto the paper. The printing element heats up, boiling the ink. A tiny bubble of ink forms on the end of the print nozzle. Once the bubble becomes sufficiently enlarged, it pops, at which point electrically charged plates deflect the ink onto the paper. Sounds kind of messy, but it's actually precise. An inkjet print head contains between 300 and 600 nozzles, each about the diameter of a human hair. When the inkjet cartridge is not in use, pump pressure keeps the ink from leaking out the nozzle.

Canon and Hewlett-Packard inkjet printers use this thermal process. Epson printers use a different, proprietary inkjet technology featuring a special *crystal* at the back of the ink reservoir that flexes when an electric current is applied to it. When the crystal flexes, it forces a drop of ink out of the nozzle. The way it flexes determines the size and placement of the resulting drop.

A common problem with inkjet printers is the tendency for the ink inside the jets to dry out when it's not used, even for a relatively short time. To counter this problem, all inkjet printers move the printhead to a special park position that keeps the ink from drying.

Laser Printers

Laser printers rely on the photoconductive properties of certain organic compounds. *Photoconductive* means that particles of these compounds, when exposed to light (that's the *photo* part), will conduct electricity. Laser printers use lasers as a light source because of their precision.

Like inkjet printers, laser printers are nonimpact page printers. The print mechanism never touches the paper and they image the entire page before transferring it to paper. Some laser printers even support *duplexer* technology, which enables you to print on both sides of the paper.

Laser Printer Parts

Laser printers have many components, and the A+ exams expect you to know them. Let's run through the list.

Toner Cartridge Components   To reduce maintenance costs, many laser printer parts, in particular, those that suffer the most wear and tear, have been incorporated into the *toner cartridge* (see Figure 12-2).

While this makes replacement of individual parts nearly impossible, it also greatly reduces the need for replacement. Those parts most likely to break are replaced every time you replace the toner cartridge. Unlike inkjet printers, the relatively high initial cost of laser printers makes their repair a common and popular option.

Travel Assistance

If you're looking for a company that sells laser printer parts, try The Printer Works–a large mail-order outfit with very knowledgeable sales folks. Like an auto parts store, they can often help you determine the problem, and then sell you the part. The Printer Works is on the Web at http://www.printerworks.com.

FIGURE 12-2   Laser printer's toner cartridge

The Photosensitive Drum

The *photosensitive drum* is an aluminum cylinder (see Figure 12-3) coated with particles of photosensitive compounds. The drum itself is grounded to the power supply, but the coating is not. When light hits these particles, whatever electrical charge they may have had drains out through the grounded cylinder. The drum, usually contained in the toner cartridge, can be wiped clean if it becomes dirty. If you do this, however, *exercise extreme caution!* If the drum becomes scratched, the scratch will appear on every page printed from that point on. The only repair in the event of a scratch is to replace the toner cartridge.

Erase Lamp

The *erase lamp* exposes the entire surface of the photosensitive drum with light, making the photosensitive coating conductive. Any electrical charge present in the particles bleeds away into the grounded drum, leaving the surface particles electrically neutral.

Primary Corona Wire

The *primary corona wire,* located close to the photosensitive drum, never touches the drum. When charged with an extremely high voltage, an electric field (or corona) forms, allowing voltage to pass to the drum and charge the photosensitive particles on its surface. The *primary grid* regulates the transfer of voltage, ensuring the surface of the drum receives a uniform negative charge of between ~600 and ~1,000 volts.

Laser

The *laser* is the printer's writing mechanism. Any particle on the drum struck by the laser becomes conductive, allowing its charge to be drained away into

FIGURE 12-3   Toner cartridge with photosensitive drum exposed

the grounded core of the drum. In this way, the laser *writes* a positive image onto the drum. Particles struck by the laser are left with a ~100 volt negative charge, compared to the ~600 to ~1000 volt negative charge of the rest of the drum surface.

Toner   The *toner* in a laser printer is a fine powder, made up of plastic particles bonded to iron particles. The *toner cylinder* charges the toner with a negative charge of between ~200 and ~500 volts. Because that charge falls between the original uniform negative charge of the photosensitive drum (~600 to ~1000 volts) and the charge of the particles on the drum's surface hit by the laser (~100 volts), particles of toner are attracted to the areas of the photosensitive drum that were hit by the laser, that is, to the areas with a positive charge *relative to* the toner particles.

Transfer Corona   To transfer the image from the photosensitive drum to the paper, the paper must be given a charge that will attract the toner particles off the drum and on to the paper. The transfer corona applies a positive charge to the paper, drawing the negatively charged toner particles to the paper. The paper, with its positive charge, is also attracted to the negatively charged drum. To prevent the paper from wrapping around the drum, a *static charge eliminator* removes the charge from the paper.

Fuser   In most printers, the *fuser* assembly is outside the toner cartridge, but it can be an integrated component. After the static charge eliminator has removed the paper's static charge, the toner is still merely resting on top of the paper. The toner must be fused to the paper to make the image permanent. Two rollers—a pressure roller and a heated roller—work together to fuse the toner to the paper. The pressure roller presses against the bottom of the page, while the heated roller presses down on the top of the page, melting the toner into the paper. The heated roller has a nonstick coating, such as Teflon, to prevent the toner from sticking to it.

The Laser Printing Process

Let's put these steps together to see how a typical laser printer does its job. Remember, some brands of laser printers may depart from this exact process, although most do work in exactly this order. The printing process contains six steps, in this order:

     Clean → Charge → Write → Develop → Transfer → Fuse

Exam Tip

Know the order of a laser printer's printing process! To help you keep the steps in order, remember: Careful Computer Weenies Don't Trade Files!

Step 1: Clean the Drum   The printing process begins with the physical and electrical cleaning of the photosensitive drum. Before printing each new page, the drum must be returned to a clean, fresh condition. All residual toner left over from printing the previous page must be removed, usually by a rubber cleaning blade that scrapes the surface of the drum. If residual particles remain on the drum, they appear as random black spots and streaks on the next page. The physical cleaning mechanism either deposits the residual toner in a debris cavity or recycles it by returning it to the toner cartridge. Damage to the drum during the physical cleaning process causes a permanent mark to be printed on every page.

The printer must also be electrically cleaned, as shown in see Figure 12-4. One or more erase lamps bombard the surface of the drum with the appropriate wavelengths of light, causing the surface particles to discharge into the grounded drum. After the cleaning process, the drum should be completely free of toner and have a neutral electrical charge.

Step 2: Charge the Drum   To make the drum receptive to new images, it must be charged. The corona wire applies a uniform negative charge to the entire surface of the drum, normally between ~600 and ~1000 volts.

Steps 3 and 4: Write and Develop the Image   Next the laser writes a positive image on the surface of the drum, as shown in Figure 12-5. Every particle on the drum hit by the laser will release most of its negative charge into the drum. Those particles are then positively charged relative to the toner particles, and will attract them, creating a developed image on the drum.

Step 5: Transfer the Image   To transfer the image from the drum on to the paper, the transfer corona charges the paper with a positive charge. Once in proximity to this positive charge, the negatively charged toner particles leap from the drum to the paper. Then the static charge eliminator removes the paper's positive charge, leaving the particles resting on the paper.

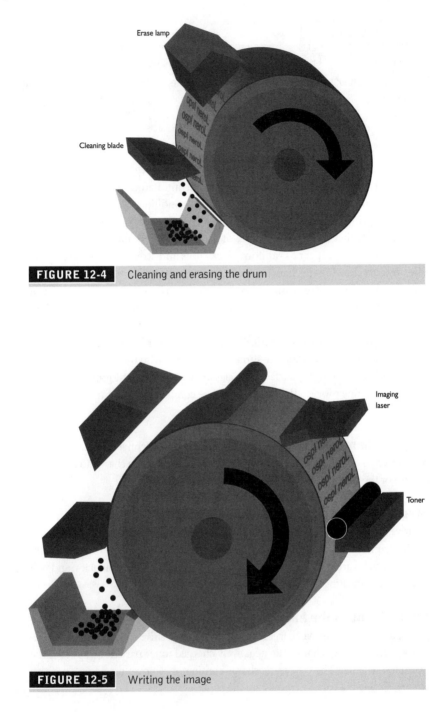

FIGURE 12-4 Cleaning and erasing the drum

FIGURE 12-5 Writing the image

Step 6: Fuse the Image   For the final step in the process, the fuser melts the toner on to the paper. (See Figure 12-6.) The printer then ejects the final printed copy, and the process begins again with the physical and electrical cleaning of the printer.

Travel Advisory

The heated roller of the fuser produces enough heat to melt some types of plastic media, particularly overhead transparency materials. *Never* use transparencies in a laser printer unless they are specifically designed for use in laser printers. Use of nonapproved materials can seriously damage a laser printer and void the warranty!

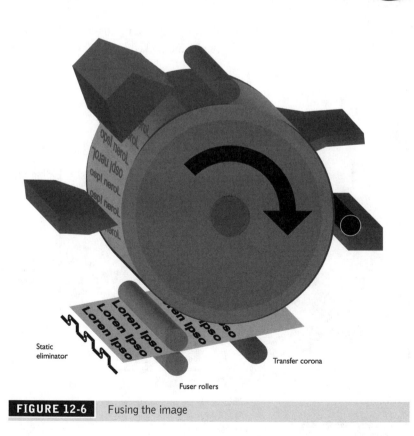

Static
eliminator

Transfer corona

Fuser rollers

FIGURE 12-6   Fusing the image

Other Laser Printer Components

Although the majority of the printing activity takes place within the toner cartridge, many other parts of the laser printer are hard at work outside the cartridge, as you can see in Figure 12-7.

Power Supplies   All laser printers have at least two separate power supplies. The first power supply is called the *primary* power supply or sometimes just the *power* supply. The primary power supply powers the motors that move the paper, the system electronics, the laser, and the transfer corona.

The second power supply is the *high-voltage* power supply. It usually only powers the primary corona. The extremely high voltage of this power supply makes it one of the most dangerous devices in the world of PCs! Therefore, it's imperative that—except when inserting a new toner cartridge or paper—you *always turn off* a laser printer before you open it!

Turning Gears   A laser printer performs many mechanical operations. The paper must be picked up, fed through, and kicked out of the printer. The

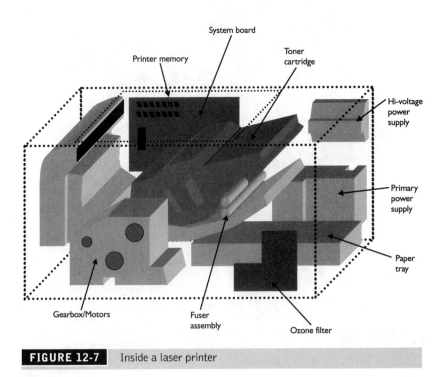

FIGURE 12-7   Inside a laser printer

photosensitive roller must be turned and the laser, or a mirror, must be moved from left to right. The toner must be evenly distributed and the fuser assembly must squish the toner into the paper. All these functions are performed by complex gear systems. In most laser printers, these gear systems are packed together in discrete units, generically called *gear packs* or *gearboxes*. Most laser printers have two or three gearboxes. These are relatively easy to remove in the rare case where one of them fails. Most gearboxes have their own motor, or solenoid, that moves the gears.

Fuser Assembly   The *fuser assembly* is almost always separate from the toner cartridge. It's usually positioned near the bottom of the toner cartridge. Look for the two rollers that fuse the toner. In some printers, the fuser is relatively enclosed and the rollers are hidden from view. When hunting for the fuser, think about the data path of the paper and remember fusing is the final step in the printing process.

Transfer Corona   In some laser printers, the transfer corona may also be outside the toner cartridge. The *transfer corona* is a thin wire, usually protected by other thin wires. An exposed transfer corona is a particularly troublesome part—it's prone to dirt build-up and must be cleaned, yet it's also quite fragile. Most printers with an exposed transfer corona come with a special tool to clean it.

System Board   Every laser printer has at least one electronic board containing the main processor, the printer's ROM, and the RAM it uses to store the image before it's printed. Many printers divide these functions among two or three boards dispersed around the printer. The printer may also have an extra ROM chip and/or a slot where you can install an extra ROM chip, usually for special functions such as Postscript printing. When the printer doesn't have enough RAM to store the image before it prints, it generates a Memory Overflow error.

Travel Advisory

Adding RAM is usually a simple job—just snapping in a SIMM stick or two—but getting the *right* RAM is important. Call the printer manufacturer and ask what type of RAM you need. Although most printer companies will happily sell you their expensive RAM, most printers can use generic DRAM like the kind you use in your PC.

Ozone Filter   The coronas inside laser printers generate ozone (O_3). While the amount generated isn't harmful to humans, high concentrations of ozone will damage printer components. To counter this problem, most laser printers have a special ozone filter that must be replaced periodically.

Sensors and Switches   Every laser printer contains a large array of sensors and switches. The sensors are used to detect a broad range of conditions such as paper jams, empty paper trays, or low toner levels. Many sensors are really tiny switches that detect conditions like open doors. Most of the time, these sensors and switches work reliably, but they can occasionally become dirty or broken and send a false signal to the printer. Simple inspection is usually sufficient to determine if a problem is real or just the result of a faulty sensor or switch.

Exam Tip
Know and understand the various laser printer components!

Objective 12.02   Printer Connections and Configurations

As a technician, you should know how to connect and configure parallel, serial, USB, and network printers.

Serial Printers

Most printers use parallel or USB connections, but some older printers use serial connections. *Serial printers* connect to a serial port on the back of your PC.

To connect a serial printer, you need a cable with a DB9 or DB25 female connector that plugs into the serial port on the back of your PC and a DB25 male connector that plugs into the back of the printer. Serial cables can reach lengths of up to 25 feet without significant EMI or crosstalk problems.

Exam Tip
Serial is the slowest printer connection.

Parallel Printers

Although the parallel port is being overtaken by USB, it remains the connection type most identified with computer printers.

The Parallel Port

The parallel port was included in the original IBM PC as a faster alternative to serial communication. The IBM engineers considered serial communication, limited to one bit at a time, to be too slow for the high-speed devices of the day, such as dot matrix printers. Like so much of the technology used in PCs today, the standard parallel port has been kept around for backward compatibility.

The speed of a standard parallel port has remained the same, despite speed improvements in almost every other part of the PC. The maximum data transfer rate of a standard parallel port is approximately 150 kilobytes per second (KB/s). Standard parallel ports aren't capable of true bidirectional communication. Standard parallel communication on a PC relies heavily on software, eating up a considerable amount of CPU time.

Despite the "standard" label, the lack of standardization remains a source of incompatibility problems for some parallel devices. Because manufacturers are not required to adhere to a single standard for electromagnetic shielding on the cables to protect against EMI and crosstalk, for example, parallel cables longer than six feet are not recommended.

The IEEE 1284 Standard

In 1991, a group of printer manufacturers proposed to the Institute of Electrical and Electronics Engineers (IEEE) that a committee be formed to devise a standard for a backward-compatible, high-speed, bidirectional parallel port for the PC. The committee was the IEEE 1284 committee, hence, the name of the standard. The IEEE 1284 standard attempts to deal with both the poor performance and lack of standardization of standard parallel ports, while maintaining backward compatibility.

The IEEE 1284 standard requires the following:

- Support for all five modes of operation (Compatibility, Nibble mode, Byte mode, EPP, and ECP).
- A standard method of negotiation for determining which modes are supported both by the host PC and by the peripheral device.
- A standard physical interface (the cables and connectors).
- A standard electrical interface (termination, impedance, and so forth).

Because only one set of data wires exists, all data transfer modes included in the IEEE 1284 standard are *half-duplex,* that is, data is transferred in only one direction at a time

Compatibility Mode/Centronics Mode

The standard parallel port used in the original IBM PC is often referred to as a *Centronics* port. This connection normally manifests itself as a female DB25 (25-pin) connector on the PC and as a female Centronics 36-pin connector on the printer.

The pins or wires on the DB25 connector are assigned various tasks. Four control wires are used for control and handshaking signals going from the PC to the printer. Five status wires are used for handshaking signals from the printer to the PC, and for standardized signals from the printer to the PC, such as out of paper, busy, and offline. Only eight wires are used for passing data and that data travels in only one direction: from the PC to the printer. The remaining eight wires are used as grounds.

The advantage to Centronics mode is backward compatibility, but its disadvantages are clear. Data passes in only one direction, from the PC to the peripheral device, or forward. In addition, the CPU must constantly poll the status wires for error messages and handshaking signals, using up significant numbers of CPU clock cycles. Standard/Centronics mode transfers are limited to approximately 150 KB/s.

Nibble Mode

Nibble mode is the simplest way to transfer data in *reverse* direction—from the printer to the PC. Nibble mode requires no special hardware, and can normally be used with any standard parallel port (that is, it doesn't require an IEEE 1284 parallel port). When used in concert with compatibility/Centronics mode, it provides a limited form of bidirectional communication using any parallel port.

All parallel ports have five status wires designed to send signals from the peripheral to the PC. Using four of these wires at a time, we can transfer a byte (8 bits) of data in two pieces, one nibble (4 bits) at a time. Nibble mode is even more software-intensive than compatibility/Centronics mode, eating up many CPU clock cycles. This intensive use of CPU time, combined with the limitation of passing data in small chunks, limits Nibble mode data transfers to approximately a whopping 50 KB/s.

Byte Mode/Enhanced Bidirectional Port

Byte mode enables reverse direction (peripheral to PC) parallel communication by using extra hardware that handles the negotiation between the PC and the peripheral. With *Byte* mode, two-way communication can achieve speeds approaching the speed of the one-way

Centronics data transfers, approximately 150 KB/s. Parallel ports capable of Byte mode transfers are sometimes referred to as *enhanced bidirectional ports*. Byte mode is often supported by parallel ports and devices that don't support the entire IEEE 1284 standard.

Enhanced Parallel Port (EPP)
The Enhanced Parallel Port (EPP) protocol outperforms, but remains compatible with, the standard parallel port. EPP is used primarily by peripherals *other* than printers, such as hard drives, CD-ROM drives, and network adapters, which require constant two-way communication with the PC. The EPP protocol offers high-speed, two-way data transfers with relatively little software overhead. Hardware handles the handshaking and synchronization between the peripheral device and the PC, allowing the CPU to transfer data to and from the port with a single command. Data transfers using the EPP protocol can approach the speed of an ISA bus, transferring between 500 kilobytes and 2 megabytes per second.

Extended Capabilities Port (ECP)
The Extended Capabilities Port (ECP) protocol is designed to provide high-performance parallel communication for operations that involve moving large chunks of data, but don't require much monitoring, like a print job going out to a printer or an image coming in from a scanner. In contrast to EPP, once an ECP data transfer has begun, the software that initiated the transfer (a printer driver, for example) cannot monitor the progress of the transfer. The software must wait for a signal that shows the transfer was completed. Even more than with EPP, this reduces the number of clock cycles used by the transfer to a bare minimum.

ECP ports use a data compression method called Run Length Encoding (RLE). With RLE, data can be compressed by a ratio of up to 64:1. This enhances performance significantly because printers and scanners deal with raster graphics, which tend to compress well. For RLE to work, both the device and the parallel port must support it. Note, RLE compression isn't actually part of the IEEE 1284 standard but, instead, is part of Microsoft's standard for implementing the ECP protocol.

Like EPP, the ECP standard provides a great degree of flexibility to hardware manufacturers. As long as the parallel port and devices respond to the standardized ECP commands, manufacturers can enhance performance any way they want. Because data transfers that use ECP don't require manipulation of the data, many manufacturers have added special capabilities to the ports, especially Direct Memory Access (DMA) channels, something never seen on any other form of parallel port.

Local Lingo

Raster Graphics   *Raster graphics* is another term for *bit-mapped graphics,* which refers to the way an image is represented in a computer's memory. *Bit-mapping* means dividing an image into rows and columns of dots, and recording a value for each dot as one or more bits of data.

Vector Graphics   Other than bit-mapping to represent images on computers, mathematical formulas are used to record the various parameters of an image. Because they're recorded as formulas, vector images can easily change size without looking different. Vector images are used to create scalable fonts.

Some parallel modes are more appropriate for some types of devices than for others. With the highest throughput of all the parallel modes, ECP excels at handling large blocks of data via DMA channels, making it ideal for printers and scanners. External devices that must frequently switch back and forth between read-and-write operations, such as external CD-ROMs, are better served by EPP's capability to change the direction of the data flow without additional handshaking and overhead. Because Centronics mode and Nibble mode are controlled through software, any parallel port ever made for an IBM PC can do both. If the parallel port lacks appropriate hardware support, however, expensive devices capable of high-speed communication using Byte mode, ECP, or EPP must slow down to the speed of the parallel port. Check the parallel port settings in CMOS, as shown in Figure 12-8, to verify that a parallel port is set to the appropriate mode.

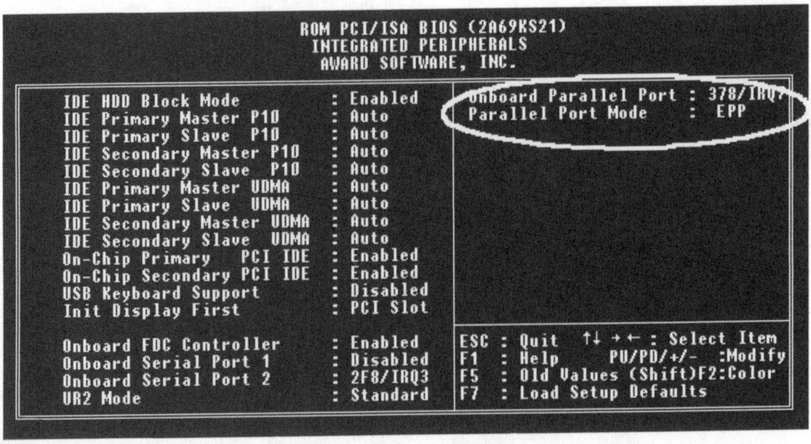

FIGURE 12-8   Parallel port settings in CMOS

USB Printers

USB is the newest type of printer connection. USB printers can connect to a USB port on the back of your PC or to a USB hub. As with any USB device, you can add or remove a USB printer at any time without powering down your machine.

Network Printers

You can set up a printer in two different ways on a network: you can configure the printer as a shared printer or it can be a true network printer.

Shared Printers

A *shared printer* is attached to a computer on the network, referred to as a *print server,* which shares its printer with other computers on the network. The computers on the network can only use the shared printer if the print server is on the network and has given the other computers permission to access its printer.

Network Printers

Network Printers contain a Network Interface Card (NIC) and are configured on the network, just like any other computer on the network. These printers have a small keypad, so you can enter configurations.

A network printer needs a lot of memory to accept multiple print jobs. If the printer memory is insufficient, some print jobs might not print and memory errors might pop up.

Objective 12.03   # Troubleshooting and Preventive Maintenance

Preventive maintenance keeps a printer in good working order. If a problem arises, printers can be one of the most difficult computer peripherals to troubleshoot and diagnose. *Assume nothing when it comes to printers.* Try the obvious first, and then graduate to more advanced troubleshooting techniques.

Exam Tip
Know the basic troubleshooting procedures for all printer types.

Feed and Output

Printers often develop problems with the paper-feed mechanism. When paper-feed problems occur, the paper can become jammed in the feed mechanism, halting the printing process.

Problems with Friction Feed Mechanisms

The most common problem with friction-feed mechanisms is a form of operator error: too much paper in the paper tray. This can cause the feed mechanism to pick several sheets of paper and try to send them through the printer simultaneously. Sometimes you get lucky, but usually you get a paper jam. Most paper trays have a line or symbol on the edge to show the maximum allowed paper in the paper tray at one time.

Static buildup in friction-feed mechanisms causes pages to stick together, which again results in several pages being fed through the printer at the same time. To prevent paper jams caused by static, fan the stack of papers on a desk or other surface before placing them in the paper feed tray. This looses the pages and reduces the static cling.

When a print job claims to have executed but no pages come out, the problem might be not enough paper in the paper tray. If the paper level is too low, the rollers can have trouble catching hold of the top sheet. If sufficient paper seems to be in the tray, check to see if you're using recycled paper, which can sometimes be thinner than normal paper and harder for the rollers to grab.

Problems with Tractor-Feed Mechanisms

Tractor-feed mechanisms require you to line up the spokes on the wheels with the holes in the paper. If the holes on either side of the paper aren't lined up evenly, the text might print diagonally on the page. If the holes are uneven, the paper will crease, wrinkle, and, eventually, jam. Because they use continuous form paper, tractor-feed printers can require your assistance to position the paper vertically. Each model of printer has its own special way of positioning the paper vertically, making trial and error an essential part of this process. If you get this wrong, your top and bottom margins will be off, and sometimes lines of text will even split across two sheets of paper.

Printer Errors

In a typical office environment, A+ techs are called upon to fix printer problems, ranging from completely bizarre I/O errors to simple paper jams. The A+ exams recognize *printer guru* as yet another hat you'll often wear, and so requires you to know several common printer errors.

Out of Paper Errors

The cause of a *Paper Out* error should be pretty obvious: no paper is in the printer. To correct this problem on a tractor-feed printer, lift the printer's lid and carefully feed the first sheet onto the tractor wheels. To fix this problem on a friction-feed printer, simply add paper to the paper tray.

Input/Output Errors

Input/Output errors occur when the computer is unable to communicate with the printer. When troubleshooting an Input/Output error, start with these possibilities:

- Is the printer plugged in?
- Is the printer turned on?
- Are all cables firmly connected?
- Is the proper driver for your printer installed? If so, could it have become corrupted?
- Are the IRQ and I/O settings for the printer correct?

If all these check out, try restarting your computer. Simply restarting can sometimes fix a multitude of problems. If the printer still produces the Input/Output error, connect the printer to another computer. If the printer does not work on the other computer, you know you have a printer problem. If it works fine on the other computer, you have a configuration problem.

Incorrect Port Mode Errors

An *Incorrect Port Mode* error indicates the parallel port you connected the printer to isn't using the correct port mode. If you receive this error, use the CMOS settings program to change the port mode to one that's compatible with your printer.

No Default Printer Errors

A *No Default Printer* error indicates no printer has been installed or that you haven't set a default printer. To set a default printer:

1. Click the Start button.
2. Select Settings.
3. Select Printers. The Printers dialog box will appear.

4. Alternate-click the icon of the printer you want to set as the default.

5. Select Set As Default from the Shortcut menu.

If no printer has been installed, follow these steps:

1. Click the Start button.

2. Select Settings.

3. Select Printers. The Printers dialogue box will appear.

4. Double-click the Add Printer icon and follow the instructions.

Toner Low and Ink Low Errors

When the toner cartridge in a laser printer runs low, it issues a warning before the cartridge runs out completely. Replace the cartridge as soon as you see the error to avoid half-finished or delayed print jobs. You should also replace inkjet cartridges promptly to prevent clogged print nozzles.

Consumable Refills   Ink and toner refill kits are much less expensive than purchasing new cartridges and may seem like an economic solution to the consumable problem. However, because you're reusing the original cartridge components, like the pump and heating element, you risk damaging your printer. Purchasing new cartridges is more economical than fixing your laser printer because of damage caused by old cartridges.

Paper Jams

Many things such as static or dust can cause paper jams. To prevent paper jams, use the correct weight paper for your printer, and keep your printer free from dust and other debris by vacuuming it regularly. If the problem persists, you might have to replace the rollers.

To fix a paper jam, open the printer and gently extract the paper. Whenever possible, move the paper in the direction it would normally go. Remember your physics, and pull slowly and gently. This minimizes the likelihood that you'll rip off the exposed part of the paper. Also, pulling too hard can damage the rollers in the feed mechanism. Some printers won't continue printing after you fix the problem until you press the Online or Reset button.

Print Quality

Depending on the printer type you're using, several factors might affect print quality.

Dot-Matrix Print Quality Issues

One downside to dot matrix is the need for ongoing maintenance. Keep the *platen* (the roller or plate on which the pins impact) and the printhead clean. Be sure to lubricate gears and pulleys according to the manufacturer's specifications. Never lubricate the printhead, however, because the lubricant will smear and stain the paper.

White Bars on Text   White bars going through the text point to a dirty or damaged printhead. Try cleaning the printhead with a little denatured alcohol. If the problem persists, replace the printhead. Printheads for most printers are readily available from the manufacturer.

Chopped Text   If the characters look chopped off at the top or bottom, the printhead probably needs to be adjusted. Follow the manufacturer's instructions for proper adjustment.

Pepper-Look   If the paper is covered with dots and small smudges—the "pepper look"—the platen is dirty. Clean the platen with a soft cloth.

Faded Image   If the image is faded and you know the ribbon is good, try adjusting the printhead closer to the platen.

Light to Dark   If the image is okay on one side of the paper, but fades on the other, the platen is out of adjustment. Platens are difficult to adjust, so your best plan is to send it to the manufacturer's local warranty/repair center. The $30–$50 you'll spend is far cheaper than the frustration of trying to do it yourself!

Inkjet Print Quality Issues

Inkjet printers are more complicated than dot-matrix printers, which also means more things can go wrong.

Unclear Images   If an inkjet printer is producing unclear images, the ink cartridges are probably running low on ink and need to be replaced.

Blank Printouts If an inkjet printer is producing blank printouts, either the ink level is low or the nozzles have become clogged. First check the ink and replace the cartridge if it's low. If the ink is at an acceptable level, the nozzles have probably become clogged. To unclog the nozzles, dip a cotton swab in denatured alcohol and gently remove any dried ink.

Confetti Printouts Printouts with ink speckles, or *confetti,* always indicate an ink problem. Over time, ink can escape into the body of an inkjet printer, eventually finding its way onto subsequent printouts. To fix or prevent speckling, clean the insides of the printer with a damp cloth.

Wrong Colors in Printouts If an inkjet produces printouts using the wrong colors, check for low ink in one or more cartridges, or a dirty nozzle. First check the ink cartridges. If they're full, clean the nozzles with a cotton swab dipped in denatured alcohol.

Smudges on Printouts Smudges on printouts are most often caused by the user touching the printout before the ink has completely dried. Other causes include dirty printers and worn-out nozzles. Worn-out nozzles cannot be fixed. You must replace the ink cartridges if the nozzles have become worn out.

Laser Print Quality Issues

Laser printers usually manifest problems by creating poor output. One of the most important tests you can do on any printer—not only a laser printer—is called a *diagnostic print page* or an *engine test page.* You can print a test page by holding down the Online button as the printer is started or by selecting the menu option on the printer's operator panel. You can also select Start | Settings | Printers in Windows and issue the test page command from the printer's Properties dialogue box. The A+ exam is *very* concerned that you understand laser printer maintenance. Make sure you know the causes and solutions for their various maintenance problems.

Blank Paper Blank sheets of paper usually mean the printer is out of toner. If the printer does have toner and nothing prints, print a diagnostic print page. If that's also blank, remove the toner cartridge and look at the imaging drum inside.

If the image is still there, you know the transfer corona or the high-voltage power supply has failed. Check the printer's maintenance guide to see how to zero in on the bad part and replace it.

Ghosting

Sometimes ghost images appear at regular intervals on the printed page. Either the imaging drum hasn't fully discharged and is picking up toner from a previous image, or a previous image has used up so much toner that either the supply of charged toner is insufficient or the toner hasn't been adequately charged.

Light Ghosting vs. Dark Ghosting

A variety of problems can cause both light and dark ghosting, but the most common source of *light ghosting* is *developer starvation*. If you ask a laser printer to print an extremely dark or complex image, it can use up so much toner that the toner cartridge won't be able to charge enough toner to print the next image. The proper solution is to use less toner by doing the following:

- Lowering the resolution of the page (print at 300 dpi instead of 600 dpi)
- Using a different pattern
- Avoiding 50 percent gray scale and dot-on/dot-off patterns
- Changing the layout, so gray scale patterns don't follow black areas
- Making dark patterns lighter and light patterns darker
- Printing in landscape orientation
- Adjusting print density and Resolution Enhancement Technology (RET) settings
- Printing a completely blank page immediately prior to the page with the ghosting image and as part of the same print job

Low temperature and low humidity can aggravate ghosting problems. Check your users' manual for environmental recommendations.

Dark ghosting can sometimes be caused by a damaged drum. It can be fixed by replacing the toner cartridge. Light ghosting cannot be solved in this way. Switching other components usually won't fix ghosting problems because they're a side effect of the entire printing process.

Vertical White Lines

Vertical white lines are usually caused by clogged toner. Clogs prevent the proper dispersion of toner on the drum. Try shaking the toner cartridge to dislodge the clog or, if that doesn't work, replacing the toner cartridge.

Blotchy Print This is most commonly because of uneven dispersion of toner—especially if the toner is low. Try shaking the toner from side to side. Also be sure the printer is level. Finally, make sure the paper isn't wet in spots. If the blotches are in a regular order, check the fusing rollers and the photosensitive drum for foreign objects.

Spotty Print If spots appear at regular intervals on the printout, the printer's drum might be damaged or toner might be stuck to the fuser rollers. Try wiping off the fuser rollers. Check the drum for damage. If the drum is damaged, you must get a new toner cartridge.

Embossed Effect If your prints have an embossed effect (like putting a penny under a piece of paper and rubbing it with a pencil), a foreign object is almost certainly on a roller. Use regular water with a soft cloth to try to remove it. If the foreign object is on the photosensitive drum, you'll have to use a new toner cartridge.

Incomplete Characters Incompletely printed characters on laser-printed transparencies can sometimes be corrected by adjusting the print density. Remember to use only materials approved for use in laser printers.

Creased Pages Laser printers have up to four rollers. In addition to the heat and pressure rollers of the fusing assembly, rollers are designed to move the paper from the source tray to the output tray. These rollers crease the paper to avoid curling, which would cause paper jams in the printer. If the creases are noticeable, try using a different paper type. Cotton bond paper is usually more susceptible to noticeable creasing than other bonds. You might also try sending the output to the face up tray, which eliminates one roller. No hardware solution exists to this problem. This is simply a side effect of the process.

Warped, Overprinted, or Poorly Formed Characters Poorly formed characters can indicate either a problem with the paper (or other media) or a problem with the hardware.

Incorrect media causes a number of problems. Avoid too rough or too smooth paper. Paper that's too rough interferes with fusing of characters and their initial definition. If the paper is too smooth (like some coated papers, for example), it might feed improperly, causing distorted or overwritten characters. While you can purchase laser printer-specific paper, all laser printers will run acceptably on standard photocopy paper. Because paper picks up humidity from the air, don't open a ream of paper until you're ready to load it into the printer. Always fan the paper before loading it into the printer—especially if the paper has been left out for more than a few days.

The durability of a well-maintained laser printer makes hardware a rare source of character-printing problems, but it is a possibility. Fortunately, checking the hardware is easy. Most laser printers have a self-test function, often combined with a diagnostic printout, that's quite handy to verify those "Is it the printer or is it the computer?" questions. Run the self-test to check for connectivity and configuration problems. Possible solutions:

- Replace the toner cartridge, especially if you hear popping noises.
- Check the cabling.
- Replace the data cable, especially if bends or crimps exist, or objects are resting on the cable.
- If you have a Front Menu Panel, turn off Advanced Functions and High Speed Settings to determine if they aren't working properly or aren't supported by your current software configuration (check your manuals).

If these solutions don't work, the problem might not be user serviceable. Contact an authorized service center.

General Print Quality Issues

Now that you understand some of the print quality issues that can affect the individual printer types, you need to understand the print quality issues that can affect all three. Let's look at the most common print problems in Windows 9x/2000.

Print Job Never Prints   If you press the Print button, but nothing comes out of the printer, first check all the silly things. Is the printer on? Is it connected? Is it online? Does it have paper? Assuming the printer is in good order, it's time to look at the spooler. You can see the spooler status either by double-clicking the printer's icon in the Printers applet or by clicking the tiny printer icon in the System Tray if it's present (if you're having a problem, it's almost always there).

Print spoolers easily overflow or become corrupt because of a lack of disk space, too many print jobs, or one of a thousand other factors. The Printers window shows all the pending print jobs and enables you to delete, start, or pause print jobs. The best answer is usually to delete the print jobs and try again.

Strange Sizes   A print job that comes out a strange size usually points to a user mistake in setting up the print job. Check the Print dialogue box for incorrect print parameters. Also check the Page Setup option in the relevant application. Make sure the user is setting up the page properly.

If you know the page is set up correctly, recheck the printer drivers. If necessary, uninstall and reinstall the print drivers. If the problem persists, you might have a serious problem with the printer's print engine, but that is only a possibility when you continually get the same strangely sized printouts using a number of different applications.

Garbage Characters in Printout   Misaligned or garbage printouts invariably point to a corrupted or incorrect driver. Make sure you're using the right driver (it's hard, but not impossible, to mess this up), and then uninstall and reinstall the printer driver. If the problem persists, you might be asking the printer to do something it cannot do. For example, you might be printing to a PostScript printer with a PCL driver. Check the printer type to verify you haven't installed the wrong type of driver for that printer! Try some of these diagnostic avenues:

- Make sure the printer cables are attached firmly and haven't become loose.
- Turn the power to the printer off, and then on again.
- To check the basic communication between the PC and the printer, try printing a plain text file—Notepad is excellent for this.
- Restart your computer. Many Windows and application problems can be resolved simply by restarting your system.
- Reinstall your printer drivers. Drivers occasionally become corrupted and might need reinstalling.
- Check your resource settings for the parallel or USB port to verify no resource conflicts exist.
- Connect the printer to a different computer. If the printer continues producing garbage characters on the second computer, you know the problem lies within the printer.
- Try printing a smaller document. If you can print a smaller document, the problem could be insufficient memory in the printer. Insufficient memory can be remedied by adding more RAM to the printer.

Printer Not Responding   If the printer isn't responding, check the easy things first. Make sure the printer is turned on, and the cables are securely and correctly attached. Make sure the printer is on line. Make sure the application you're printing from is sending the print job to the correct printer. Try to print a test page.

Try attaching it to a new computer. If nothing works, your printer might have to go to a printer repair facility.

Preventive Maintenance

The best thing you can do for your printer is to perform regular preventive maintenance. Good technicians know preventive maintenance is the key to preventing printer problems.

Cleaning your printer regularly can prevent many problems from occurring. Paper dust and ink deposits are the root of many printer problems. Paper dust causes ESD and can be removed with compressed air or an anti-static vacuum. Excess ink and toner need to be removed from printers regularly to prevent poor quality printouts.

> **Exam Tip**
>
> Know the proper cleaning procedures for all printer types.

Cleaning Dot Matrix Printers

Dot matrix printers require regular cleaning. Before you begin cleaning a dot matrix printer, you need to disconnect all cables and wait for the printhead to cool down and the capacitors to discharge. To clean a dot matrix printer, follow these steps:

1. Remove the plastic casing and carefully pull the printhead away from the platen.
2. Inspect the ribbon and replace it, if necessary.
3. Remove paper dust from the printer by using compressed air or an anti-static vacuum.
4. Clean the printhead with denatured alcohol.
5. Remove paper from the platen.
6. Inspect the carriage belt and replace it, if necessary.

After you finish cleaning the printer, lubricate the gears and pulleys. Never lubricate the printhead or your printouts will appear stained. Once you service the printer, carefully put it back together.

Cleaning Inkjet Printers

You need to clean your inkjet printer regularly to keep it working optimally. Before you begin servicing an inkjet printer you need to unplug all the cables and wait for the capacitors to discharge. To clean inkjet printers, follow these steps:

1. Remove the plastic housing and ink cartridges.
2. Remove paper dust from the printer by using compressed air or an anti-static vacuum.
3. Wipe off the ink cartridges with a damp cloth.
4. Wipe excess ink from the inside of the printer with a damp cloth.
5. Clean the platen.
6. Inspect the carriage belt and replace it, if necessary.

Once you clean the printer, carefully put it back together.

Cleaning Laser Printers

Generally, you can only get your laser printer dirty in two ways. The first way is excess toner. Toner is hard to see inside a dark printer but, over time, it will coat the entire printer. The second way is paper dust, sometimes called *paper dander*. This tends to build up where the paper is bent around rollers or where pickup rollers grab paper. Unlike toner, paper dust is easy to see and it's usually a good indicator a printer needs to be cleaned. Without being printer-specific, usually the best maintenance procedure is a thorough cleaning using a can of deionized, compressed air (do this outdoors or you might end up looking like a chimney sweep!) or an anti-static vacuum designed especially for electronic components.

To clean a laser printer, follow these steps:

1. Remove all cables and wait for the fuser to cool and the capacitor to discharge.
2. Remove your antistatic wrist strap.
3. Remove and wipe off the toner cartridges.
4. Use compressed air or an anti-static vacuum to remove paper dander and toner from the inside of the printer.
5. Use denatured alcohol to clean the transfer corona.
6. Clean the fusing rollers and replace the roller pad.
7. Replace the ozone filter.
8. Clean the rubber guide rollers with a little general purpose cleaner, such as Formula 409 or even just a little water.
9. When you finish, carefully put everything back where it belongs!

CHECKPOINT

✔ **Objective 12.01: Printers**   Know the types of printers—dot matrix, inkjet, laser—and how each one works. Understand the laser printing process and know its six discrete steps in the order they occur.

✔ **Objective 12.02: Printer Connections and Configurations**   Four types of printer connections exist: serial, parallel, USB, and network. You should know the various connectors for the first three types and the requirements for accessing a printer over a network.

✔ **Objective 12.03: Troubleshooting and Preventive Maintenance** Common printer problems include paper jams and problems with paper-feed mechanisms, I/O errors, No Default Printer errors, low toner/ink, a huge variety of print-quality issues, and non-responsive printers.

REVIEW QUESTIONS

1. What are the six steps of the laser printer process?

   A. Paper In, Charge, Develop, Transfer, Fuse, Paper Out
   B. Clean, Charge, Write, Develop, Transfer, Fuse
   C. Charge, Clean, Write, Transfer, Print, Fuse
   D. Clean, Charge, Develop, Transfer, Write, Fuse

2. What type of feed mechanism do dot matrix printers use?

   A. Tractor feed
   B. Friction feed
   C. Paper feed
   D. Spoke feed

3. Which printer types use friction-feed mechanisms?

   A. Dot matrix
   B. Laser
   C. Inkjet
   D. Daisy wheel

4. What is the maximum recommended length for a parallel printer cable?

   A. 10 feet
   B. 25 feet
   C. 6 feet
   D. 3 feet

5. Garbage characters are appearing in a printout. What's the problem?

   A. The printer is old and needs to be replaced
   B. You have the wrong language set up for the printer
   C. The printer needs to be cleaned
   D. The computer isn't communicating correctly with the printer

6. What does the primary corona wire in a laser printer do?

   A. Cleans the drum
   B. Charges the drum
   C. Creates the image on the drum
   D. Transfers the image from the drum to the paper

7. What do inkjet printers use to deflect ink onto a page?

   A. A printhead
   B. Electrically charged plates
   C. Fusers
   D. Rollers

8. Which parallel port mode is the fastest?

   A. Centronics
   B. Byte mode
   C. ECP
   D. EPP

9. Which component of a laser printer needs to be replaced regularly?

   A. Ozone filter
   B. Fusing rollers
   C. Primary corona
   D. Transfer corona

10. What can cause ghosted images to appear in printouts from a laser printer?

    A. The writing stage of the laser printer process has failed
    B. The charging stage of the laser printer process has failed
    C. The transferring stage of the laser printer process has failed
    D. The cleaning stage of the laser printer process has failed

11. Which part of a dot matrix printer is most dangerous?

    A. The printhead
    B. The ribbon
    C. The feed mechanism
    D. The wheels

12. Which parts of a laser printer are most dangerous?

    A. Laser
    B. Primary corona
    C. Fuser
    D. Traction feed

13. Which printer connection is the slowest?

    A. Parallel
    B. USB
    C. Serial
    D. Network

14. Which type of printer can create carbon copies?

    A. Laser
    B. Inkjet
    C. USB
    D. Dot matrix

15. What component of a laser printer transfers the image from the drum to the paper?

    A. Primary corona
    B. Fusing rollers
    C. Transfer corona
    D. Friction feed

REVIEW ANSWERS

1. **B** The steps of the laser printer process are Clean, Charge, Write, Develop, Transfer, Fuse.

2. **A** Dot matrix printers use a tractor-feed mechanism.

3. **B** **C** Both inkjet and laser printers use a friction-feed mechanism.

4. **C** The maximum length for a parallel printer cable is six feet. Cables any longer are subject to crosstalk and EMI.

5. **D** Garbage characters in a printout mean the computer isn't communicating correctly with the printer. One possible reason for this is incorrect or corrupted drivers.

6. **B** The primary corona wire charges the drum after it has been cleaned.

7. **B** Electrically charged plates deflect ink onto the paper.

8. **C** ECP is the fastest parallel port mode.

9. **A** The ozone filters in a laser printer need to be replaced regularly.

10. **D** Ghosted images in laser-printer printouts indicate the cleaning stage of the laser printer process has failed.

11. **A** The printhead on a dot matrix printer gets very hot and can burn you.

12. **A** **C** The laser in a laser printer can harm your eyes, and the fusing rollers get very hot and can burn you.

13. **C** Serial is the slowest type of printer connection.

14. **D** Dot matrix printers are impact printers and can create carbon copies.

15. **C** The transfer corona in laser printers transfers the image from the drum to the paper.

CHAPTER

13

Troubleshooting Hardware

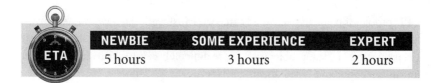

	NEWBIE	SOME EXPERIENCE	EXPERT
ETA	5 hours	3 hours	2 hours

Troubleshooting makes up a large part of the A+ exam. Knowing how to troubleshoot hardware is also a vital part of your job as a technician. This chapter looks at three major areas of troubleshooting: system components, such as the CPU, motherboards, and RAM; mass storage devices, such as hard drives, SCSI devices, CD-media drives, and floppy drives; and expansion cards and peripherals, such as monitors, video cards, modems, and sound cards. That's a ton of material to cover in such a short chapter, so let's get started!

Objective 13.01   System Components

Diagnosing problems with system components, such as the CPU, motherboard, and RAM, often takes time and diligence on the part of the technician. If you have a dead PC that you just put together, the best option is almost always to check your connections and cabling, and *simplify* the system to eliminate possibilities.

A lot of techs get caught up in the "put it all together and then flip the switch" mode when building systems. This works, of course, often enough that such techs have this behavior reinforced. When it doesn't work, however, what do you have to do? When you flip the switch on a new build and nothing happens, you need to take it all apart, and then build and test a piece at a time. A couple of quick stops to test CPU, RAM, and video during the initial build can end up saving you a lot of time in troubleshooting after the fact. Let's look at specific issues for CPUs.

CPUs

CPU problems come in two broad categories: installation issues and heat problems. Installation issues result in a dead PC at boot up or a CPU not running at the proper speed. Heat problems are more difficult because they result in random lockups, reboots, and other general problems.

Installation Issues

Dealing with installation issues involves stripping down the system, checking the jumpers or dip switches on the motherboard, and verifying the connection between CPU and motherboard. If you have some power and boot, but the CPU doesn't register properly, also check the CMOS settings.

One of the more common installation problems happens when, for some reason, the connectivity between CPU and motherboard fails. The result is a dead PC, but not permanently so. Undo the ZIF socket lever and press down firmly before you lower the lever on PGA-style CPUs. Press firmly on SEC-style CPUs or remove and reinstall.

Travel Advisory

SEC-style CPUs can creep up in the slot when you install other expansion cards or RAM. If you just added something to the motherboard and suddenly have a dead PC, it might not be the fault of what you just added.

One other install-related issue comes with truly dead CPUs. It's impossible to insert a modern CPU incorrectly into a ZIF socket unless you break a pin—a bad thing and a dead CPU. As noted in earlier chapters, you can also crack modern PGA-style CPUs by inserting a fan and heat sink assembly. Take caution!

Heat Issues

Heat kills CPUs but, before they die, they crash a lot! Heat problems stem from dead or clogged fans, or inadequate airflow in a case. If you have a PC that sits in a high-debris environment and it ran great for a while, but has started locking up, open the case and check the fans. Animal hair, smoke, dust, rodents—any or all of these can get into a CPU fan and cause it to run poorly or stop altogether. I opened a dead PC the other day, for example, and found a fried lizard inside. No joke! Excessive heat can kill a CPU (or a stray lizard) quickly and permanently.

Inadequate airflow causes PCs to overheat and lock up or spontaneously reboot. This often manifests in summer when the air conditioning doesn't quite hold up to a hot day. The power supply fan is designed to draw air through the system unit, but missing slot covers can disrupt that flow. Too many unrestrained ribbon cables can also disrupt the flow. Adding a front fan or secondary exhaust fan and tying down ribbon cables usually does the trick.

Exam Tip

Missing slot covers on the system unit can cause the PC to overheat.

Motherboards

When the computer is turned on or reset, it initiates a special program, also stored on the ROM chip, called the power-on self test (POST). Chapter 4 touched on POST, but let's look at it in detail here.

The POST program checks out the system every time the computer boots. To perform this check, the POST sends out a standard command that says to all the devices "check yourselves out!" All the devices in the computer then run their own internal diagnostic—the POST doesn't specify what to check. The quality of the diagnostic is up to the people who made that particular device.

Let's consider the POST for a moment. Some device, let's say the 8042 keyboard controller chip, runs its diagnostic and determines it isn't working properly. What will the POST do about it? There's only one thing to do—tell the human being sitting in front of the PC! So, how does the computer tell the human? The first thought is to put some information on the monitor. That's fine, but what if the video card is faulty? What if some low-level device isn't operational? All POSTs first test the most basic devices. If anything goes wrong on this first group of devices, the computer will beep using its built-in speaker. But what if the speaker doesn't work? Trouble! The POST assumes it always works. All PCs beep on startup to let the user know the speaker is working. Now you know why every computer always beeps when it first starts!

The POST can, therefore, be divided into two parts. First is the test of the most basic devices—up to and including the video. If anything goes wrong, the computer will beep. Second is a test of the rest of the devices. If anything goes wrong here, a text error message appears on the screen.

Before and During the Video Test: The Beep Codes

The computer tests the most basic parts of the computer first. If anything goes wrong, the computer sends a series of beeps. The meaning of these beeps varies from one BIOS manufacturer to another. Additionally, BIOS makers have changed the beep codes over time. Award BIOS no longer uses beep codes except for when the video card fails—it gives one long beep followed by two short beeps. Refer to your motherboard book for your POST's beep codes.

Travel Assistance

If the motherboard book failed to include beep codes, go to these BIOS maker's web sites for exhaustive listings:

AMI BIOS   http://www.ami.com/support/doclib.cfm

Phoenix BIOS   http://www.phoenix.com/pcuser/BIOS/phoenix_home.htm

Award BIOS   http://www.phoenix.com/pcuser/BIOS/
award_error_codes.htm

And, remember, web sites often change!

Table 13-1 lists the most common POST problems and how to deal with them. Watch out for false beep codes. Many computers with a bad power supply generate intermittent beep codes. The secret to determining if you have a bad power supply is to turn the computer on and off three or four times to see if you generate the same beep code every time. If you get the same beep code, it's probably legitimate. If the beep codes change, if the machine stops working, or if the computer seems to heal itself, check the power supply.

TABLE 13-1	Common POST Beep Errors and Solutions
Problem	**Solution**
RAM refresh failure Parity error RAM bit error Base 64K error	1. Reseat and clean the RAM chips. 2. Replace individual chips until the problem is corrected.
8042 error Gate A20 error	1. Reseat and clean keyboard chip. 2. Replace keyboard. 3. Replace motherboard.
BIOS checksum error	1. Reseat and clean ROM chip. 2. Replace BIOS chip.
Video errors	1. Reseat video card. 2. Replace video card.
Cache memory error	1. Reseat and clean cache chips. 2. Verify cache jumper settings are correct. 3. Replace cache chips.
Everything else	1. Clean motherboard. 2. Replace motherboard.

After the Video Test: The Error Messages

Once the video has been tested, the POST displays any error messages on the screen. In the old days (as in pre-Pentium), most systems displayed a numeric code that you needed to decipher. Today's systems use text error messages that simply say where the problem lies in the system. Let's look at both.

Numeric Error Codes   When an old computer's POST generated a numeric error code, the machine locked up and a numeric error code appeared in the upper-left corner of the screen. There were hundreds of numeric error codes and, fortunately, they've been replaced with simple text messages. However, you must be aware of their existence. Table 13-2 lists the five most common numeric error codes and the probable causes of the problem.

TABLE 13-2 Common Numeric Errors Codes	
Problem	**Solution**
301	The keyboard is broken or isn't plugged in.
1701	The hard drive controller is bad.
7301	The floppy drive controller is bad.
161	The battery is dead.
1101	The serial card is bad.

Text Error Codes

BIOS programs no longer use numeric error codes. After years of PC technicians trying to memorize a bunch of cryptic codes, AMI realized the overwhelming majority of numeric error codes are never used. So, AMI reduced the number of error codes to about 30 and substituted text that described the problem. Today, instead of mysterious numbers, you get text that's usually, but not always, self-explanatory (Figure 13-1).

Text errors are far more useful because you can simply read the screen to determine the bad device. I should add here that a few PC makers (read: IBM) still use numeric error codes in some models. But, in these cases, they invariably also add a text code for clarity.

```
PhoenixBIOS 4.0 release 6.0
Copyright 1985-2000 Phoenix Technologies Ltd.
All Rights Reserved


CPU = Pentium III  500MHz
640K System RAM Passed
47M Extended RAM Passed
USB upper limit segment address:  EEFE
Mouse initialized

HDD Controller Failure
Press <F1> to resume
```

FIGURE 13-1 Text error messages

Troubleshooting RAM

Memory errors show up in a variety of ways on modern systems, including parity errors, ECC error messages, system lockups, and page faults in Windows. These errors can indicate bad RAM, but often point to something completely unrelated to RAM. The challenge for techs is to determine which part of the system caused the memory error.

System lockups and page faults (they often go hand-in-hand) in Windows can indicate a problem with RAM. Certainly page faults look like RAM issues, because Windows generates frightening error messages filled with long strings of hexadecimal digits, such as KRNL386 caused a page fault at 03F2:25A003BC. Just because the error message contains a memory address, however, doesn't mean you have a problem with your RAM. Write down the address. If it repeats in later error messages, you probably have a bad RAM stick. If Windows displays different memory locations, then you need to look elsewhere for the culprit.

Objective 13.02 # Mass Storage Devices

The A+ Certification exams test heavily on troubleshooting mass storage devices, requiring you to know about issues of connectivity, physical damage, BIOS and drivers, and much more. About the only thing you don't have to know is what to do with a client who thinks the CD-ROM tray is a drink holder! Let's look at hard drives first, and then move to other mass storage devices.

Troubleshooting Hard Drives

The hard drive receives a bad reputation as the problem child of the computer. This might be because many fixes for problems unrelated to a hard drive boil down to reinstalling software—maybe people assume the hard drive caused the problem. Certainly, hard drives do fail a considerable amount of times, but good maintenance and a few good repair tools can keep a hard drive running for many years.

When Good Drives Go Bad

All hard drive failures fit into one of four groups, listed from most to least common:

- Installation errors
- Corrupted data on good sectors
- Corrupted data on physically bad sectors
- Drives physically damaged beyond repair

Installation errors are covered in Chapter 17, but you already know the issues from earlier chapters: power, connectivity, jumper settings, and CMOS. For the other problems, the A+ exams assume you've performed a good backup of essential files (see Chapter 18 for details on backup) and know how to run the built-in disk checking utilities ScanDisk and Check Disk. Let's look at some of the other possible problems.

All hard drives occasionally get corrupted data in individual sectors. Power surges, accidental shutdowns, corrupted install media, viruses, along with hundreds of other issues can cause this corruption. In most cases, this type of error shows up while Windows is running. Here is a classic example:

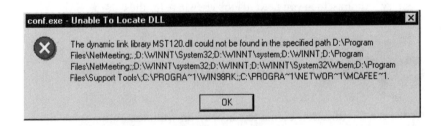

You might also see Windows errors messages saying one of the following:

- The following file is missing or corrupt
- The download location information is damaged
- Unable to load file

If core boot files become corrupted, you might see text errors at boot, such as the following:

- Cannot find COMMAND.COM
- Error loading operating system
- Invalid BOOT.INI

On older programs, you might see a command prompt open with errors such as this one:

```
Sector not found reading drive C: Abort, Retry, Fail?
```

These problems occur with such frequency that all versions of Windows provide a disk-checking utility. The most common way to access this tool is by alternate-clicking on the suspected drive and selecting Properties. Under the Tools tab, click the Check Now button to the start the system-checking tool.

While the look and feel (and name) of this tool varies between Windows 9*x* (ScanDisk, see Figure 13-2) and Windows 2000 (Check Disk, see Figure 13-3), it performs the same function in both operating systems. The disk-checking program scans your drive, verifying proper drive structures, that is, it checks to see if the directories point to other directories and the filenames are valid. Then it runs a disk scan to verify that the bad clusters are all marked in the FAT tables and, if it finds any bad clusters, the disk-checking utility marks those as bad. Before the program marks a cluster bad, it attempts to move the data to a good cluster. This marking of bad clusters is where the disk-checking utility does its best work. This process usually works successfully and often recovers otherwise lost data.

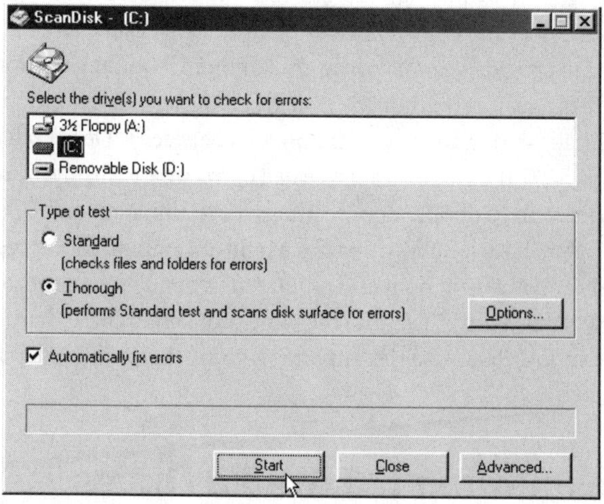

FIGURE 13-2   The disk checker in Windows 9*x*: ScanDisk

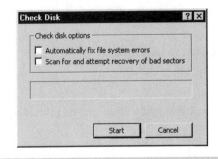

FIGURE 13-3   The disk checker in Windows 2000: Check Disk

Note some of the options available for Windows 9x. The *Thorough* option checks the entire drive. *Standard* checks file and folders areas only. Both Windows 2000 and Windows 9x give the option to fix errors automatically. I don't like to use this—if errors begin to show, I want to see them. If I intend to run the program overnight (it can take a long time) however, the automatic fixing option works wonders! Just remember to turn off the screen saver!

Troubleshooting SCSI Devices

SCSI problems can be reduced to certain categories, some of which overlap and not all of which apply to every problem. You know the issues from Chapter 8: power, cabling, BIOS, ID, and termination.

What kinds of power problems could prevent a device from showing up? It's usually nothing more exotic than forgetting to plug it in. Make sure both internal and external devices have power. Most SCSI devices, especially external ones, require power to provide termination and all of them require power for operation.

Make sure the devices are properly installed. Is the termination set properly (one terminator at each end of the chain and none in between)? Does each device have its own unique SCSI ID? Are the cables seated correctly and firmly? You'll probably need documentation to double-check settings for termination and SCSI IDs. Most SCSI host adapters have a ROM chip with a built-in configuration program. Make sure the adapter shows up at boot and if not, remove and reseat the card.

Finally, SCSI hard drives run into the same problems as EIDE hard drives, with bad sectors and lost data. Use the same tools to fix the problems: ScanDisk and Check Disk.

Troubleshooting CD Media Drives

CD media drives are extremely reliable and durable PC components, but at times, that reliable and durable device decides to turn into an unreliable, nondurable pile of plastic and metal frustration. This section covers a few of the more common problems with CD media drives and how to fix them.

The single biggest problem with CD media drives, especially in a new installation, is the connections—your first guess should be that the drive hasn't been properly installed in some way. A few of the more common problems are forgetting to plug in a power connector, inserting a cable backwards, and misconfiguration of jumpers/switches. Although you need to know the type of drive (ATAPI or SCSI), the test for an improper physical connection is always the same: using BIOS or DOS-level device drivers to see if the system can see the CD media drive.

How a BIOS detects a CD media drive depends on the system. Most of the CD media drives used today are the ATAPI type. Knowing this, most BIOS makers have created intelligent BIOS software that can see an installed CD media drive. Here's a modern Award Software, Inc. BIOS recognizing an ATAPI CD-ROM during startup:

```
Award Plug and Play BIOS Extension v1.0A
Copyright (C) 2001, Award Software, Inc.
Found CDROM : TOSHIBA CD-ROM XM-6702B
```

This text tends to move by rather quickly during bootup, so a good eye and/or a fast press on the PAUSE key might be necessary to see this operation. Note that, not every BIOS can recognize a CD media drive and not even the most advanced BIOS will see a SCSI CD media device, with one possible exception. If the system has a SCSI host adapter with onboard BIOS, it usually displays text at boot that says something like:

```
Press Ctrl-A for SCSI BIOS Selection
```

This option enables the user to access configuration options. The goal here is to make the host adapter scan the SCSI bus and return a list of devices on the bus. If the SCSI CD-ROM doesn't appear, there is a problem with the hardware. Look for options similar to *Scan SCSI Bus* or *Diagnostic.* Different SCSI host adapter makers give the function different names but, in any case, the result is a screen that looks something like this:

```
SCSI ID 0   Seagate ST4302
SCSI ID 1   No Device Detected
SCSI ID 2   No Device Detected
SCSI ID 3   No Device Detected
SCSI ID 4   No Device Detected
SCSI ID 5   IOMEGA ZIP100
SCSI ID 6   HITACHI CD20032
SCSI ID 7   ADAPTEC 2940
```

The fact that the CD-ROM is visible shows it has a valid SCSI ID, is properly connected and powered, and the SCSI chain is properly terminated.

If no type of BIOS support exists, the only option is to boot to a DOS-level device driver. This is where a startup disk really comes in handy. Just boot off the startup disk and watch for the CD-ROM device driver:

```
DEVICE=C:\DOS\TRICD.SYS /D:MSCD001
Triones ATAPI CD-ROM Device Driver, Version 3.6
Copyright (c) 1994-1997 Triones Technologies, Inc.
All rights reserved.
Secondary/Master: MATSHITA CD-ROM CR-584, Multi-word DMA 1
ATAPI CD-ROM Device Driver installed.
```

Here's the same boot with the data cable intentionally inverted:

```
DEVICE=C:\DOS\TRICD.SYS /D:MSCD001
Triones ATAPI CD-ROM Device Driver, Version 3.6
Copyright (c) 1994-1997 Triones Technologies, Inc.
All rights reserved.
Error: No CDROM detected.
```

Of course, you should be sure to have the correct DOS driver for the CD-ROM drive that's being tested! The file MSCDEX.EXE must be installed before a CD-ROM will work in DOS. If the device is detected, yet can't read a CD media disc, first try a commercial CD-ROM disc. CD-R and CD-RW discs often have compatibility issues with CD-ROM drives. No CD media drive will read badly scratched discs.

Cleaning Your CD Media Drive and Discs

If the drive still doesn't see a disc, try cleaning the CD media drive. Most modern CD media drives have built-in cleaning mechanisms but, occasionally, you need to use a commercial CD-ROM cleaning kit.

We don't clean CD media drives too often, but we do often clean CD media discs. While a number of fine CD-ROM disc cleaning kits exist, most CD media discs can be cleaned quite well with nothing more than a damp, soft cloth. Use a smooth clean cloth and gently wipe the CD-ROM, starting at the center and moving to the edges. *Never* use a circular motion when cleaning a CD-ROM. Occasionally, a mild detergent can be added.

A common Old Tech's Tale about cleaning CD media discs is they can be washed in a dishwasher! Although this may seem laughable, the tale has become so common that it requires a serious response. This is *untrue* for two reasons. First, the water in most dishwashers is too hot and can cause the CD media discs to warp. Second, the water pushes the CD media discs around, causing them to hit other objects and get scratched. Don't do it!

Troubleshooting Floppy Drives

No single component fails more often than the floppy drive. This isn't that surprising because floppy drives have more exposure to the outside environment than anything but the keyboard. Only a small door divides the read/write heads from dust and grime. Floppy drives are also exposed to the threat of mechanical damage. Many folks destroy floppy drives by accidentally inserting inverted disks, paper clips, and other foreign objects. Life is tough for floppy drives!

As a result of this abuse, the only preventative maintenance we perform on floppy drives is cleaning. Above all, keep the floppy drive clean! All electronic stores sell excellent floppy drive cleaning kits. You should use them to ensure the best possible performance from your floppy drives.

Floppy disks run into the same problems you find with hard drives, including bad sectors and clusters, problems with format, and such. Use the same tools for floppy disk repair that you use for hard drive repair: ScanDisk or Check Disk.

Objective 13.03 Expansion Cards and Peripherals

Now that you've mastered mass storage troubleshooting, it's time to dive into the rest of the pieces. We'll look at monitors and video cards first, and then move to modems and sound cards.

Troubleshooting Monitors

Because of the inherent dangers of the high-frequency and high-voltage power required by monitors, and because proper adjustment requires specialized training, this section concentrates on giving a support person the information necessary to decide whether a trouble call is warranted. Virtually no monitor manufacturers make schematics of their monitors available to the public because of liability issues regarding possible electrocution. To simplify troubleshooting, look at the process as two separate parts: external and internal adjustments.

External Adjustments

Monitor adjustments range from the simplest—brightness and contrast—to the more sophisticated—pincushioning and trapezoidal adjustments. The external controls provide users with the opportunity to fine-tune the monitor's image. Many monitors have controls for changing the tint and saturation of color, although plenty of monitors put those controls inside the monitor. Better monitors enable you to square up the visible portion of the screen with the monitor housing.

Finally, most monitors have the capability to degauss themselves with the push of a button. Over time, the shadow mask picks up a weak magnetic charge that interferes with the focus of the electron beams. This magnetic field makes the image look slightly fuzzy and streaked. Most monitors have a special built-in circuit called a *degaussing coil* to eliminate this magnetic buildup. When the degaussing circuit is used, an alternating current is sent through a coil of wire surrounding the CRT and this current generates an alternating magnetic field that demagnetizes the shadow mask. We activate the degaussing coil using the Degauss button or menu selection on the monitor. Degaussing usually makes a rather nasty "thunk" sound and the screen goes crazy for a moment—don't worry, that's normal. Whenever a user calls me with a fuzzy monitor problem, I always have them degauss first.

Internal Adjustments

As shipped, most monitors don't produce an image out to the limits of the screen because of poor convergence at the outer display edges. Convergence defines how closely the three colors can meet at a single point on the display. At the point of convergence, the three colors combine to form a single white dot. With misconvergence, a noticeable halo of one or more colors will be around the outside of the white point. The farther away from the center of the screen, the more likely the chance for misconvergence. Low-end monitors are especially susceptible to this problem. While adjusting the convergence of a monitor isn't difficult, it does require getting inside the monitor case and having a copy of the schematic, which shows the location of the variable resistors. For this reason, it's a good idea to leave this adjustment to a trained specialist.

I don't like opening a CRT monitor. I avoid doing this for two reasons: 1) I know very little about electronic circuits, and 2) I once almost took my finger off with a jolt of electricity. Be that as it may, the A+ exams expect you to have a passing understanding of adjustments you might need to perform inside a monitor. Before we go any further, let me remind you about a little issue with CRT monitors.

Inside every CRT monitor is a piece of equipment called the high-voltage anode, as shown in Figure 13-4. If you lift that suction cup, you'll almost certainly

FIGURE 13-4   High-voltage anode

get seriously electrocuted. Underneath that cup is a wire—the actual *high-voltage anode*. On the other side of that wire leading into the high-voltage anode is the fly-back transformer. Don't worry about what they do—just worry about what they can do to you! There's a big capacitor that holds upwards of 25,000 volts. The capacitor will hold that charge if the monitor is turned off. It will hold the charge if the monitor is unplugged. That capacitor (depending on the system) can hold a charge days, weeks, months, or even years.

Sufficiently warned? The A+ Certification exams test your knowledge of common internal adjustments you can make on a monitor. These include adjusting the focus on a fuzzy monitor (after first trying the substantially less-risky degaussing), dealing with convergence issues as previously outlined, and increasing the brightness and color saturation of an aging monitor. If you happen to be electronically inclined, you can resurrect dead monitors, replacing the flyback transformer, the monitor power supply, or the yoke or yoke coil.

Troubleshooting Video Cards

AGP is typically the default video bus on a system. The qualities of AGP have been mentioned in other chapters. The only great downside to AGP lies in the close connection tolerances required by the cards themselves. It's common to snap in a new AGP card and power up just to get a "no video card beep" or a system that doesn't boot. Always take the time to insure that an AGP card is snapped down securely and screwed down before starting the system.

Fortunately, video cards rarely break. The majority of problems in video can be attributed to improper drivers, poor connections, and bad monitors. Unfortunately, when they do break, invariably the only option is to throw them away. One area for possible repair is the video RAM. You'll know bad RAM by the cool, unintended effects displayed on the screen, such as fixed speckles or spots, bizarre colors in Windows, or a filmy, hazy look. Replace the card.

Troubleshooting Modems

A broken modem is probably the most frustrating repair problem in the PC world. But, by following these steps, you can make the problem much easier (I didn't say easy—just easier) to repair.

Is the Modem Using a Non-Conflicting COM Port and IRQ?

To find out, I turn to a powerful shareware program called *Modem Doctor*, made by Hank Volpe. This program queries all your COM ports, looking for a modem (Figure 13-5). Modem Doctor does an excellent job detecting COM ports and determining whether a modem is at a particular COM port.

Travel Assistance

You can download the latest version of Modem Doctor from http://www.modemdoctor.com.

Many technicians make the mistake of not considering a COM port or IRQ conflict unless the modem or some other hardware has just been installed. Don't do that! Software or corrupted files can change many different cards. Assume nothing!

Modem Doctor does far more than simply verify COM ports. Many times a technician wants to know, "Is this modem still good?" This is where Modem Doctor shines. Modem Doctor will test your modem thoroughly and give you a complete description of its quality. The one nice thing about modems is they

Comm Parameters   ☒

Ports	Speed	Mode	
	300		✔ OK
◇ Com2	▷ 1200	◆ Test Modem	
◆ Com3	◆ 2400	◇ Test Driver Only	✖ Cancel
		Modem(s) may be found on	
		Com3	? Help

Only Valid Port/Speed Options are displayed

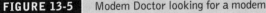

FIGURE 13-5   Modem Doctor looking for a modem

never get sick; they just die. Modem Doctor will let you know, without a doubt, if your modem is alive or dead (Figure 13-6 shows a modem passing with flying colors). If Modem Doctor says your modem is okay, then it's time to look at the software. At this point, you need to zero in on the type of problem.

The Software Says There's No Modem

Make sure the modem is looking at the right port and make sure no conflict exists with another device. Reinstall the modem software and reconfigure to make sure you haven't corrupted a driver. If the modem is plug and play, and you're using Windows 9x or Windows 2000, make sure the Device Manager shows the modem and the modem is working properly.

The Modem Works Sporadically

Make sure you have the right modem installed or try another modem type. Check the phone lines in the house or call the phone company and complain about the phone lines.

Troubleshooting Sound Cards

When something goes wrong with your computer's sound, certain factors point to the problem. The trick is to appreciate that all sound problems can be broken down into three groups: physical problems, driver issues, and support resources.

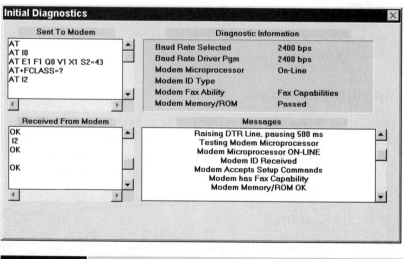

FIGURE 13-6   A diagnostic display of Modem Doctor

Physical Problems

Simply stated, something isn't turned on, plugged in, or turned up. Of all problems with sound cards, this is probably the easiest, most common, and also the most overlooked. Fortunately, physical problems are easy to diagnose—the software says everything is great, but no sound comes out (or in the case of a microphone, no sound goes in). A good triple-check is important here to verify all connections are good and to make sure devices that need power are getting what they need.

Be careful with volume controls. There can be up to four places to change the volume and if any of these are turned down, the system will have no sound. Many speakers have a volume control, and a few of the older sound cards have a volume control wheel on the card itself. In the software world, individual applications have a volume control and the operating system itself may have a volume control.

If you have a problem with no sound coming out of your sound card or the sound from your 4-speaker sound card being reversed, check the cabling in the back. With older sound cards, the jacks in the back weren't labeled clearly, if at all, so it was easy to put the speaker plug in the wrong jack. If you find the front and back speakers reversed, reverse the jacks they're plugged into.

Finally, remember speaker and microphone wires are exposed to all the trauma that shoes, chairs, vacuum cleaners, and general abuse can provide. Most of the time, wires fray on the inside and slowly come apart without anything noticeable happening to the outside jacket. Listen for cracking sounds coming from the speakers and in recordings made by the microphone. This is usually a sign of bad wires.

Drivers

As with any device, sound card device driver issues come up frequently. Make sure you install the latest drivers and don't fear a quick uninstall/reinstall.

Support Resources

I use the phrase *support resources* to describe the many little programs Windows puts between the device drivers and the applications. These support programs divide into two groups: codecs (compressor/decompressors) and DirectX. The latter did not make the cut for the A+ exams, so we'll concentrate on codecs here.

Travel Assistance

For more information on DirectX, go straight to the source:
http://www.microsoft.com/directx

Pure waveform files are huge—near-CD-quality WAV files average about 10MB/minute of sound. No big deal for system sounds like short beeps, but complete songs get really big! Try downloading a WAV file that size—even on a high-speed connection it takes a while. As a result, a large number of compression methodologies exist. Some are quite famous—have you ever heard of an MP3 file? An MP3 is nothing more than a WAV file that uses a special compression program called the Fraunhofer IIS MPEG Layer-3 Codec. For a sound application to play the sound file, it needs access to the algorithm that decodes the MP3 format into a waveform. While some applications use their own built-in codecs, Windows provides a broad cross-section of codecs that any sound application may access, leaving the sound application to do other jobs.

Different compression formats meet different needs. Some codecs do a better job of compression, but lose some of the sound quality. Others keep all the quality, but may not compress as well. Without the proper codec, the sound file, or the sound built into a video file, won't play. If an application refuses to play a particular sound file or if a video file plays without sound, you need to verify you have the correct codec installed. Granted, later generation sound and video applications, such as WinAmp or Windows Media Player, will attempt to access the proper codec on their own—Windows Media Player even tries to download the proper one—but they often fail with some type of error that implies an *I don't have the right codec* type of problem.

Earlier sound applications usually give no clue other than a useless *Unable to read file* message. When receiving a multimedia file, it's common to ask about both the file format and the codec to ensure you can play the file.

CODEC Problems

If you're having a problem with a particular audio or video file, check the file's properties. Most, but not all, sound and all video files show their codec in their properties.

You can fix most codec problems by downloading the desired codec. All codec installation programs load the codec files and update the Registry—installing codecs is akin to loading a regular application.

Unfortunately, I've yet to find an established, one-stop web site for codec downloads. If you find one, let me know. I usually just fire up my web browser and search on the codec name I want and the word "download."

Folks love to look at all the codecs in their Multimedia settings and try to figure out which codec goes with which type of audio or video file. Who cares? The A+ Certification exams certainly don't care whether you know the msg723 codec is used for compression of videoconferencing and telephony applications. The A+ exams do want you to understand why codecs exist and that you might need to download one occasionally. The only time I have even the slightest interest in a codec is when I can't get some application to run!

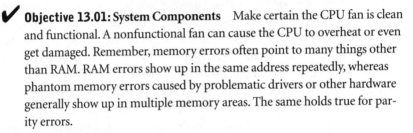

Exam Tip

Don't panic about understanding all the different codecs! Just make sure you know what they do and that you occasionally need to download them!

CHECKPOINT

✔ **Objective 13.01: System Components** Make certain the CPU fan is clean and functional. A nonfunctional fan can cause the CPU to overheat or even get damaged. Remember, memory errors often point to many things other than RAM. RAM errors show up in the same address repeatedly, whereas phantom memory errors caused by problematic drivers or other hardware generally show up in multiple memory areas. The same holds true for parity errors.

✔ **Objective 13.02: Mass Storage Devices** Prevention is the best hard-drive cure. Back up all important data regularly! If you run into problems with a drive, run the built-in disk-checking utility first. SCSI drive troubleshooting covers the same issues as EIDE drives, such as power, connectivity, and BIOS, but also adds SCSI ID settings and termination into the mix. If the LED comes on and stays on when you install a new floppy disk drive, you've reversed one end of the 34-pin cable-select ribbon cable.

✔ **Objective 13.03: Expansion Cards and Peripherals** If you must go inside a monitor to adjust the focus, convergence, or brightness, practice extreme caution. Make sure to push the AGP video card into the slot fully on installation. If you're experiencing problems with video and sound cards, check the drivers and support software, such as sound codecs and DirectX.

REVIEW QUESTIONS

1. Tom has just installed a four-speaker sound card into his system. When he turns up the volume for the front speakers, the back speakers get louder. When Tom adjusts the volume for the back speakers, it affects the front ones. Which of the following is the most likely problem?

   A. Tom forgot to switch the controls in Windows

   B. Tom disabled the back speakers

   C. Tom needs to run the SNDCHK utility

   D. The speaker cables are switched on the sound card

2. Jackie is trying to retrieve her e-mail. She doesn't hear the modem dialing out as she normally hears. What is least likely to have caused this problem?

   A. The RJ-11 isn't plugged into the modem

   B. The phone is disconnected

   C. Someone is on the line

   D. The Internet is down

3. The message "missing operating system" appears when booting up the PC from the hard drive. To attempt a repair to the drive without losing data, you should first try which of the following?

   A. Boot to a bootable floppy disk and type **FORMAT C: /S**

   B. Boot to a bootable floppy disk and type **SYSTEM C:**

   C. Repartition the drive using FDISK

   D. Boot to a bootable floppy disk and type **SYS C:**

4. Jill installs a new SCSI host adapter in a system. When she boots up the system, a new text message appears and seems to cause the system to halt for a minute. Then the system continues and Windows loads normally. The host adapter appears in Jill's Device Manager and seems to be working. What could be the cause of the odd text message and slowdown at boot?

   A. The SCSI host adapter must have buggy drivers

   B. The SCSI host adapter has option ROM that loads BIOS for the card

   C. The SCSI host adapter must need drivers loaded

   D. The SCSI host adapter has option RAM that has to search the hard drive for drivers before it can load

5. What program must be run from a bootable floppy to allow access to a CD-ROM drive?

   A. EMM386.EXE

   B. CDEX.EXE

   C. MSCDEX.EXE

   D. MSCDEX.SYS

6. An old IBM PC gives you a POST error code of 1701. This points to:

   A. keyboard

   B. video

   C. CPU

   D. hard drive controller

7. If the CPU fan dies, what are the two most likely effects?

   A. Dead CPU

   B. System lockup

   C. Hard drive failure

   D. RAM failure

REVIEW ANSWERS

1. **D** Most four-speaker soundcards have a front and back jack. He probably switched them.

2. **D** An extension phone could be in use. The cable might not be connected. The phone line might not be connected.

3. **D** The SYS command puts the system files on the hard drive in the appropriate areas and enables you to boot from the C: drive.

4. **B** The SCSI host adapter has option ROM that loads BIOS for the card.

5. **C** The file MSCDEX.EXE must be installed before a CD-ROM will work in DOS.

6. **D** This is an old POST text hard-drive error code.

7. **A** **B** The system will lock up like a stone and, if you leave it on with no fan running for the CPU, the CPU will fry.

Portable
Computers

	NEWBIE	SOME EXPERIENCE	EXPERT
ETA	2 hours	1 hour	1/2 hour

The computing world today differs vastly from that of earlier years; a fact perhaps most evident in the world of portable PCs. As battery and screen technology improved dramatically and more wireless peripherals were developed, more folks opted for portables.

As the chances to work on these machines increase, it's more important than ever that you know how to upgrade and repair them. The A+ Certification competencies have portable PC topics liberally sprinkled here and there. This chapter puts it all together for you.

Objective 14.01 Configuration

For years, portable PC makers engineered entirely proprietary components for each system model they developed. For the most part, this proprietary attitude still prevails, but some modularity is appearing in today's portable PCs, enabling you to make basic replacements and upgrades without going back to the manufacturer for expensive, proprietary components. You need to surf the Web for companies that sell the components because few storefronts stock them. The following sections highlight the most common components.

RAM

Every recent laptop has upgradeable RAM slots. These slots all use either 72-pin or 144-pin SO-DIMMs. Be sure to check with the manufacturer of the laptop to find out if any special features, such as PC100 or ECC, are required.

Hard Drives

ATA drives in the 2.5-inch drive format now rule in all laptops. While much smaller than regular ATA drives, they use the same features and configurations. Some manufacturers might use strange settings, such as requiring the drive to use the cable select setting instead of master or slave. Again, check with the laptop maker. Otherwise, no difference exists between 2.5-inch drives and their larger 3.25-inch brethren.

Modular CPUs

Both Intel and AMD have long sold specialized, modular CPUs for laptops, yet many folks don't realize they can easily upgrade many systems by removing the old module and replacing it with a new one, as shown in Figure 14-1. Be careful to follow the manufacturer's specifications!

Video Cards

Video card makers have now begun to enter the modular laptop component arena. While no single standard works in all systems, a quick phone call to the tech support department of the laptop maker often reveals upgrade options. Video cards are the least upgraded modular components but, as standards begin to tighten, we'll be replacing video cards in laptops more often.

PC Cards

PC Cards are standard on today's mobile computers. *PC Cards* are credit-card sized, hot-swappable devices that can, and do, perform virtually every PC function. Although originally visualized as memory cards, today PC Cards hold hard drives, modems, network cards, sound cards, SCSI controllers—the list can continue indefinitely. PC Cards, as shown in Figure 14-2, are easy to use, inexpensive, and convenient.

Local Lingo

PCMCIA   Personal Computer Memory Card International Association. PCMCIA card is the original name, still in common use, for PC Card.

FIGURE 14-1   Modular CPU

FIGURE 14-2   Assorted PC Cards

Unfortunately, this same convenience and ease of use can make PC Cards a real challenge to configure and troubleshoot. As with so many other parts of the PC, the secret is to understand the individual components of PC Cards, so you can recognize symptoms when they appear. The place to start with PC Cards is to recognize they come in three different physical sizes, as determined by the PCMCIA committee. They are called Type I, Type II, and Type III. While the PCMCIA standard only recommends, rather than mandates, that certain sizes of cards perform certain functions, most PC Cards follow their recommendations (listed in Table 14-1).

TABLE 14-1   Types of PC Cards

	Length	Width	Thickness	Recommended Use
Type I	85.6 mm	54.0 mm	3.3 mm	Flash Memory
Type II	85.6 mm	54.0 mm	5.0 mm	I/O (Modem, NIC, and so forth)
Type III	85.6 mm	54.0 mm	10.5 mm	Hard Drives

The only difference among these three types is the thickness of the card. All PC Cards share the same 68-pin interface, and assuming the slot is high enough to accept the card, any PC Card will work in that slot. Type II cards are by far the most common type of PC Cards. Most laptops have two Type II slots—one above the other—so they can accept two Type I or II cards or one Type III card, as shown in Figure 14-3.

The PCMCIA standard defines two levels of software drivers to support PC Cards. The first, lower level is known as socket services. *Socket services* are device drivers used to support the PC card socket, enabling the system to detect when a PC Card is inserted or removed, and providing the necessary I/O to the device. The second, higher level of software drivers, known as *card services,* recognizes the function of the particular PC Card in the slot and provides the specialized drivers necessary to make the card work.

In the early PCMCIA days, most of the responsibility for making PC Cards work rested with individual laptop manufacturers. This meant if you wanted to be sure a PC Card worked, you purchased the PC Card from the same place you got the laptop. This problem persisted until the advent of Windows 95 and modern laptop chipsets.

In today's laptops, the socket services are standardized and are handled by the System BIOS. Windows itself handles all card services and has a large preinstalled base of PC Card device drivers, although most PC Cards come with their own drivers. Access Windows 9*x* Card Services via the PCMCIA option in the Control Panel.

Many PC Card makers advertise a Type IV slot. This slot is not part of the PCMCIA standard. The Type IV slot is used to describe any PC Card thicker than the Type III.

FIGURE 14-3   Two PC cards in a laptop

CardBus

The newest type of PC Card is called CardBus. *CardBus* provides a 32-bit multiplexed address/data path operating at PCI local-bus speeds of up to 33 MHz. CardBus uses the synchronous burst-transfer orientation of PCI and what is essentially a PCI bus protocol. This means CardBus devices are capable of acting as system-bus masters. This compares to PC Cards, which use an 8- or 16-bit interface operating at ISA bus speeds (8 MHz) and an ISA-like asynchronous protocol.

A single CardBus card can perform up to eight functions. Regular PC Cards can perform a maximum of two functions. An example of a two-function PC Card is a modem/network PC Card. Thanks to CardBus, don't be surprised if you can purchase a modem/network/ISDN/sound/SCSI card soon!

CardBus uses the same form factors and the same 68-pin connector as a regular PC Card. This allows a regular PC Card to work in a CardBus slot. Unfortunately, a CardBus card won't work in a regular PC Card socket. In fact, because CardBus uses 3.3-volt power instead of the regular 5-volt PC Card power, CardBus cards have special keying that prevents you from accidentally plugging one into a regular PC Card socket.

Finally, for CardBus to operate, the laptop should be running Windows 95 OSR2 or later. CardBus has become the PC card of the future and is standard equipment on most new laptops.

Objective 14.02   # Power Management

The typical laptop has dozens of components and each part uses power. Every part used power continuously in early laptops, whether or not the system needed that device at that time. The hard drive would continue to spin whether or not it was being accessed, for example, and the screen would continue to display, even when the user walked away from the machine.

The optimal situation would be a system where the user could instruct the PC to shut down unused devices selectively, preferably by defining a maximum period of inactivity after which the PC would shut down the inactive device. Longer periods of inactivity would trigger the entire system to shut itself down, leaving critical information loaded in RAM, ready to restart when a *wake-up event,* such as mouse movement or a keystroke, occurs. The system would have to be sensitive to potential hazards, such as shutting down in the middle of writing to a drive. To do all this, a laptop would need specialized hardware, as well as a specialized BIOS and operating system. This process of cooperation between the hardware, BIOS, and operating system to reduce power usage is known generically as *power management.*

System Management Mode

Intel's 386SX CPU was the first to employ power management features. These new features, collectively called System Management Mode (SMM), allowed the CPU to slow down or stop its clock without erasing the register information and enabled power saving in peripherals. From its humble beginnings in the 386SX, SMM slowly started to show up in more CPUs and is now common. Using only a power-saving CPU meant power management was relegated to special sleep or doze buttons that would stop the CPU and all the peripherals on the laptop. To take real advantage of SMM, you must also have a specialized BIOS and operating system. To this end, Intel proposed the Advanced Power Management (APM) specification in 1992 and the Advanced Configuration and Power Interface (ACPI) standard in 1996.

Requirements for APM/ACPI

APM and ACPI require four features to function fully. The first is an SMM-capable CPU, which virtually all CPUs now are. The second requirement is an *APM-compliant BIOS,* which enables the CPU to shut off the peripherals as desired. The third requirement is devices that will accept being shut off. These devices are usually called *Energy Star* devices, which signals their compliance with the EPA's Energy Star standard. To be an Energy Star device, a peripheral must have the capability to shut down without actually turning off. Finally, the system's operating system must know how to request that a particular device be shut down and the CPU's clock be slowed down or stopped.

ACPI goes beyond the APM standard by supplying support for hot-swappable devices, always a huge problem with APM. This feature aside, it's a challenge to tell the difference between an APM system and an ACPI system at first glance.

APM/ACPI Levels

The APM specification defines five different power usage operating levels for a system: Full on, APM enabled, APM standby, APM suspend, and Off. These levels are left intentionally fuzzy to give manufacturers considerable leeway in their use. The only real difference among them is the amount of time each takes to return to normal usage.

Full On Everything in the system running at full power. No power management.

APM Enabled CPU and RAM running at full power. Power management enabled. An unused device may or may not be shut down.

APM Standby CPU is stopped. RAM still stores all programs. All peripherals are shut down, although configuration options are still stored, so you won't have to reinitialize the devices to get back to APM Enabled state.

APM Suspend Everything in the PC is shut down or at its lowest power consumption setting. Many systems use a special type of Suspend called *Hibernation,* where critical configuration information is written to the hard drive. Upon a wake-up event, the system is reinitialized and the data is read from the drive to return the system to the APM Enabled mode. The recovery time between Suspend and Enabled states is much longer than the time between Standby and Enabled states.

Off When in the Off state, your computer or device is powered down and inactive. Data and operational parameters may or may not be preserved.

ACPI handles all these levels, plus a few more, such as *Soft Power On/Off,* which enables you to define the function of the Power button.

Configuration of APM/ACPI

You can configure APM/ACPI via CMOS settings or through Windows. Windows settings will override CMOS settings. Although the flexibility of APM/ACPI standards can cause some confusion among different implementations, some settings are usually part of CMOS configuration. First, CMOS can initialize power management, which enables the system to enter the APM Enabled mode. CMOS configuration often includes options for setting time frames for entering Standby and Suspend modes, as well as settings to determine which events take place in each of these modes. Finally, many CMOS versions include settings to determine wake-up events, such as directing the system to monitor a modem or a particular IRQ, as you can see in Figure 14-4.

```
       CMOS Setup Utility - Copyright (C) 1984-1999 Award Software
                           Wake Up Events
┌─────────────────────────────────────────────────┬──────────────────────┐
│  UGA                      OFF                     │     Item Help        │
│  LPT & COM                LPT/COM                 │                      │
│  HDD & FDD                ON                      │  Menu Level    ▶     │
│  PCI Master               OFF                     │                      │
│  PowerOn by PCI Ca┌──────────────────────────┐   │                      │
│  Wake Up On LAN/RI│ Wake Up On LAN/Ring      │   │                      │
│  RTC Alarm Resume  │                          │   │                      │
│ x Date (of Month)  │                          │   │                      │
│ x Resume Time (hh:m│ Disabled ..... [ ]       │   │                      │
│ ▶ IRQs Activity Mon│ Enabled  ..... [■]       │   │                      │
│                    │                          │   │                      │
│                    │                          │   │                      │
│                    │                          │   │                      │
│                    │ ↑↓:Move ENTER:Accept ESC:Abort│                     │
│                    └──────────────────────────┘   │                      │
└─────────────────────────────────────────────────┴──────────────────────┘
```

FIGURE 14-4   Setting a wake-up event in CMOS

A true ACPI-compliant CMOS provides an ACPI setup option. Figure 14-5 shows a typical modern BIOS that provides this setting.

APM/ACPI settings can be found in two areas in Windows 9x. Because the monitor is one of the biggest power users on a computer, a great place to start the power management configuration process is in the Control Panel. Select Display | Settings tab | Advanced Settings.

With the exception of adding the Suspend option to the Start button, Windows 9x hides the APM/ACPI Standby and Suspend features. Instead, Windows provides individual control for the big power eaters—monitors, PC Cards, and hard drives—and makes its own assumptions for everything else in the PC. These controls can be found in the Power section of the Control Panel, as shown in Figure 14-6.

```
       CMOS Setup Utility - Copyright (C) 1984-1999 Award Software
                         Power Management Setup
┌─────────────────────────────────────────────────┬──────────────────────┐
│ ▶ Power Management        Press Enter            │     Item Help        │
│   ACPI Suspend Type       S1(POS)                │                      │
│   PM Control by APM       Yes                     │  Menu Level    ▶     │
│   Video Off Option        Suspend -> Off          │                      │
│   Video Off Method        U/H SYNC+Blank          │                      │
│   MODEM Use IRQ           NA                       │                      │
│   Soft-Off by PWRBTN      Instant-Off             │                      │
│ ▶ Wake Up Events          Press Enter             │                      │
│                                                   │                      │
│                                                   │                      │
│                                                   │                      │
│                                                   │                      │
│                                                   │                      │
└─────────────────────────────────────────────────┴──────────────────────┘
```

FIGURE 14-5   CMOS with ACPI setup option

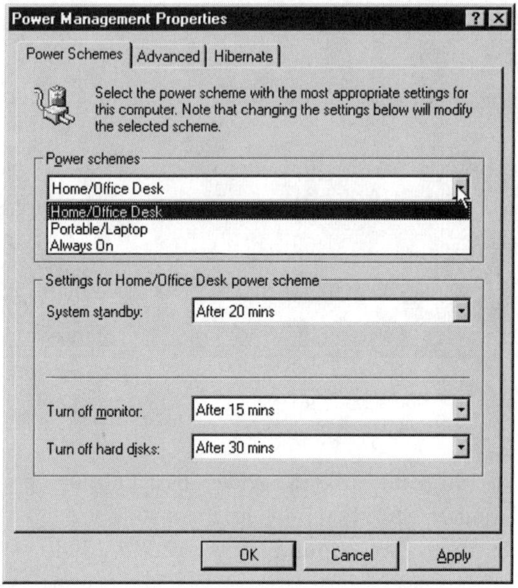

FIGURE 14-6   Power Management controls

Objective 14.03   Batteries

O f all the many technologies unique to mobile PCs, batteries are the most obvious, the most frustrating, and yet the most easily supported component. The secret to understanding batteries is understanding the different types of batteries used by mobile PCs and appreciating each of their special needs/quirks. Once this is clear, battery problems are usually easy to spot and fix. To begin with, only three types of batteries are commonly used in mobile PCs: Nickel-Cadmium (Ni-Cd), Nickel-Metal Hydride (Ni-MH), and Lithium-Ion (Li-Ion). Let's investigate each of these types.

Nickel-Cadmium (Ni-Cd)

Ni-Cds were the first batteries commonly used in mobile PCs, which, unlike flash-lights or Walkmans, must have a steady voltage. Before Ni-Cd, a cheap battery technology didn't exist that could provide that steady voltage. Ni-Cd, being the first of its type, was full of little problems. Probably most irritating was a little thing called *battery memory*: the tendency of a Ni-Cd battery to lose a significant amount of its capability to recharge if it was charged repeatedly without being totally discharged. A battery that originally kept a laptop running for two hours would eventually only keep that same laptop going for 30 minutes or less.

To prevent memory problems, a Ni-Cd battery had to be discharged completely before each recharging. Recharging was tricky as well because Ni-Cd batteries dislike being overcharged. Unfortunately, there was no way to verify when a battery was fully charged without an expensive charging machine. As a result, most Ni-Cd batteries lasted an extremely short time. One quick fix was to purchase a *conditioning* charger, which would first totally discharge the Ni-Cd battery, and then generate a special reverse current that electrically cleaned the internal parts of the battery, so it could be recharged more often and would run longer on each recharge.

Ni-Cd batteries would at best last for 1,000 charges or far fewer with poor treatment. Ni-Cds were extremely susceptible to heat and would self-discharge over time if not used. Leaving a Ni-Cd in the car in the summer was like throwing it in the garbage. And Ni-Cd batteries didn't stop causing trouble after they died. The highly toxic metals inside the battery made it unacceptable simply to throw them in the trash. Ni-Cd batteries must be disposed of via specialized disposal companies—most recycling centers are glad to take them. Also, many battery manufacturers and distributors will take them. Even though Ni-Cd batteries aren't used in PCs often anymore, many devices, such as cellular and cordless phones, still use Ni-Cds.

Nickel Metal Hydride (Ni-MH)

Ni-MH batteries were the next generation of mobile PC batteries and are still quite common today. Basically, Ni-MH batteries are like Ni-Cd batteries without most of the headaches. Ni-MH batteries are much less susceptible to memory problems, can better tolerate overcharging, can take more recharging, and last longer between rechargings. Like Ni-Cds, Ni-MH batteries are still susceptible to heat, so it's better not to leave them in a hot car. While they're considered nontoxic to the environment, it's still a good idea to do a special disposal. Unlike a Ni-Cd, recharging a Ni-MH with shallow recharges, as opposed to a complete discharge/recharge, is usually better. Ni-MH is a popular replacement battery for Ni-Cd systems.

Lithium Ion (Li-Ion)

The most common type of battery used today is Li-Ion. These batteries are extremely powerful, completely immune to memory problems, and last at least twice as long on one charge compared to Ni-MH batteries. Li-Ion batteries can't take as many charges as Ni-MH batteries but, in return for a shorter total battery life span, users get longer periods between charges. Li-Ion batteries will explode if they're overcharged, so all Li-Ion batteries sold with PCs have built-in circuitry to prevent accidental overcharging. Lithium batteries can only be used on systems designed to use them and they can't be used as replacement batteries for the older types.

Smart Batteries

In an attempt to provide better maintenance for laptop batteries, manufacturers have developed a new type of battery called the *smart battery*. Smart batteries tell the computer when they need to be charged, conditioned, or replaced.

In general, remember five basics. First, always store batteries in a cool place. Although a freezer might sound like an excellent storage place, moisture, metal racks, and food make it a bad idea. Second, condition your Ni-Cd and Ni-MH batteries—they'll last longer. Third, keep battery contacts clean with a little alcohol or a dry cloth. Fourth, *never* handle a battery that has ruptured or broken—battery chemicals are extremely dangerous. And, fifth, always recycle old batteries.

Objective 14.04 USB and FireWire

Two of the newest external bus standards used for desktop PCs—Universal Serial Bus (USB) and IEEE 1394, better known as *FireWire*—are also quite popular in portable PCs. Let's review these two standards briefly.

USB

USB ports are present on all PCs, not only on portable ones, but they're most heavily used on laptops. Let's discuss USB in a bit more depth to help you appreciate the power—and problems—of USB.

In theory, up to 127 devices can use a single USB port. In reality, USB's maximum throughput of 12 Mb/s limits most USB sharing to three or four devices, depending on their functions. USB ports also supply power to connected devices, but too many devices on a single USB chain can overtax its power capabilities.

USB devices run at one of two speeds: a low speed of 1.5 Mb/s and a high-speed of 12 Mb/s. Some low-speed devices don't like to share a port with high-speed devices. Fortunately, most systems that support USB also provide more than one USB port. USB is also full duplex, which we discuss later in this chapter.

USB allows for a maximum cable length of five meters, although you can add a powered USB hub every five meters to extend this distance. While most USB devices never get near this maximum, many devices such as digital cameras try to use five-meter cables, which can cause problems. Because USB is a bidirectional connection, even a standard, well-shielded, 20-gauge, twisted-pair USB cable will begin to suffer from electrical interference as the cable grows longer. Personally, I stick to no more than two-meter cables.

USB Configuration

Improper USB CMOS and driver configuration will make your USB installations nightmarish. Always make sure to follow these steps:

1. Make sure the CMOS provides an IRQ for the USB ports. Look for a setting similar to Figure 14-7.
2. Make sure your operating system supports USB. USB is supported by every version of Windows, except Windows NT and Windows 95A. For the latter, Microsoft supplies a USB supplement you can download from the Microsoft web site.
3. Always install the device driver for a new USB device *before* you plug it in. Once you install the device and you know the ports are active, you can feel free to hot-swap devices to your heart's content. USB makes device installation a breeze once the drivers are installed!

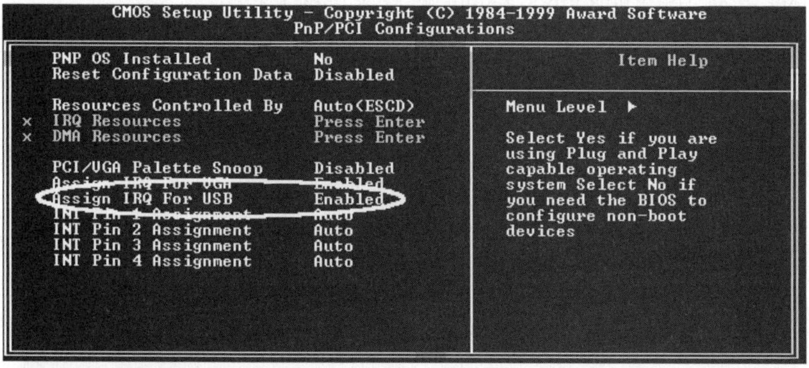

FIGURE 14-7 IRQ for USB in CMOS

Windows 2000 has a large number of built-in drivers for USB devices. You can count on Windows 2000's built-in drivers to recognize keyboards, mice, and other basic devices. If your new mouse or keyboard has some extra features, however, the default USB drivers probably won't support them. Thus, it's good policy to install the driver that comes with the device.

FireWire

The emergence of PC multimedia in the 1990s created an intense demand for a low-cost, high-speed, bi-directional cabling standard to replace the aged and notoriously slow serial communication mode. This demand led to the amazing IEEE 1394 standard, better known by the name *FireWire*. Apple Computers designed FireWire and the IEEE standardized it at the end of 1995. Even though FireWire has existed as a standard for many years, the standard only recently has been widely adopted.

FireWire consists of a special 6-wire cable and a unique FireWire connector, as shown in Figure 14-8. Sony Corporation has also developed a smaller, 4-pin version.

The 6-pin connection provides power, in addition to data transfer. Devices that use the 4-pin version must use a separate power supply. You can purchase cables that convert the Sony 4-pin to the standard 6-pin connection.

Most devices use the larger standard connector, while the smaller one is found on devices such as digital video cameras. In fact, this is one of the most popular uses for FireWire. Any single FireWire cable can be no longer than 5 meters, often referenced as 15 feet in the United States.

IEEE 1394 allows devices to run at speeds of 100, 200, and 400 Mb/s. Virtually all FireWire devices now use the 400 Mb/s speed. Because few portable PCs have built-in FireWire ports, most require a FireWire PC Card.

FIGURE 14-8   FireWire connectors

Finally, FireWire supports daisy chaining, allowing up to 63 devices to run from a single controller. FireWire is totally hot-swappable, runs at full duplex, and is fully compliant with plug and play, making it amazingly simple to use.

Objective 14.05 Duplex Explained

B ecause you learned that both USB and FireWire are duplex, it's a good time to bring up what this means! Anyone who's spent more than three minutes hanging out with a modem, network card (NIC), or sound card has, no doubt, run into the magical term "duplex" or one of its two offshoots: full duplex and half duplex. In most cases, we simply ignore these terms, trusting in that magical beast called plug and play (or the other handy tool called ignorance is bliss) to deal with this duplex thingamabob. We pray our little bit of hardware du jour will work, even though we chose not to deal with the duplex animal—whatever the heck it is.

The scary aspect of duplex is, in most cases, you don't need to deal with it at all. Usually, the whole concept of a hardware device's *duplexity* (my word) is totally academic. So, arm in arm, we trot happily down the yellow brick road of PC repair, confident—nay, smug—that we wouldn't know a duplex device if it bit us. However, as techs we do need to understand duplex.

Sound cards, NICs, and modems all share one important characteristic: they send and receive data. While most of us can easily visualize NICs and modems sending and receiving data, we forget that sound cards come with microphones and input ports to receive sound, and speakers for output. So where does duplex come into play? That's easy. *Duplex* simply refers to a device's capability to send and receive data at the same time. A half-duplex device can only send *or* receive at any given moment. A full-duplex device can *both* send and receive simultaneously. The term "duplex" used alone means full duplex.

Duplex Capability

Is duplex capability something we can turn on or off? In most cases, the answer is no. You simply need to know whether a device is full or half duplex, to understand why certain things you ask a device to do may or may not work. In most cases, duplex capability is clearly advertised on the box. One great example is Internet phone applications like Microsoft's NetMeeting or Net2Phone. These applications enable you to talk to another user over the Internet using your sound card.

However, if your sound card isn't capable of full duplex, you can forget it! Many cheap sound cards on the market today are only half duplex. Some sound applications provide a setting that enables you to use the full-duplex capability of your hardware.

When you see the term full duplex with a modem, it usually refers to a voice modem, capable of handling advanced Telephony Application Program Interface (TAPI) functions like voice recordings. For regular data modems, neither a means nor a reason exists for you to mess with duplex settings.

Duplex and NICs

NICs often have the capability to switch between full- and half-duplex communication. Which one you use depends on your network. Most modern networks using twisted-pair cable have hubs that support both full-duplex and older half-duplex NICs. Use the much faster full-duplex mode if at all possible.

Most NICs let you change their duplex settings. In Windows 9x, open Device Manager, and then select the Advanced tab under the device's Properties. When you look at the computer settings for a NIC, note that it has an Auto Detect setting. This usually works, although some hubs insist you force the card to use either full or half duplex. In that case, always try full duplex first, only switching to half duplex if you encounter problems.

Duplex isn't limited to only these three types of devices. In fact, everything that performs I/O inside and outside your PC uses either half or full duplex. Serial, FireWire, SCSI, IDE, and USB connections all use full duplex. Only parallel connections use half duplex. So, if someone asks you whether a generic device is half or full duplex, you can play the resident Duplex Super Genius and answer with confidence: unless it's parallel, it's capable of full duplex.

Objective 14.06   ## Docking Stations

Until recently, it was almost always true that a person who owned a portable PC also had a desktop PC. You could take your portable to a job site or on a trip—and that was cool—but when you wanted to get real work done, you used your desktop computer. To keep these multiple-PC users on the near side of sanity, Microsoft has long provided a number of handy tools such as the Microsoft briefcase to assist you in synchronizing the data on your laptop with the data on your PC.

The power of laptops has reached a point today where many people forgo the desktop PC entirely and replace it with a laptop. The only downside to this arrangement is in the hardware. Desktop PCs can more affordably have a big monitor, big storage devices, and extra groovy features, such as a CD-RW drive. Recognizing this problem, manufacturers of portable PCs provide (for a price) a *docking station* that gives the laptop access to big monitors, full-sized mice, network connections, secondary mass storage, and so on. Figure 14-9 shows a typical laptop connected to a docking station.

Docking stations provide fantastic convenience, but there's a catch. If the laptop is connected to a docking station, it must have some method of knowing what hardware is available on the docking station and be able to use that equipment. Equally, if the laptop is disconnected, it must know what hardware isn't available. Windows handles this problem via hardware profiles.

Hardware Profiles

A *hardware profile* is a list of devices Windows automatically enables or disables in the Device Manager, depending on what devices the system detects. Or, the user can manually choose a profile from a list at bootup. The manual method has become less prominent because smarter laptops can detect their current state and easily choose the proper profile via the PnP process.

Both Windows 9*x* and Windows 2000 configure their hardware profiles in the System Properties window on the Hardware Profiles tab. Figure 14-10 shows the hardware profiles for a laptop running Windows 98. One profile is for what this user calls *Standalone*—not connected to the docking station. The other hardware profile is used when the laptop is connected to the docking station.

FIGURE 14-9   Laptop computer in a docking station

Hardware profiles

In theory, you can create hardware profiles for any system but, in reality, hardware profiles are for laptops. In fact, the hardware profiles features in Windows 2000 simply assume if you use hardware profiles, as shown in Figure 14-11, you're using a laptop. The only trick to hardware profiles is some devices show as disabled in the Device Manager, depending on which profile is active. Don't panic if you see a red *X* on a device in Device Manager on a laptop—this might only mean a particular device isn't being used by the current profile!

Hardware profile settings in Windows 2000

CHECKPOINT

✔ **Objective 14.01: Configuration** Most portables are made up of proprietary components, although if you look hard enough, you can find modular replacement components. Know how to replace or upgrade RAM, hard drives, modular CPUs, and video cards, as well as PCMCIA (PC) and CardBus cards. Also know the three types of PC cards and how they differ from one another.

✔ **Objective 14.02: Power Management** Understand the APM (Advanced Power Management) and ACPI (Advanced Configuration and Power Interface) standards. The five power usage operating levels defined by the APM specification are Full On, APM Enabled, APM Standby, APM Suspend (Hibernate), and Off. The biggest advantage of ACPI is it supports hot-swappable devices.

✔ **Objective 14.03: Batteries** Three types of batteries are commonly used in mobile PCs: Nickel-Cadmium (Ni-Cd), Nickel-Metal Hydride (Ni-MH), and Lithium-Ion (Li-Ion). The most common type used today is Lithium-Ion.

✔ **Objective 14.04: USB and FireWire** USB devices run at either 1.5 Mb/s or 12 Mb/s. A single USB port can, in theory, support up to 127 devices but, in reality, most USB sharing is limited to three or four devices. FireWire devices can run at speeds of 100, 200, and 400 Mb/s, but most now run at 400 Mb/s. FireWire supports daisy chaining of up to 63 devices, is totally hot-swappable, runs at full duplex, and is fully compliant with plug and play.

✔ **Objective 14.05: Duplex Explained** Duplex refers to a device's capability to send and receive data at the same time. A half-duplex device can only send or receive at any given moment, while a full-duplex device can both send and receive simultaneously. The term "duplex" used alone means "full duplex." Serial, FireWire, SCSI, IDE, and USB connections all use full duplex. Only parallel connections use half duplex.

✔ **Objective 14.06: Docking Stations** Laptops that connect to docking stations use hardware profiles to determine what devices are available. A hardware profile is a list of devices that Windows automatically enables or disables in the Device Manager, depending on what devices the laptop detects.

REVIEW QUESTIONS

1. Which of the following is *not* true about PC Cards?

   A. Socket Services need to be set to detect whether a card is installed
   B. PCMCIA services must be set up in CMOS
   C. Card Services need to be set up to detect the function of the card installed
   D. PC Cards are hot-swappable

2. How many Type III cards can typically fit into a laptop at one time?

   A. 1
   B. 2
   C. 3
   D. 4

3. What is the theoretical maximum number of devices a Universal Serial Bus (USB) port can support?

   A. 1
   B. 16
   C. 32
   D. 127

4. In meters, what is the maximum length between two full-speed USB devices using 20-gauge shielded cables?

   A. 6
   B. 5
   C. 3
   D. 2

5. When a new USB mouse is plugged into a Windows 95 portable, the laptop doesn't recognize that a device has been added. What's the most likely cause for this problem?

   A. The device was plugged in while the system was running
   B. The device was plugged in while the system was off
   C. The system is running Windows 95A
   D. The system doesn't yet have the proper drivers loaded

6. How many Type II cards can typically fit into a laptop at one time?

   A. 1
   B. 2
   C. 3
   D. 4

7. Which of the following is not possible?

   A. Having two Type II cards in a laptop at one time
   B. Having a Type I and a Type II card in a laptop at one time
   C. Having two Type I cards in a laptop at one time
   D. Having a Type II and a Type III card in a laptop at one time

8. If the USB port is active and Windows 2000 includes a driver for the peripheral, what is the minimum number of steps it takes to install the peripheral?

   A. Shut down the system, plug in the device, start the system, run the Add/Remove Hardware Wizard, select the device, load the driver, restart the system
   B. Plug in the device, start the system, run the Add/Remove Hardware Wizard, select the device, wait for Windows 2000 to recognize the device automatically, install the drivers, initialize the device
   C. Turn off the system, plug in the device, start the system, wait for Windows 2000 to recognize the device automatically, install the drivers, initialize the device
   D. Plug the device into a running system, wait for Windows 2000 to recognize the device automatically, install the drivers, and initialize the device

9. Which of the following is *not* a recommended maintenance procedure for laptop batteries?

   A. Keep the contacts clean using alcohol or a dry cloth
   B. Store them in the freezer if they won't be used for a long period of time
   C. Recycle them according to the manufacturer's specifications
   D. Store them in a cool place

10. How many pins do PC Cards have?

   A. 30
   B. 40
   C. 68
   D. 168

REVIEW ANSWERS

1. **B** There's no need to set up PCMCIA services in CMOS.

2. **A** Only one Type III PC Card can fit into a laptop at a time because of the thickness of these cards.

3. **D** A USB port can theoretically support up to 127 devices.

4. **B** The maximum length between two full-speed USB devices using 20-gauge shielded cables is five meters.

5. **C** Windows 9x did not support USB until Windows 95B.

6. **B** A typical laptop can fit two Type II cards at the same time.

7. **D** If you use a Type III card, no other card will fit into the socket.

8. **D** Plug the device into a running system, wait for Windows 2000 to recognize the device automatically, install the drivers, and then initialize the device.

9. **B** Storing batteries in the freezer for a long period of time isn't advisable because of the presence of moisture, metal racks, and food.

10. **C** There are 68 pins on PC Cards and sockets.

Networks: Hardware

	NEWBIE	SOME EXPERIENCE	EXPERT
ETA	3 hours	2 hours	1 hour

Early on in the life of PCs, it became obvious that individual PCs needed to share data and peripherals with other PCs. Certainly, any PC can read another PC's data off floppy disks. But that requires time to copy the data to a floppy disk, take the floppy to the other machine (aka *SneakerNet*), insert the floppy, and access the data. This works, but it's a slow process and, for certain types of data, completely useless. In particular, the PC world likes to have one database that many users can access simultaneously. The data stored in databases includes customer lists, product inventories, and student enrollment—examples of this type of data are endless. Next, there is a great demand for sharing devices. Why buy everyone in the company a laser printer when a single laser printer, accessible to everyone, would suffice?

Objective 15.01   Networking Basics

Clearly, there was a strong motivation to create a grouping of PCs—a network—that could enable users to share data and peripherals. So the big question is—How? It's easy to say, "Well, just run a wire between them!" Although most networks do manifest themselves via some type of cable, this barely touches the thousands of questions that come into play here. Here are a few of the *big* questions.

- How will each computer be identified? If two or more computers want to talk at the same time, how do you ensure all conversations are understood?
- What kind of wire? What gauge? How many wires in the cable? Which wires do which things? How long can the cable be? What type of connectors?
- If more than one PC is accessing the same file, how can they be prevented from destroying each other's changes to that file?
- How can access to data and peripherals be controlled?

Obviously, there's a lot more to making a network than just stringing up some cable! To give a clearer picture of how networks *network*, I'll break the subject into four major areas: Hardware, Protocols, Network, and Shared Resources. Let's take a quick look at these categories, so you know what to expect.

Hardware   Hardware is probably the most self-explanatory of the four categories. This section covers the many different ways data can be moved from one

PC to another. Here, we discuss the different types of cabling. This section also explains how network cards are installed and tested. Plus, the Hardware category hits on the interesting boxes, such as hubs, switches, or repeaters, among which all the wires in the network run. Finally, this section explains hardware terms like *Ethernet, 10BaseT,* and *topology.*

Protocols   I should call this section "Network Protocols," but I don't want you confusing it with the next section. *Protocols* are the languages of networks. These languages have interesting names, such as NetBEUI, IPX/SPX, and the ever-popular TCP/IP. A protocol is a highly standardized language that handles most of the invisible functions on a network, like determining which computer is SERVER1, or disassembling/reassembling data passed over the network. In early computer networks, there was only one protocol. Today, it's common for the same network to run more than one protocol, primarily to enable that network to connect to other networks. This section covers the most common protocols used today and shows how they are installed, configured, and repaired.

Network   Once the hardware is installed and the protocol determined, the next step is to decide which systems will share resources. Then we need to come up with some way to name the systems, so they can "see" each other. This section clarifies the concepts of client/server, peer-to-peer, and domain-based. This section also describes in detail how networks make resources available and how they control access to those resources.

Shared Resources   Once all the systems have names, we need to identify the resources they'll share, like files, folders, and printers. If a drive, directory, or file is to be shared, there must be a way to identify it as available for sharing. The rules for naming shared resources are called *naming conventions.* A great example would be a system that offers its D:\FRED directory for sharing. This D:\FRED directory needs a network name, such as SERVE_FRED. This network name is displayed to all of the devices on the network. The process of creating shared resource names is covered in this section.

A network also needs to control access to resources. A laser printer, for example, might be available for sharing, but might best be used solely by the accounting department, excluding other departments. Individual systems need to be able to access the shared resources. There needs to be a process where a PC can look out on the network and see what's available. Having found those available resources, the PC then needs to make them look and act as though they were local resources. For example, say another computer has offered a shared resource called SERVE_FRED. The local machine might want to create a phony drive called H:, which is actually the SERVE_FRED resource. The process of taking network resources and making them perform like local resources is popularly called *redirecting*.

This chapter covers hardware, which makes sense for the hardware section of the book! We jump into the latter subjects in Chapter 21 with the more OS-oriented networking issues. So, let's get started with the most fun of all four topics—the hardware.

Objective 15.02   Networking Hardware for the PC

Every network needs hardware to move the bits of data between computers. For the overwhelming majority of networks, this means that all the PCs are linked together through some type of cabling. The cable connects to an individual PC into a network adapter. Invariably, all the cables from all the PCs come together in some mysterious box called a *hub*. This objective looks at issues specific to installing Network Interface Cards (NICs) for cabled networks and infrared technology for cable-free networking.

Installing NICs

Installing a NIC into any version of Windows is usually a no-brainer, because most NICs today are completely plug and play. For the most part, this is simply a matter of turning off the PC, installing the card, and turning the system on again. The only trick is to remember that you should use the disk that comes with the NIC, even if Windows offers to use its own drivers. All the issues discussed with respect to installing devices also hold true for NICs—just because they are network adapter cards doesn't mean anything else special needs to happen. If the NIC shows up in the Device Manager, you're done with this step. If it doesn't, well, go back to any of the previous chapters and review what it takes to install a device! Figure 15-1 shows a typical network adapter, nicely installed in Windows 2000 Device Manager.

A few legacy NICs survive out there, so you still might need to install a NIC manually. As with all cards in the PC, NICs use an I/O address and IRQ. Some even use memory locations or DMA channels. It is important to remember that with legacy NICs, the card first needs to be configured using its setup program, which usually means first booting to Safe Mode Command Prompt Only (in

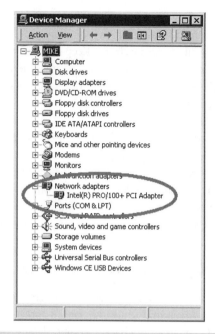

FIGURE 15-1   Windows 2000 showing a NIC installed

Windows 9x) to run the configuration program that came with the NIC. After setting up the NIC's I/O address, IRQ, and so on, you restart Windows, install the NIC's driver, and manually set the system resources for the NIC in the Device Manager. Although some cards still use jumpers, most NICs use a software-based resource setting manifested by a setup/install program on an accompanying floppy disk.

Travel Advisory

If the Hardware Compatibility List (HCL) does not contain the NIC, don't even bother to try to install the legacy card under Windows 2000.

After you've installed the card, you can then install the drivers manually. Click the Add New Hardware icon in the Control Panel. Although Windows often finds a legacy card automatically, it's usually faster to do the install manually. Select Network Adapters, and then click the Have Disk button to tell Windows where to locate the driver.

If the NIC didn't come with a diskette, check to see if Windows has a driver. If Windows doesn't have the driver, contact the company from which you purchased the card or try the manufacturer's web site. Keep in mind that many of the no-name Ethernet cards use a driver called NE2000-compatible. Most of the time, the card then installs itself with a series of preset resources. Always verify that these settings don't wind up causing a resource conflict because it's not unusual for these settings to be wrong!

Restart Windows one more time and re-open the Device Manager. Verify that the network card is operating properly.

At this point, you're ready to plug a piece of network cable into the PC and connect to the network, right? But how does the PC communicate with another PC? You need software for that, specifically software protocols. Chapter 21 covers protocols in detail, but let's glance at them now so you can see the hardware connection.

Software Protocols and Packets

Protocols handle the details of data transfer, such as making sure the sending PC packages the data properly in uniformly understood *packets*, and that the receiving PC knows how to put the data back together. Each protocol uses its own unique "language" for a packet, so packets created with one protocol cannot be read by a machine that does not have that protocol installed.

Windows 95 automatically installs both the IPX/SPX and NetBEUI protocols whenever a network adapter is installed. Windows 98 and Windows 2000 automatically install TCP/IP. So which protocol should you use? If the PC is part of a network, the network people usually tell you which protocol or protocols to install. Virtually the entire world uses only TCP/IP, but Windows comes with lots of other protocols. On the rare occasion where you need to install another protocol, go to the Network window in the Control Panel, select Add Protocol, and choose the protocol you want to install, as shown in Figure 15-2.

If you're using anything *but* the TCP/IP protocol, that's all you need to do. If you're using TCP/IP—and everybody is using TCP/IP these days—you need to do a lot of configuration! I've given TCP/IP its own section at the end of Chapter 21 in Part II of this book, just to talk about all the fun configuration work you need to do!

Hardware and Packets

Packets contain many components, from the data to unique identifying numbers for the sending NIC. Here's the hardware connection.

Every NIC in the world has a built-in identifier called a Media Access Control (MAC) address. The *MAC address* is a binary address that is unique for every network card. Yup, that's right! Every network card in the world has a unique MAC address.

Select Network Protocol ☒

Click the Network Protocol that you want to install, then click OK. If you have an installation disk for this device, click Have Disk.

Manufacturers:
- Banyan
- Digital Equipment (DEC)
- IBM
- Microsoft
- Novell
- SunSoft

Network Protocols:
- IPX/SPX-compatible Protocol
- Microsoft DLC
- NetBEUI
- TCP/IP

Have Disk...

OK Cancel

FIGURE 15-2 Adding a network protocol

The MAC address is 48-bits long, giving over 281 *trillion* MAC addresses, so there are plenty of MAC addresses to go around. Note that on the vast majority of NICs, the MAC is hard-coded on to the card and can't be reset. Some (very few) NICs permit you to configure this value in the card properties.

Local Lingo

Packet A container for data that includes the MAC address of the sending NIC.
Frame A commonly used synonym for *packet*.

All the many varieties of packets share certain common features. First, packets contain the MAC address of the network card to which the data is being sent. Second, they have the MAC address of the network card that sent the data. Third, is the data itself (at this point, we have no idea what the data is—software handles that question), which can vary in size depending on the type of packet. Finally, there is some type of data check to enable the receiving network card to verify if the data was received in good order (Figure 15-3).

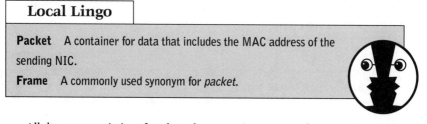

Recipient MAC	Sender MAC	Data	CRC

FIGURE 15-3 Generic packet

At this point, you have the basic PC hardware installed for a cabled network, but various wireless network hardware and protocols compete for market share. The one that shows up consistently on the A+ exams, and thus concerns us now, is *infrared*. Let's take a look.

Infrared

Wireless networking through the Infrared Data Association *(IrDA)* protocol is largely overlooked these days, probably because of the explosion of interest in the newer and faster 802.11b wireless Ethernet standard. This is a shame, because IrDA provides an easy and reasonably fast way to transfer data.

IrDA works through a piece of hardware called an *Infrared Transceiver,* which is basically a kind of modem that uses light instead of sound. IrDA uses a focused beam of Infrared light to send bits of data to another device.

All sorts of devices use infrared, from laptop computers to the popular PDAs, handheld computers, and tablet computers you find at your local Fry's. And, let's not forget all the cool gadgets that gave rise to the popular term *convergence*: digital cameras, cell phones, even pagers and watches are capable of talking to a computer through Infrared.

The IrDA protocol stack is a widely supported industry standard and has been included in Macintosh computers, all versions of Windows since Windows 95, and now Linux. IrDA uses a one-to-one connection between devices. IrDA has a mode that emulates full-duplex communication, but it's really half-duplex. A device communicating over an infrared connection, therefore, can only send or receive—but not both—at one time.

Exam Tip	
IrDA communicates in half-duplex.	

The latest versions of Windows solidly support IrDA devices—in fact, there's not much for techs to configure. Devices make IrDA links dynamically, without user interaction. When two IrDA-enabled devices "see" each other, the sending (primary) device negotiates a connection to the receiving (secondary) device, and voilà! It's just point and shoot!

Now, as far as networking goes with IrDA, your choices are somewhat limited. IrDA is designed primarily to connect only two systems together. Typically, this will be two laptops because they already have the hardware built-in, but you can find adapters to make a desktop infrared-capable. Most motherboards have an input for an infrared transceiver. The "eye" is usually mounted into an external drive bay. You can also get infrared to USB adapters that plug into an available USB port.

Any of those options is okay if you only need to hook up the two systems, but to connect to a LAN through IrDA, you need a different device: an Infrared Access Point. This gadget combines an Infrared transceiver with an Ethernet NIC. Through one of these guys, you just point your laptop at the eye of the access point, wait a couple of seconds while they negotiate a link, and you're ready to log on.

Now that I've sung IrDA's praises, let's talk about the limitations. For one, IrDA's speed isn't that impressive. Most IrDA devices transfer data from 2400 Kb/s to about 115 Kb/s, depending on the devices. The latest version of IrDA, version 2.0, supports transfer speeds of up to 4 Mb/s. Not too shabby, but hardly stellar.

Further, IrDA devices have a limited range. The maximum distance between devices is about 1 meter. Worse, IrDA links are limited to a direct line-of-sight and can be broken by things like a badly placed can of Mountain Dew or even by bright sunlight hitting the Infrared transceiver eye.

Clearly, IrDA is not the best solution for a dedicated network connection, but for a quick file transfer without getting your hands dirty, it'll do in a pinch.

Now that you've looked at hardware options for the PC, it's time to cable the network together. So, let's move into the stuff that goes on behind closed wiring closet doors—network topologies.

Objective 15.03   Network Topologies

Even though most networks share the same basic look and feel, the way the data moves around inside those wires may be quite different from one network to the next. The *topology* of a network describes these different configurations of the cabling between computers.

Since the first networks were invented over 30 years ago, many types of topologies have been invented, but most have disappeared. Networks today use only two competing topologies: bus topology and ring topology. Each of these topologies has advantages and disadvantages. The best topology for a specific situation depends on a variety of factors, including cost, speed, ease of installation, the physical position of the PCs, and the number of PCs in the network.

Bus Topology

The first type of topology was bus topology. *Bus topology* means all the PCs are connected via *a single cable that runs to all the PCs*. Bus topologies look something like Figure 15-4.

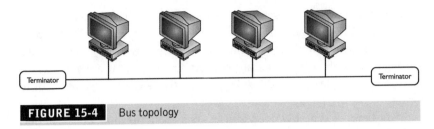

FIGURE 15-4   Bus topology

Bus topology works like a big telephone party line: all devices must first listen to see if anyone else is sending packets before they can send a packet. If the cable is not being used, the device sends its packet on the line. Every network card on the bus sees and reads the packet. This is called Carrier Sense Multiple Access/Collision Detection (CSMA/CD).

Sometimes two cards do talk at the same time. This is called a *collision* and the cards themselves arbitrate to see who gets to resend their frames first.

Reflection and Termination

Any time a device sends voltage along a wire, some voltage bounces back or reflects when it reaches the end of the wire. This *reflection* poses a big problem for a bus topology network. As soon as one PC sends a packet, that packet will bounce off the end and back up the wire, making the cards that want to send data wait for no reason. Worse, the uselessly reflecting packets create a *packet storm*, where no other card can send data. To prevent a packet storm, every bus network needs a device called a *terminator* plugged into both ends of the bus cable. A terminator is nothing more than a resistor that absorbs the signal, thus preventing reflection.

This need for termination is a weak spot in bus topology. If the cable breaks anywhere, a packet storm is instantly created and no device can send data, even if the break isn't between the devices exchanging data.

Ring Topology

Ring topology is more recent than bus topology (although that does not make it more popular). A *ring topology* connects all the PCs together on a single cable, much like bus topology. As the name implies, however, this bus functions like a ring.

Ring topologies use a transmission method called token passing. In *token passing*, a mini-packet called a *token* constantly passes from one card to the next in one direction, as shown in Figure 15-5. If one PC wants to talk to another, it must wait until it gets the token. The PC's NIC then attaches data to the token and sends the packet back out the ring. If another PC wants to send data, it must wait until a free token (one that doesn't have an attached packet) comes around.

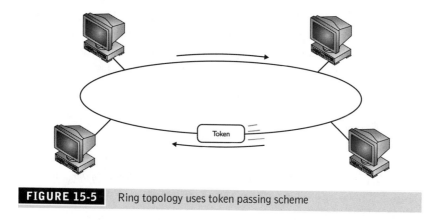

FIGURE 15-5   Ring topology uses token passing scheme

Because ring topologies use token passing, we tend to use the term "token ring" when describing ring networks. There were a few exceptions where a ring topology used features other than token passing, but they were few and are long gone. All current ring networks use an IBM-trademarked version of token passing called, rather appropriately, *Token Ring*. So, if it is a ring topology, it's Token Ring.

Star Ring

Token Ring topology was, if not invented, perfected and packaged by IBM. Token Ring actually uses a topology called *star ring*. Instead of running a ring of cable all around the LAN, the ring is stored inside a special box called a Multistation Access Unit (MSAU). We often just call it a MAU or hub, although all in-the-know Token Ring techs would have a heart attack if you said it within earshot of them! Although Token Ring is a ring, it looks more like a star, as you can see in Figure 15-6.

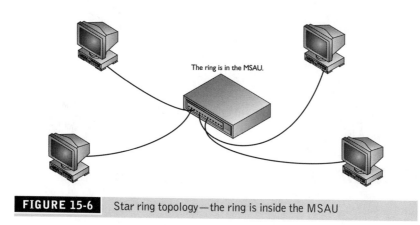

FIGURE 15-6   Star ring topology—the ring is inside the MSAU

Token Ring is slowly losing market share to bus-type topologies because of its cost and because it was proprietary IBM technology. Token Ring is still, however, heavily used in hundreds of thousands of networks. Because Token Ring normally uses a more robust type of cabling, it's also still popular in areas with a lot of electrical interference.

Star Bus

The star configuration used in Token Ring made it dependable and easy to expand. This led to a variation of the bus topology called *star bus topology.* Imagine if you were to take a bus network and shrink the bus down so it would fit inside a hub, as in Figure 15-7.

The bus topology would sure look a lot like a star, wouldn't it? This type of star bus topology is the single most popular topology today. Cheap and centralized, a star bus network does not go down if a cable breaks. True, the network would go down if the hub itself failed, but that is rare. Even if a hub fails, replacing a hub in a closet is much easier than tracing a bus running through walls and ceilings trying to find a break!

Objective 15.04   **Hardware Protocols**

When Digital Equipment, Intel, and Xerox invented the first network in the mid-1970s, they wrote a series of standards that defined everything necessary

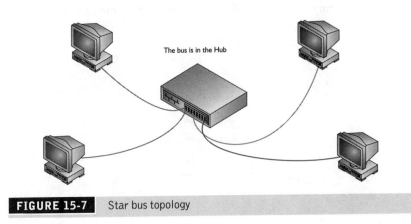

The bus is in the Hub

FIGURE 15-7   Star bus topology

to get data from one computer to another, including cabling types, connectors, and more. This series of standards, called *Ethernet*, is the dominant standard for today's networks. IBM entered the field a bit later with a competing network standard called Token Ring. This objective looks at Ethernet cabling and devices and then finishes with a brief overview of Token Ring technology.

Ethernet

The Ethernet standard—now controlled by the 802 committee of the IEEE standards body—has appeared in several physical forms, such as 10Base5, 10BaseT, and 100BaseFX. Each form or technology defines different hardware for the data transfers, but it's all Ethernet, so for the most part you can mix and match with the right hardware without losing the ability to communicate.

Thick Ethernet—10Base5

The original Xerox Ethernet specification defined a specific type of cabling for the first Ethernet networks. This type of cable is called thick Ethernet. *Thick Ethernet,* also known as *ThickNet,* is a thick (about half an inch in diameter) coaxial cable manufactured under the Belden 9580 standard. (Belden is a *big* cable manufacturer and their internal part number (9580) for thick Ethernet is a popular way to define ThickNet.)

Local Lingo

Coaxial cable or coax   Coax consists of a center cable (core) surrounded by insulation. This, in turn, is covered with a shield of braided cable. The inner core actually carries the signal and the shield effectively eliminates outside interference. The entire cable is then surrounded by a protective insulating cover.

ThickNet or 10Base5 networks use a true bus topology, which means that all PCs attach to a single cable called the *segment*. ThickNet supports up to 100 devices hooked to one segment. The maximum length of one segment is 500 meters. 10Base5 networks run at 10 Mb/s.

ThickNet is clearly marked every 2.5 meters. These marks show where to connect devices to the cable. All devices on a ThickNet must be connected at these marks. This assures that all devices are some multiple of 2.5 meters apart. This spacing is required to reduce noise because of oscillations in the signal.

Devices connect to ThickNet by means of a vampire connector. The *vampire connector* literally pierces the cable, creating the connection. The vampire connector is also a *transceiver,* a device that both receives and sends data. The transceiver is the device that allows connections between devices and the common cable. Transceivers also detect when collisions take place. Actually, all networks use transceivers, but ThickNet uses an external transceiver. The cable from the vampire connector/transceiver to the device must be no more than 50 meters.

Thick Ethernet uses a bus topology, as mentioned above, so it needs terminators. As you might guess, the 50-Ohm ThickNet terminator must be placed on each end of the segment. ThickNet connects to a PC's network card via a 15-pin male connector. This connector is called the AUI or sometimes the DIX (Digital, Intel, Xerox) connector.

Thick Ethernet is on the way out. Bus topology is always risky because one break on the cable causes the entire network to fail. In addition, ThickNet is expensive and hard to work with. The cable, transceivers, and terminators cost far more than those in any other network. Nevertheless, there is a massive installed base, and it is still actively used, especially where longer distances or heavy shielding are needed.

Thin Ethernet—10Base2

Thin Ethernet, also known as *ThinNet* or *Cheapernet,* was invented as an inexpensive alternative to ThickNet. ThinNet cable is much easier to handle than ThickNet cable and is used in many small networks.

ThinNet uses a specific type of coax called RG-58. RG stands for Radio Grade, which is an industry standard for measuring coax cables. This type of coax looks similar to the coax used with cable television, but it's quite different. Your television cable uses RG-6, a slightly thicker cable.

The RG rating should be clearly marked on the cable. If it isn't, it will say something like ThinNet or 802.3 to let you know you have the right cable.

While thin Ethernet also runs at 10 Mb/s on a true bus topology, it has several big limitations that thick Ethernet doesn't share. Thin Ethernet supports only 30 devices per segment and each segment can be no more than 185 meters long.

On the plus side, cabling with ThinNet is a snap compared with ThickNet. The cable is much thinner and more flexible than ThickNet. In addition, the

> **Exam Tip**
>
> Know the ThinNet (10Base2) numbers—10 Mb/s speed, 30 devices per segment, and 185-meter segment maximum length.

transceiver is built into the ThinNet network card, so ThinNet does not require an external transceiver. Each ThinNet network card is simply connected to the bus cable with a T connector.

The ThinNet cable has twist-on connectors, called *BNC connectors,* that attach to the T connector, forming the network, as shown in Figure 15-8. Termination is handled by twisting small, specialized terminators onto the unused end of the T connector on the machines at the ends of the chain.

When installing ThinNet, it's important that one of the terminators be grounded. Special terminators can be grounded to the case of the PC, but be sure the PC is also grounded! You *must* use a T connector!

To add another PC to the network, simply remove the terminator from the last PC, add another piece of cable with another T connector, and add the terminator on the new end. Adding a PC between two systems is also easy: unhook one side of a T connector, and add another PC and cable in between.

ThinNet still enjoys popularity for small office home office (SOHO) networks. Its relatively short maximum segment lengths and small number of devices per segment, however, make ThinNet totally unacceptable for larger networks.

10BaseT

Probably the most popular of all networks today is Ethernet 10BaseT. This standard defines Ethernet running on unshielded twisted pair (UTP), at 10 Mb/s, in a

FIGURE 15-8   BNC connector

star bus topology. The segment length (the distance from the PC to a hub) is limited to 100 meters.

UTP cables come in categories that define the maximum speed at which data can be transferred (also called *bandwidth*).

Local Lingo

CAT 1-5 levels   Experienced networking techs refer to the different types of cabling as "*CAT X,*" as opposed to "*Category X.*" For instance, "Hey, Billy-Bob! Toss me that coil o' CAT 5, will ya?"

CAT Levels

UTP cable comes in five major categories (CATs) of two-pair cables. You can find the CAT level clearly marked on a cable. Table 15-1 shows the speeds.

TABLE 15-1 Standard CAT Types	
CAT 1	Standard phone line
CAT 2	Data speeds up to 4 Mb/s
CAT 3	Data speeds up to 16 Mb/s
CAT 4	Data speeds up to 20 Mb/s
CAT 5	Data speeds up to 100 Mb/s

These categories are established by the Telecommunication Industry Association/Electronics Industry Association (TIA/EIA) and are under the EIA-568 specification. Currently, just about everybody uses CAT5 cable (or the slightly superior CAT5e). Although most networks run at 10 Mb/s, the industry standard is currently shifting to fast networks designed to run at 100 Mb/s. Of the two-pair cables, only CAT5 handles these speeds, so about everyone is installing CAT5 even if they are running at speeds where CAT3 or CAT4 would do. Consequently, it's becoming harder to get anything but CAT5 cable.

A number of wire makers are pushing UTP with even higher ratings. A good example is Belden Wire and Cable's DataTwist 350 cable, designated to run as fast as 350 Mb/s. These new cables tend to get names like "CAT6," "CAT-6a," and "CAT-7" but, as of now, there are no official CAT levels above CAT5.

The 10BaseT cabling standard requires two pairs of wires: a pair for sending and a pair for receiving. 10BaseT runs on CAT3, CAT4, or CAT5 cable. These cables use a special connector called RJ-45. The RJ designation was invented by Ma Bell years ago and is still used today. Currently, you see only two types of RJ connectors: RJ-11 and RJ-45, as shown in Figure 15-9.

RJ-11 is the connector that hooks your telephone to the telephone jack. It supports up to two pairs of wires, though most phone lines only use one pair. The other pair is used to support a second phone line. RJ-11 connectors aren't used in any common network installation, although a few weird (and out of business) "network in a box"-type companies used them. *RJ-45* is the standard for UTP connectors. RJ-45 has connections for up to four pairs and is visibly much wider than RJ-11. The #1 pin on an RJ-45 jack is the first one on the *left* when pointing the jack away from you with the clip facing *down*.

Exam Tip

Know the 10BaseT numbers and names—10 Mb/s data transfers, 100-meter segment length, RJ-45 connectors, and UTP cabling.

The Electronics Industries Association/Telecommunications Industry Association (EIA/TIA) has two standards: the EIA/TIA 568A and the EIA/TIA 568B. Both are acceptable. You don't have to follow any standard as long as you use the same pairings on each end of the cable, but you will make your life simpler if you choose a standard. Make sure all your cabling uses the same standard and you will save a great deal of work in the end. Most important: *keep records!*

Like all wires, the wires in UTP are numbered, although no number is on each wire. Instead, each wire has a standardized color. Table 15-2 shows the official EIA/TIA Standard Color.

FIGURE 15-9   RJ-11 (left) and RJ-45 (right)

TABLE 15-2	UTP Cabling Color Chart	
Pin#	**568A**	**568B**
1	White/Green	White/Orange
2	Green	Orange
3	White/Orange	White/Green
4	Blue	Blue
5	White/Blue	White/Blue
6	Orange	Green
7	White/Brown	White/Brown
8	Brown	Brown

Fast Ethernet

A 10 Mb/s network works fine for sharing data and for light networking duties, but once you implement *serious* applications over a LAN, a mere 10 megabit bandwidth just won't cut it. I mean, imagine the level of frustration a good tech feels as he's about to throw down on his buddy in a serious game of Half-Life or Quake III but the network suddenly slows to a crawl because somebody in the office—at that very moment—decided to start downloading a zillion MP3 music files! It just won't do!

Thankfully, you can implement faster Ethernet standards that run at 100 Mb/s or even faster. Several standards currently compete for market share and the Fast Ethernet crown, such as 100BaseT4 and 100BaseTX, with the latter well on its way to victory. 100BaseT4 requires four-pair CAT3 or better UTP, while 100BaseTX requires only two-pair CAT5. In either case, these high-speed Ethernets need their own 100BaseT4 or 100BaseTX network cards and hubs. They are incompatible with each other.

Fiber-Optic Ethernet

Fiber-optic cable is an attractive way to transmit network packets. First, because it uses light instead of electricity, fiber-optic cable is immune to electrical problems

like lightning, short circuits, and static. Second, fiber-optic signals travel much farther, usually 2,000 meters (compared with 100 meters for 10BaseT or 100BaseT).
There are two standards for using fiber-optic cable with Ethernet. In either case,
the cabling is the same and it's called 62.5/125 multimode fiber-optic. All fiber
Ethernets need two of these cables, as shown in Figure 15-10.

The two fiber-optic standards are called 10BaseFL and 100BaseFX. As you can
guess by the names, the only real difference is the speed of the network (some
important differences occur in the way hubs are interconnected, and so on).
Unfortunately, fiber-optic cabling is delicate, expensive, and difficult to use, so it's
usually relegated to backbone-type situations. A *backbone* would be the main piece
of Ethernet to which all other hubs are connected.

Combining and Extending Ethernet

Because the many technologies involved in Ethernet follow the 802.3 standards,
you can get hardware to combine different networks, thus increasing compatibility and range. Many 10BaseT hubs, for example, have a ThinNet BNC connector
so you can hook a small 10Base2 network into a star bus network. That saves you
from having to add new NICs and run new cabling for the older network.

Combo Cards   Because 10BaseT uses the same language (Ethernet) as
10Base2 or 10Base5, you can find Ethernet combo network cards that support two
or even three different type of connections. Further, most current 100BaseTX
NICs are actually 10/100 NICs, able to handle either 10 Mb/s or 100 Mb/s speeds
depending on the rest of the network hardware.

FIGURE 15-10   Typical fiber-optic cables with connectors

Repeaters Ethernet networks have limited lengths, as noted earlier, but various devices enable you to break that limitation. A *repeater* is an electronic device that amplifies the signal on a line. Repeaters can extend the useful length of a cable segment beyond its specified maximum. Networks use two different types of repeaters.

The first type is a dedicated box that takes input from one segment, amplifies it, and then passes it to another segment. Figure 15-11 shows a photo of a common repeater for 10Base2. Using a repeater, you can link together two 10Base2 segments. This would enable you to get past the 185-meter maximum length.

The 10BaseT hub is also a repeater, and can enable a maximum separation of 200 meters between PCs on a 10BaseT network.

Hubs In a 10BaseT network, each PC connects to a 10BaseT hub. These hubs have multiple connections called *ports,* one per connected device. To add a device to the network, simply plug another cable into the hub, as in Figure 15-12.

Remember, 10BaseT uses the star bus topology. The hub holds the actual bus and allows access to the bus through the ports. Using a star bus topology creates a robust network: the failure of a single node will not bring down the entire network

The maximum distance from the hub to any device is 100 meters. No more than one PC can be hooked to each segment and the maximum number of PCs that can be hooked to any one hub is 1,024. You'll be hard pressed, though, to find a hub with that many connectors. Most hubs come with 4, 8, 16, 32, or 64 ports. 10BaseT hubs act as repeaters, amplifying the signals between devices hooked into

| **FIGURE 15-11** | Ethernet repeater |

| **FIGURE 15-12** | Typical rack-mounted hub |

the network. They need power to provide this amplification, so make sure the hubs are plugged in to a good power source.

Although just about every 10BaseT network worth its salt uses a hub of sorts to connect the PCs, in a desperate pinch you can hook two 10BaseT network cards together without a hub. Just connect the two PCs together with a *crossover cable!* Crossover cables work great as a quick way to network two PCs. You can make a crossover cable by making one end TIA586A and the other TIA568B.

Travel Advisory

To expand a network, technically called *scaling,* you simply add more hubs. Hubs are connected together by a normal patch cable through an integrated port called an *uplink port,* which performs the same action as a crossover cable.

Token Ring

Token Ring is a confusing term. The problem is Token Ring refers to two related, but different, things. First, *Token Ring* is a topology. Second, Token Ring is a set of network standards developed by IBM that define a complete network system. Token Ring is completely incompatible with Ethernet and is considered a competitor to Ethernet. Token Ring runs at either 4 Mb/s or 16 Mb/s, depending on the type of Token Ring network cards you buy. Token Ring was originally based around the IBM Type 1 cable. *Type 1 cable* is a two-pair, shielded twisted pair (STP) cable designed to handle speeds up to 20 Mb/s. Today, Token Ring can use either STP or UTP.

STP Types

STP cables also have certain categories. These are called *types* and are defined by IBM. The most common types are

Type 1	Standard STP with two pairs—the most common STP cable
Type 2	Standard STP plus two pairs of voice wires
Type 3	Standard STP with four pairs
Type 6	Patch cable—used for connecting hubs
Type 8	Flat STP for under carpets
Type 9	STP with two pairs—Plenum grade

Local Lingo

Plenum grade cabling   A type of cabling with special cladding that doesn't give off toxic fumes when burned. Plenum grade cabling is usually required by law when stringing cable through ceilings or behind walls.

Token Ring Connectors

The Type 1 Token Ring connectors are not RJ-45. Instead, IBM designed a unique *hermaphroditic* connector, which is neither male nor female: they are designed to plug into each other, as seen in Figure 15-13.

Token Ring network cards use a nine-pin female connector. A standard Token Ring cable has a hermaphroditic connector on one end and a nine-pin connector on the other.

Token Ring can also be used with CAT 3, 4, or 5 UTP. When combined with UTP, Token Ring uses an RJ-45 connector so, from a cabling standpoint, Token Ring UTP and Ethernet UTP look the same. Many Token Ring network cards are combo cards. This means they come with both a nine-pin connection for STP and an RJ-45 connection for UTP.

As discussed earlier, Token Ring uses a star-ring topology, so it also uses a hub. A Token Ring hub is *not* interchangeable with an Ethernet hub. IBM has a special name for its hubs. They are called either MAUs or MSAUs. Unfortunately, they are also sometimes just called hubs (usually by Ethernet people who don't know any better).

- Token Ring can support up to 260 PCs using STP and up to 72 PCs using UTP.

FIGURE 15-13   Hermaphroditic connector

- Using UTP, the maximum distance from any MAU to a PC is 45 meters.
- Using STP, the maximum distance from any MAU to a PC is 100 meters.

Token Ring also uses repeaters. Token Ring repeaters can only be used between MAUs. With a repeater, the functional distance between two MAUs increases to 360 meters (with UTP) and 720 meters (with STP).

CHECKPOINT

✔ **Objective 15.01: Networking Basics**   For PCs to communicate on a network, they must speak the same language, called a protocol.

✔ **Objective 15.02: Networking Hardware for the PC**   Network Interface Cards (NICs) send data on to the network cabling as discrete chunks called data packets, also called frames. Every NIC has a unique 48-bit MAC address.

✔ **Objective 15.03: Network Topologies**   Bus topology refers to a network in which all computers are physically connected by a single length of cable. Each end of the cable must be terminated. Ring topology also refers to a network in which a single length of cable connects all computers, except the ends are joined, thus making, appropriately, a ring.

✔ **Objective 15.04: Hardware Protocols**   ThickNet (10Base5) supports up to 100 devices hooked to a segment of no more than 500 meters. ThinNet (10Base2) uses RG-58 coaxial cables and supports 30 devices hooked to a segment of no more than 185 meters. Ethernet (10BaseT) uses UTP cabling (usually CAT 5) with RJ-45 connectors. Ethernet hubs and repeaters enable a maximum separation between PCs of 200 meters in 10BaseT networks. Token Ring refers to both the standard star ring topology and the network standards. Token Ring networks use STP or UTP cabling, and moves data at 4 or 16 Mb/s.

REVIEW QUESTIONS

1. To provide a computer a physical and electronic connection to a network, what must be installed?

   A. A hub
   B. A router

C. A NIC

D. A bridge

2. What is the maximum distance for a 10Base2 segment?

   A. 1,000 meters

   B. 330 meters

   C. 185 meters

   D. 100 meters

3. Which of the following is needed to configure a plug and play NIC in a Windows 2000 system?

   A. CMOS

   B. Device Driver

   C. Configuration software

   D. DMA

4. José wants to extend his 10Base2 network beyond its maximum segment distance. Which of the following does he need?

   A. Converter

   B. Expander

   C. Repeater

   D. Extender

5. Everything worked fine on your 10BaseT network yesterday but, today, no one can connect to the server. The server seems to be in good running order. Which of the following is the most likely problem?

   A. Malfunctioning hub

   B. Someone changed all the passwords for server access

   C. Someone's T connector has come loose on the bus

   D. The server's cable is wired as EIA/TIA 568A and all the other are wired as EIA/TIA 568B

6. What is the minimum specification of cable types for 100BaseTX networks?

   A. Category 2

   B. Category 3

   C. Category 4

   D. Category 5

7. How far apart can two PCs that share the same 10BaseT hub be placed?

   A. 1,000 meters
   B. 330 meters
   C. 200 meters
   D. 100 meters

8. Which component(s) prevent reflection on a bus topology network?

   A. Terminator
   B. Crossover cable
   C. Uplink port
   D. Multiple Station Access Unit

9. What equipment type limits network equipment, so it cannot send and receive at the same time?

   A. Half-duplex
   B. Single-duplex
   C. Muted
   D. IEEE

10. What must be used to set IRQs on legacy ISA network interface cards with no jumpers?

   A. COMS
   B. Device Manager
   C. Configuration software
   D. DIP switches

REVIEW ANSWERS

1. **C** A system must have a network interface card (NIC) to participate in any type of network.

2. **C** 10Base2 has a maximum distance of 185 meters.

3. **B** PnP only requires the proper driver.

4. **C** José needs a repeater.

5. **A** Although someone might have changed all the passwords or the cables during the night, a bad hub is the most probable answer.

6. **B** 100BaseTX requires CAT5 rated cabling.

7. **C** As each system can be 100 meters from the hub, any two systems can be up to 200 meters apart.

8. **A** A terminator is a resistor that absorbs voltage from the bus topology cable to prevent reflection.

9. **A** Half-duplex components can either send or receive data, but not both at the same time.

10. **C** Although some cards still use jumpers, most NICs use software-based resource settings.

Operating System Technologies

Introduction to OS Technologies

ETA	NEWBIE	SOME EXPERIENCE	EXPERT
	4 hours	2 hours	1 hour

When Bill Gates struck his deal with IBM, Windows wasn't even a gleam in his eye—it was DOS that began the Microsoft Empire, and the concepts and functions associated with DOS live on to this day. Every DOS command you see in this chapter also works in *every* version of Windows, and usually offers a quicker way to accomplish a task than its graphical alternative. Further, the A+ Operating System Technologies exam tests you on all these commands. I'd rather explain these commands in a separate DOS section than wait for a related Windows chapter and have you scratching your head and wondering, "Why in the world is this command important?"

Exam Tip

A+ tests on every DOS command in this chapter. I describe differences between versions of these commands where appropriate. Know the commands. Know them well.

You'll find this section is a lot easier to understand if you have a PC at hand. That way, you can follow along with the explanations and try exploring around your machine. Although this works best with true DOS, a computer running Windows is also acceptable.

If your system runs Windows, use the MS-DOS Prompt if available (check under Start | Programs). Or, select Start | Run, and then type **COMMAND** (**CMD** in Windows 2000) and click OK. This opens the Windows equivalent of DOS, called a *command line window* or *DOS virtual machine*. Be aware that the command line in Windows differs slightly from true DOS. Even though all the DOS commands discussed in this chapter work in Windows, many of the screens will look a little different. To make the experience even more realistic, you can press ALT-ENTER to make the DOS window full-screen. Press ALT-ENTER again to bring it back into a smaller window.

Local Lingo

Command prompt　　The general term for the command line interface in DOS and all versions of Windows. Many techs refer to the command line interface as the DOS prompt, C-prompt, or A-prompt (if booting to a floppy disk drive).

You can execute most command line commands in several ways. Showing you all those ways, however, would not only take a huge amount of time, it would also be counterproductive to the goals of this book. Therefore, I only describe one method for each command. This method might not be the fastest or easiest, but it's the one that most clearly explains the command and the command's effect on the system.

Travel Assistance

Check out these sites for in-depth information on DOS commands:

http://www.easydos.com/dosindex.html

http://www.computerhope.com/msdos.htm

Objective 16.01   **Operating System Basics**

Because vestiges of DOS and Windows 3.*x* still abound in personal computers, every A+ certified tech needs to know about the core DOS operating system and configuration files. Further, working from a command line requires you to know several basic conventions, such as filenames, directory structures, and command syntax. Let's go there now.

DOS Concepts

Microsoft designed DOS to run on an 8086 processor and never truly upgraded DOS to take advantage of the more advanced Intel processors' protected mode. DOS remains as it started, a *single-tasking* operating system. Sure, DOS runs fine on a Pentium 4, but DOS can't take advantage of any protected-mode functions on that advanced CPU. When you run DOS on a modern CPU, all you have is an extremely fast 8086! Second, DOS is text-based. Everything on the screen uses text, although individual applications may use graphical screens. All text is uppercase. If you type a lowercase letter, it's automatically changed to uppercase. Third, DOS doesn't support mice, although it supports applications that use them.

Two subjects warrant a bit more discussion, namely the ways DOS uses files and directories. Techs who grew up in a Windows world might find DOS files, filenames, and directory structures a bit less than intuitive.

Travel Advisory

DOS is completely case-insensitive.

Files

DOS manifests each program and piece of data as an individual *file*. Each file has a name, which is stored with the file on the drive. Names break down into two parts: the filename and the extension. The *filename* can be no longer than eight characters. The *extension*, which is optional, can be up to three characters long. No spaces or other illegal characters (/ \ [ ] | < > + = ; , * ?) can be used in the filename or extension. The filename and extension are separated by a period, or *dot*. This naming system is known as the 8.3 (eight dot three) system. Here are some examples of acceptable DOS filenames:

- FRED.EXE
- SYSTEM.INI

Here are some unacceptable DOS filenames:

- FRED.EXEC
- WAYTOOLONG.F

The extension tells the computer the type or function of the file. Program files take the extensions EXE (for executable) or COM (for command). Anything that is not a program is some form of data to support a program. Different programs use different types of data files. The extension indicates which program uses that particular data file. For example, Microsoft Word for DOS (yes, there was a Microsoft Word for DOS!) uses files with the extension DOC. Changing the extension of a data file does not affect its contents, but without the proper extension, DOS (or even Windows) won't know which program uses it.

DOS makes heavy use of text files for system configuration and optimization. A technician who uses DOS must be comfortable accessing and editing text files with a special program called a *text editor*. DOS comes with a text editor called EDIT, which enables technicians to manipulate text files.

Drives and Directories

At bootup, DOS assigns a drive letter to each hard drive partition and to each floppy or other disk drive. The first floppy drive is called A:, and the second, if installed, is called B:. Hard drives start with the letter C: and can continue to Z:, if necessary. CD-ROM drives usually get the next available drive letter after the last hard drive. DOS defines these letters and will not let you change them.

Like almost every OS, DOS uses a *hierarchical directory tree* to organize the contents of these drives. All files are put into groups called *directories*. Windows also uses directories, but calls them *folders*. Any file not in a directory within the tree is said to be in the *root directory*. A system may have directories inside directories, which are called *subdirectories*. Any directory can have multiple subdirectories. Two or more files with the same name can exist in different directories on a PC, but two files in the same directory cannot have the same name. In the same way, no two subdirectories under the same directory can have the same name, but two subdirectories under different directories can have the same name.

When describing a drive, you use its letter. For example, the hard drive would be represented by C:. To describe the root directory, add a backslash (\ ). The root of C:, for example, would be C:\. To describe a particular directory, add the name of the directory. For example, if a PC had a directory called TEST, the directory would be called C:\TEST.

Subdirectories in a directory are displayed by adding backslashes and names. If the TEST directory had a subdirectory called SYSTEM, it would be shown like this: C:\TEST\SYSTEM. This naming convention provides for a complete description of the location and name of any file. If the C:\TEST\SYSTEM directory had a file called TEST2.TXT, it would be C:\TEST\SYSTEM\TEST2.TXT.

The exact location of a file is called its *path*. The path for the TEST2.TXT file is C:\TEST\SYSTEM. Here are some examples of possible paths:

```
C:\DOS
F:\FRUSCH3\CLEAR
A:\REPORTS
D:\
```

DOS Structure: Three Main Files

The DOS operating system is composed of three main files, accompanied by roughly 80 support files. The three main files are IO.SYS, MSDOS.SYS, and COMMAND.COM and they load in that order. These files must be on the C: drive or the computer will not boot. IO.SYS handles talking to the BIOS and hardware. MSDOS.SYS is the primary DOS code, often called the *kernel*. COMMAND.COM actually interprets commands typed into the computer and passes that information to MSDOS.SYS. COMMAND.COM is also called the *command interpreter*. The command interpreter stores a number of commands you can enter to get work done. Commands built into COMMAND.COM are known as *internal commands*.

The core part of DOS is composed of these three files, but DOS also encompasses a large number of auxiliary files. These separate programs are usually stored in a directory called C:\DOS. The Windows *9x* equivalents are stored in a directory called C:\WINDOWS\COMMAND. These extremely important *external programs* provide DOS with extra functions that aren't built into COMMAND.COM. For example, FDISK.EXE and FORMAT.EXE are both external commands.

Objective 16.02 The DOS User Interface

The text-based DOS user interface might seem primitive when compared with the attractive, colorful, graphics-based Windows interface used by systems today, but it's quite fast and powerful. An experienced user can perform many equivalent jobs faster from the command line than in any Windows graphical interface. But the interface is picky and unforgiving: one wrong keystroke can result in the loss of crucial data with no warning.

The DOS Prompt

The DOS user interface is centered on the *prompt*, which is a path followed by a greater-than sign (>) and a flashing cursor. When you see the prompt (Figure 16-1), DOS is telling you, "I'm ready to take your commands!"

DOS is always focused on a particular directory. The prompt shows you which directory currently has DOS's focus. This is important because DOS performs any commands you issue on the files in the directory on which DOS is focused. For example, if you see a C:\> prompt, you know DOS is focused on the root directory of the C: drive. If you see a C:\DBASE\:> prompt, you know DOS is focused on the DBASE directory of the C: drive. The first trick to using DOS is remembering

FIGURE 16-1   The DOS prompt

to get DOS to focus on the drive and directory where you want to work. Let's put this idea into practice with the DIR command.

DIR Command

The *DIR command* shows you the contents of the directory that currently has DOS's focus. Let's assume DOS is focused on the root directory of the C: drive. When you type **DIR** and press the ENTER key (you must always press ENTER after every command in DOS), you see something like this:

```
C:\>DIR
 Volume in Drive C is
 Volume Serial Number is 1734-3234
 Directory of C:\

DOS                  <DIR>                 09-03-96     9:34a
COMMAND     COM              34222         04-01-94     4:33p
AUTOEXEC    BAT              14            04-03-00    11:55a
WINDOWS              <DIR>                 11-07-99     1:34a
CONFIG      SYS              34            04-03-00     4:36p
MIKE                 <DIR>                 09-03-99     8:15a
JUNK        DOC              55677         05-13-99    10:03a
COMMAND     COM              23222         09-03-96     4:33p
9 file(s)     72233 bytes
        18288834 bytes free
```

If you're following along on a PC, remember that different computers contain different files and different programs, so you'll certainly see something different from the preceding example! If a lot of text scrolls quickly down the screen, try using a switch—a combination of a forward slash and a letter—after the command; for example, type **DIR/P** (to pause the scroll) or **DIR/W** (to run the text wider), and don't forget to press ENTER! Almost all switches can be used simultaneously to modify a command. For example, try typing **DIR/W/P**.

Exam Tip

Use the /? switch after any command line command to get a help file that shows the proper use and syntax of that command.

All these entries are files. The DIR command lists the filename, extension, file size in bytes, and creation date/time. Note how all the filenames stay within the 8.3 limit.

Windows 9x and Windows 2000 support long filenames, making the DIR command look a bit different than what you would see in DOS. Windows shows both its DOS 8.3 name and its full Windows name, using a tilde (~) character and a number (in this case, the number 1) in the 8.3 name to replace the extra characters.

Directories: The CD Command

Type **DIR** once again and, this time, ignore the file listings. See if you can find any entries that are followed by <DIR>. They might look like these samples from a Windows 2000 system:

```
07/30/2000  08:04p    <DIR>      Transcender
08/10/2000  07:23p    <DIR>      ts4.3
08/19/2000  10:47a    <DIR>      Office52
08/26/2000  12:23a    <DIR>      mgafold
11/10/2000  07:13a    <DIR>      BTMAGIC.PQ
11/10/2000  07:13a    <DIR>      WINNT
```

If you type **DIR/W**, these listings display differently. Instead of <DIR> after the directory name, the name is enclosed in brackets. Do you see any listings that look like these when you type **DIR/W**?

```
[DOS]    [WINDOWS]    [QUAKE]    [OBIWAN]
```

These are *directories,* or *folders,* as we say in the Windows world. The terms are interchangeable.

The CD (or CHDIR) command enables you to change the focus of DOS to a different directory. To use the CD command, type **CD** followed by the name of the directory on which you want DOS to focus. To go to the C:\OBIWAN directory, type **CD\OBIWAN**, and then press ENTER. If the system has an OBIWAN directory, DOS will change its focus to that directory and the prompt will change to C:\OBIWAN>. If there is no OBIWAN directory or if you accidentally type something like OBIWAM, a DOS or Windows 9x system will report an *Invalid directory* error. If you use Windows 2000, the message you'll see is *The system cannot find the path specified.* If you get this error, check what you typed and try again.

To return to the root directory, type **CD** and press ENTER.

Travel Advisory

You absolutely cannot hurt your PC in any way by typing the DIR or CD commands incorrectly. Take advantage of this knowledge and experiment! Intentionally make mistakes to familiarize yourself with the error messages. Have fun! Learn from errors!

Moving Between Drives

The CD command is *not* used to move between drives. To get DOS to *point* (DOS geek-speak for *switch its focus*) to another drive, type the drive letter and a colon and press ENTER. If DOS is pointing at the C:\DOS directory and you want to see what's on the floppy (A:) drive, type A: and DOS will point to the floppy drive. You see the following on the screen:

```
C:\DOS>A:
A:\>
```

To return to the C: drive, type **C:** and you see the following:

```
A:\>C:
C:\DOS>
```

Note that DOS returns you to the same directory you left. Just for fun, try typing a drive letter you know doesn't exist. I know my system doesn't have a W: drive. If I type in a nonexistent drive on a DOS or Windows 9*x* system, I get the error

```
Invalid drive specification
```

In Windows 2000, I get the following error

```
The system cannot find the drive specified.
```

With the DIR, CD, and drive letter commands, you can access any folder on any storage device on your system. Make sure you can use these commands comfortably to navigate inside your computer.

Making Directories

So far, you learned how to navigate in a command prompt world. Now it's time to start making stuff, starting with a new directory.

To create (or make) a directory, use the MD (or MKDIR) command. To create a directory called QUAKE under the root directory of C:, for example, first ensure you are in the root directory by typing **CD**.

Now that DOS is pointing to the root directory, type **MD QUAKE**. DOS will not volunteer any information. You must use the DIR command to see that you have, in fact, created a new directory.

Travel Advisory

DOS almost never tells you a command has been performed successfully. But, rest assured, it will complain when you do something wrong! The old adage is: DOS never pats you on the back, but it will slap you on the head!

Removing Directories or Subdirectories

Removing subdirectories works exactly like making them. First, get to the directory that contains the subdirectory you want to delete. Then, execute the command by typing **RD** (or **RMDIR**), followed by a space and the name of the subdirectory you're deleting. No response from DOS? Good. That means you probably did it right! Type **DIR** to check that the subdirectory is gone.

The RD command will not delete a directory if it contains files or subdirectories. If you want to delete a directory that contains files or subdirectories, you must first empty that directory using the DEL (for files) or RD (for subdirectories) command. You can also use the DELTREE command. DELTREE deletes the directory, as well as all files and subdirectories. DELTREE is handy, but it can also be dangerous because it's easy to delete more than you want.

Running a Program

To run a DOS program, simply change DOS's focus to the directory where the program resides, and then type the name of the program. To try this, go to the C:\DOS directory by using the CD command. If you're using Windows 9x, go to the C:\WINDOWS\COMMAND directory. Type **DIR/W** to see the files in wide format. You should see a file called MEM.EXE. As mentioned earlier, all files with the extensions EXE and COM are programs, so MEM.EXE is a program. To run the MEM.EXE program, type the filename—in this case **MEM**—and press ENTER. Note that you do not have to type the .EXE extension, although you can if you want. Congratulations! You just ran your first DOS program.

Travel Advisory

The MEM program is a handy command-line program for a quick check of upper memory.

Objective 16.03   **Fun with Files**

This section deals with basic file manipulation: how to look at, copy, move, and delete files. You learn to create your own folders and how to copy files to them from other folders currently on your system.

Attributes

All files have four special values, or *attributes*, which determine how the file will act in special situations: hidden, read-only, system, and archive. A *hidden* file will not show up when you type the DIR command. A *read-only* file cannot be modified or deleted. Only system files such as IO.SYS and MSDOS.SYS get the *system* attribute. This attribute does nothing more than provide an easy identifier for these files. Finally, backup software uses the *archive* attribute to identify files that have changed since their last backup.

ATTRIB.EXE is an external DOS program that enables you to inspect and change file attributes. To inspect a file's attributes, type **ATTRIB** followed by a space and the name of the file—the letter *A* stands for archive. The letter *R* means read-only, *H* is hidden, and *S* is system.

Go to the C:\ directory and type **ATTRIB** by itself, and then press ENTER. If you're using DOS or Windows 9*x*, you see a result something like this:

```
A H      C:\AUTOEXEC.BAT
A H      C:\CONFIG.SYS
A SHR    C:\IO.SYS
```

```
A SHR    C:\MSDOS.SYS
A        C:\COMMAND.COM
```

Don't panic if you see a number of different files than the ones previously listed. No two C:\ directories are ever the same. In most cases, you see many more files than just these five. Notice that MSDOS.SYS and IO.SYS both have the system, hidden, and read-only attributes set. Microsoft does this to protect these important files.

You can also use the ATTRIB command to change a file's attributes. To add an attribute to a file, type a plus sign (+), followed by the attribute letter and the filename. To delete an attribute, use a minus sign (–).

Wildcards

Visualize having 273 files in one directory. A few of these files have the extension DOC, but the majority don't. If you're looking only for files that end with the DOC extension, wouldn't it be nice if you could get the DIR command to list only the .DOC files? You can! The answer is wildcards.

Wildcards are two special characters, * (asterisk) and ? (question mark), which can be used in place of all or part of a filename to make a DOS command act on more than one file at a time. Wildcards work with all DOS commands that take filenames. A good way to think of the * wildcard is *I don't care.* Replace the part of the filename you don't care about with *. The result of DIR *.COM would be all the files that have the extension .COM. Wildcards also substitute for extensions. CONFIG.* gives you all the files called CONFIG with any extension. The ? wildcard replaces any single character. This can be handy when you're looking for filenames with a specific number of characters.

Deleting Files

To delete files, you use the DEL or ERASE command. *DEL* and *ERASE* are identical commands and can be used interchangeably. Deleting files is simple—maybe too simple. Once a file has been erased, it can only be recovered by using a special recovery utility, such as Norton's UNERASE. A good rule here is *check twice and delete once.* To delete a single file, type **DEL** followed by a space and the name of the file to delete. Although nothing will appear on the screen to confirm it, the file is now gone. To confirm the file is no longer listed, use the DIR command.

You can use wildcards with the DEL and ERASE commands to delete multiple files. For example, to delete all files with the extension COM in a directory, you would type **DEL *.COM**.

To delete all files with the filename CONFIG in a directory, type **DEL CONFIG.***. To delete all the files in a directory, you can use the popular *.* wild-card (often pronounced star-dot-star), like this: **DEL *.***. This is one of the few DOS commands that elicits a response from DOS. On receiving the DEL *.* command, DOS responds with Are you sure? (Y/N), to which you respond with either Y or N. Pressing Y will erase every file in the directory, so be extremely careful with *.*!

Don't confuse erasing files with erasing directories. DEL erases files, but it will not erase directories. Use RD or DELTREE to erase directories.

Copying and Moving Files

The ability to copy and move files from a command prompt is crucial to all technicians. Because of its finicky nature and many options, the COPY command is also rather painful to learn, especially if you're used to simply dragging icons in Windows. The following tried-and-true five-step process makes it easier, but the real secret is to get in front of a C: prompt and copy and move files around until you're comfortable. The only difference between copying and moving is whether the original is left behind (COPY) or not (MOVE). Once you learn the COPY command, you've learned the MOVE command!

Mike's Five-Step COPY/MOVE Process

I've been teaching folks how to copy and move files for years using this handy process. Remember, there are hundreds of variations on this process. As you become more confident with these commands, try doing a COPY /? or MOVE /? at any prompt to see the real power of these commands. But, at first, follow this process step-by-step.

1. Point DOS to the directory containing the files to be copied or moved.
2. Type **COPY** or **MOVE** and a space.
3. Type the name of the file(s) to be copied/moved (with or without wildcards) and a space.
4. Type the path of the new location for the files.
5. Press ENTER.

XCOPY

The standard COPY/MOVE commands can only work on one directory at a time, making them a poor choice for copying or moving files in multiple directories. To help with these multidirectory jobs, Microsoft added the XCOPY command. (Note that there is no XMOVE, only XCOPY.)

XCOPY works similarly to COPY, but it has extra switches that give XCOPY the power to work with multiple directories. If I want to copy a bunch of files and directories to my D:\ drive in one command, I would use XCOPY.

The power and utility of the DEL, COPY/MOVE, and XCOPY commands make them indispensable for a PC technician, but that same power and utility can cause disaster. Think twice and execute the command once. The data you save may be your own!

Objective 16.04   Communicating with Hardware

All hardware needs BIOS. New devices snapped into an expansion slot require specific programming to function properly with the OS.

DOS provides two special text files for adding control to new hardware: device drivers via CONFIG.SYS and certain programs via AUTOEXEC.BAT. Because most Windows 9x systems retain and use these files, A+ techs need to know them intimately.

Device Drivers and CONFIG.SYS

The most common way to add BIOS is through special files called device drivers. A *device driver* is little more than a file containing all the programming necessary to talk to a new device. Device drivers usually come from the same company that makes the hardware. If you buy a sound card or network card, it will come with a diskette or CD-ROM containing the necessary files. Most DOS device driver files use the extension SYS, such as DRIVER.SYS.

Device drivers load through a special file called CONFIG.SYS, a text file that must be in the root directory of the C: drive. The most common way to add device drivers in DOS is first to copy the device driver on to the C: drive from the floppy drive or CD-ROM, either manually using the COPY command or automatically by running an installation program that does the copying for you. Either way, the result is a device driver on the C: drive, usually in its own directory. Once the device driver is copied to the C: drive, a line is added to the CONFIG.SYS file. This line starts with DEVICE= or DEVICEHIGH=, followed by the path/name of the device driver.

Travel Advisory

If you use Windows, type SYSEDIT in the Start | Run box and click OK to open the System Configuration Editor. This handy program opens CONFIG.SYS, as well as other important startup files.

If you change CONFIG.SYS, the change will not be reflected until you reboot the computer.

TSRs and AUTOEXEC.BAT

The second way to add support for devices is through a terminate and stay resident (TSR) program. TSRs are less common than CONFIG.SYS device drivers, but they work equally well. You run a TSR like any other program, by typing its name at the prompt. Unlike other programs, however, a TSR immediately returns you to a DOS prompt (terminate), but will still be in RAM (stay resident). One of the most common DOS TSRs provides support for a mouse. Most mice come with a diskette that includes a TSR, so you can use it in DOS. These TSR programs usually have a catchy name like MOUSE.COM. When a program such as MOUSE.COM runs, it seems as though nothing has happened, but it has. The MOUSE program has loaded into memory and will now support DOS programs that use a mouse. Try running the EDIT program and move your mouse. Ta-da! You have a mouse cursor! That's a classic use of a TSR. Relatively few devices use TSRs in DOS. Most use device drivers in CONFIG.SYS.

AUTOEXEC.BAT

Now let's say you decide you like MOUSE.COM and you are going to use a mouse. Every time you reboot, you need to enter MOUSE.COM before you start working. Wouldn't it be great if you could tell DOS to start certain TSRs automatically? That's the job of *AUTOEXEC.BAT*, which is a text file that resides in the root directory of the C: drive, just like CONFIG.SYS.

Using the EDIT program, you can create a text file with this line:

```
MOUSE
```

Save it with the name AUTOEXEC.BAT in the root directory of C:. Now, every time you boot the PC, MOUSE.EXE starts automatically. Any command you can type at the prompt can be added to the AUTOEXEC.BAT file.

Some errors, bad drivers, or buggy TSRs in CONFIG.SYS or AUTOEXEC.BAT can cause a DOS PC (or Windows 9x machine, for that matter) to lock up at startup. If you run into such a circumstance, reboot and press the F5 key when the system says Starting MS-DOS. DOS will load but bypass CONFIG.SYS and AUTOEXEC.BAT. Alternatively, if you press F8, DOS enables you to step through CONFIG.SYS and AUTOEXEC.BAT line by line.

Working with Drives

One of the most important items in your toolbox is a bootable floppy diskette. This floppy has many uses, the most useful of which is booting up a system when the hard drive isn't working properly. You can make a bootable floppy from any properly operating PC. *Do not* wait to make one until you need it. You might not have a properly operating PC available! Insert a blank floppy and use the SYS command to make it bootable (see the following).

Most techs use the fabulous Windows 98 Startup diskette as a general purpose tool because of the built-in CD-ROM drive support (see Chapter 18 for details). If you must use a DOS diskette, in contrast, you'll need to copy a few extra utilities to the diskette. As a minimum, copy

- FDISK.EXE or FDISK.COM (depending on the version of DOS)
- FORMAT.EXE or FORMAT.COM (depending on the version of DOS)
- SYS.COM
- EDIT.COM (from Windows 95, but also works with old DOS)

You should add three other utilities:

- ATTRIB.EXE
- DEFRAG.EXE
- SCANDISK.EXE

SYS

The SYS command copies the three DOS system files to a partition, making it bootable. Although you can use the FORMAT command with the /S option to format a drive and copy the system files, sometimes you don't want to reformat a drive. Sometimes, you only want to add or replace the system files. To do this, run the SYS command followed by the letter of the drive you want to make bootable. This command is handy for making preformatted floppy diskettes bootable. The SYS command looks like this:

```
C:\>SYS A:
System transferred
```

The SYS command works equally well to replace a suspect system file on a hard drive. Whenever you lock up on boot after the POST, a quick **SYS C:** after booting to a bootable floppy disk is a handy way to verify the system files are intact. Make certain you SYS only with the same version of DOS or Windows.

ScanDisk

The ScanDisk program is a disk utility to be included as a part of DOS, as shown in Figure 16-2. ScanDisk identifies and repairs lost cluster chains. It can reliably detect and fix a wide range of disk problems. Earlier versions of DOS come with a similar disk utility called the CHKDISK program.

> **Travel Advisory**
>
> Windows 2000 has brought back CheckDisk as a valuable disk utility. DOS and Windows 9x don't need CHKDSK, but Windows 2000 does!

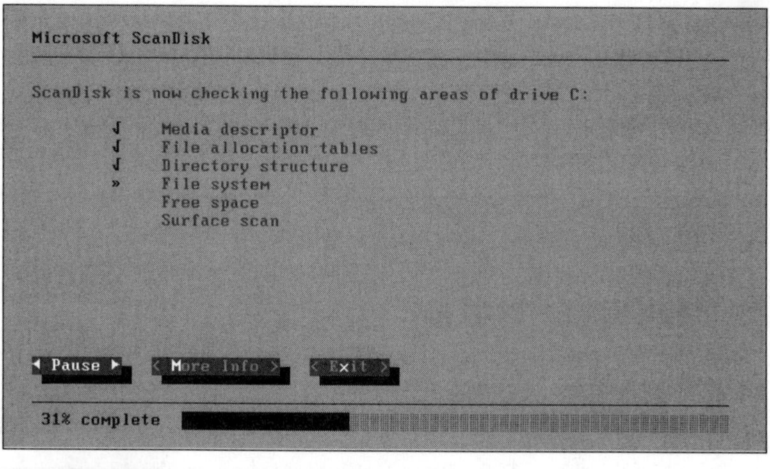

```
Microsoft ScanDisk

ScanDisk is now checking the following areas of drive C:

        √       Media descriptor
        √       File allocation tables
        √       Directory structure
        »       File system
                Free space
                Surface scan




    ◄ Pause ►      < More Info >    < Exit >


    31% complete    ████████████████
```

FIGURE 16-2   DOS ScanDisk

Disk Defragmenter

As discussed earlier in the book, hard drives need to be defragmented regularly, about once a week. DOS's Disk Defragmenter program is a simple defragmentation program that does an admirable job of clearing up file fragmentation without any user intervention. It works similarly to the Windows versions.

The A+ Certification exams continue to stress the command prompt because good PC techs need to be as comfortable starting at the C: prompt as they are looking at My Computer. Understand the DOS commands shown in this chapter, not to prove you can use an obsolete operating system, but to make better use of today's most advanced operating systems. DOS may be dead, but the legacy of DOS lives on in every PC used today.

Objective 16.05 Memory Management

The introduction of Windows 95 substantially reduced the need to understand DOS memory management, but the installed base of DOS applications still thrives—alive and well—happily humming under the hood of millions of PCs. So, until that final faraway day when we get to throw out COMMAND.COM for good and load up that next generation of Windows 200x or whatever operating system, the nasty specter of DOS-based memory management still can sneak up on the unprepared PC technician. Good technicians—read, *A+ Technicians*—still need to understand memory and the basic principles of memory management. The A+ Certification exam's memory management questions are fairly simple. You need to know how to make DOS programs function inside Windows 9x/2000 systems.

Microsoft wrote DOS to take advantage of the relative power of the 8086 and 8088 processors, way back in the Stone Age of the PC. This meant, however, that DOS shared the 20-bit address bus limitation as well, and so could only handle a 1MB address space, even on CPUs that exceeded that limit (such as the i386 and later processors).

Conventional and Reserved Memory

The 1MB of memory locations available to a DOS PC breaks down into two distinct areas—*conventional* and *reserved*. The area from 0 to 640K (00000h to 9FFFFh) is called conventional memory. Conventional memory contains all the memory addresses set aside for RAM to run programs. All the addresses from

A0000 to FFFFF are set aside for other chips that the CPU may need to access, primarily ROM chips and specialized RAM. This memory is called reserved memory. Conventional memory has 655,360 memory locations (640K), and reserved memory has 393,216 memory locations (384K), for a total of 1,048,576 memory locations (1,024K or 1MB).

Travel Assistance

Memory addresses, just like I/O addresses, are written in hexadecimal notation. For a refresher on hex, check out the Tech File at http://www.totalsem.com/techfiles.htm.

The Reserved Area

The reserved area is a rather complex compilation of different ROMs and RAMs that use memory. Most of these devices have distinct memory locations—either determined by IBM long ago or by a de facto process of clone makers and device manufacturers taking over certain memory locations. All programs take up a range of memory locations. By far the most important device in the reserved area is the System BIOS. Although some variation can occur, the System BIOS is classically located in the memory locations from F0000 to FFFFF.

Video cards all have RAM mapped into the reserved area in three different areas. When your video card is in a color text mode (like in DOS), its RAM uses the memory locations from B8000 to BFFFF. When the video card is in graphics mode, its RAM is mapped from A0000 to AFFFF. The first generations of video cards displayed monochrome text. Their video RAM was mapped from B0000 to B7FFF. Most modern video cards have begun to ignore these memory divisions and simply use the entire area from A0000 to BFFFF.

None of the reserved memory addresses from C0000 to EFFFF were initially dedicated to any particular device. They are for optional ROM and RAM that peripheral makers might install on their cards. Different types of cards can come with ROM or RAM, although no hard and fast rule exists. By tradition and long usage, however, all video card ROM chips use the memory range from C0000 to C7FFF. Figure 16-3 illustrates the first 1MB of memory addresses.

Exam Tip

Take some time to memorize these hex locations for the exam!

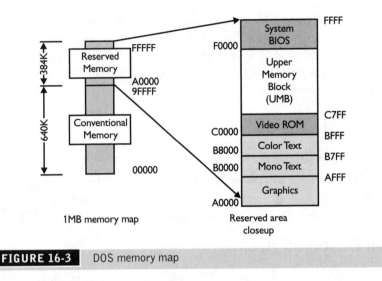

FIGURE 16-3   DOS memory map

Reducing Conventional Memory Use

The goal of DOS memory management is to reduce the amount of conventional memory used by anything other than the currently running application. The secret to reducing conventional memory use is to find some unused memory in which to store programs.

The upper memory block (UMB) is the unused portion of reserved memory, as illustrated in Figure 16-3. That unused area can be used to reduce the amount of conventional memory used by running applications.

Moving programs into the UMB takes two steps. First, you have to open the door or gateway to the UMB by running a special program called EMM386.EXE. To do this, add the following line to CONFIG.SYS somewhere *after* the line DEVICE=C:\DOS\HIMEM.SYS:

```
DEVICE=C:\DOS\EMM386.EXE
```

EMM386.EXE prepares the UMB for device drivers and programs, but it doesn't load them. To tell DOS you will be loading high (into the UMB), you need to add the following line to CONFIG.SYS:

```
DOS=UMB
```

To load a device driver in CONFIG.SYS in to the UMB, change its DEVICE= line to DEVICEHIGH=. To load a TSR in AUTOEXEC.BAT into the UMB, insert the command LOADHIGH or LH in front of the TSR command.

Extended Memory

In ancient times, DOS computers could access only the first 1MB of memory, even on systems with greater than 20-bit wide memory address buses. But one, bright and glorious day, someone at Intel or Microsoft (there's still some argument on this) discovered that if you ran a certain BIOS routine through the 8042 (keyboard) chip, you could unmask the 21st address wire and, suddenly, DOS could see more memory! Why they ran this routine, one can only guess, but it worked and the world was better for it. The newly awakened and accessible memory wasn't that much, only 64K minus 16 bytes of memory, but oh how techs loved it! This tiny area available only to 286 or better processors is called the high memory area (HMA).

Note that the HMA is simply more memory addresses. To use these addresses, RAM chips must populate the addresses above FFFFF. In other words, the system must have physical RAM beyond 1MB, what is called *extended memory*.

Exam Tip

Know your memory locations! *Conventional* is the first 640K. *Reserved* is the next 384K. Everything beyond 1MB is *extended* memory. The HMA is the first 64K of extended memory.

DOS cannot directly use extended memory. Generally, only portions of the OS files and the buffers can load into the HMA. Here again, you must perform two steps to access extended memory. First, you have to open the door or gateway to the HMA, by adding the following line to CONFIG.SYS:

```
DEVICE=C:\DOS\HIMEM.SYS
```

HIMEM.SYS has two functions—it opens the extended memory, which is cool, and it scans your RAM thoroughly when your PC boots up. That's a nice bonus! If you get a HIMEM.SYS error at boot, you might have a bad stick of RAM.

The second step is to load what you can into the HMA. To do that, you need to add the following line to CONFIG.SYS:

```
DOS=HIGH
```

The only rule with using UMB and HMA is the HIMEM.SYS line needs to be first. DOS=HIGH and DOS=UMB can be written in several ways. DOS=HIGH, UMB; DOS=UMB, HIGH are also acceptable.

> **Exam Tip**
>
> Remember, UMB and EMM386.EXE are for the unused areas of reserved memory; HMA and HIMEM.SYS are for extended memory.

Objective 16.06 The Computer Virus

The words "I think your machine has a virus" can send shudders down the back of even the most competent PC technician. The thought of megabytes of critical data being wiped away by the work of some evil programmer is, at best, annoying, and, at worst, a serious financial disaster. Although computer viruses aren't limited to DOS, this chapter provides a number of concepts necessary to understand the function of computer viruses. Because these concepts are still fresh in your mind, this is a good point to learn about viruses and their prevention/removal.

So, where do viruses come from? Just like many human viruses, they live in host bodies—in this case—computers. Your computer can only catch a virus if it interacts with other computers, or with programs or data from an infected computer. The problem is, these days, almost everyone's computer (aside from folks like the CIA) is connected to the Internet and, thereby, to many, many other computers. Also, many viruses are spread through the sharing of programs or information on floppy disks or CD-ROMs.

How do you know if you've caught a virus? You feel sluggish, start sneezing and coughing, and want to sleep. In the case of your computer, it might seem unusually sluggish, generate strange error messages or other odd emissions, or possibly even lock up and refuse to function entirely. All these are classic symptoms, but you cannot assume your computer is virus-free because it seems fine. Some viruses do their work in secret, as I'll discuss shortly.

The secret to avoiding viruses is to understand how a virus works. A virus is a program that has two functions: 1) *proliferate* (make more copies of itself), and 2) *activate* (at some signal, count, or date, *do* something—frequently something bad like delete the boot sector). Not all viruses do damage to your system. In fact, some of the first viruses written were harmless and downright amusing.

Types of Viruses

Without going into too much gritty detail, there are basically only four types of viruses: boot sector, executable, macro, and Trojan. A fifth type, bimodal/bipartite, is a combination of two other virus types.

Boot Sector

A *boot sector* virus changes the code in the Master Boot Record (MBR) of the hard drive. Once the machine is booted, the virus resides in memory, attempting to infect the MBRs of other disks and drives, such as floppy and Zip disks or connected network machines, and wreaking whatever havoc the programmer who designed it had in mind.

Executable

Executable viruses reside in executable files. They are literally extensions of executables and are unable to exist by themselves. Once an infected executable file is run, the virus loads into memory, adding copies of itself to other EXEs that are subsequently run and, again, doing whatever evil deed the virus was designed to do.

Macro

Macro viruses are specially written application macros. Although they aren't truly programs, they perform the same functions as regular viruses. These viruses autostart when the particular application is run, and then they attempt to make more copies of themselves. Some even try to find other copies of the same application across a network and propagate.

Trojan

A *Trojan* is a true, freestanding program that does something other than what the person who runs the program thinks it will do. An example of a Trojan is a program that a person thinks is a game, but that's a CMOS eraser instead. Some Trojans are quite sophisticated. It might be a game that actually works but, when the user quits the game, the program causes some type of damage.

Bimodal/Bipartite

A *bimodal* or *bipartite* virus uses both boot sector and executable functions.

Antivirus Programs

The only way to protect your PC permanently from getting a virus is to disconnect from the Internet and never permit any potentially infected software to touch your precious computer. Because neither scenario is likely these days, you need to use a specialized antivirus program to help stave off the inevitable virus assaults.

An antivirus program protects your PC in two ways: it can be both sword and shield, working in an active *seek and destroy* mode and in a passive *sentry* mode. When ordered to seek and destroy, the program scans the computer's boot sector and files for viruses, and if it finds any, presents you with the available options for removing or disabling them. Antivirus programs can also operate as virus shields that passively monitor your computer's activity, checking for viruses only when certain events occur, such as a program executing or a file being downloaded.

Antivirus programs use different techniques to combat different types of viruses. They detect boot sector viruses simply by comparing the drive's boot sector to a standard boot sector. This works because most boot sectors are basically the same. Some antivirus programs make a backup copy of the boot sector. If they detect a virus, the programs uses that backup copy to replace the infected boot sector.

Executable viruses are a little more difficult to find because they can be on any file in the drive. To detect executable viruses, the antivirus program uses a library of signatures. A *signature* is a code pattern of a known virus. The antivirus program compares an executable file to its library of signatures. There have been instances where a perfectly clean program coincidentally held a virus signature. In this case, the antivirus program's creator usually provides a patch to prevent further alarms. Antivirus programs detect macro viruses through the presence of virus signatures or of certain macro commands that indicate a known macro virus.

Now that you understand the types of viruses and how antivirus programs try to protect against them, let's review a few terms often used when describing certain traits of viruses.

Polymorphics/Polymorphs

A *polymorph* virus attempts to change its signature to prevent detection by antivirus programs, usually by continually scrambling a bit of useless code. Fortunately, once the antivirus makers become aware of the virus, the scrambling code itself can be identified and used as the signature. One technique that's sometimes used to combat unknown polymorphs is to have the antivirus program create a checksum on every file in the drive. A *checksum,* in this context, is a number generated by the software based on the contents of the file rather than the name, date, or size of that file. The algorithms for creating these checksums vary among different antivirus programs. They are also usually kept secret to help prevent virus makers from coming up with ways to beat them. Every time a program is run, the antivirus program calculates a new checksum and compares it with the earlier calculation. If the checksums are different, it's a sure sign of a virus.

Stealth

The term "stealth" is more of a concept than an actual virus function. Most *stealth* virus programs are boot sector viruses that use various methods to hide from antivirus software. One popular stealth virus hooks on to a little-known, but often-used, software interrupt, running only when that interrupt runs. Others make copies of innocent-looking files.

Virus Prevention Tips

The secret to preventing damage from a virus attack is to keep from getting one in the first place. As discussed earlier, all good antivirus programs include a virus shield that automatically scans floppies, downloads, and so on. Use it! Another good idea is to scan a PC daily for possible virus attacks. Again, all antivirus programs include TSRs that run every time the PC is booted. And, last, but not least, know where software has come from before you load it. While the chance of commercial, shrink-wrapped software having a virus is virtually nil (although there have been a few well-publicized exceptions), that illegal copy of Quake Tournament you borrowed from a local hacker should definitely be inspected with care.

Get into the habit of keeping around an antivirus floppy disk: a bootable, copy-protected floppy with a copy of an antivirus program. If you suspect a virus, use the diskette, even if your antivirus program claims to have eliminated the virus. Turn off the PC and reboot it from the antivirus diskette. Run your antivirus program's most comprehensive virus scan. Then check all removable media exposed to the system and any other machine that might have received data from, or is networked to, the cleaned machine. A virus can often go for months before anyone knows of its presence.

CHECKPOINT

✔ **Objective 16.01: Operating System Basics**   The concepts and functions associated with DOS remain relevant for the A+ technician. This section covers DOS concepts, DOS commands, DOS 8.3 filenames, DOS file structure, and the three main DOS files: IO.SYS, MSDOS.SYS, and COMMAND.COM.

Objective 16.02: The DOS User Interface   The DOS user interface is quite different from the Windows GUI. You must be comfortable with the DOS prompt, the DIR and CD commands, working with drives and directories, and running a program in DOS.

 Objective 16.03: Fun with Files   To use DOS efficiently, you must understand basic DOS file management concepts and procedures, including file attributes, wildcards, and file manipulation (copy, move, delete) procedures.

 Objective 16.04: Communicating with Hardware   When Microsoft invented DOS, it knew new devices would be invented in the future, so DOS had to support the capability to add extra BIOS for new devices. DOS does this using device drivers and CONFIG.SYS, and TSRs and AUTOEXEC.BAT. Related issues for the PC tech include making a bootable floppy disk and using certain key DOS tools.

 Objective 16.05: Memory Management   Good technicians need to understand memory and the basic principles of memory management, including how to make DOS programs function inside Windows 9*x*/2000 systems. Understand conventional memory, extended/upper memory, high memory, expanded memory, HIMEM.SYS, and EMM386.EXE.

 Objective 16.06: The Computer Virus   More than ever it's important to understand how viruses work and how to avoid them. Key information here includes the different types of viruses, how antivirus programs work, terms used when describing certain traits of viruses, and techniques for virus prevention.

REVIEW QUESTIONS

1. Which of the following shows a typical DOS prompt?

   A. A:\\

   B. D:/>

   C. C:\>

   D. C://

2. Which command(s) can DOS use to remove files from a drive? (Select all that apply.)

   A. REMOVE

   B. DEL

   C. DELTREE

   D. ERASE

3. Which of the following is true about DOS files?

   A. Names are broken down into filenames and extensions

   B. Filenames can be no longer than eight alphanumeric characters

   C. The optional extension usually defines the function of the file

   D. All of the above

4. Which command run from the C:\ prompt enables you to create a bootable floppy disk?

   A. SYS A:

   B. BOOT A:

   C. BOOT A: SYS

   D. A: /S

5. The three main files that make up DOS are

   A. MSDOS.SYS, CONFIG.SYS, and AUTOEXEC.BAT

   B. IO.SYS, MSDOS.SYS, and CONFIG.SYS

   C. IO.SYS, MSDOS.SYS, and COMMAND.COM

   D. COMMAND.COM, CONFIG.SYS, and AUTOEXEC.BAT

6. A computer virus can be categorized as which of the following? (Select all that apply.)

   A. Always destructive

   B. Self-replicating

   C. Self-activating

   D. Self-destructive

7. Which of the following statements accurately describe(s) CONFIG.SYS? (Select all that apply.)

   A. Your system can run fine without a CONFIG.SYS file

   B. CONFIG.SYS is known as a BIOS loader

   C. CONFIG.SYS is a static file; it cannot be modified

   D. If you notice an unfamiliar line in CONFIG.SYS, it's best to delete that line

8. What is conventional memory?

   A. Conventional memory is the first 640K of the first megabyte of RAM, needed by all DOS programs

B. Conventional memory is the last 640K of the first megabyte of RAM, needed by all DOS programs

C. Conventional memory is the first 640K of extended memory, needed by all DOS programs

D. Conventional memory is the last 640K of extended memory, needed by all DOS programs

9. What two lines need to be in CONFIG.SYS to load a portion of DOS into the HMA?

A. DEVICE=EMM386.EXE HIGH

B. DEVICE=HIMEM.SYS

C. DOS=HIGH

D. DOS=UMB

10. Which of the following statements about reserved memory is *incorrect*?

A. It is 384K

B. It is set aside to run DOS programs

C. Its memory address range is from A0000h to FFFFFh

D. Device drivers can sometimes load into reserved memory

REVIEW ANSWERS

1. **C** C:\> is a typical DOS prompt.

2. **B** **C** **D** All three of these are correct commands for removing files from a drive. DELTREE is the dangerous one because it permanently deletes files, directories, and subdirectories.

3. **D** All the statements are true for DOS files.

4. **A** Run the SYS A: command from the C:\ prompt to create a bootable diskette. This works in DOS and all versions of Windows 9x.

5. **C** IO.SYS, MSDOS.SYS, and COMMAND.COM.

6. **B** **C** For a program to be considered a virus, it must be self-replicating and self-activating.

7. **A** **B** A DOS system can run fine without CONFIG.SYS, although it needs the file to load device drivers for all but the most basic hardware. Deleting lines in CONFIG.SYS without knowing what they do can lead to system errors or nonresponsive hardware.

8. **A** Conventional memory is the first 640K of the first megabyte of RAM, needed by all DOS programs.

9. **B** **C** Both DEVICE=HIMEM.SYS and DOS=HIGH must be loaded in CONFIG.SYS. DOS=UMB, although often combined with DOS=HIGH, is for the upper memory blocks, not the high memory area.

10. **B** Reserved memory is not set aside to run DOS programs.

Windows 9x Installation and Configuration

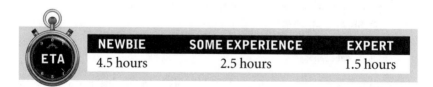

	NEWBIE	SOME EXPERIENCE	EXPERT
ETA	4.5 hours	2.5 hours	1.5 hours

After you've set up a PC's hardware, you need to install an operating system. And, although it's cool and important to know how to work from a command-line interface, such as DOS, most folks want more: pictures, icons, a mouse-driven interface … I want my Macint… err … I mean, I want Windows! This chapter covers essential installation issues for Windows 9*x*.

Objective 17.01   Partitioning and Formatting Hard Drives

Once you've installed a hard drive in a new system, you need to boot to a Startup disk and perform two steps to make the drive usable to the system: partition and format the drive. The process of partitioning and formatting a drive varies dramatically from one operating system to the next. The A+ Certification exams test your knowledge of *what* these processes do to make the drive work, as well as *how* to partition and format in both Windows 9*x* and Windows 2000. This chapter covers in detail the *what* part of the question and the *how* for the Windows 9*x* operating system. Windows 2000 is covered in Chapter 20.

But First … Creating a Windows 9*x* Startup Disk

All versions of Windows 9*x* provide the capability to create a Startup disk. A *Startup disk* is a bootable floppy disk that enables you to boot to an A: prompt. To create a Startup disk, follow these steps:

1. Click Start | Settings | Control Panel to open the Control Panel.
2. Locate the Add/Remove Programs applet and open it.
3. Click the Startup Disk tab.
4. Get a blank floppy disk and insert it into the floppy drive.
5. Click Create Disk.

Windows now creates a Startup disk. This disk contains just enough files to perform basic troubleshooting. On some systems, Windows prompts for the Windows installation CD—on others it won't. After Windows has created the Startup disk, take it out of the floppy drive and set it aside for later.

Exam Tip

Know where to go and how to create a Windows 9*x* Startup disk.

One of the most important jobs for a Startup disk is to let you gain access to your CD-ROM drive. Windows 95 Startup disks do not provide access to the CD-ROM drive. Windows 98, 98 SE, and ME Startup disks *do* provide CD-ROM access, so if possible, always use a 98 or later Startup disk. The process of creating bootable diskettes in Windows 2000 differs quite a bit from that of Windows 9x and is covered separately in Chapter 20.

Travel Advisory

Windows 9x installs only on a partitioned, formatted drive. Many Windows installations come with a Setup disk that will detect unpartitioned/unformatted drives, and then do the partitioning and formatting for you automatically. Many techs, myself included, use only Windows 98 Startup disks when we work on Windows 95 systems—they work great!

Partitioning

Partitions are electronic, logical divisions of a hard drive that provide tremendous flexibility in hard drive organization. A computer might have only one physical hard drive, for example, but it can have anywhere from 1 to 24 logical drives, named C: to Z:.

When the computer first boots to a hard drive, it looks for a special sector called the *boot sector*, which contains two critical pieces of information: the Master Boot Record (MBR) and the partition table, as shown in Figure 17-1. The *MBR* takes control of the boot process from the system BIOS and begins to look for a partition with a valid operating system. It does so by looking in the partition table. The *partition table* defines all the partitions on the hard drive, but a hard drive can also have different partitions with different capabilities. Let's discuss the types of partitions and see how they work to appreciate the power of partitioning.

Partition Types

A hard drive can have up to four partitions. These partitions divide into two types: primary and extended. Each type of partition performs a different function, and you create these partitions based on the needs of the particular PC system.

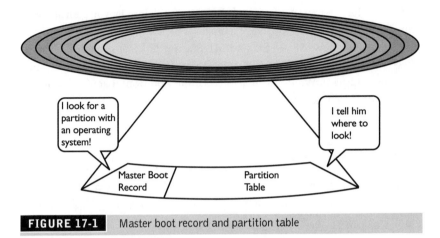

FIGURE 17-1   Master boot record and partition table

Primary Partitions   *Primary partitions* store the operating system(s). If you want to boot from a hard drive, it must have a primary partition. Therefore, the MBR must check the partition table for a primary partition. In Windows 9*x* and 2000, the name of the primary partition on the primary hard drive controller is always C: and you cannot change the name of the C: drive. It's worth noting that a hard drive can have up to four primary partitions but, in the DOS/Windows 9*x* world, the built-in partitioning program, called *FDISK,* can only create one primary partition on the drive. My guess is Microsoft, being a seller of operating systems, didn't want you to install other operating systems! So, even though hard drives support up to four primary partitions, we almost never see this in the Windows 9*x* world. Other operating systems, such as Windows 2000 and Linux, fully support multiple primary partitions on one drive. We use a number of terms for this function, but dual-boot and multiboot seem fairly common.

Travel Advisory

Don't confuse a primary partition with the primary controller. These are totally different animals: they just happen to share a similar name.

Active Partition   If a hard drive stores multiple primary partitions—each with a valid operating system—how does the system know which one to boot? That's where the concept of active partition comes into play. For a primary partition to boot, you must set it as the *active partition*. Only one primary partition can be set active at a time. Earlier, I mentioned that the MBR looks for an operating system to boot. This can now be defined a little more precisely. The MBR looks for a primary partition set to active.

Extended Partition   Your hard drive may or may not have the other partition type: an extended partition. *Extended partitions* are not bootable and one hard drive can only have one extended partition. If a hard drive has an extended partition, it takes up one of the areas in the partition map for the primary partitions. You can only have up to three primary partitions on a drive with an extended partition.

The beauty of an extended partition is in the way it handles drive letters. When you create a primary partition, it gets a drive letter and that's it. But when you create an extended partition, it does not automatically get a drive letter. Instead, you divide the extended partition into *logical drives*. An extended partition can have as many logical drives as you want, limited only by the letters of the alphabet for Windows 9*x* systems, enabling a maximum of 24 logical drives on one system (remember, A: and B: are reserved for floppy drives). You can turn an extended partition into one logical drive or into multiple logical drives, whatever suits you. You set the size of each logical drive to any size you want.

All this flexibility creates a little problem, especially for folks new to partitioning. Because a newly created extended partition doesn't yet have logical drives, working with extended partitions always requires two steps: (1) make the extended partition and (2) create logical drives within that extended partition.

Partition Examples   There are an almost infinite number of possible combinations for physical hard drives and partitions, but Figure 17-2 shows some common ones.

FDISK

To partition a drive only requires a few steps. First, you need to run FDISK. From a Startup disk, simply type the word **FDISK** at the A: prompt, and then press the ENTER key. From within Windows, click Start | Run, and then type FDISK in the dialog box. Click the OK button to start the program.

When you run FDISK, you'll see one of two things on your screen—a bunch of text or the main menu. Windows 95 version B and later versions of FDISK place a message onscreen that starts with *Your computer has a disk larger than 512MB* and ends by requiring you to select yes (Y) or no (N), as you can see in Figure 17-3.

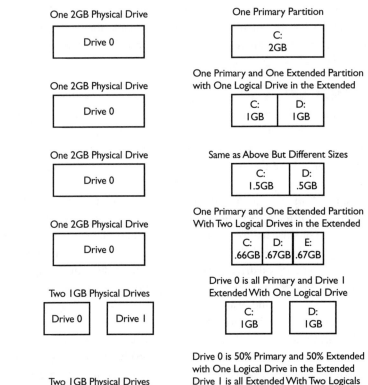

FIGURE 17-2   Examples of partitions

```
Your computer has a disk larger than 512 MB.  This version of Windows
includes improved support for large disks, resulting in more efficient
use of disk space on large drives, and allowing disks over 2 GB to be
formatted as a single drive.

IMPORTANT: If you enable large disk support and create any new drives on this
disk, you will not be able to access the new drive(s) using other operating
systems, including some versions of Windows 95 and Windows NT, as well as
earlier versions of Windows and MS-DOS. In addition, disk utilities that
were not designed explicitly for the FAT32 file system will not be able
to work with this disk. If you need to access this disk with other operating
systems or older disk utilities, do not enable large drive support.

Do you wish to enable large disk support (Y/N) ...........? [ ]
```

FIGURE 17-3   Opening Windows 98 FDISK screen

> **Travel Advisory**
>
> If you get the error *No Fixed Disks Present,* I'll bet you forgot
> to tell the CMOS to look for the drive. Reboot, access CMOS,
> and try setting up the drive again.

All this is simply Windows asking you whether you want to use FAT16 or
FAT32. If you press Y, everything you do will be FAT32. If you press N, everything
you do will be FAT16. For this example, select Y for yes. This brings up the famous
FDISK main menu, as shown in Figure 17-4.

> **Travel Advisory**
>
> If you boot directly to the FDISK main menu without seeing the long
> paragraph about FAT32, you are using a Windows 95 or even a
> DOS FDISK. There's nothing wrong with those FDISKs,
> assuming FAT16 is acceptable to you.

The FDISK main menu provides four choices. By pressing the first selection,
you can create a primary partition, an extended partition, or logical drives in an
extended partition. The second selection enables you to select the active partition.
Selection 3 enables you to delete partitions and logical drives. Selection 4 displays
current information. Note, all versions of FDISK—from MS-DOS to Windows
ME—call the partitions DOS partitions. Don't let that throw you off! If you have

```
                     Microsoft Winodws 98
                   Fixed Disk Setup Program
             (C)Copyright Microsoft Corp.  1983 - 1998

                        FDISK Options

Current fixed disk drive: 1

Choose one of the following:

1. Create DOS partition or Logical DOS Drive
2. Set active partition
3. Delete partition or Logical DOS Drive
4. Display partition information

Enter choice: [1]


Press ESC to exit FDISK
```

FIGURE 17-4   FDISK main menu

more than one drive installed, FDISK adds a fifth option—Change Current Fixed Disk Drive—which enables you to choose the drive on which you want to work.

The key to partitioning with FDISK is to *read the screens!* FDISK has clear instructions on what to do, but you have to obey the rules for it to work right. When you create a partition and FDISK says you need to exit and reboot so the changes can go into effect, exit and reboot before you try to access that partition! Let FDISK guide you.

High-Level Formatting

The last step in the process of preparing a drive to hold data is to format the drive. The official term for this last step is high-level formatting, although most of us simply refer to it as *formatting*. The high-level format performs two major functions: creating and configuring the file allocation tables (FATs) and creating the root directory. The root directory provides the foundation on which the operating system builds files and folders. The FAT requires a bit more explanation.

File Allocation Table (FAT)

Every operating system has a FAT, although some of the more recent operating systems (Windows 2000) might use a different term.

FAT in Concept　　The FAT keeps track of stored data on the hard drive. The base storage area for hard drives is a *sector*, with each sector storing up to 512 bytes of data. If an OS stores a file smaller than 512 bytes in a sector, the rest of the sector goes to waste. So what happens when an OS stores a file larger than 512 bytes? The OS needs a method to fill one sector, find another that's unused, fill it, find another, and so on, continuing to fill sectors until the file is completely stored. Once the OS has stored a file, it must remember which sectors hold that file, so it can retrieve that file later.

The official jargon description of a FAT calls it a *data structure,* but it's more like a two-column spreadsheet. The left column gives each sector a number—from 0000 to FFFF (in hex, of course). This means there are 65536 (64K) sectors. Notice the left-hand side contains 16 bits. We call this type of FAT a *16-bit FAT* or *FAT16*. Not only hard drives have FATs. Floppy drives also use FATs, but because they store so much less data, their FATs are only 12 bits.

One of the functions of high-level formatting is to map bad sectors. The right-hand side of the FAT contains information on the status of sectors. All hard drives, even brand-new drives fresh from the factory, contain faulty sectors that cannot store data because of imperfections in the construction of the drive. The OS must locate these bad sectors, mark them as unusable, and then prevent any files from being written to them. After the format program creates the FAT, it then proceeds through the entire partition, writing and attempting to read from each sector sequentially. If it finds a bad sector, it places a special status code (FFF7) in the sector's FAT location, which indicates the sector is unavailable for use. Formatting also marks the good sectors as 0000.

Using the FAT to track sectors, however, creates a problem. The 16-bit FAT addresses a maximum of 64K (2^{16}) locations. Therefore, the size of a hard-drive partition should be limited to 64K × 512 bytes per sector, or 32MB. When Microsoft first unveiled FAT16, this 32MB limit presented no problem because most hard drives were only 5MB to 10MB. But, as hard drives started to become much larger, Microsoft realized the 32MB limit for drives was unacceptable.

Modern FATs use a method called clustering to break this early limit. Clustering simply means to combine a set of contiguous sectors and treat them as a single unit in the FAT, as in Figure 17-5. These units are called *file allocation units* or *clusters*. Each row of the FAT addressed a cluster instead of a sector. Unlike sectors, the size of a cluster is not fixed, but varies according to the size of the partition.

Sectors and Clusters   The introduction of clustering meant a cluster, rather than a sector, became the basic unit of storage. Although this change enabled larger partition sizes—a good thing—it also increased the inherent wastefulness of FAT

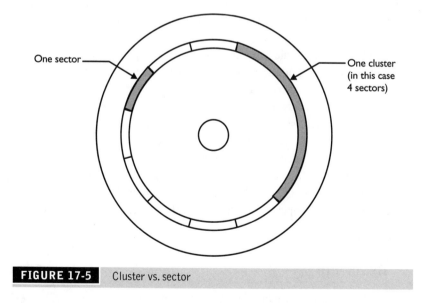

FIGURE 17-5   Cluster vs. sector

storage. With a sector-based FAT, when you saved a file of fewer than 512 bytes, the excess unused space in the sector went to waste. For example, saving a file of only 100 bytes left 412 bytes unused. We could accept this amount of waste because a typical file usually used a large number of sectors. For example, if you had a 15,000-byte file, you needed 30 sectors (15,000 bytes / 512 bytes per sector) to store the entire file. The last sector was only about 25 percent full, wasting roughly 125 bytes. Big deal! Compared to the total amount of storage used by all the sectors to store the file combined, this produced (125 / 15,000 = .008) or less than 1 percent waste.

This changed when clusters became the smallest storage area in a hard drive. Let's say you stored that same 15,000-byte file on a 1200MB (1.2GB) partition. A FAT16 partition of that size used 64 sectors/cluster, making each cluster ~32,000 bytes. In this case, the 15,000-byte file took one 32,000-byte cluster, leaving 17,000 bytes wasted. Storing the same file in clusters created much greater waste because clusters were so much larger.

Fragmentation

FAT drives store files in one or multiple sectors, depending on the size of the file. One big drawback to FAT drives comes when some of the parts of a single file reside in different areas of the drive. This is called *fragmentation*. The key to understanding fragmentation is one simple rule: the computer saves data in the *first available* locations in the file allocation table. Data does not get moved *up* in the table automatically when you delete something listed earlier in the FAT.

Fragmentation takes place all the time on FAT16 systems. While the system can easily handle a small file fragmented into only two parts, in the real world, a file might fragment into hundreds of pieces, forcing the read/write heads to travel all over the hard drive to retrieve a single file. Too much fragmentation slows a system down during hard drive reads and writes. Thus, you can dramatically improve a hard drive's read/write speed by eliminating this fragmentation. Every version of Windows—except NT—comes with a program called *Disk Defragmenter*, as shown in Figure 17-6, which is specially designed to rearrange files back into neat contiguous chunks. To access Disk Defragmenter, click Start | Programs | Accessories | System Tools and select Disk Defragmenter. You can also get there when you access the properties of a hard drive. (Right-click the drive and select Properties, remember?)

Exam Tip

To keep a system running optimally, run Disk Defragmenter once a week.

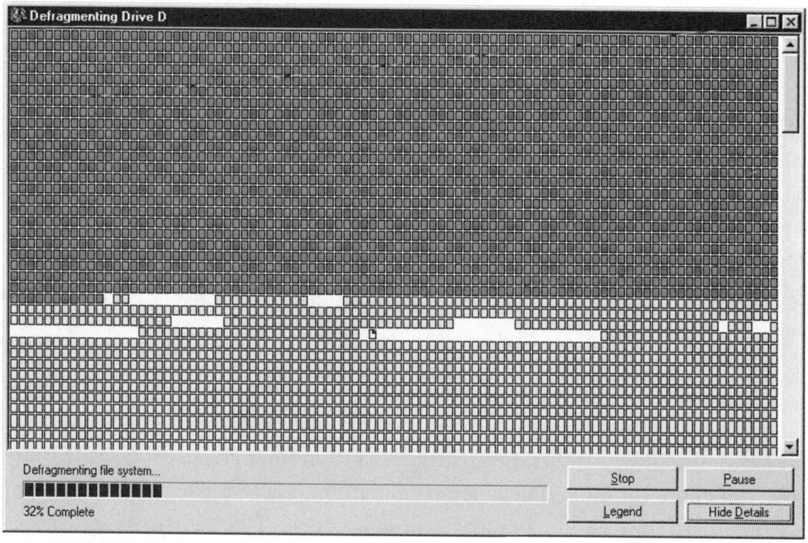

FIGURE 17-6 Windows Disk Defragmenter

Improved Formats

FAT16 continues to soldier on to this day. In fact, all versions of Windows, including Windows 2000, completely support FAT16 drives. However, two new format types, called FAT32 and NTFS, are the dominant types used with Windows 9x and Windows 2000, respectively. Both offer many advantages over FAT16, including more efficient use of disk space and, with NTFS, better security. In addition, Windows 95 introduced long filenames for FAT partitions.

Long Filenames   Before Windows 95, FAT16 forced us to limit filenames to eight letters/numbers (the *filename*), followed by a period, and then three more letters/numbers (the *extension*). Windows 95 broke free of this 8.3 format by using unused space in folders to store long filenames of up to 255 characters. This is not some new file format: long filenames can use simple FAT16-formatted partitions. The power of long filenames lies with Windows, not FAT16.

FAT32   Later versions of Windows 9x and 2000 can use an improved FAT that has 32 rather than 16 bits to address the hard drive clusters. The appropriately named FAT32 has some advantages over FAT16. First, the vast numbers of entries for clusters makes FAT32 cluster sizes much smaller and thus much more efficient. Second, FAT32 has no limits on the number of root directory entries. FAT16 has a limit of 255 entries. Third, FAT32 stores two copies of the boot sector, so if one copy gets corrupted, you can still boot and repair. FAT16, as you might suspect, only has one boot sector. If it goes, life is bad for the drive.

> **Exam Tip**
>
> Windows 98 and Windows 2000 support FAT32 right out of the box. With Windows 95, however, only OSR 2 supports FAT32.

NTFS   Windows 2000 and its predecessor, Windows NT, use the vastly more powerful, more robust and flexible NT file system (NTFS). The big discussion of NTFS is saved for Chapter 19 but, for now, let's say NTFS is virtually indestructible and provides ultrahigh security for files, on-the-fly file and folder compression, encryption, and a wealth of other features.

Windows 2000 supports FAT16, FAT32, and NTFS. Windows 9x systems capable of FAT32 cannot read NTFS, although they have FDISK programs that recognize them and let you delete them. (This is nice when you need to turn a Windows 2000 system back to Windows 98.) DOS and Windows 95 FAT16 systems see only FAT16 drives. If you run their FDISKs, they don't even see the FAT32 or NTFS partitions. FAT32 is completely compatible with all DOS and Windows applications, but you must never use any disk utilities unless they are designed for FAT32!

Formatting a Drive

Formatting a drive is a relatively simple process. In Windows 9x, you can format a drive from a command prompt, from My Computer, or from Windows Explorer. If you prefer the command prompt, start a DOS window and, at the command prompt, type **FORMAT** followed by the drive letter you want to format. Make sure you leave a *space* between the command and the drive letter. For example, to format your D: drive, type **FORMAT D:** at the command prompt and press ENTER. The screen shown in Figure 17-7 then appears. Because formatting a drive wipes out all the data on it, Windows asks if you're sure this is what you want to do. If you're sure, press Y to start the formatting process.

```
A:\>format C:/s

WARNING:   ALL DATA ON NON-REMOVABLE DISK
DRIVE C:   WILL BE LOST!
Proceed with Format  (Y/N)?y


Formatting  30709.65M
Format complete.
System transferred

Volume label (11 characters, ENTER for none)?

32,197,017,600 bytes total disk space
        262,144 bytes used by system
32,196,755,456 bytes available on disk

        491,520 bytes in each allocation unit.
        982,455 allocation units available on disk.

Volume Serial Number is 3166-11D9
```

FIGURE 17-7   DOS FORMAT screen

To format a drive from My Computer or Windows Explorer, alternate-click (right-click) on the icon of the drive you want to format and select Format. Windows 98 displays the screen shown in Figure 17-8. By the way, this also works in Windows 95 and Windows 2000, although the options vary a little in Windows 95 and a lot in Windows 2000. Remember, you already have a bootable system (how could you be in Windows if you didn't?), so you *do not* need to copy system files.

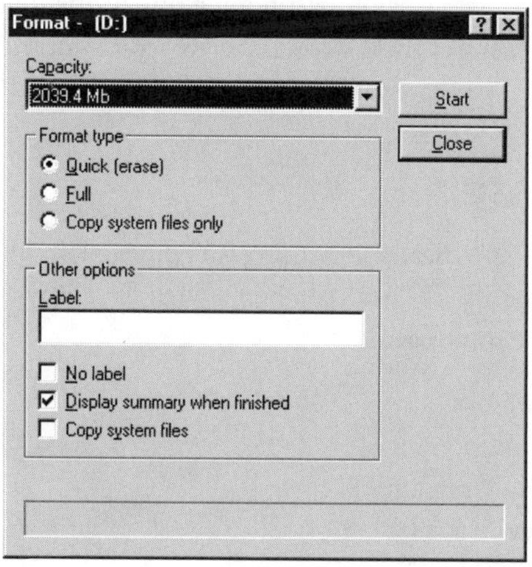

FIGURE 17-8   Windows 9*x* Format dialog box

A Final Warning   Please *be careful* using FDISK and FORMAT. Carelessly employed, these powerful tools can easily wipe out everything on a partition. Many organizations delete these files from working systems to keep untrained folks from accidentally erasing their hard drives! If you only want to *see* your partitions, use the System Information program. If you don't yet have Windows installed—often the case when you're building a new system—boot to a floppy disk, get to an A: prompt, and type **FDISK /STATUS**. This handy command tells FDISK to report the current partition information, as shown here:

```
C:\>fdisk/status
                         Fixed Disk Drive Status
   Disk   Drv   Mbytes   Free   Usage
    1             9590            100%
          C:      9590
    (1 MByte = 1048576 bytes)
C:\>
```

Objective 17.02
Troubleshooting Drive Installation Errors

Installing a drive and getting to the point where it can hold data requires four distinct steps: connectivity, CMOS, partitioning, and formatting. If you make a mistake at any point on any of these steps, the drive won't work. The beauty of this is, if you make an error, you can walk back through each step and check for problems.

Connectivity

A *connectivity* problem means something isn't plugged in right or something has managed to unplug itself. These problems virtually always show themselves at boot time. Here are some classics:

- Hard-drive error
- No fixed disks present
- HDD controller failure
- No boot device available
- Drive not found

If you plug an IDE drive cable in backwards, the computer simply won't boot. It's a famous error and everyone who has ever installed a hard drive has done it. Just reinsert the cable properly and turn the machine back on.

You can usually conquer connectivity errors by carefully inspecting the entire connection system, including electricity, and finding the mistake (welcome to the club). When you get an HDD controller failure, always remove the controller and reseat it if it's on an expansion card because they are prone to static build-up. I also keep an extra controller around to verify whether the controller is good. Cables can go bad, but this is rare unless the cable is obviously ripped or pinched. If your BIOS has an IDE autodetection function, use it! It won't detect a drive unless everything is installed correctly. It's a great, quick connectivity verifier. If you just installed the drive, also check the jumper settings. You can't have two masters or two slaves on a single controller. And, don't forget the 1 Drive or Standalone setting on some drives!

CMOS

Modern systems rarely get CMOS errors because the autodetection feature handles most drives. The errors that do occur generally fall into two groups: forgetting to run Autodetect and selecting the wrong sector translation in Autodetect. Two rules apply here: *always* run Autodetect and *always* select LBA.

Older systems could lose CMOS data for a variety of reasons, including static electricity buildup, insertion of an expansion card, or blinking too hard (okay, I'm kidding about the last one, but you get the idea). It's a trivial task to do a quick check of the CMOS with autodetection to verify the drive's geometry is correct. Here are some of the more common errors that might point to CMOS problems:

- CMOS configuration mismatch
- No boot device available
- Drive not found
- Missing operating system

If Autodetect fails to see the drive in question, remember, it's probably a connectivity problem. Grab a screwdriver and look inside the system!

Partitions

Partitioning errors generally fall into two groups: failing to partition at all and making the wrong size/type of partition. The first error invariably shows up when you try to access the non-partitioned drive. The operating system gives you a nice, clear Invalid Drive Specification error and you find you can't see the drive except in CMOS and FDISK. Simply add your partition of choice and go on.

The most common sizing issue comes from selecting less than the full remaining space when you make an extended partition. This problem usually begins with, "Hey! Why do I only have *X* megabytes of space? My drive is bigger than that!" Check the partitions in FDISK and redo them if necessary.

Format

Failing to format a drive makes the drive unable to hold data. Accessing the drive in Windows results in a "drive is not accessible" error. Accessing it from a C:\ prompt generates the famous Invalid Media Type error. Format the drive unless you're *certain* the drive has already been formatted. Review the information on corrupted data in Chapter 13 for other possible answers.

Objective 17.03   Windows 9*x* Installation Procedures

Installing or upgrading Windows 9*x* is usually a surprisingly painless, roughly hour-long process. The combination of PnP with an amazingly intelligent installation program, makes most installs a matter of typing in commands and trying to stay awake as files are copied and the system goes through a number of reboots. The A+ exam is extremely interested in your ability to install Windows 9*x* on a blank (unpartitioned) drive and to upgrade a Windows 95 system to Windows 98. This section covers both of these situations.

The upgrading or installing process always require three distinct operations:

- Preparing to upgrade or install
- Performing the upgrade or installation
- Debugging

This section assumes a standalone system without networking. Chapter 21 covers the networking installation steps and issues.

Preparing to Upgrade/Install

Most Windows upgrades and installs fail for one simple reason: the tech fails to perform a few basic checks before installing/upgrading Windows 9*x*. Follow these few steps—they work.

Minimum Requirements

Microsoft defines some fairly low-hardware requirements for both Windows 95 and Windows 98. To make things more confusing, different types of Microsoft documentation give different values. After some serious research and a few phone calls to some folks who ought to know at Microsoft, here are the official minimum hardware requirements for Windows 9x:

- 486DX/66 CPU with 24MB of RAM
- Hard drive space up to 400MB—average Windows install takes 200MB
- Video capable of 640 × 480 at 16 colors

Microsoft also recommends a mouse, a CD-ROM, and a sound card. Personally, I find these requirements to be laughably low. Even Microsoft admits this, but it is possible to run—maybe a better term would be "to walk"—Windows 9x with this hardware.

Hardware Compatibility

Assuming your system meets these requirements, we need to see how well Windows supports your hardware. Check the Microsoft hardware compatibility list at http://www.microsoft.com/hcl/default.asp for the definitive list. Don't panic if you don't see your device—many supported devices don't appear on that list. Check the floppies or CD-ROMs that come with your hardware for proper devices. Even when the HCL lists a piece of hardware, I still make a point to check the web site for later drivers. Resist the temptation to use a Windows 95 driver on a Windows 98 system, unless you simply have no choice.

Antivirus and Backup

If you're upgrading, take a moment to run an antivirus utility on the system. An active virus during install will, at the very least, infect every file you place on the drive. In most cases, it simply destroys the installation process, requiring a complete reinstall from the top.

Also, make a point to backup any data before upgrading. Windows installations do fail occasionally, in some cases, destroying everything on the drive.

Right CD-ROM Disc

Make sure you use the correct CD-ROM! Windows comes in both Upgrade and Full versions. Some systems require a special OEM version made just for that system, particularly laptops. Don't bother trying to use an upgrade version on a blank drive unless you also have a full earlier version of Windows.

FAT16 or FAT32?

You need to decide ahead of time what type of partition you want to use. While you almost always pick FAT32 for both clean installs and upgrades, three situations exist that might make you want to keep at least one FAT16 partition. First, consider if you might want to boot to the previous version of MS-DOS to support a DOS program that won't run in Windows, even in a DOS box. Second, you might have a version of Windows 95 that simply doesn't support FAT32. Third, you might want to set up some wild multiboot functions. But, in almost all cases, you'll choose to use FAT32.

Installing vs. Upgrading

The only real difference between installing and upgrading takes place at the beginning. In a scenario where you upgrade from Windows 95 to Windows 98, you already have an operating system and a number of nicely installed applications that you'd prefer not to reinstall. In a clean install, you have a blank, unpartitioned drive with nothing on it. This means a clean install requires a few extra steps because you must partition and format the drive before you can begin to install Windows 9x. To do a clean install, boot to the Startup disk and run FDISK to partition as you would like (here's your big chance to make a D: drive to store backups!), and then format the C: drive.

Many techs are aware of the CVT.EXE (used at a command prompt) or the CVT32.EXE (in Windows, select Programs | Accessories | System Tools | Drive Converter) utility that comes with Windows 98. These tools enable you to convert a FAT16 drive to FAT32 without losing data. With such handy conversion tools, why bother worrying about using FAT16 or FAT32? Well, don't forget the 2GB partition size limitation of FAT16! A brand new 30GB drive will need a lot of drive letters. Also, the convert tools have been known to fail disastrously on rare occasions. Better to play it safe and decide ahead of time!

The Install/Upgrade Process

Once the blank drive is formatted, the install and upgrade processes become virtually identical. If you're upgrading, just boot normally into Windows 95 and toss in the upgrade Windows 98 disk to see the upgrade prompt that tells you an older version of Windows is running currently on the computer and wants to know if you want to upgrade.

If you're doing a clean install, run the SETUP.EXE program on the CD-ROM. If the Setup software doesn't automatically show you a prompt, manually start the SETUP.EXE program from the CD-ROM. Be sure your Setup disk supports the CD-ROM or you won't get a CD-ROM drive letter!

A common installation trick is to copy the contents of the \WIN9*x* folder from the CD-ROM to a folder on your hard drive. Copying the installation files to your hard drive does two things. First, it makes the installation of Windows 9*x* faster because CD-ROMs are slow. Second, Windows 9*x* is notorious for needing the original CD-ROM disc virtually every time you make a change to the system's configuration. Windows remembers where it was installed from and prompts for you to insert the Windows Installation CD-ROM disc. If you put the files in a folder on a local drive, Windows remembers that and immediately goes straight to those files, saving you the hassle of trying to find the Install CD-ROM disc.

DOS Part

Both Windows 95 and 98 clean installs always begin with a DOS-level install process. This performs a quick scandisk, and a quick check for video and mouse, and then loads a few critical files needed for installation, usually then initiating the first of many reboots.

Graphical Install

The first part of a clean install consists of the Install Setup Wizard. This wizard begins by installing a second set of critical installation files. It then uses these files to:

Verify Disk Space   Windows needs to make sure enough space exists to install all temporary installation files, as well as the minimum amount of disk space needed for the actual operating system.

Prompt for Component Options   Windows 9*x* prompts for you to install with options that look like Figure 17-9.

For most users, a Typical installation is the safest bet. Once they become familiar with the many options of the Windows 9x install, however, most folks prefer to use the Custom option. The Portable and Compact options are rarely used because they skip too many features most users want.

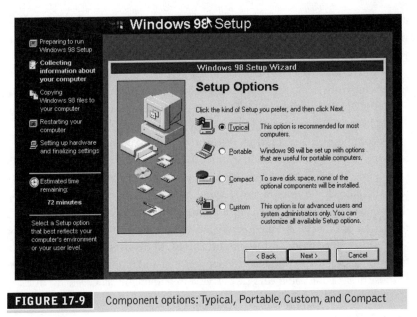

FIGURE 17-9   Component options: Typical, Portable, Custom, and Compact

Never worry about this screen. You can always add or remove components after Windows installs by using the Add/Remove Software feature in the Control Panel.

Prompt for Product Key   Microsoft makes money by selling Windows, not by giving it away. Thus, you need to install the product key, invariably located on the CD-ROM disc container. My smart techs learn the hard way that these covers tend to disappear when you need them most and they write the product code directly on the CD itself.

Windows 95 used to wait until near the end of the install process to ask for the product key, driving techs crazy when they realized they spent 20 minutes installing to discover their key was missing. Windows 98 and 2000 both are kind enough to ask for the key early on in the process, saving considerable inconvenience when you're juggling 23 different CDs, all in the wrong cases, trying to punch in the correct product key.

Prompt for Installation Directory   Clean installs always prompt for an installation directory, recommending C:\WINDOWS. Use this default unless you're compelled not to do so. When upgrading from Windows 95 to Windows 98, you must use the same folder that contains the Windows 95 files or Windows 98 simply performs a clean install. This leaves you with a useless copy of Windows 95 on your system and requires you to reinstall all your applications.

Prompt for Startup Disk   You should already have a Startup disk, but you can make another one now, if you like. If you choose not to make a Startup disk, simply click Cancel when given the opportunity.

Network Options   The Windows 9x Installation Wizard is kind of brainless here because it always prompts for networking information, even if it doesn't detect a network card. Because our current installation example assumes a stand-alone system, this discussion is saved for Chapter 21.

Save System Files   When upgrading from Windows 95 to Windows 98, you're given the opportunity to save the Windows 95 system files. If you save these files, you can uninstall Windows 98 from the Control Panel. Go to the Windows Setup tab in the Add/Remove Programs applet.

The Big Copy

No matter what your version of Windows, you always get to the point where Windows begins to install itself on the system. I call this the *Big Copy* and use this time to catch up on my reading, eat a sandwich, or count ceiling tiles.

Hardware Detection

The point where the hardware detection phase begins varies between Windows 95 and Windows 98. They both work the same way, but Windows 98 is a bit more automated. Windows follows the classic PnP search methodology. Windows first tries to find legacy devices (Windows 95 *cheats* by asking you if you have a sound card or a network card), and then kicks in the PnP hardware detection functions, searching for and configuring the detectable hardware on the system. In a completely PnP environment, you usually just sit and watch the installation process. As Windows detects devices, it loads the appropriate device drivers if it has them. If not, it prompts you for a driver disk. This process is identical to the process described earlier of installing a device into an existing system.

Making the System Operational

Most installations go flawlessly (if you've done your homework properly, of course!), but when things go wrong, you need to know what to do. The A+ OS Technologies exam tests your knowledge of error messages, recovery from a failed installation, log files, and the Startup menu. Let's take a look.

Install Problems

The term "install problem" is rather deceptive. The install process itself almost never fails. Usually, something else fails during the install process that makes us points at some intangible problem called an *install failure*. Here are some typical installation problems and how to correct them.

DOS Level Errors

If I'm going to have an install problem, this is the place to get one. It's always better to have the error right off the bat, as opposed to when the installation is nearly complete. DOS errors only take place during clean installs and usually point to one of the following:

- *No boot device present* when booting off the Startup disk. Either the Startup disk is bad or the CMOS isn't set to look to the floppy disk first.
- *Windows has detected that drive C does not* contain *a valid FAT partition.* You forgot to partition the hard drive or you're trying to install on a partition type that Windows doesn't understand.
- *Windows Setup requires XXXX amount of* available *drive space ...* You forgot to format the C: drive or there's a bunch of stuff on the drive already.
- *MSCDEX error No CD-ROM detected.* The CD-ROM settings are messed up. Check the CONFIG.SYS and AUTOEXEC.BAT settings.
- *Not ready error* on CD-ROM. You probably need to give the CD-ROM a moment to catch up. Press R for retry a few times. You might also have a damaged Install CD or the CD-ROM might be too slow for the system.

Errors During Install

Once the install passes the DOS level and moves into the graphical portion, a whole new crop of problems can arise. These two are by far the most common:

Can't Read CAB Files   Probably the most common of all installation errors. Check the CD for scratches. Try copying all the files from the \WIN9x drive in to a directory on your hard drive and running Setup from there. Finally, try another CD-ROM drive.

This System Already Has an Operating System ...   A common error when upgrading from 95 to 98. You're probably trying to use a full-install CD for an upgrade. There's a perfectly legal way around this:

1. Exit Setup.
2. Type **C:**.
3. Type **CD\SYSTEM**.
4. Type **ren setupx.dll setupx.ol1**.
5. Type **ren setupx.w95 setupx.ol2**.
6. Start Setup again.

Lockups During Install

Lockups during install vary considerably, depending on whether you install Windows 95 or 98. In Windows 95, lockups are fairly common. In Windows 98, they're rare.

Safe Recovery

Most system lockups occur when Windows queries the hardware. If a system locks up once during an install, turn off the computer. Literally unplug the system. Do not press ctrl-alt-del. Do not press the Reset button on the case. Turn the system back on with the bootable floppy still inserted, and then rerun the Setup program. Windows will see the partial installation and prompt you for a Safe Recovery mode. This mode ignores all but the most critical hardware to complete the installation.

CD-ROM/Hard Drive

Bad CD-ROM discs, CD-ROM drives, or hard drives can cause lockups. Check and replace the drive, if necessary.

Log Files

Windows 95 generates a number of special text files called *log* files that track the progress of certain processes. While Windows makes a number of different log files for different purposes, three files, all located in the root directory of your C: drive, are of the most interest to us:

- SETUPLOG.TXT tracks the complete installation process, logging the success or failure of file copying, registry updates, reboots, and so forth.
- DETLOG.TXT is created during the hardware detection process. It tracks the detection, query, and installation of all devices.
- BOOTLOG.TXT tracks the boot process, logging as each device driver and program loads.

Honestly, the chances of you ever actually reading a log file, understanding it, and then getting something fixed as a result of that understanding, is pretty darn small. What makes log files handy is when you call Microsoft or a hardware manufacturer. They *love* to read these files and have people who understand them. Don't worry about trying to understand log files for either the A+ exam or for real life—just make sure you know the names of the log files and their location. Leave the details to the *Ubergeeks*.

Exam Tip

Know the names of each log file and what would be included in each file. Also know what utility will open a log file.

No Install Is Perfect

Even when the installation seems smooth, issues may slowly surface, especially in the case of upgrades. Be prepared to reinstall applications or deal with new functions absent in the previous operating system. If things really fall apart, you can always go back to the previous operating system.

Windows Startup Menu

The Windows Startup menu, especially the Safe mode option, is an important tool for diagnosing problems that occur during the boot process.

The Startup Menu (F8)

By pressing the F8 key during the Windows 9x boot process, you can access the Startup menu. Some systems turn off the *Starting Windows 9x* text. In that case, start pressing F8 at boot up. Don't hold down the key—press it about once a second until the boot menu appears. If you miss, restart the system and try again.

If you want to examine the Startup menu, be sure to press the DOWN ARROW a few times. Otherwise, the timer in the lower-right hand corner of the screen will boot the default option (usually Normal).

Here's a list of the common boot menu options for Windows 9x.

- **Normal**   This boots Windows normally.
- **Logged (\BOOTLOG.TXT)**   This logs the boot process in a file called BOOTLOG.TXT.
- **Safe mode**   This boots Windows into Safe mode. You can boot directly into Safe mode by pressing the F5 key at boot. Safe mode boots the system using the default settings for Windows 9x and is a great troubleshooting tool.
- **Safe mode with network support**   This boots Safe mode, but still loads the network drivers, so you can access the network. This option only appears on networked systems—that does not include Dial-up Networking!
- **Step-by-step confirmation**   Similar to the old DOS F8 step-by-step, this includes a number of auto-loading features that are normally invisible.
- **Command prompt only**   This processes all startup files, but does not start the GUI. You can type WIN from the C: prompt to start the GUI, if desired.
- **Safe mode command prompt only**   This skips all startup files to get to a C: prompt. You must reboot to start Windows.
- **Previous version of MS-DOS**   If you installed Windows over a true DOS system, Windows keeps the original DOS boot files in the root directory with the extension DOS and shows this option. You can boot to them. Don't use this option if you don't have a previous version of DOS or if the version of Windows uses FAT32.

Take the time to make sure you can access the boot menu. Try all the options except for Previous Version of MS-DOS. I especially suggest using the step-by-step option. You can see a number of interesting options there!

Exam Tip

Know the difference between F5 and F8 keys. Know when to use them. Each key produces different results when pressed at boot.

Objective 17.05   Windows Boot Problems

Many Windows troubleshooting issues deal with boot problems. In most cases, these are fairly simply fixes. A few of the classics follow.

No Operating System Found   This points to a corrupted or missing IO.SYS or MSDOS.SYS. Pop in the Startup disk and use the SYS program to put back the missing file. From the A: prompt, type **SYS C:**.

This automatically restores the IO.SYS, MSDOS.SYS, and COMMAND.COM files. If you edited the MSDOS.SYS file, you need to restore any edits.

Bad or Missing COMMAND.COM   An easy one to fix. Use your Startup disk to copy the COMMAND.COM file back on to the C:\ drive.

Error in CONFIG.SYS (line XX)   This one rarely happens unless you've been working in CONFIG.SYS file or installing some older device that tossed something into CONFIG.SYS. Edit the CONFIG.SYS file and count the line numbers until you get to the one in question. Look for typos. Because most Windows systems pretty much ignore the CONFIG.SYS file anyway, put a semicolon (;) at the beginning of the line. If everything runs fine for a few days, go back in and remove the line completely.

Device Referenced in SYSTEM.INI Not Found   This is exactly the same scenario as described before for CONFIG.SYS, except this usually shows the device name in question. See Chapter 18 for details on SYSTEM.INI and WIN.INI.

HIMEM.SYS Not Loaded or Missing or Corrupt HIMEM.SYS
Windows must load the HIMEM.SYS file at each boot. Because Windows does this automatically, this is rarely an issue. This error tends to result from a hard drive that needs some serious ScanDisk action! As a quick fix, boot off the Startup disk and add this line to the CONFIG.SYS file using EDIT

```
DEVICE=C:\HIMEM.SYS
```

and then copy the HIMEM.SYS file from the Startup disk to C:\. Now, boot normally and check that hard drive!

Won't Boot to GUI   Ever booted a copy of Windows just to get stuck at the pretty Windows startup screen? Failure to boot into the GUI can have many causes. The first thing you should try is to boot into Safe mode and check Device Manager and the configuration files (CONFIG.SYS, SYSTEM.INI, and the rest). If you don't find the culprit, try a step-by-step configuration from the Startup menu. This usually gives you a good sense as to which of the following areas should be checked next.

You might need to restore the previous registry copy. Use whatever tool you have to restore your copy of the registry. If you don't have one, try replacing SYSTEM.DAT and USER.DAT with SYSTEM.DA0 and the USER.DA0. All these files are hidden and read-only, so use the ATTRIB command from the Startup disk to turn off the attributes. It would look something like this:

```
ATTRIB -r -s -h c:\WINDOWS\SYSTEM\*.dat
COPY c:\WINDOWS\SYSTEM\*.da0 C:\WINDOWS\SYSTEM\*.dat
```

For Windows 98, boot to the Startup disk and run the Windows Registry Checker tool. From the A: prompt, type **C:\WINDOWS\COMMAND\ SCANREG /fix**. Try booting again. If the registry was the problem, you should now boot normally.

Resource conflicts can sometimes prevent the GUI from booting. A quick boot to Safe mode and a check of the Device Manager should confirm this. Fix resource conflicts as described previously.

A bad driver can cause problems. For this, use the Automatic Skip Driver (ASD) tool in Safe mode. You can find it under the Tools menu in the System Information tool, although I usually just do a Run… and type in ASD. The ASD looks over your LOG files and prevents any drivers that failed previously from loading at the next boot. If this works, check for a driver update or remove the offending device.

✔ **Objective 17.01: Partitioning and Formatting Hard Drives**   The first step in a Windows 9x installation is partitioning and formatting the hard drive. Know the types and functions of partitions, how to format a drive, which versions of Windows can use which FATs, and how to use tools like FDISK and Disk Defragmenter.

✔ **Objective 17.02: Troubleshooting Drive Installation Errors**   Installing a drive and getting to the point where it can hold data requires four distinct steps: connectivity, CMOS, partitioning, and formatting. Know how to partition and format a drive properly, how to recognize and troubleshoot a connectivity problem, and how to run Autodetect and select LBA sector translation.

✔ **Objective 17.03: Windows 9*x* Installation Procedures**   You must know all the proper steps to install Windows 9*x* on a blank (unpartitioned) drive and how to upgrade a Windows 95 system to Windows 98. Know how and why to check the Microsoft hardware compatibility list.

✔ **Objective 17.04: Making the System Operational**   No install is perfect. Know the typical installation problems and how to correct them. Know the features of the Startup menu, and know the difference between accessing the Startup menu and Safe mode.

✔ **Objective 17.05: Windows Boot Problems**   Even after you troubleshoot your installation, your job as a PC tech might not be over. Know the classic Windows boot problems and how to solve them.

REVIEW QUESTIONS

1. Tammy loaned her laptop to Fay. When Fay returned it, Tammy booted the laptop and got a text error that said *No operating system present*. She called Fay, who said the machine worked perfectly only one hour ago as she was copying her Word documents in preparation of returning the laptop. What should Tammy suspect first?

   A. Fay left a non-bootable floppy disk in the floppy drive
   B. Fay must have deleted the \WINDOWS directory accidentally
   C. Fay accidentally cleared the CMOS
   D. Fay might have introduced a virus into the laptop

2. Which file(s) does the Windows Startup disk needs to access a CD-ROM?

   A. IO.SYS
   B. AUTOEXEC.BAT
   C. COMMAND.COM
   D. CONFIG.SYS

3. In Windows 9*x*, what is the way to create a Startup disk?

   A. Start | Run, and from the command entry type **FORMAT A: /S**

B. Start | Programs | MS-DOS prompt, and, from the command line, type
FORMAT A: /S

C. Start | Settings | Control Panel; double-click the Add/Remove Programs
applet, and then go to the Startup Disk tab

D. Start | Settings, double-click the Add/Remove Programs applet, and then
go to the Startup Disk tab

4. Which key do you press at the Starting Windows 95 prompt to boot directly
to Safe mode?

A. F1

B. F4

C. F5

D. F8

5. During Windows 9x installation, which of these log files tracks the complete
installation process?

A. SETUPLOG.TXT

B. DETLOG.TXT

C. BOOTLOG.TXT

D. WINLOG.TXT

6. Which of the following is not a Windows 9x upgrade/installation error?

A. No boot device present

B. Can't read CAB files

C. MSCDEX error No CD-ROM detected

D. Memory not detected

7. Which of the following best describes Windows 9x Safe mode?

A. Safe mode is a troubleshooting tool that boots the system using the
default settings for Windows 9x

B. Safe mode enables the PnP options to load safely

C. Safe mode enables antivirus applications to safely check the system

D. Safe mode limits system changes to those specified as safe

8. What is the most likely cause of a *No operating system found* error at bootup?

A. A corrupted WIN.INI file

B. A corrupted or missing IO.SYS or MSDOS.SYS file

C. A corrupted registry key

D. A corrupted or missing SYSTEM.INI file

9. Which of the following is *not* a function performed by the Install Setup Wizard?

 A. Prompt for Installation Directory
 B. Prompt for Component Options
 C. Verify Disk Space
 D. Verify Windows Version

10. What do you type at the A: prompt to run the Windows Registry Checker tool in Windows 98 after booting to the Startup disk?

 A. C:\WINDOWS\COMMAND\CHECKREG /REPAIR
 B. C:\WINDOWS\COMMAND\SCANREG /FIX
 C. C:\WINDOWS\SYSTEM\REGSCAN /REPAIR
 D. C:\WINDOWS\SYSTEM\REGCHECK /FIX

REVIEW ANSWERS

1. **A** Fay probably left a non-bootable floppy disk in the floppy drive.

2. **A** **C** The Windows Startup Disk needs the IO.SYS and COMMAND. COM files to access a CD-ROM.

3. **C** To create a Startup disk in Windows 9x, select Start | Settings | Control Panel. Double-click the Add/Remove Programs applet, and then go to the Startup Disk tab. Running a FORMAT A: /S command on a floppy disk will certainly create a bootable floppy, but not an official Windows Startup disk.

4. **C** Press the F5 key at the Starting Windows 95 prompt to boot directly to Safe mode.

5. **A** During Windows 9x installation, SETUPLOG.TXT tracks the complete installation process.

6. **D** Memory not detected is not a Windows 9x upgrade/installation error.

7. **A** Safe mode is a troubleshooting tool that boots the system using the default settings for Windows 9x.

8. **B** The most likely cause of a *No operating system found* error at bootup is a corrupted or missing IO.SYS or MSDOS.SYS file.

9. **D** Verify Windows Version is not a function performed by the Install Setup Wizard.

10. **B** Type C:\WINDOWS\COMMAND\SCANREG /FIX at the A: prompt to run the Windows Registry Checker tool in Windows 98.

Optimizing and Maintaining Windows 9x

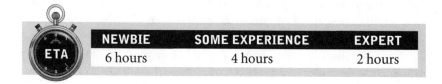

	NEWBIE	SOME EXPERIENCE	EXPERT
ETA	6 hours	4 hours	2 hours

Every A+ certified technician worth his or her salt knows how to optimize and maintain Windows 9*x* PCs. The tools of the trade come in a variety of packages, from intuitive graphical interfaces to the hard school of the command line, and you need to know them all. This chapter first outlines the structure and core files that make up Windows, and then launches into specific discussion of tools and procedures to keep those PCs purring happily for your clients.

As you know, Windows has two parts—the command line environment that differs little from that of DOS, and the graphical user interface (GUI) that provides a more intuitive, easy-to-use experience. While regular Windows users rarely see the DOS side of Windows 9*x*, technicians spend an inordinate amount of time staring at a C: prompt in Windows. Make sure you are comfortable working with a command prompt because I won't cover in this chapter basic command prompt functions, such as creating folders (we need to stop calling them directories now), moving around among folders, and performing basic file manipulations. Refer back to Chapter 16 for a refresher if necessary. In the meantime, let's look at the Windows system files.

Objective 18.01   Windows 9*x* System Files

Windows 9*x* has many holdover system files and system configuration files from the DOS and Windows 3.*x* days, and you need to know them all to some degree. IO.SYS, MSDOS.SYS, and COMMAND.COM still live in Windows 9*x*, albeit somewhat changed, and every Windows 9*x* system still can make use of both CONFIG.SYS and AUTOEXEC.BAT. Windows 9*x* uses three key system files not yet discussed in depth that you must know: IO.SYS, WIN.INI, and SYSTEM.INI. Further, you must have a solid understanding of the Windows Registry. The *Registry* is composed of two binary files—SYSTEM.DAT and USER.DAT—that reside in the \WINDOWS folder. The \WINDOWS folder contains many important resources for a PC tech.

IO.SYS

One of the many jobs of IO.SYS is to check to see if the F8 key (left CTRL key in Windows 98) has been pressed as Windows loads. If it has, the Windows Startup menu loads.

The Windows Startup menu provides a method for technicians to perform a number of boot methods on-the-fly to allow for many different troubleshooting scenarios. Be warned that not all systems show the same boot options. Figure 18-1 shows a Startup menu from a typical Windows 98 system.

```
Microsoft Windows 98 Startup Menu
━━━━━━━━━━━━━━━━━━━━━━━━━━━━━━━━━━

   1. Normal
   2. Logged (\BOOTLOG.TXT)
   3. Safe mode
   4. Step-by-step confirmation
   5. Command prompt only
   6. Safe mode command prompt only

Enter a choice: 1




F5=Safe mode  Shift+F5=Command prompt  Shift+F8=Step-by-Step confirmation [N]
```

FIGURE 18-1   F8 Windows 98 Startup menu

WIN.INI

Although not needed by Windows 9x/2000, both operating systems can incorporate a WIN.INI file into their boot routines. *WIN.INI* defined all the personalization of Windows 3.x, such as fonts, screen savers, and display colors, and how resources interacted with applications. WIN.INI was also the dumping ground for settings that did not have a home anywhere else. Finally, WIN.INI functioned like an AUTOEXEC.BAT, used to launch many programs automatically. Because Windows 9x/2000 act on settings in a WIN.INI file, you sometimes find sneaky programs or buggy features residing in here. Use the System Configuration Editor or Notepad to edit the WIN.INI file. To access the former, go to Start | Run, type **SYSEDIT** and click OK.

Exam Tip
Know how to edit SYSTEM.INI and WIN.INI on a Windows 9x and 2000 system. Know why they exist and when they're needed!

SYSTEM.INI

SYSTEM.INI was the CONFIG.SYS of Windows 3.x. The SYSTEM.INI file determined all the resources initialized, and defined a number of global settings for resource allocation. We often edited this file on Windows 3.x systems to tweak a large number of settings. And guess what? You still find SYSTEM.INI on all

Windows 9*x* and 2000 systems today. Keeping the SYSTEM.INI file allows for backward-compatibility with older Windows 3.*x* applications that still look for a SYSTEM.INI file to load or determine critical settings. All Windows 9*x* systems still require SYSTEM.INI, even though the settings are no longer critical. If you don't believe me, rename the SYSTEM.INI file to YODA.INI on any version of Windows 9*x* and reboot the system. You'll get this nasty error:

```
Cannot find SYSTEM.INI.
You need to run Windows Setup again to install this file
Press any key to continue...
```

You know what? On second thought, *don't* do this—at least not until you learn how to access the Windows 9*x* Startup menu! If, by any chance, you already did this, read ahead to see how to boot to the Windows Startup menu. Boot to *Safe mode command prompt only* to get to a C: prompt. Get into the WINDOWS directory and type **REN YODA.INI SYSTEM.INI** to put it back to normal. REN is the *rename* command.

Dealing with SYSTEM.INI and WIN.INI

Windows 9*x* and Windows 2000 systems rarely need to bother with these two files. This is because all the sections in SYSTEM.INI and WIN.INI are properly created when Windows is installed and should never be changed. However, two situations warrant an occasional peek at these two files. First, you occasionally see an error in Windows 9*x* systems at boot that looks like:

```
Cannot find a device file that may be needed to run Windows
or a Windows application.
The Windows Registry or SYSTEM.INI file refers to this device
file, but the device file no longer exists.
If you deleted this file on purpose, try uninstalling the
associated application using its uninstall or setup program.
If you still want to use the application associated with this device
file, try reinstalling that application to replace the missing file.
chimchim
Press a key to continue.
```

Notice the word "chimchim"? That's a line in the SYSTEM.INI file that probably needs correcting. Many applications and hardware install programs dump lines into the SYSTEM.INI, which are, in most cases, useless. To edit the

SYSTEM.INI file, use the handy System Configuration Editor program, as shown in Figure 18-2.

The [386Enh] section of SYSTEM.INI stores all the drivers for 386-Enhanced mode. Most of the problems associated with SYSTEM.INI on Windows 9x and 2000 systems can be attributed directly to drivers within this section. When I find these errors, I add a semicolon (;) to the beginning of the offending line (turning it into a comment that Windows will ignore on startup), and then reboot. These lines are rarely needed.

WIN.INI has two problem areas that can cause trouble on modern systems: LOAD= and RUN=. These lines automatically load programs when Windows starts, acting like a hidden Startup folder. If you find a program keeps running, but it isn't in the Startup folder, check here to see if one of these lines is starting the program.

The Windows 9x Registry

The *Registry* stores nearly everything about your PC, including information on all the hardware in the PC, network information, user preferences, file types, and virtually anything else you might run into with Windows 9x. Think of the Registry as the central repository of all configuration information for your system. Almost any form of configuration done to a Windows 9x system involves editing the Registry. The Registry is composed of two binary files: SYSTEM.DAT and USER.DAT. These files reside in the \WINDOWS directory. Fortunately, you rarely have to access these massive files directly, but instead can rely on an entire set of relatively user-friendly applications—the Control Panel applets—to edit the Registry for you.

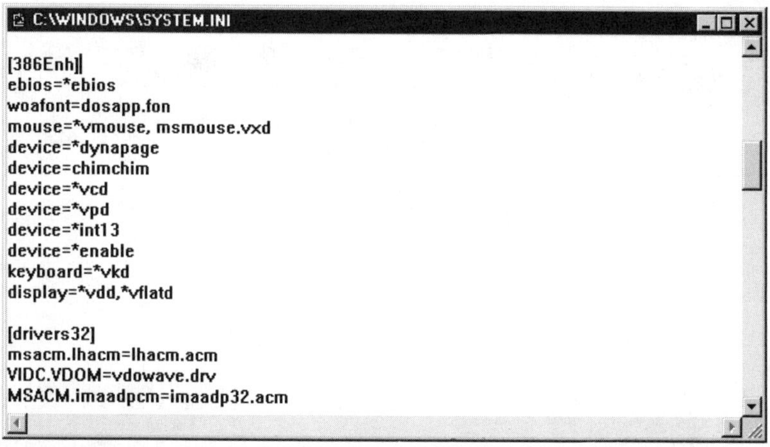

```
C:\WINDOWS\SYSTEM.INI                                    _ □ ×

[386Enh]
ebios=*ebios
woafont=dosapp.fon
mouse=*vmouse, msmouse.vxd
device=*dynapage
device=chimchim
device=*vcd
device=*vpd
device=*int13
device=*enable
keyboard=*vkd
display=*vdd,*vflatd

[drivers32]
msacm.lhacm=lhacm.acm
VIDC.VDOM=vdowave.drv
MSACM.imaadpcm=imaadp32.acm
```

FIGURE 18-2 Editing the SYSTEM.INI file

Exam Tip

Know the files SYSTEM.DAT and USER.DAT. Also know that Windows 95/98 creates backups of these files named SYSTEM.DA0 and USER.DA0.

The main way to access the Registry is through the Control Panel, as shown in Figure 18-3. You can get to the Control Panel in several ways. Double-click the My Computer icon on your desktop and then double-click the Control Panel icon. Alternately, click Start | Settings | Control Panel. Notice all the *applets* in the Control Panel; they provide fairly intuitive interfaces whose only function is to help you update the Registry.

In Windows 9*x*, everything necessary to configure the system can be handled from the Control Panel, although occasionally you'll need to tweak some parameter that requires direct Registry access.

When you want to access the Registry directly, you must use the Registry Editor. To start the Registry Editor, click Start | Run, and then type **REGEDIT**. This

FIGURE 18-3   Windows 9*x* Control Panel

will start the Registry Editor. Remember, the Registry is a binary file! You cannot edit it with EDIT, Notepad, or any other text editor. You must use REGEDIT.

Registry Components

The Registry is organized in a tree structure similar to the folders in the PC. Once you open REGEDIT, you see six main subgroups or *keys*:

> HKEY_CLASSES_ROOT
> HKEY_CURRENT_USER
> HKEY_LOCAL_MACHINE
> HKEY_USERS
> HKEY_CURRENT_CONFIG
> HKEY_DYN_DATA

Try opening one of these keys and note that more subkeys are underneath them. A *subkey* also has other subkeys and/or values. Figure 18-4 shows an example of a subkey with some values. Notice that REGEDIT shows keys on the left and values on the right, just as Windows Explorer shows folders on the left and files on the right.

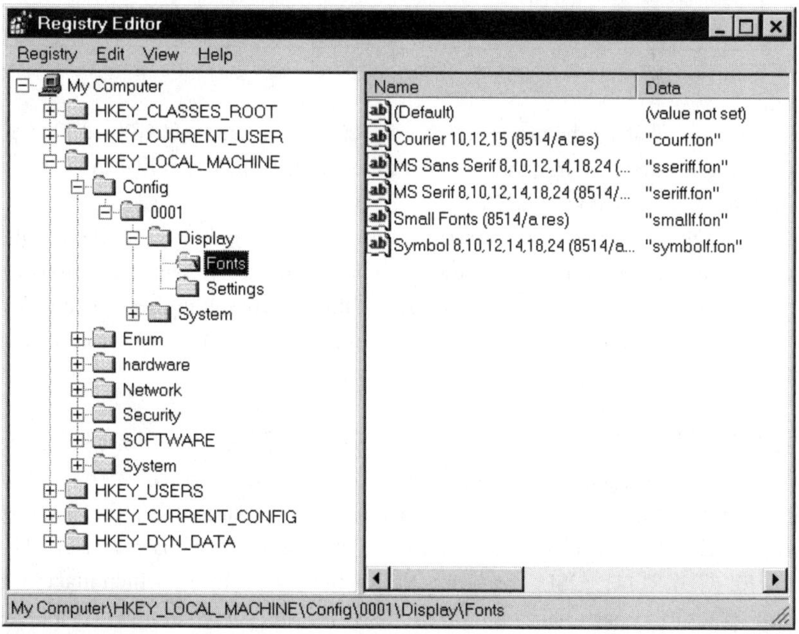

FIGURE 18-4   Typical Registry keys and values

The secret to understanding the Registry is first to understand the function of the six main keys. Each of these subgroups has a specific function, so let's look at them individually.

HKEY_CLASSES_ROOT   This key defines the standard class objects used by Windows 9x. A *class object* is a named group of functions. Pretty much everything that has to do with files on the system is defined by a class object.

For example, a Musical Instrument Digital Interface (MIDI) sound file is defined using two class objects. If you search the Registry for the .MID file extension, you'll find the first class object, which associates the *.mid* file extension with the name *midfile*, as shown here:

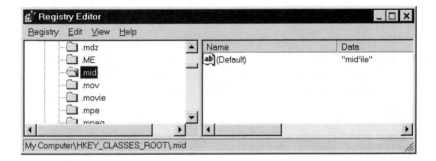

Ah, but what are the properties of *midfile*? That's what the HKEY_CLASSES_ROOT key is designed to handle. Search this section again for midfile and you can see what's associated with it.

This key tells the system everything it needs to know about a particular software item. The file associations are defined here, icons are shown, and options are displayed when an item is right-clicked. Although changing these settings via REGEDIT is possible, the normal way is to use the \View\Options menu from Windows Explorer.

HKEY_USERS AND HKEY_CURRENT_USER   Windows 9x can be configured to support more than one user on the same PC, storing personalized information such as colors, screen savers, and the contents of the desktop. HKEY_USERS stores all the personalization information for all users on a PC. The HKEY_CURRENT_USER key stores the current user settings, which makes it a good place to fix personalizations like fonts, icons, and colors on systems set up to support multiple users.

HKEY_LOCAL_MACHINE   This key contains all the data for a system's non-user-specific configurations. This includes every device in your PC, including devices you removed. For example, Figure 18-5 shows the description of a SCSI Zip drive. Remember HKEY_LOCAL _MACHINE when you have to configure or repair hardware in Windows 9*x*.

HKEY_CURRENT_CONFIG   If values in HKEY_LOCAL_MACHINE have more than one option, such as two different monitors, this defines which one is currently being used. Because most people have only one type of monitor and similar equipment, this area is almost never touched.

HKEY_DYN_DATA   This key is Registry data stored in RAM to speed system configuration. A snapshot of all hardware in use is stored here. It is updated at boot and when any changes are made in the system configuration file.

Exam Tip

Make sure you know the six main keys of the Registry and what system information would be stored in each.

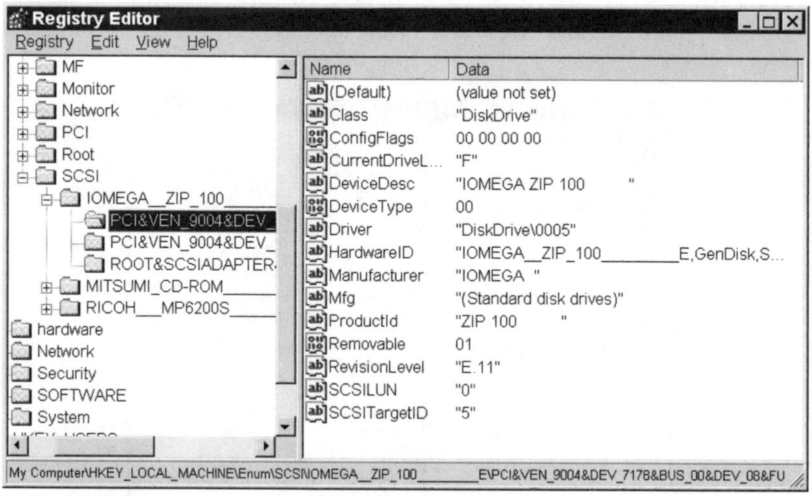

FIGURE 18-5   Registry information for a SCSI Zip drive

The Windows 9x Directory Structure

For this section, assume you installed Windows 98 on the C: drive in a folder called \WINDOWS—the default installation setting. Not all systems follow this: you can install Windows into any folder name. You can even install Windows into another drive letter! Don't get too excited, though. The Windows boot files, IO.SYS, MSDOS.SYS, and COMMAND.COM still must sit in the root folder of the C: drive, so even though it looks as if you installed Windows on the D: drive, you only installed most of Windows there. Windows still must boot from the C: drive, just like DOS.

Travel Advisory

Windows 2000 varies dramatically from Windows 95 and Windows 98 in both its boot method and directory structure. The discussion of the Windows 2000 directory structure is in Chapter 20. This section only covers Windows 9x!

The best way to see the directory structure is graphically, using the popular Windows Explorer, shown in Figure 18-6. Find Windows Explorer by clicking Start | Programs | Windows Explorer.

All Windows 9x systems share several folders in common, such as \Program Files for applications and \Windows for the operating system files. Techs most

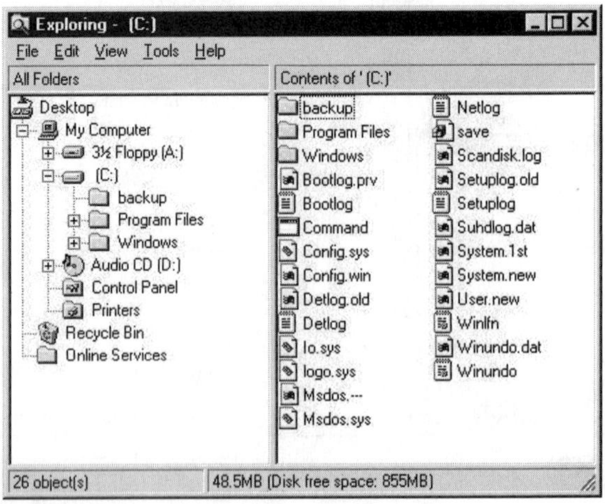

FIGURE 18-6 Windows Explorer

often need to access files or commands in the \Windows, \Windows\Command, and \Windows\System folders. You also need to know about the two temporary folders, \Windows\Temp and \Windows\Temporary Internet Files.

C:\Windows   This folder contains all the subfolders used by Windows. This is the general dumping ground for many different types of files. You can find a backup copy of COMMAND.COM here. Also, notice all the INI files! You'll see a number of programs, mostly simple ones like CALC.EXE (the Windows calculator program) and a few throwbacks from the Windows 3.*x* days, such as WINFILE.EXE (the ancient Windows File Manager). You might also see graphics files with the BMP extension and lots of TXT files. The latter files contain wonderful information that most Windows techs never even bother to read. I read every one of these files (double-click them and they open in Notepad) whenever I get a new Windows version. You should also read them! Take a moment to locate the Registry files, SYSTEM.DAT and USER.DAT. Finally, see if a file called WIN386.SWP resides in this folder. That's the Windows virtual memory swap file.

Travel Advisory

You need to tell Windows to show the file extensions, because that feature is disabled by default. In Explorer or My Computer, select View | Folder Options | View tab. Uncheck the Hide File Extensions Of Known File Types option and click the OK button. Microsoft keeps changing the location of this option with each new version of Windows, so you might need to look around to find it.

\Windows\Command   This folder stores all the DOS-equivalent command line programs. You'll see FDISK.EXE and FORMAT.COM, among others. Do you see EDIT.COM? Open that program—it looks just like the EDIT you run from a real DOS prompt! Close the EDIT program.

\Windows\System   This is the real heart of Windows 9*x*. Here you see the core operating system files for the graphical user interface: GDI.EXE, KRNL386.EXE, and USER.EXE. This folder also stores almost all the DLL files used by Windows. Many Windows 9*x* systems also have a \WINDOWS\SYSTEM32 folder. This folder stores DLLs and other support files for programs designed to run under both Windows 9*x* and Windows NT/2000 systems.

\Windows\Temp   This is the default folder for temporary files. Many applications create temporary files for one reason or another. Windows dictates they should always go in here, although you'll find that even some Microsoft programs ignore this rule. This folder fills up with temporary files and folders, requiring you to clear it out periodically.

\Windows\Temporary Internet Files   This folder stores your browser's cache files, mostly graphics from web pages you visited. This is a great place to snoop into what folks have been browsing, even better than the \Windows\History folder because users rarely think to clear this cache.

Other Tools to Use

Most techs rely on a few select tools to do the bulk of their jobs, such as Explorer and the Device Manager. A+ techs need a few extras thrown into their kits. Here are tools I use often:

- **Run**   Found above the Shut Down option on the Start button menu, the Run command enables you to execute commands without clicking an icon. Select Start | Run, and then type **REGEDIT**, for example. This executes the Registry Editor program that enables you to edit the Registry files. You can also use the Browse button in the Run command to find executable commands in Windows. Finally, if you know the path to an executable, you can simply type in the whole string; for example, C:\Windows\Program Files\MicrosoftOffice\Office\Winword.
- **MS-DOS Prompt**   As you no doubt recall from Chapter 16, you can access a command prompt and execute DOS commands while still in Windows. Go to Start | Programs | MS-DOS Prompt to create a virtual DOS window that can handle any DOS commands. This was included for backwards-compatibility with software that still required manual DOS commands to load, but it turns out to be very useful for techs.
- **System Configuration Editor**   This handy utility opens the SYSTEM.INI, WIN.INI, CONFIG.SYS, and AUTOEXEC.BAT files in separate windows while still in Windows. From here, you can edit each file and save any changes you make. Remember, any changes you make to an .INI file won't take effect until you reboot the computer. To access the System Configuration Editor, go to Start | Run, type **SYSEDIT**, and click OK.

- **System Configuration Utility**   This system utility included in Windows 98/ME enables you to include or exclude files that would be read by Windows during boot up. You can also edit other system configurations from the tabs provided in the utility. To access the System Configuration Utility, go to Start | Run, type MSCONFIG, and click OK. You can also access the tool by going to Start | Program Files | Accessories | System Tools | System Information. From the Tools menu, select System Configuration Utility.

Objective 18.02

Optimizing and Maintaining Windows 9x

If you were looking forward to getting the "Hotrodder's Guide to Windows 9x" in this section, you're in for a big disappointment. All versions of Windows 9x come pretty well optimized out of the box. You can't do much to make a Windows system run faster or better by tweaking the system. Sure, I read the same web sites and magazines you do, all touting some bizarre Registry setting that makes a Windows system better but, on the whole, I've found them hardly to be worth the effort and certainly way outside the scope of the A+ exams! Optimization these days means little more than checking the status of a few settings, which, in all probability, are already set properly by Windows, and making sure a Windows system takes advantage of the latest updates.

Maintenance, as you might expect, focuses on running ScanDisk, Disk Defragmenter, antivirus, System Cleanup, and System Backup utilities. When installed properly, all these work automatically, or nearly automatically, freeing you up for more interesting problems. Let's begin with the most important of all jobs: updating Windows with Service Packs and patches.

Service Packs, Patches, and Windows Update

Since its inception, Windows 9x has received a number of patches and upgrades to correct or improve many problems. You can update Windows in three different ways: patches, service packs, and new versions.

Patches are EXE files that you get from Microsoft to fix a specific problem. You run these programs and they do whatever they're supposed to do—update DLLs, reconfigure Registry settings, or whatever else is necessary to fix a particular problem. For example, you download a patch to fix a problem Windows had with extended partitions on LBA drives. Once the patch is downloaded, you double-click the EXE file to install the patch to your system. This patch installs a TSD virtual device that handles the partition issue. What's a TSD virtual device? Who cares? What matters is that these patches are required to keep Windows running properly. This doesn't mean that Windows 9*x* requires *every* patch produced. Ignore the patches that have nothing to do with what you do or fix a problem you don't have. There are roughly 200 patches for Windows 95 and about 10–20 for Windows 98. The majority of them are important. I'll show you how to determine what you need in a moment.

Sometimes a patch might not totally fix a particular problem or it might even cause other problems. In this case, you need a patch for the patch. Also, some patches must be installed before another patch can be used. This creates a unique situation where the patch order is quite important.

Travel Advisory

The order in which you install patches in Windows 9*x* can be crucial!

The first Windows 95 release was followed by a long series of patches over the next few months, fixing everything from password problems to memory leaks. Microsoft packaged these together into a single EXE file that would perform the patches simultaneously. This grouping of patches is called a *service pack*.

There are currently two Windows 95 service packs, predictably called Service Pack 1 and Service Pack 2, both of which you should install, assuming you have an original version of Windows 95. Microsoft eventually sold Windows 95 with Service Pack 1 already installed. This version was called OSR 1 (OEM service release 1). After OSR 1, more patches were created and so, roughly a year later, another set of patches was combined into OSR 2. There have been a number of patches since OSR 2.

As time goes by, Microsoft continues to redefine the names for patches. For example, a patch that fixes a security problem is now called a *security update*. Don't let terminology prevent you from getting what you need!

Windows 98 only had one major update, which Microsoft calls the *Customer Service Pack*. Windows 98 SE includes the Customer Service Pack, plus a number of other enhancements, such as new versions of Internet Explorer, Outlook Express, and other applications. A number of minor patches have also been released.

Okay, you're convinced of the need to update Windows. You now need to be able to answer the question, "What service packs/patches are on my system now and what should I install?" This is one area where the power of Windows 98 shines through. Just go to the Windows Update utility, as shown in Figure 18-7, and let Microsoft tell you!

> **Travel Assistance**
>
> To help determine what patches or upgrades you need, visit
> http://windowsupdate.microsoft.com/.

Windows Update Utility Tells All ...

The Windows Update utility queries your system and provides a list of the updates you require. Simply read about them and select the ones you want. Know ahead of time, though, that most of these updates are huge and, therefore, a pain to download using a 56K modem. If you prefer, Microsoft will gladly provide them on CD for a nominal fee.

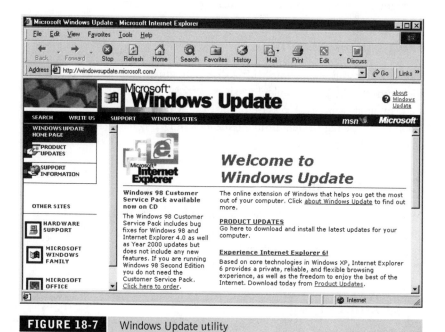

FIGURE 18-7   Windows Update utility

Identifying needed patches in Windows 95 is tougher. Running Microsoft's QFECHECK tool is the best way to determine which patches are currently loaded on your Windows 95 system.

QFECHECK can be downloaded from the Microsoft web site and generates a detailed list of all patches performed on your machine. Note that the listed patches can be expanded to show the details of the updated files. Remember, service packs and OSRs are compilations of patches. When you install a service pack or purchase a machine with an OSR, QFECHECK shows all the patches performed by that service pack or OSR.

Make sure you understand the needs of your system before you download that latest security update or service pack. When a new one comes out, let other folks test it out for a few weeks, and then do a search on the Internet to see if any problems exist with that update. Believe me, it's no fun to install a patch to improve a system only to find you've made it worse!

Drive Maintenance

Drive maintenance is one of the most boring, tedious, mind-numbing jobs a PC support person must perform. It's also the single most important way to ensure the long-term health of a PC system. The most important functions are disk defragmentation, scanning, and the occasional disk cleanup.

Defragmentation

Windows 9x and 2000 come with a disk defragmentation utility called Disk Defragmenter. Most techs still refer to it as Defrag—the name of the old DOS disk defragmentation utility. Access Defrag by clicking Programs | Accessories | System Tools | Disk Defragmenter. Although the look of Defrag has changed along with Windows, the job it does has not.

Disk Scanning

Windows 9x and 2000 also include a disk scanning program that checks for errors, just like the old ScanDisk utility used to do. As with the term "Defrag," you still refer to any tool of this type as ScanDisk. In Windows 9x, you access ScanDisk by clicking Programs | Accessories | System Tools | ScanDisk.

Exam Tip

Know the difference between defragging and disk scanning.

Disk Cleanup

As mentioned earlier, Windows puts a lot of junk files on the system. These junk files fall into six categories:

- Application temporary files that failed to delete
- Installation temporary files that failed to delete
- Internet Browser cache files
- Files in the Recycle Bin
- Internet cookie files
- Identical files in separate locations

In time, these files can take up a large percentage of your hard drive. As long as you have lots of extra drive space, these files matter little. But, as you begin to fill drives, you'll need more space. Windows 95 brought this problem to light and created an industry of third-party cleanup programs that enabled you to eliminate these files selectively. Not all programs choose the six file categories previously listed. Most delete fewer and some delete more. Either way, disk cleanup has become a critical part of drive maintenance.

Starting with Windows 98, Microsoft introduced a built-in disk cleanup program called, cleverly enough, Disk Cleanup (see Figure 18-8). Most third-party disk cleanup tools do a far better job than Disk Cleanup, but it's not a bad little program. Personally, I find that some of the better third-party utilities are more flexible. I want a tool, for example, that only deletes Internet cookies that haven't been accessed in the last 60 days. I hate typing in all my Amazon.com data over again!

Task Scheduling

Why bother running these programs manually when you can just tell the Windows Task Scheduler to run them at a certain time? Born from the same third-party utilities, handy task-scheduling utilities now come with Windows 98 and Windows 2000. I simply choose the program I want to run, when and how often I want it to run, and disk maintenance no longer becomes a part of my job description. To use the Task Scheduling Wizard, click Start | Accessories | System Tools | Scheduled Tasks. To schedule a task, click Add Scheduled Task and use the set up wizard.

Virtual Memory

All versions of Windows require the use of *virtual memory*—mapping a portion of the hard drive with memory addresses to mimic RAM. Windows creates a swap file that allows it to have more programs open on the screen than it could normally

FIGURE 18-8   Disk Cleanup utility

hold in real RAM. Unlike Windows 3.*x*, the swap file in Windows 9*x* is called WIN386.SWP, while the Windows 2000 swap file is called PAGEFILE.SYS. Windows sets the initial size of the swap file automatically based on the amount of free space on the C: drive. While this automatic setting works fairly well, you can optimize Windows' use of that swap file with a few judicious alterations. The Windows 9*x* swap file is configured in the Device Manager. Click the Virtual Memory button on the Performance tab to bring up the Virtual Memory dialog box, as shown in Figure 18-9.

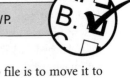

Exam Tip

Know the filename of the Windows 9*x* swap file: WIN386.SWP.

The most common reason to change the default swap file is to move it to some drive other than C:. Many systems tend to fill up the C: drive, so little or no room is left for the swap file. The swap file can use only the free space on a drive. When that space is filled, the swap file can't get any larger, resulting in nasty Not Enough Memory errors. The solution is to move the swap file to another drive.

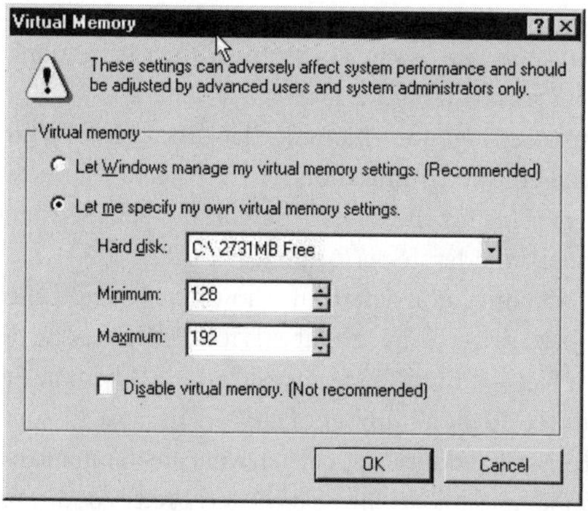

FIGURE 18-9   Configuring the Windows 9x swap file

To move the swap file in Windows 9x, click the *Let me specify my own virtual memory settings* radio button and select another drive. Notice the minimum and maximum swap-file sizes. Windows 9x sets the minimum to zero and the maximum to the size of the free space on the drive. Experimentation has shown that leaving these settings at these defaults creates enormous swap files, far larger than you really need. The current consensus is to reduce the swap-file size down to around two or three times the amount of RAM, meaning a system with 128MB of RAM should have its swap file set somewhere around 256MB to 384MB. Set both the minimum and maximum to the same number. Certain programs demand large swap files. If you use heavy-duty graphics programs like CorelDraw, you'll probably find two or three times your RAM isn't a big enough swap file. Gradually increase the size settings until the Not Enough Memory errors go away.

Occasionally a swap file will become corrupted and start causing lots of bizarre problems. These often manifest as lockups and KERNEL32.DLL errors. The fix is simple and painless. Navigate to the WIN386.SWP file, delete it, and reboot. Windows will create a new, squeaky clean swap file on the fly.

Disk Cache

The disk caching that comes with Windows installs automatically and is virtually maintenance-free. Windows 9x uses the powerful Vcache to replace the venerable SmartDrive used in DOS and Windows 3.x. The size of the disk cache is roughly one-fourth the total size of the RAM. Windows automatically sets the size of the disk cache holding pen based on settings given at setup. You can change these settings by accessing the File System button on the Performance tab in System Properties, as you can see in Figure 18-10.

There are two settings for changing the disk cache: Typical Role of This Machine and Read-Ahead Optimization. The Typical Role button determines how much RAM to set aside for the disk cache holding pen. Setting this to Network Server can produce a moderate performance boost.

Read-Ahead Optimization determines how much to read ahead when the system goes to the hard drive. Think about this for a minute. The disk cache doesn't think in terms of files—it thinks in terms of clusters. When the hard drive asks for data, it's actually asking for a number of clusters because files tend to span many clusters. So, if the system asks for one cluster, what are the chances it will come back in a few milliseconds and ask for the next cluster? Pretty good, it seems. So why not have the disk cache grab a few more clusters, on the assumption that the program will ask for them? This is called the *read-ahead*. You can adjust the read-ahead using a sliding bar. It should always be set to Full. This allows the disk cache to read ahead 64K worth of clusters, or two to four clusters ahead on most systems.

Resource Tracking Tools

Even though default Windows installations come well optimized, many Windows systems experience substantial system degradation over time. Good disk maintenance and basic optimization take you only so far on systems before they begin to suffer slowdowns. Most of the trouble stems from software bloat—too many programs

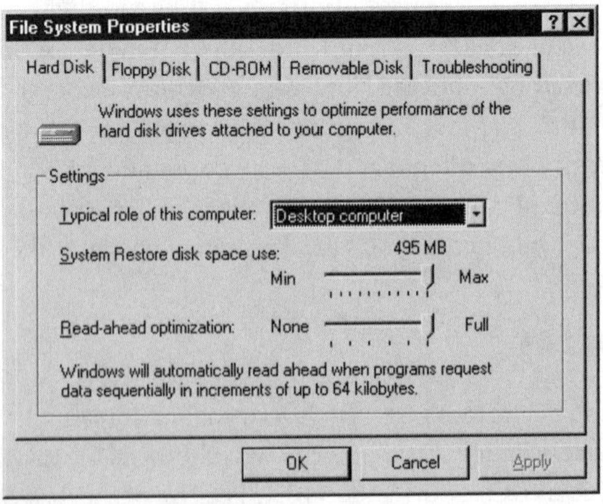

FIGURE 18-10   Change the disk cache settings

trying to run at the same time. Sure, you probably know that opening a number of applications at once eats memory, but the average system is also stuffed with background programs that consume memory. Before you inspect the culprits, you need to know how to use the necessary tools to watch for these problems. These tools will also come into play for other problems.

System Applet

One area many techs look toward for system resource information on a Windows 9x system is the System Resources percentage under the Performance tab, as shown in Figure 18-11, of the System applet in the Control Panel.

> **Exam Tip**
>
> Know how to navigate to the Performance tab of the System applet.

While the A+ Certification exam puts great stock in this setting, I find it too incomplete to be much help. Windows 9x uses a number of *heaps*—discrete areas of RAM—to store many types of general housekeeping information, such as which application uses a particular resource. To calculate this value, Windows

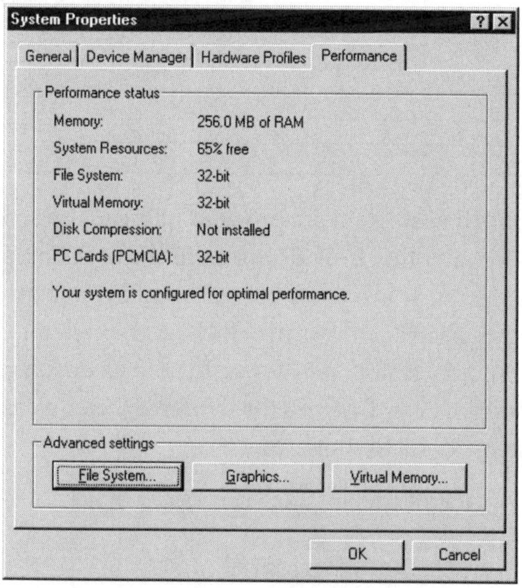

FIGURE 18-11 System Resources percentage

takes a snapshot of the heap usage of all resources at boot time. It then monitors all heaps, dividing the current usage by the boot usage, and shows the lowest value for the System Resource usage. Many systems can run down into the low 20s with absolutely no ill effect.

System Monitor and Resource Meter

My favorite tool for checking system problems is the *System Monitor,* which provides a detailed snapshot of a broad number of system processes. You can track free physical memory, CPU usage, network throughput—in fact, almost any process where you need to see what's happening on your PC, as shown here:

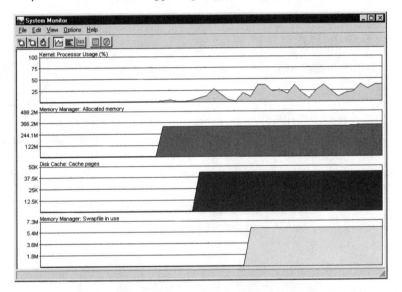

Heaps are limited in size and are prone to filling up on some systems. While an overfilled heap sometimes provides an error message box, such as "Warning! Your system is dangerously low on resources! Would you like to close application *xxxxxxx.exe*?", other heap overflows may lock up the system. One clear result of heap filling is substantial system slowdown. To keep an eye on your heaps, use the Resource Meter, shown here. To access the Resource Meter, go to Start | Programs | Accessories | System Tools | Resource Meter.

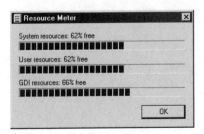

This handy tool does a much better job of showing you where problems lie. I always load this when I notice a system slowdown—it runs quite nicely from the system tray. As I load applications, I see what's eating heap space. If I don't see any substantial heap space usage, I usually head for the System Monitor to look for other problems.

Close Program

You access the Close Program dialog box by pressing CTRL-ALT-DEL. Also commonly called the Task Manager, the Close Program dialog box shows all running programs, including hidden ones, as you can see in Figure 18-12. I often use this tool in concert with the Resource Meter to close background programs that seem to defy closing anyplace else. Just remember *never* to close Explorer or Systray because these two programs must run to keep Windows running.

Autostarting Programs

It seems that every third application installed on a PC today uses some form of background program. In most cases, this is perfectly acceptable—I want my antivirus program to run constantly, invisibly inspecting the system for problems. Yet, when someone brings me a sluggish system, my first step is to boot normally, and then check the processor usage, the available physical memory, and the amount of the swap file in use, using the System Monitor. If the CPU constantly runs at near 100 percent, or if most the physical memory is in use, and worse yet, if any swap file is in use, I know I have way too many autostarting programs. Go

FIGURE 18-12   Close Program dialog box shows all running programs

to the system tray and say to yourself, "Which of these can I live without?" You'll be amazed how many of these programs provide simple *Do you want me to start at next boot?* options you can turn off. Don't go crazy here—keep the programs you need or want.

If you have Windows 98, fire up the System Information program, and then open the System Configuration Utility from the Tools menu. Go to the Startup tab and uncheck suspicious programs. *Don't* turn off the System Tray. While you're there, click the WIN.INI tab and open the Windows folder to make sure no programs are starting under Run= or Load=, as shown in Figure 18-13.

Finally, see what's running under AUTOEXEC.BAT. TSRs rarely have much effect on Windows memory, but it never hurts to check.

If you use Windows 95, locate the \WINDOWS\STARTMENU\PROGRAMS\ STARTUP folder to find the autostarting programs. Also, run SYSEDIT to check the SYSTEM.INI and WIN.INI files.

Control Panel

The Control Panel (refer back to Figure 18-3) enables you to handle most of the maintenance, upgrade, and configuration needs of Windows. This makes the Control Panel, naturally, one of the most important features of Windows for techs! Click Start | Settings | Control Panel to open the Control Panel.

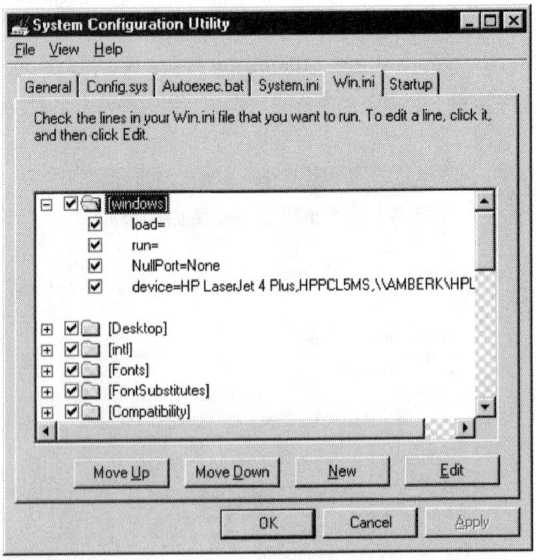

FIGURE 18-13   Check for programs loading in WIN.INI

A large number of programs, called *applets,* populate the Control Panel. The names and number of applets vary among versions of Windows and according to whether any installed programs added applets, but all versions of Windows share most of the same applets. A+ techs use every applet eventually, but a few jump out as the ones you access every day and should have completely mastered: Add New Hardware, Add/Remove Programs, Date/Time, Display, Internet Options, Network, Printers, and, especially important, System.

Travel Assistance

For detailed descriptions of every common Control Panel applet, check out the Tech Files at http://www.totalsem.com/techfiles.htm

---

Add New Hardware   The Add New Hardware applet provides a step-by-step process, or *wizard,* to enable you to install devices your PnP does not support. Use the Add New Hardware Wizard to install legacy devices or if the PnP has a problem, such as no driver or a resource conflict. In some versions of Windows, this wizard may start automatically if the PnP cannot find a valid INF file for the detected device.

Add/Remove Programs   This applet's original function was to assist in both adding and uninstalling applications, as shown in Figure 18-14. Every Windows install program now provides some level of uninstall function, however, making the install aspect rarely used. One aspect of the Add/Remove Programs applet that comes in handy is the capability to remove or modify components of installed applications, rather than simply removing the whole program. This applet also enables you to add/remove Windows components and create a Startup disk.

Date/Time   This sets the system date, time, and time zone. You can also set the date and time by double-clicking the clock on the taskbar or by accessing a command prompt and typing in the DATE and TIME commands.

Display   The Display applet handles almost all display functions. You can also access this applet by alternate-clicking any unused area on the Desktop and selecting Properties.

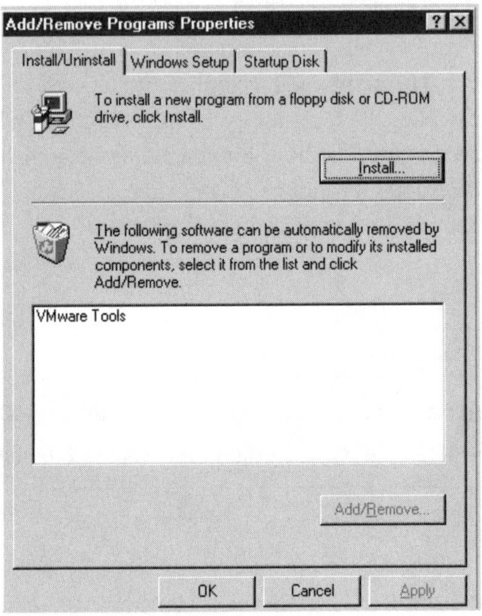

FIGURE 18-14   Add/Remove Programs

Most of the tabs in the Display applet are fairly obvious. The Background tab enables you to choose a background picture or pattern. The Screen Saver tab has settings for choosing and configuring a screen saver. The Appearance tab provides various color schemes. The Effects tab enables you to change the look and effects of Desktop icons, animations, and font quality. The Web tab enables you to activate the Active Desktop, making your Desktop, in essence, a web browser. Neither the Effects nor Web tabs are available in Windows 95. The tab of most interest to PC techs is the Settings tab, where you set the color depth and resolution of the display, change video card and monitor drivers, and set the video refresh rate.

Internet Options   The Internet Options applet (just called "Internet" in Windows 95) configures the settings for the web browser. You can also access this option from within the web browser. Note that double-clicking the Internet Options applet opens the Internet Properties dialog box. This applet enables you to set up an Internet connection, specify a home page, and modify the History, Web cache, and cookies settings, as well as a number of other things. When a browser doesn't browse, this is one of the first places to check.

Network   The Network applet configures all network functions. You can also access this applet through Network Neighborhood properties. Chapter 21 covers this applet in detail.

Printers   If it has to do with a printer, the Printers applet does the job. Every version of Windows provides many other methods to access this applet. The most common way to access this applet is by opening My Computer. The main printer window shows the installed printers and the Add Printer Wizard.

System   Of all the applets in the Windows 9x Control Panel, PC techs use the System applet the most. You can also access this applet via My Computer's properties. The following describes the tabs of the System applet (refer back to Figure 18-11):

- **General**   This tab tells you the version of Windows, registration information, and a few bits of information about the CPU and RAM.
- **Device Manager**   This is the most important place in the entire computer for hardware troubleshooting. You'll see lots of this in the next section.
- **Hardware Profiles**   Hardware Profiles enable you to turn off selected hardware for different system states. You'll see this used most often with laptops.
- **Performance**   This enables you to optimize a disk cache, swap file, and graphics settings.

Exam Tip

Many exam questions test your ability to use essential Control Panel applets. Know the important applets.

Device Installation

Device installation, once the private domain of only the nerdiest of computer techs, has been completely transformed by the advent of Plug and Play (PnP). With the right equipment and a little advance planning, PnP makes a tech's installation jobs fairly easy. If you don't plan, however, even a simple seeming device installation can make your life hell, so you need to follow a few tried-and-true guidelines to avoid any messes.

Most of the procedures and specifics of device installation have been covered in previous chapters, so I won't bore you with repetition here. Instead, let's look at four issues for installation specific to operating systems: drivers, backup, Device Manager, and troubleshooting.

Driver Check

PnP devices as you know, require four pieces in place in order to install and work perfectly. You need a PnP operating system, a PnP System BIOS, a PnP piece of hardware (always useful, that!), and proper drivers. The first three issues you can deal with before you walk out of the computer store with a new device. If you have Windows 9*x*/2000 installed, you have a PnP OS. If you have a Pentium or later system, you have a PnP System BIOS. Check the box for the expansion card. If it's PCI or AGP, it's PnP. That leaves only drivers as the primary sticking point on installations.

It'll come as no surprise to any of you with experience working on PCs to know that drivers often suck, especially for brand new models of hardware. Nothing quite makes a bad tech day like spending 300+ dollars on a new state-of-the-art video card, installing it, and then having your favorite game slap down your PC the first time you try to run the game! Hardware changes much faster than programmers can turn out solid drivers. In fact, you can almost always find updated drivers for a piece of hardware as soon as you can find that hardware in a computer store!

The bottom line is that you need to use the latest, non-beta drivers for your hardware. A quick check at the manufacturer's web site always settles this issue quickly.

Driver installation in a PnP system is highly anticlimatic in most cases. You get to watch Windows discover the new device and show the famous "Windows has discovered new hardware" alert. Windows either has the driver built in or it prompts you to provide the driver.

The seemingly absurd message "Windows has found unknown hardware and is installing software" usually results from installing two devices at once, where one depends on the other for connection to the system, like a new video card and monitor. Don't panic. Windows will eventually find the unknown device, although it might take a few reboots, especially with Windows 95.

Backup

Let's list the five most important backup items before you install.

1. Back up the Registry.
2. Back up the Registry.

3. Back up the Registry.
4. Back up the Registry.
5. And ... back up the Registry.

When you install a new device, Windows changes the Registry to reflect that new device. If you've backed up the Registry and something goes wrong with the install, you just restore the Registry and try again. But if you've failed to back up the Registry and something goes awry, your day just got a lot longer and will probably fill up with pain, heartache, and a possible complete system rebuild. Ouch!

You can back up the Registry in so many ways that listing them all here would take forever. Depending on the version, Windows 9*x* provides a number of methods to back up the Registry and many third-party vendors provide excellent backup tools. Both Windows and third-party programs contain many powerful extras and conveniences that make them worthwhile. But you don't need them just to back up the Registry. Use My Computer or Windows Explorer to perform these backup steps. If you really want to, you can do it from a DOS prompt, but why make life hard? Here's the way I do it:

1. Create a folder called C:\BACK.
2. Open the C:\WINDOWS\SYSTEM folder.
3. Make sure to set the View option to show all files.
4. Turn off all the file attributes on SYSTEM.DAT and USER.DAT (Forgot how? Here's your clue: Properties!). If you can't see SYSTEM.DAT or USER.DAT, you might have to have Windows reveal hidden files. Go to Explorer | View | Folder Options | View tab, and select the *Show all files* radio button.
5. Copy SYSTEM.DAT and USER.DAT to the C:\BACK folder.

Alternatively, you can use the Windows Registry Checker tool, SCANREG, to perform a backup. Get to a command prompt, type **SCANREG /BACKUP**, and then press ENTER.

Congratulations! You just backed up the Registry.

If anything doesn't go the way you want and you want to return the system to exactly the way it was before you tried installing that @#^%$ device, just restore the Registry. To restore the Registry, boot from a Startup floppy disk. When you get to an A: prompt, type the following line if you used my method.

```
COPY C:\BACK\*.DAT C:\WINDOWS\SYSTEM
```

Otherwise, type **SCANREG /RESTORE** and let Windows do it for you.

Although the A+ exam always says to do a full system backup (completely back up everything) before you even look at a computer, I rarely do a system backup for basic device installs—the chance of messing up a drive by snapping in a card or plugging something into a port is almost nil. If I'm installing for someone else, however, I always give the same speech before I touch anything. I won't quote the whole routine, but it boils down to this: "I am not responsible for your data." If they want me to back up their system, fine, but they get charged for my time. Ever taken a system into a shop for repair? That little piece of paper you sign invariably includes a "we're not responsible for your data" clause. Follow their lead and cover yourself—or at least have a boss you can hide behind if you wipe out all their data. Believe me, it can happen!

The Device Manager

Once you've installed a device, it's time to check it out in the Device Manager. The *Device Manager* is the primary tool for dealing with devices and device drivers in Windows. The Device Manager displays every device Windows recognizes. Alternate-click on My Computer and select Properties to open the Device Manager, and then double-click Computer to view the listings for all the IRQs, I/O addresses, and DMA settings for the entire system. Figure 18-15 shows a typical Device Manager screen with all installed devices in good order. If Windows detects a problem, it shows the device with a red X or an exclamation point.

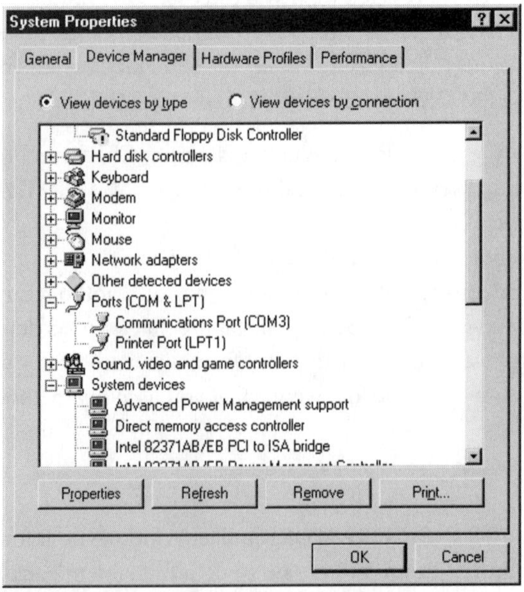

System Properties	? X

General | Device Manager | Hardware Profiles | Performance |

○ View devices by type   ○ View devices by connection

- Standard Floppy Disk Controller
- ⊞ Hard disk controllers
- ⊞ Keyboard
- ⊞ Modem
- ⊞ Monitor
- ⊞ Mouse
- ⊞ Network adapters
- ⊞ Other detected devices
- ⊟ Ports (COM & LPT)
  - Communications Port (COM3)
  - Printer Port (LPT1)
- ⊞ Sound, video and game controllers
- ⊟ System devices
  - Advanced Power Management support
  - Direct memory access controller
  - Intel 82371AB/EB PCI to ISA bridge

Properties | Refresh | Remove | Print... |

OK | Cancel |

FIGURE 18-15 Device Manager

The Device Manager organizes devices in special groups called *types*. All devices of the same type are grouped under the same type heading. To see the devices of a particular type, you must open that type's group by double-clicking the group. For example, if you select the group type Ports, you see the COM and LPT ports that are enabled on your system. By double-clicking a device (or by selecting the device and clicking the Properties button), and then clicking the Resources tab, you can view the resources used by that device.

Device Manager enables you to print a summary of a PC, a very useful tool when you have a problem with a remote PC. To print, simply open Device Manager and click the Print button on the tab. At that point, you can elect to print a *System summary*, which shows allocated resources (IRQs, I/O addresses, and such), or the far more useful *All devices and system summary*. The latter shows resources, but also lists all the drivers installed for all hardware. Having a computer-challenged user fax a copy of the device and system summary can go a long way in helping you troubleshoot!

Dealing with PnP Problems

Believe it or not, PnP sometimes doesn't work! Although increasingly rare, you'll still on occasion run into problems on a PnP install, primarily dealing with drivers, but sometimes with resource conflicts. Very rarely, a buggy driver or a conflict can corrupt your Registry, so be prepared!

Windows PnP Can't Find Driver   Most techs feel that failure to find a correct device driver stands as the most common PnP install issue. While you see some variance among Windows versions, basically every version of Windows always brings up the Add New Hardware Wizard and immediately moves to the screen that says "please tell me the location of the device."

The issue boils down to the fact that Windows PnP queried the new device and knows the device exists, but cannot find the correct INF for that device. In most cases, you click the Have Disk button and point the installer to the proper directory location. You know the correct directory location because you looked this up in the documentation. If you didn't look (like that would ever happen!), use the Browse feature to navigate around the install CD/floppy until the Add New Hardware Wizard finds an INF file.

Use a little common sense here! If you have a Windows 98 system and the install floppy for the device shows the following folders, guess where to look first for the driver:

        A:\LINUX
        A:\NETWARE4

A:\NETWARE5
A:\NT4
A:\WIN2K
A:\WIN95
A:\WIN98

Please tell me you picked the A:\WIN98 folder!

Make sure you insert the correct install disk, especially with Windows 9x, or you might install the wrong driver, requiring you to delete the device from the Device Manager and try again. In some cases, installing the wrong driver wreaks havoc: Windows copies the INF file to the \INF folder, so even if you delete the device from the Device Manager, Windows keeps reinstalling the wrong driver! To stop this action, you must first watch Windows as it installs. This happened to me recently (yes, I screw up every day!) and I documented it. I purchased the Compaq iPAQ Personal Digital Assistant (PDA), which comes with a little USB cradle that lets you synch your e-mail, web sites, contacts, and so forth between a desktop system and the PDA. When I installed the cradle, I didn't bother reading the instructions, which clearly told me to install the synch program before plugging in the device. I just plugged in the device and quickly installed the wrong driver. When I dropped the PDA into the cradle, the system locked up. After a quick scan of the documentation, I said "oops!" and promptly deleted the Compaq Aero PDA device from the Device Manager, as you can see in Figure 18-16.

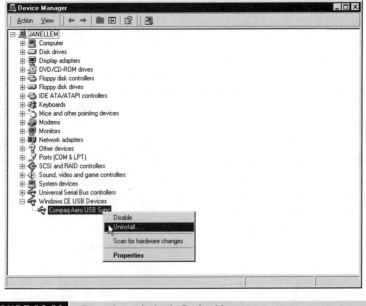

FIGURE 18-16   Removing a device in Device Manager

I rebooted and it immediately reinstalled itself. Ouch. The fix to this problem required using the Search/Find menu to locate the INF file that contained the offending device. I knew I needed to find the INF containing the text "Compaq Aero," so I searched for it in the \INF folder and up it came! Once I found it, I simply deleted it and did a complete uninstall/reinstall, this time according to the directions provided (and a phone call to Compaq tech support). I'll never neglect reading the documentation again—well at least for another two weeks!

Many times hardware makers hide device drivers and INF files in a SETUP program. You must run the program to get all the files you need. In many cases, these SETUP programs don't set up anything; they just uncompress themselves into a folder on the hard drive. Watch them as they unpack themselves—they always clearly show the destination folder. You can then rerun the install wizard and point it to the folder the SETUP program created.

Device Manager Errors   Windows often sees a PnP device and tries to install it but, for one reason or another, fails to install the device properly. Unlike errors where the PnP simply fails to see the device, these devices show in the Device Manager, but they show one of two possible errors. If a device has a problem, it shows up with an exclamation point surrounded by a small yellow dot. A small red *x* on a device means the device has been disabled by Windows. The following shows an example of both problem icons.

There's really no difference between the two errors in terms of how I deal with them. The bottom line is the device isn't working and I need to fix it. Anyone reading the Microsoft Knowledge Base support documentation can see that probably 50 different types of problems cause these errors but, in my experience, the vast majority of errors boil down to two cards that want the same resources by default. You might have to do some juggling in both CMOS and Device Manager to make the devices play well together. Sometimes simply uninstalling both devices and installing in reverse order will fix the problem. Try it!

Corrupted Registry   In most cases, the device error will report this one very clearly: Registry corrupted. No problem since you kept that backup copy, right!

Right? If you didn't back up the Registry, you still have a bit of hope. Try the Windows Registry Checker's repair feature. Get to a command prompt, type **SCANREG /FIX**, and then press the ENTER key. That sometimes works and is worth a try!

Windows Shortcuts

Windows provides a number of handy keyboard shortcuts that enable you to switch quickly between applications. Know these shortcuts!

Exam Tip

All these shortcuts work with Windows 2000.

ALT-TAB   This brings up a small window that enables you to choose from all running programs. Hold down the ALT key, and then press tab repeatedly to cycle through all running programs. Release the keys after selecting the program to make it active. If you select a minimized program, Windows restores the program.

ALT-ESC   This shortcut cycles around all windows, including minimized ones, but doesn't open minimized windows.

CTRL-ESC   This opens the Start Menu without using a mouse.

CTRL-ALT-DEL   This brings up the Close Program dialog box, as mentioned earlier in this chapter (refer back to Figure 18-12), which enables you to close any running program. I'm adding it to this list in case you missed it!

Windows Enhanced Keyboard Shortcuts

Those of you lucky enough to have a Windows keyboard get some extra keys. The two most common are the Windows logo key (WIN key) and the MENU key. These keys—either alone or in combination with other keys—give a number of handy shortcuts. Here are a few of my favorites:

- **WIN** This opens the Start menu—extremely handy.
- **MENU** This opens the default pop-up menu for that window. Usefulness varies by application.
- **WIN-TAB** This shortcut cycles around all windows, including minimized ones, but doesn't open minimized windows. It functions similarly to ALT-ESC.
- **WIN-M** This is one of the most underused of all Windows shortcuts. This minimizes all windows. Handy for getting all open windows out of the way. Windows 98 and Windows 2000 users get the Show Desktop icon on the Quick Launch toolbar on the taskbar, which accomplishes the same thing.

Printers

Windows 9*x* systems use a fairly simple approach to printing. The *print mechanism* is divided into three distinct parts: the printer, the print driver, and the print spooler. When you send out a print job (that is, when you click Print), the application sends the print job to the print spooler. The *print spooler,* working with the print driver, formats the print job in a language the printer can understand and stores it as a temporary file on the hard drive. Once the print job has been spooled to the hard drive, the print job is then sent to the printer. To speed things along, you can also have the computer send the beginning of the print job to the printer *before* the entire print job has spooled. You can enable that feature at Start | Settings | Printers and select the properties for your printer. In properties, select the Details tab and click on the Spool Settings button to configure.

Adding a Printer

Setting up a printer is so easy, it's almost scary. Most printers are PnP, so installing a printer is reduced simply to plugging it in and loading the driver, if needed. If the system doesn't detect the printer or if the printer isn't PnP, click Start | Settings | Printers to open the Printers applet. The icon for this applet can also be found in the Control Panel. As you might guess, you install a new printer by starting the Add New Printer applet. This starts the Add New Printer Wizard. As the wizard starts, select Next. You have a choice to make now. You can choose to install a printer plugged directly into your system—Local Printer—or a network printer. If you choose a local printer (you learn about networked printers in Chapter 21), Windows 9*x* asks you to select a printer manufacturer on the left of the Printer

Wizard window and the Printer model on the right. If you find your printer listed, great! If not, click Have Disk and place the manufacturer's install disk that came with the printer into the floppy or CD-ROM drive.

Next, Windows 9x wants to know the port to which the printer connects. By default, LPT1 is selected because earlier in the wizard, you indicated this printer will be a local printer. After confirming the port by clicking Next, you're then asked to name the printer. You can leave the name automatically placed in the space provided or type a new name and click Next.

The Printer Wizard then asks if you want to send a test page. Go ahead, you'll want to make sure the driver for the printer is working correctly. Then click Finish. You'll be asked in a separate window if the print job came out correctly. If it did, then all is well. If it did not, you can either delete the printer by selecting it in the printers windows and pressing the DELETE key, or right-click the printer and select Delete from the short-cut menu. Once the printer is deleted, start the Printer Wizard over again and reinstall the printer you need.

Figure 18-17 shows a typical printer applet with one printer installed. Note the small checkmark in the corner, which shows the device is the default printer. If you have multiple printers, you can change the default printer by selecting the printer's properties and checking *Make default printer*.

Installing printers in Windows 9x is one of the easiest processes in any version of Windows. If only everything was this easy!

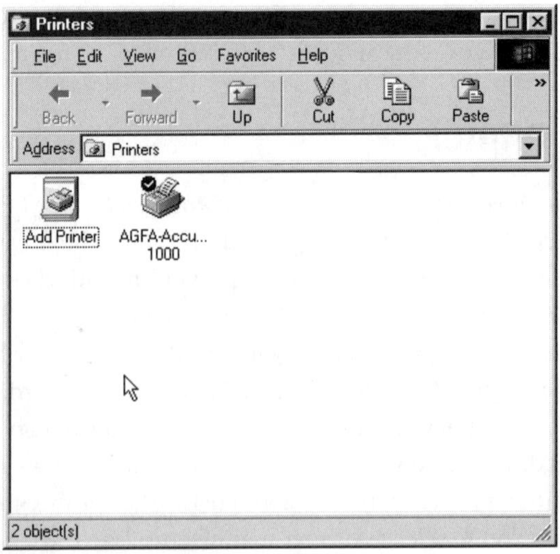

FIGURE 18-17 Default printer properly installed

Objective 18.03 # Troubleshooting Windows 9*x*

Windows 9*x* is unfortunately far from rock solid in many situations. This section reviews some of the more common troubleshooting situations you'll encounter as a PC tech.

Be Prepared

In almost every case, you fix Windows problems by restoring some kind of backup of some kind of data. You already know how to back up the Registry, but we need to discuss the concept of backing up in a more generic sense.

Backup

People get terribly confused by the word "backup." Simply put, *back up* means to take a copy of a file and place it somewhere else, so it can be retrieved if you have a problem with the original. I advise backing up four different groups of files (some of these overlap):

- Personal data files (usually all the stuff in My Documents)
- Personal data used by applications (for example, address book entries, favorites, or data files used by accounting programs like Quicken and Peachtree)
- Current system state files—the Registry
- The complete contents of the hard drive

The answer lies in backup software. Every version of Windows comes with a backup program and, although they vary in quality, they can all do any of the previous jobs. To start the Backup program in Windows 9*x*, go to Start | Program Files | Accessories | System Tools, and select Backup. If you have a tape drive installed, the Backup program starts immediately, but if not, it'll give you an error message. In the latter event, simply ignore the error and run the program. You can use all sorts of media for backing up, including Iomega Zip drives, spare hard drives, and CD-RW drives. Backup has a very intuitive interface, enabling you to decide quickly whether to back up all or some of your programs, data, and operating system files. The A+ Certification exams do not expect mastery of the specific application, but you should know the location. In the field, most of us use more advanced, third-party software, such as Veritas Backup MyPC.

Lockups/Reboots

All system lockups fit into one of two groups. The first group is the lockups that take place immediately after you add a new program or device. These almost always point to resource conflicts or software version incompatibilities. Use the techniques described in earlier chapters to fix these problems.

The second group is the lockups from nowhere. These invariably point either to a virus attack (see the big virus discussion in Chapter 16) or to a hardware problem, usually the power supply, RAM, or hard drive. Test/replace until the problem goes away.

Spontaneous reboots always point to bad hardware or a virus. The power supply is the first item to check, followed closely by the CPU. Overheated CPUs love to reboot spontaneously. Make sure the fan works. Most CMOS setup utilities have a screen that enables you to set overheat alarms to monitor the CPU, as Figure 18-18 shows.

General Protect Faults

General Protection Faults (GPFs) occur when one program tries to stomp on another program's memory area. If I get an occasional GPF (say, once every two

```
        CMOS Setup Utility - Copyright (C) 1984-1999 Award Software
                             PC Health Status
 ┌─────────────────────────────────────┬──────────────────────────────┐
 │                                      │            Item Help         │
 │  CPU Temp Alarm          60°C/ 140°F │                              │
 │  Current System Temp.    26°C/  78°F │                              │
 │  CPU (FAN1) Speed        4854  RPM   │  Menu Level  ▶               │
 │  PWR (FAN2) Speed           0  RPM   │                              │
 │  Vcore                   1.77  V     │                              │
 │   2.5V                   2.45  V     │                              │
 │   3.3V                   3.36  V     │                              │
 │    5V                    4.92  V     │                              │
 │   12V                   11.76  V     │                              │
 │                                      │                              │
 └─────────────────────────────────────┴──────────────────────────────┘
  ↑↓→← :Move Enter:Select +/-PU/PD:Value  F10:Save  ESC:Exit  F1:General Help
        F5:Previous Values  F6:Fail-Safe Defaults  F7:Optimized Defaults
```

FIGURE 18-18   Set CPU overheat alarms in CMOS setup

weeks), I usually ignore it. Static and subtle incompatibilities make GPFs something you live with in Windows. Consistent GPFs that always point to the same filename as the culprit, however, require attention. If the system hasn't been changed, the named file may be corrupt. Try reloading the file from the installation CD. If it's a Windows file, use the EXTRACT command to locate the file on the CD and copy it to the same location as the potentially bad one. Use the search function to find the location of the bad file.

Windows Protection Errors

Windows protection errors take place when a special type of driver file, called a virtual device driver (VxD) fails to load or unload. *VxDs* are used to support older Windows programs and you usually see this error when a device somehow gets a device driver in both CONFIG.SYS and SYSTEM.INI on the Registry. Running SYSEDIT shows you any drivers in CONFIG.SYS. Put semicolons in front of DEVICE= lines until the problem goes away. If this doesn't fix it, check for resource conflicts in the Device Manager, and then restore the Registry.

Fatal Exception Errors

Fatal exception errors are caused by software or hardware that sends a particular type of error Windows is not designed to contain. If these arise from a new device or software, uninstall the offending beast, and check the manufacturer's web site and the Microsoft Knowledge Base for known issues related to that software or device.

Dr. Watson

In some cases, these problems simply defy the best of your repair attempts. At this point, you'll probably need to call tech support. But, before you call, run the Dr. Watson utility and re-create the error. Dr. Watson generates a detailed report log on the status of the system at the time of the error. While the information in that report goes way outside the knowledge needed for A+ Certification, it provides critical insight to high-level techs.

Shutdown Problems

I find it interesting that most shutdown problems are identical to startup issues. Bad drivers, corrupted registries, and faulty page files all cause shutdown problems. Let's add a few other fixes unique to shutdown problems.

Application Not Closing   Some applications refuse to close. Windows 98 does a good job of closing them anyway, but Windows 95 often needs you to close an application manually before it can shut down. Try to close the application normally but, if that fails, use the Close Program dialog box to shut it down. If you click End Task and nothing happens, try again—I sometimes have to *end* Microsoft Word three or four times before it obeys.

Sound File   If the Windows Shutdown sound file corrupts, the system won't shut down. Use the Sounds applet in the Control Panel to turn off the shutdown sound.

CHECKPOINT

✔ **Objective 18.01: Windows 9x System Files**   Windows 9x uses three key system files you must be familiar with: IO.SYS, WIN.INI, and SYSTEM.INI. You should also be completely comfortable with the Windows 9x Registry. The \WINDOWS directory contains many important resources you should know. Finally, make sure you know where, how, and why to use the tools available in Windows to help you deal with system issues.

✔ **Objective 18.02: Optimizing and Maintaining Windows 9x**   All versions of Windows 9x come pretty well optimized out of the box, but some maintenance is necessary for optimal performance. Understand how to update Windows using Windows Updater, Service Packs, and patches. Know the procedures for drive maintenance, including ScanDisk, Disk Defragmenter, and Drive Cleanup. Be completely familiar with the Windows 9x swap file, the System applet and other resource tracking tools. Know your Control Panel! Know how to install and troubleshoot PnP devices. Be comfortable using keyboard shortcuts—they're not only fast, they're tested.

✔ **Objective 18.03: Troubleshooting Windows 9x**   Despite any tech's best efforts, a Windows 9x system will encounter problems sooner or later. Know the common Windows 9x troubleshooting issues, including lockups, GPFs, Windows protection errors, and shutdown problems, and know how to deal with them.

REVIEW QUESTIONS

1. Which of the following is the way to start an application in Windows 9x?

   A. Use the System applet in the Control Panel
   B. Use the FILE FIND option
   C. Click once on the application
   D. Use Windows Explorer to navigate and double-click on the application's executable file

2. The majority of configuration information for Windows 9x is stored in which files?

   A. AUTOEXEC.BAT and CONFIG.SYS
   B. USER.DAT and SYSTEM.DAT
   C. STARTUP.SYS and SYSTEM.SYS
   D. USER.SYS and SYSTEM.SYS

3. Which of the following is not one of the six Registry keys?

   A. HKEY_DYN_DATA
   B. HKEY_CLASSES_ROOT
   C. HKEY_USERS
   D. HKEY_SYSTEM_DATA

4. In Windows 95, where would you find the listings for all the IRQs, I/O Addresses, and DMA settings for the entire system?

   A. Alternate-click Start menu, and then select Open | Properties
   B. In the Startup menu, choose View All System Resources
   C. Alternate-click My Computer, select Properties | Device Manager, and then double-click Computer to view the IRQs, I/O Addresses, and DMA settings
   D. Double-click My Computer | Devices | Properties

5. In Windows 98, what is the key combination to toggle between running programs?

   A. ALT-ESC
   B. ALT-space
   C. ALT-TAB
   D. ALT-F10

6. What's the best way to restore a corrupt Registry?

    A. Replace the SYSTEM.INI and WIN.INI files with backup copies

    B. Copy USER.DAO to USER.DAT, and SYSTEM.DAO to SYSTEM.DAT

    C. Use a new Startup disk

    D. Run the System Configuration Editor

7. In Windows 9*x*, how would you remove an application from your system? (Select two.)

    A. My Computer | Control Panel | Add/Remove Programs, select the program and Uninstall

    B. Start | Settings | Taskbar and Start menu | Options | Start Menu Programs tab, and select the icon you want to delete

    C. Start | Settings | Control Panel | Add/Remove Programs, select the program and Uninstall

    D. Start | Settings | Taskbar and Start menu | Start Menu Programs tab, and select the icon you want to delete

8. What's the best way to access the Registry Editor in Windows 9*x*?

    A. Start | Programs | DOS prompt icon

    B. Start | Programs | Registry Editor

    C. Start | Run, type REGEDIT and click OK

    D. Start | Run, type REGEDIT32 and click OK

9. The three main files that control system resources in Windows 9*x* are

    A. KRNL386.EXE, GDI.EXE, and USER.EXE

    B. HIMEM.SYS, EMM386.EXE, and COMMAND.COM

    C. GDI.EXE, KRNL286.EXE, and USER.EXE.

    D. PROGMAN.INI, WIN.INI, and SYSTEM.INI

10. In which folder can you find the Windows 98 Disk Defragmenter utility?

    A. Disk Administrator

    B. Control Panel

    C. Disk Defrag

    D. System Tools

REVIEW ANSWERS

1.   **D** Use Windows Explorer to navigate and double-click on the application's executable file.

2.   **B** The majority of configuration information for Windows 9*x* is stored in USER.DAT and SYSTEM.DAT.

3.   **D** HKEY_SYSTEM_DATA is not a valid Registry key.

4.   **C** Alternate-click My Computer, select Properties, select Device Manager, and then double-click Computer to view the IRQs, I/O Addresses, and DMA settings.

5.   **C** ALT-TAB.

6.   **B** The best way to restore a corrupt Registry is to copy USER.DAO to USER.DAT, and SYSTEM.DAO to SYSTEM.DAT.

7.   **A** **C** My Computer | Control Panel | Add/Remove Programs, select the program and Uninstall. Or, Start | Settings | Control Panel | Add/Remove Programs, select the program and Uninstall.

8.   **C** Start | Run, type REGEDIT and click OK.

9.   **A** The three main files that control system resources in Windows 9*x* are KRNL386.EXE, GDI.EXE, and USER.EXE.

10. **D** The Windows 98 Disk Defragmenter utility is found in the System Tools folder.

Windows NT

ETA	NEWBIE	SOME EXPERIENCE	EXPERT
	2.5 hours	1.5 hours	1 hour

Early in the life of Windows, way back when Windows 3.*x* still ruled the land, Microsoft began to develop a new, super-powerful version of Windows that sacrificed backward compatibility with DOS and many Windows 3.*x* applications in exchange for stability, scalability, and cross-platform support. Microsoft knew the hardware and power of this new Super Windows would make it useful only for the most powerful user needs. They ended up with two operating system (OS) lines—what I call Regular and Super. *Regular* Windows is made up of the Windows 3.*x*, Windows 95, Windows 98, and Windows ME lines. The *Super* Windows line is called Windows New Technology (NT).

Exam Tip

Even though the Operating System exam doesn't stress NT as hard as Windows 9*x* or Windows 2000, a number of questions pop up that require you to know this stuff! Read on!

Objective 19.01

NT Structure and System Files

Windows NT first burst on to the scene in the early 1990s as version 3.1 to compete with the then quite popular Novell NetWare 3.1. Like regular Windows, NT went through many versions after the first one: Windows NT 3.5, Windows NT 3.51, and Windows 4.0. The other version of Super Windows tested on the A+ Certification exams—Windows 2000—drops the NT, but don't let that fool you! Although Windows 2000 boasts a number of powerful enhancements over the previous versions, the heart of NT still beats inside every Windows 2000 system.

NT Operating System Organization

From the outside, Windows NT 4.0 looks pretty much like Windows 95 but, for the most part, that's where the similarities end. Windows NT has so many features beyond Windows 9*x*, it takes a moment to decide where to start! Let's begin with the organization of the operating system.

Three words best describe NT's organization: robust, scalable, and cross-platform. NT takes an object-oriented approach to the OS, separating the OS into three distinct parts: the drivers, the NT Executive, and the subsystems, as shown in Figure 19-1.

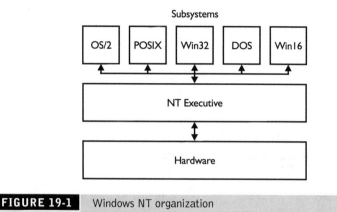

FIGURE 19-1 Windows NT organization

NT was designed to support different CPU platforms beyond the x86, such as DEC Alpha, MIPS, and PowerPC. To achieve this, the NT Executive holds the Hardware Abstraction Layer (HAL) to separate the system-specific device drivers from the rest of the NT system. Although Windows 2000 shares this organization, Microsoft chose to drop support for all but Intel x86 systems in Windows 2000.

NT and 2000's robustness comes from the separation of running processes into a myriad of subsystems. NT is fully POSIX-compliant (a UNIX thing) and has support for OS/2, DOS, and 16- and 32-bit Windows applications via these numerous subsystems. Windows 2000 keeps all the same support with the exception of OS/2. NT's scalability made it the first Microsoft OS to support symmetric multiprocessing (SMP), providing support for systems with up to 32 CPUs. Windows 2000, by the way, goes beyond SMP by adding the power of clustering, enabling multiple systems to share redundant data for ultimate protection. If one system goes down, the other systems continue to run.

Windows NT File Structure—NTFS

From the beginning, Microsoft designed and optimized every aspect of Windows NT (and Windows 2000) for multiuser, networked environments. This is most evident in the file system—how NT stores files on your hard drive(s). Whereas all other previous Microsoft operating systems used FAT16 or FAT32 formats, NT and 2000 use a far more powerful and robust file system, appropriately called, NT File System (NTFS). While NT runs fine on a FAT16 partition, NTFS is the way to go. NT doesn't support FAT32. NTFS goes way beyond the capabilities of the old FAT-based file systems in Windows 9x. NTFS offers the following excellent features:

- Larger partition sizes
- Long filenames
- Redundancy
- Backward compatibility
- Recoverability
- Security

Larger Partition Sizes   NTFS supports partitions of up to 2 terabytes, making it the obvious choice for large partitions.

Long Filenames   NTFS supported long filenames long before FAT32 even existed. Like LFNs, NTFS filenames can be up to 255 characters.

Redundancy   NTFS has an advanced FAT called the *Master File Table* (MFT). An NTFS partition keeps a backup copy of the most critical parts of the MFT in the middle of the disk, reducing the chance that a serious drive error can wipe out both the MFT and the MFT copy. Whenever you defrag an NTFS partition, you'll see a small, immovable "chunk" in the middle of the drive; that's the backup MFT.

Backward Compatibility   For all its power, NTFS is amazingly backward-compatible. You can copy DOS or Windows 9x programs to an NTFS partition. NTFS in Windows 2000 even keeps the same LFNs used by FAT32!

Recoverability   Accidental system shutdowns, reboots, and lockups in the midst of a file save or retrieval wreak havoc on most systems. NTFS avoids this with *transaction logging,* which determines incomplete file transactions and restores the file to the original format automatically and invisibly.

Security   NTFS truly shines with its powerful security functions. When most people hear the term "security," they tend to think about networks. NTFS security works perfectly in a network environment but, for the moment, let's pretend only one Windows NT system exists in the entire world. Three different people use this computer. Each person has one personal folder he or she doesn't want others to access. On a Windows 9x system, anyone who can get in front of the keyboard of a system can access any folder; the password only allows him or her on the network. This isn't so with Windows NT running NTFS! NTFS security adds user accounts that users must have to access a NT system running NTFS. Virtually every part of the NT system has a set of access rules called permissions to limit what a user account may or may not do to that particular item. You'll see much more on NTFS security in a moment.

Booting NT

Windows 9x and Windows NT share a surface resemblance—both are graphical operating systems. Inside, however, they differ significantly in the level of integration between the graphical interface and text-based functions. Both versions of Windows make a strong distinction between booting the OS and "going graphical." Windows NT and Windows 9x have primary boot files that start the OS. Once these files have started the system, a completely different set of files starts the graphical user interface (GUI). The boot files are usually quite small in size and few of them exist, compared to the size and the number of the GUI files. The distinction between text-based OS and GUI files is sharp in Windows 9x, but much muddier in Windows NT.

In Windows 9x, a clear distinction exists between the boot files and the GUI files. This can be easily shown by the many ways you can skip the GUI completely, such as the Command Prompt Only option in the Startup Options menu discussed in Chapter 17. Windows NT doesn't have a pure command prompt environment. Certainly, you can access a command prompt within NT, but the Windows 9x separation of GUI from command prompt is not valid in NT. In Windows 9x machines, the boot files must be installed on to the C: partition, but the GUI files can be installed on to any other drive letter. Of course, most installations place the GUI files in a directory called \WINDOWS on the C: drive, but this isn't at all required. The boot files and the GUI files are totally separate issues in Windows 9x.

Windows NT also separates the boot from the GUI files. Like Windows 9x, the boot files must be on the boot partition and the GUI files can be anywhere else. Unlike Windows 9x, however, the boot and GUI files are closely linked. There's no way to boot NT to a command prompt only, as is possible in Windows 9x. The boot files only start the OS and pass control to the GUI. The only way to get to a command prompt in NT is after the GUI is started. The Windows NT OS itself consists of NTOSKRNL.EXE (the Windows NT kernel), the \WINNT\SYSTEM32\CONFIG\SYSTEM file (which controls the loading of device drivers), and the device drivers themselves. Even though these files are the core of the Windows NT OS, they aren't capable of booting the system. They can reside on any partition in the system. So how does a computer find those files so they can be run to start the

OS? The answer is this: Windows NT needs boot files that can point to these critical files.

It's time for a little Microsoft terminology. The NTOSKRNL.EXE, SYSTEM, and device driver files that make up the OS are stored on the boot partition. The files that help you find the OS when the system boots up are stored on the system partition (no, that isn't a typo). In Microsoft's terminology, the partition you boot from, the bootable partition, is the *system partition*. The partition that holds the actual NT or 2000 OS is called the *boot partition*. It's completely backwards from what we would expect. Everyone knows it's backwards and it's too late to change it. In an NT system, there will be only one system partition and one boot partition. If you have the system and boot files on the same partition, of course, then that one partition serves as both.

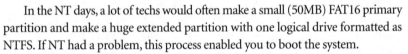

Local Lingo

Boot partition   The files that make up the OS are stored on the boot partition.

System partition   The files that help find the OS when the system boots up are stored on the system partition.

In the NT days, a lot of techs would often make a small (50MB) FAT16 primary partition and make a huge extended partition with one logical drive formatted as NTFS. If NT had a problem, this process enabled you to boot the system.

NT can coexist with Windows 9x on the same boot partition, as long as the partition is FAT16. Although you *could* do this, your inability to use NTFS makes this idea ludicrous. Using Windows NT without NTFS removes most of the power of NT—you might as well just use Windows 9x!

NTFS Security

NTFS offers three major security advantages over FAT—Accounts, Groups, and Permissions. Let's go there now.

Accounts

To use a Windows NT system, you must have a valid account and password. Without that account, you cannot use the system. Unlike with Windows 9x where you could cancel the login screen and still use the PC, with NT it's all or nothing.

Every Windows NT system has a super account called *administrator*. When you first install a Windows NT system, it prompts you for a password for the administrator account. As you might imagine, this account has access to everything—a dangerous thing in the wrong hands!

> ### Exam Tip
>
> Windows 2000 uses all these same aspects of NTFS security, but adds a few more items. Be sure to check out Chapter 20 for the extra power of Windows 2000 security!

Groups

The administrator creates user accounts with a special program called User Manager, as in seen Figure 19-2. Note the account list has three columns: User Name, Domain, and Group. To understand domains requires extensive networking discussion, so let's leave that for Chapter 21 and, instead, focus here on user names and groups. A *user name* defines an account for a person who has access to the PC. A *group* is simply a collection of accounts that share the same access capabilities. A single account can be a member of multiple groups.

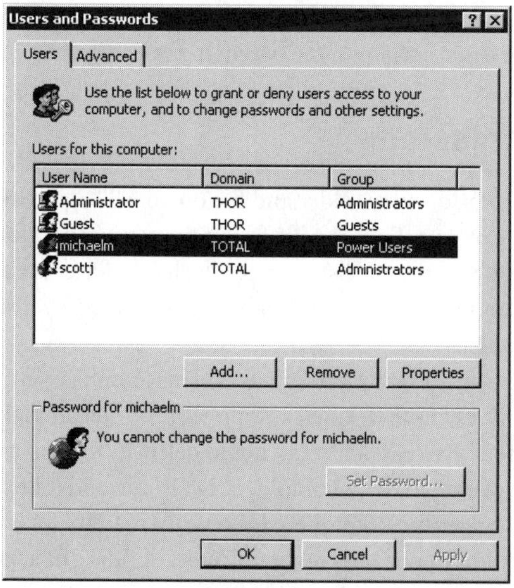

FIGURE 19-2 Users and Passwords dialog box

Groups make Windows administration much easier in two ways. First, you can assign a certain level of access for a file or folder to a group instead of an account. You can make a group called Accounting and put all the accounting user accounts in that group. If a person quits, you needn't worry about deleting her account, and then creating a new one for her replacement, including reassigning all the proper access levels. You can simply make a new account and add that new person to a group! Second, Windows provides built-in groups: Administrators, Users, Backup Operators, Replicator, Everyone, and Guests. These built-in groups have a number of preset capabilities. You cannot delete these groups.

- **Administrators**   Any account that's a member of this group has complete administrator privileges. It's common for the primary user of a Windows NT system to have his or her account in the Administrators group.
- **Users**   Users cannot edit the Registry or access critical system files. While they can create groups, users can only manage the ones they create.
- **Backup Operators**   Backup operators have the same rights as users, but they can run backup programs that access any file or folder—for backup purposes only.
- **Replicator**   Members of the Replicator group can replicate files and folders in a domain.
- **Everyone**   This account applies to any user who can log on to the system. You cannot edit this group.
- **Guests**   Someone who doesn't have an account on the system can log on using the Guest account if the system has been set up to enable that feature.

NTFS Permissions

In the NT/2000 world, every folder and file on an NTFS partition has a list that contains two sets of data. First, the list details every user and group with access to that file or folder. Second, the list specifies the level of access each user or group has to that file and folder. The level of access is defined by a set of restrictions called permissions.

Permissions define exactly what a particular account can or cannot do to the file or folder and are quite detailed and powerful. You can make it possible, for example, for a person to edit a file, but not to delete it. You can create a folder and not allow other people to make subfolders. NTFS file and folder permissions are so complicated that entire books have been written on them! Fortunately for us, the A+ Certification exams only test your understanding of a few basic concepts of NTFS permissions: Ownership, Changing permissions, Folder permissions, and File permissions.

Ownership   When you create a new file or folder on an NTFS partition, you become the owner of that file or folder. A newly created file or folder by default gives Full permission to Everyone to access, delete, and otherwise manipulate that file or folder. Owners can do anything they want to the files or folders they own, including changing the permissions to prevent anybody, even administrators, from accessing them. One special permission, however, called Take Ownership, enables anyone with that permission to do just that—seize control of a file or folder. Administrator accounts have Take Ownership permission for everything. Note the difference here between owning a file and accessing a file. If you own a file, you can prevent anyone from accessing that file. An administrator who you blocked, however, can take that ownership away from you, and *then* access that file! Get it?

Change Permissions   Another important permission for all NTFS files and folders is Change. As you might expect, an account with the Change permission can give or take away permissions for other accounts.

Folder Permissions   Let's look at a typical folder in my Windows NT system to see how all this works. My D: drive is formatted as NTFS. On the D: drive, I created a folder called D:\MIKE. I set the permissions for the folder by accessing the folder's properties and clicking the Security tab, as shown in Figure 19-3.

In Windows NT, nearly everything in the computer has a security tab in its properties. Every security tab contains two main areas. The top area shows the list of accounts with permissions for that resource. The lower area shows exactly what permissions are assigned to that account. The permissions shown in the permission area, for example, are not permissions, but rather, they are preset combinations of permissions that cover the most common types of access. Click the Advanced button, and then click View | Edit to see the real NTFS permissions. Microsoft calls them special permissions. Even the most advanced NT support people rarely need to access these.

Exam Tip

Don't panic about memorizing special permissions. Just appreciate they exist and the permissions you see in the Security tab cover the vast majority of needs.

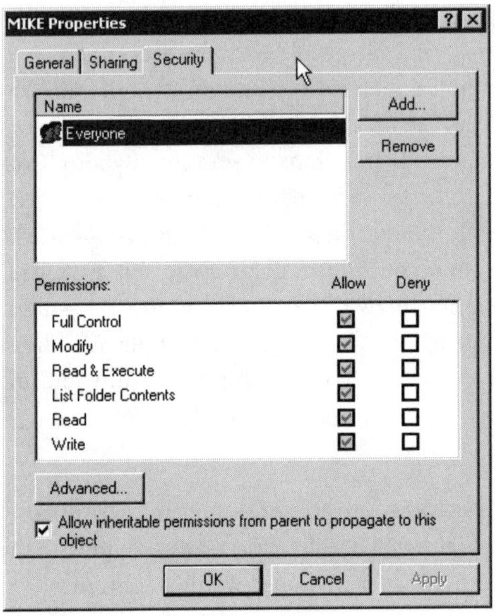

FIGURE 19-3 Security tab for folder permissions

Here are the standard permissions for a folder:

- *Full Control* enables you to do anything you want!
- *Modify* enables you to do anything except delete files or subfolders.
- *Read & Execute* enables you to see the contents of the folder and any sub-folders.
- *List Folder Contents* enables you to see the contents of the folder and any subfolders. (This permission seems the same as the Read & Execute permission, but it's only inherited by folders.)
- *Read* enables you to read any files in the folder.
- *Write* enables you to write to files, and create new files and folders.

If you look at the bottom of the Security tab, you'll see a little check box that says, Allow inheritable permission from parent to propagate to this object. In other words, any files or subfolder created in this folder get the same permissions for the same users/groups that the folder has. This enables you to stop a user from getting a specific permission via inheritance.

File Permissions   File permissions are quite similar to Folder permissions. Look at the Security tab on a typical file, as shown in Figure 19-4.

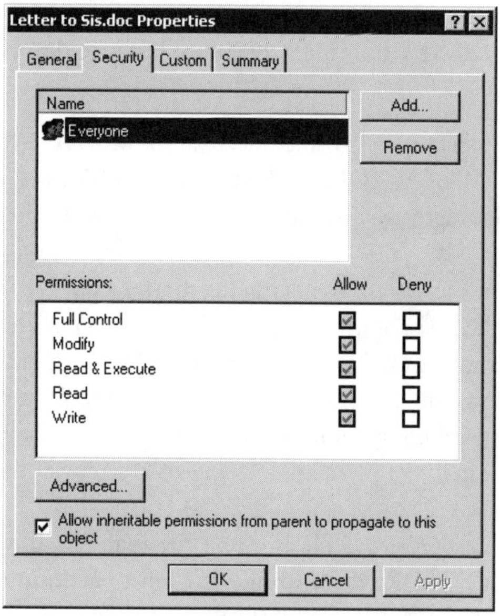

FIGURE 19-4   Security tab for file permissions

- *Full Control* enables you to do anything you want!
- *Modify* enables you to do anything except take ownership or change permissions on the file.
- *Read & Execute* means that if the file is a program, you can run it.
- *Read* means that if the file is data, you can read it.
- *Write* enables you to write to the file.

Take some time to think about these permissions. Why would Microsoft create them? Think of situations where you might want to give a group Modify permission. Also, you can assign more than one permission. In many situations, we like to give users both the Read, as well as the Write, permission. Permissions are cumulative. If you have Full Control on a folder and only Read permission on the file, you get Full Control on the file.

System Partition Boot Files

Windows NT requires these four files in the root directory of the system partition:

- NTLDR (pronounced *NT loader*)
- BOOT.INI

- NTDETECT.COM
- NTBOOTDD.SYS (only for SCSI controllers who don't have their own ROM BIOS)

Note that this list does not include IO.SYS, MSDOS.SYS, CONFIG.SYS, COMMAND.COM, or AUTOEXEC.BAT. Windows NT/2000 doesn't use these files, although you might see them in the root directory of a dual-boot system.

NTLDR   When the system boots up, the master boot record (MBR) on the hard drive starts the NTLDR program. The NTLDR *program* then launches either Windows NT or another OS. To find the available OSs, the NTLDR program must read the BOOT.INI configuration file. To accomplish this, the NTLDR program loads its own minimal file system, which enables it to read the BOOT.INI file off the system partition.

BOOT.INI   The *BOOT.INI* file is a text file that lists the OSs available to NTLDR and tells NTLDR where to find the boot partition (where the OS is stored) for each of the OSs. The BOOT.INI file has sections defined by section headings enclosed in brackets. A basic BOOT.INI in Windows NT looks like this:

```
[boot loader]
timeout=10
default=multi(0)disk(0)rdisk(0)partition(2)\WINNT [operating systems]
multi(0)disk(0)rdisk(0)partition(2)\WINNT="Microsoft Windows
NT"/fastdetect
```

A more complex BOOT.INI may look like this:

```
[boot loader]
timeout=10
default=multi(0)disk(0)rdisk(0)partition(2)\WINNT
[operating systems]
multi(0)disk(0)rdisk(0)partition(2)\WINNT="Microsoft Windows
NT"/fastdetect
C:\CMDCONS\BOOTSECT.DAT="Microsoft Windows NT Recovery Console"
/cmdcons
C:\="Previous Operating System on C:"
```

Such a BOOT.INI would result in the boot menu that appears in Figure 19-5.

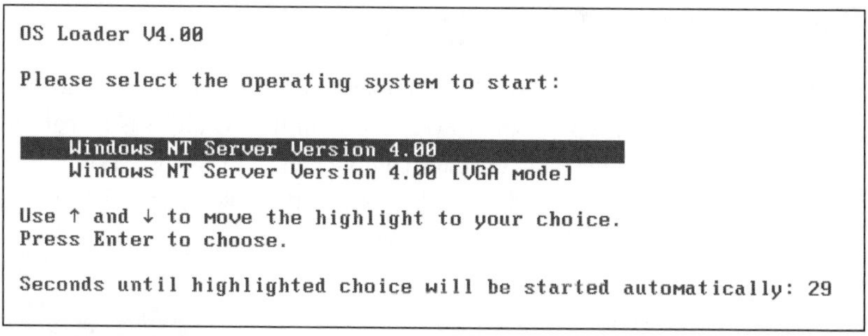

```
OS Loader V4.00

Please select the operating system to start:

   Windows NT Server Version 4.00
   Windows NT Server Version 4.00 [VGA Mode]

Use ↑ and ↓ to move the highlight to your choice.
Press Enter to choose.

Seconds until highlighted choice will be started automatically: 29
```

FIGURE 19-5 Boot menu

BOOTSECT.DOS   If the NTLDR detects that you chose to run another OS, such as Windows 9x, it reads the BOOTSECT.DOS file to locate the IO.SYS file, and then lets the other OS start.

NTDETECT.COM   If the NTLDR determines you chose to start NT/2000, it boots the system into protected mode, and then calls on NTDETECT.COM to detect the installed hardware on the system.

NTBOOTDD.SYS   If the NTLDR detects that the boot partition resides on a SCSI drive that connects to a host adapter lacking a ROM chip for BIOS support, it uses the NTBOOTDD.SYS to provide access to the SCSI boot partition. (See Chapter 8 for more information about SCSI drives and host adapters.)

Critical Files

Naming all the critical files for NT and 2000 (both operating systems share the same core files) is akin to naming every muscle in the human body—completely possible, but time-consuming and without any real use. In the next section, you'll see it takes four floppy disks to boot Windows 2000 from the floppy drive! However, a few of the *most* important files certainly deserve a short notice. Once NTLDR finishes detections, it loads NTOSKRNL.EXE, HAL.DLL, some of the Registry, and some basic device drivers. Then it passes control to the NTOSKRNL. EXE file. NTOSKRNL.EXE completes the Registry loading, initializes all device drivers, and starts the WINLOGON.EXE program, which displays the Windows NT logon screen.

The Windows NT Registry

Windows NT and Windows 2000 share similar registries. The A+ Certification exams don't expect you to memorize every aspect of the Windows NT Registry. You should, however, understand the basic components of the Registry, know how to edit the Registry manually, and know the best way to locate a particular setting.

Exam Tip

All Registry functions in NT work exactly the same in Windows 2000!

Microsoft included a new Registry Editor in Windows NT (REGEDT32.EXE), although they also left in the older Registry Editor (REGEDIT.EXE). Most techs refer to the two Registry Editor applications by their filenames: Regedt32 and Regedit.

Although Regedt32 has far more power than Regedit, we still use the older Regedit to perform searches because Regedt32's search capabilities aren't good. The best practice: search with Regedit, but only make changes with Regedt32! Figure 19-6 shows Regedit in action with a typical Windows NT system. Note, Windows NT dumps the HKEY_DYN_DATA folder seen in Windows 9x but, otherwise, it looks the same.

```
Registry Editor                                              _ □ ×
Registry  Edit  View  Favorites  Help
⊟ 🖳 My Computer          Name          Type          Data
  ⊞ 🗀 HKEY_CLASSES_ROOT
  ⊞ 🗀 HKEY_CURRENT_USER
  ⊞ 🗀 HKEY_LOCAL_MACHINE
  ⊞ 🗀 HKEY_USERS
  ⊞ 🗀 HKEY_CURRENT_CONFIG



         ⬚

My Computer
```

FIGURE 19-6 Regedit in Windows NT

As you'll recall from Chapter 18, Windows 9x uses two binary files to hold the Registry: SYSTEM.DAT and USER.DAT. Windows NT, in contrast, approaches the Registry files differently. Windows NT uses the term "hives" to describe a group of files that each add something to the Registry. These hive files are located in the \WINNT\SYSTEM32\CONFIG folder and the \WINNT\PROFILES folder. If you want to back up a Registry in Windows NT, copy these folders to a safe place. Take the time to memorize the primary boot files and the boot process for Windows NT. Most boot errors are easily repaired if you know which files are used for boot and in which order they load. Because the boot files and problems for NT and 2000 are identical, we'll save the methods for dealing with boot errors for Chapter 20.

Objective 19.02   Basic Disk Management

Windows NT requires some amount of basic disk management. Like Windows 9x, these include the usual partitioning, formatting, scandisk, and defrag. Unlike Windows 9x, the way to perform these jobs isn't always obvious.

Disk Administrator

Windows NT doesn't use FDISK to partition drives. Instead, it relies on the graphical Disk Administrator to perform all the necessary partitioning duties. While NT does have good old FORMAT, most NT techs also use the Disk Administrator to handle all the formatting chores.

Defragmentation

If you alternate-click a volume in Windows NT, select Properties, and then click the Tools tab, you'll see three tools: Error-checking, Backup, and Defragmentation. On most systems, the defragmentation button is grayed out! Amazingly, Windows NT doesn't come with any disk defragmentation tools. You need to install a third-party defragmentation utility.

Travel Assistance

O&O defrag is a popular NT defragmentation utility. Check it out at http://www.oo-software.com.

ScanDisk

Windows NT doesn't provide the classic ScanDisk tool. Instead, click the Check Now button from the Tool tab to perform a basic disk scan. Many companies provide a much better disk-scanning tool than the one provided with NT.

Objective 19.03 Troubleshooting and Upgrading Windows NT

B ecause I already covered the boot files and boot sequence earlier in this chapter, let's concentrate on creating a boot disk, and on an option for installation, upgrading, and startup in Windows NT.

Exam Tip
Every one of these topics is quite different in Windows 2000! Make sure you know the difference, for example, on how 2000 makes an emergency boot disk vs. how NT makes one!

Emergency Repair Disk

Those with experience using Windows 9x like to have a Startup disk handy to let them boot to a floppy disk if any of the critical boot files get corrupted. Knowing this, they assume they can do the same thing for Windows NT. Sadly, this is not the case. NT doesn't have boot disks other than the installation floppy disks.

However, you can create an Emergency Repair Disk (ERD) using the RDISK command at any command prompt. An ERD stores critical information about the system on a single floppy disk, enabling you to recover a system that fails at boot. To use an ERD, you boot from the install floppies and select Repair when prompted. While the ERD isn't a perfect fix for all boot problems under NT, it fixes enough common problems to make it worthwhile to do for every NT system.

Exam Tip
Use RDISK in Windows NT to create an Emergency Repair Disk.

Startup Options

Windows NT lacks the powerful startup options seen in Windows 9x and Windows 2000. Windows NT doesn't have a Safe mode or a Command Prompt startup feature. When you start a Windows NT system, you see two points in the boot process to let you do something other than a regular boot. The first one occurs when you see the boot menu, as shown earlier in Figure 19-5.

Unless the system is configured for dual boot, you only see two options: a normal boot and VGA mode boot. The VGA mode boots NT normally, but only loads the default VGA drivers—a handy way to fix a video setting that messes up the monitor.

After you select a boot option, you then see some text:

```
OS Loader V.4.01
.

Press Spacebar NOW to invoke Hardware Profile/Last Known Good menu
```

If you press the spacebar, you see the Hardware Profile/Configuration Recovery menu. From that menu, you simply press the L key to invoke the Last Known Good Configuration. Every time NT boots successfully, it keeps a copy of that configuration. If you're having problems starting up, using this option often brings the system back up to boot, although you loose any configurations done since the last good boot.

Exam Tip

Know how to access both VGA mode and the Last Known Good Configuration options.

Upgrading NT

While the A+ Operating System Technologies exam wants you to know how to install Windows 9x and Windows 2000, it doesn't expect you to know the process for installing Windows NT. It does expect you to understand one important aspect of NT: upgrading or *patching* the OS. Just as it does for Windows 9x, Microsoft provides service packs for Windows NT. The last service pack issued for NT was Service Pack 6.

CHECKPOINT

✔ **Objective 19.01: NT Structure and System Files**   NT supports FAT16
and NTFS partitions. NTFS supports partitions up to 2 terabytes. NTFS is
also the primary tool for system security in NT.

✔ **Objective 19.02: Basic Disk Management**   Windows NT uses the graphical Disk Administrator program for drive partitioning. ScanDisk and
Defragmentation are *not* a built-in part of this operating system.

✔ **Objective 19.03: Troubleshooting and Upgrading Windows NT**   NT does
not have a proper Safe mode, but if you run into trouble you can boot to VGA
mode. You can create an Emergency Repair Disk using the RDISK utility.

REVIEW QUESTIONS

1. Alice must divide her 20GB hard drive into a maximum of two partitions on
   her Windows NT system. Which of the listed drive formats can Alice use?
   (Choose two.)

   A. FAT
   B. FAT32
   C. NTFS
   D. CDFS

2. Which of the following files are not necessary for all Windows NT/2000
   systems?

   A. NTLDR
   B. NTBOOTDD.SYS
   C. NTDETECT.COM
   D. BOOT.INI

3. Windows NT and 2000 consider the initial boot partition as the system partition. They see the area that stores the operating system's _____ files as the
   boot partition.

   A. DLL
   B. GUI

    C. EXE

    D. DAT

4. With Windows NT and 2000, the robustness of these operating systems stems from the separation of running processes into a diversity of subsystems. Which of the subsystems are supported by Windows NT?

    A. Win32

    B. OS/2

    C. Win16

    D. All of the above

5. Which of the following procedures would create a Windows NT Emergency Repair Disk?

    A. Run RDISK from a command prompt

    B. Run ERD from a command prompt

    C. In the Backup program, click Create an Emergency Repair Disk

    D. In the Add/Remove Programs applet, click Create an Emergency Repair Disk

6. Every Windows NT system contains a premade account that has complete and absolute control over the entire system called:

    A. Power User

    B. Administrator

    C. Root

    D. Supervisor

7. Tim wants to use Sally's NT computer, but doesn't have any account or password. What can he do to access the system?

    A. Press the ESCAPE key at the logon screen

    B. Press the left CTRL key while booting

    C. Use the Administrator account with the password "guest"

    D. Tim cannot access Sally's system

8. Windows NT organizes user accounts into _____ that provide the same permissions to all members.

    A. Groups

    B. Teams

    C. Account headers

    D. Workgroups

9. Which of the following files must be in the root directory of the bootable volume for Windows NT?

   A. NTLDR
   B. CONFIG.SYS
   C. WIN.COM
   D. BOOT.INI

10. What is the name of the Windows NT boot mode that starts the system with only VGA video drivers?

    A. Safe mode
    B. MSDOS mode
    C. VGA mode
    D. Last Known Good Configuration mode

REVIEW ANSWERS

1. **A** **C** Windows NT can use FAT (also called FAT16) or NTFS. The size of the partitions was not specified, so either format will work.

2. **B** NTBOOTDD.SYS is only required for SCSI drives without ROM support on the host adapter.

3. **B** Windows NT and 2000 see the area that stores the operating system's GUI files as the boot partition.

4. **D** Windows NT supports applications written for all these subsystems.

5. **A** The RDISK program creates an Emergency Repair Disk in Windows NT.

6. **B** Administrator is the premade "super" account in Windows NT. This account has access to any program or device on the network and has complete control over the system.

7. **D** Tim cannot access Sally's system without a user account and password.

8. **A** Groups get permissions and every member of that group gets those permissions.

9. **A** **D** Windows NT requires NTLDR, NTDETECT, and BOOT.INI to boot.

10. **C** The Windows NT boot mode that starts the system with only VGA video drivers is called VGA mode. This option appears when Windows NT boots.

Windows 2000 Professional

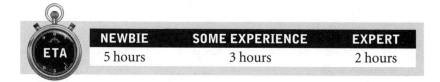

	NEWBIE	SOME EXPERIENCE	EXPERT
ETA	5 hours	3 hours	2 hours

Windows 2000 combines an improved Windows NT core with many ease-of-use and tech-friendly elements from Windows 9x. In addition, Windows 2000 adds some excellent new features; for example, the Microsoft Management Console creates a central point for the important tools techs use.

This chapter starts with a discussion of the important new or improved features of Windows 2000. It then launches into the specific tasks techs will face: installing and optimizing the operating system (OS), installing new hardware, and maintaining the system, including dealing with drives. The chapter finishes with a discussion on troubleshooting Windows 2000. Let's get started!

Objective 20.01 Installation

Windows 2000 comes in four versions—Professional, Server, Advanced Server, and Data Center Server. For the exams, you need to know Professional, the replacement for the client-side Windows NT Workstation. Although the various server versions offer some cool extra features, such as support for up to 32 CPUs in a single system and a whopping 64GB of RAM, A+ naturally cares about the stuff you'll be dealing with as an A+ tech.

Preinstallation Tasks

Installing an OS can be a time-consuming task, even when everything goes right. Nothing sets the teeth to grinding as much as an indecipherable error message or "blue screen of death" (BSOD) 55 minutes into an hour-long system installation.

With this in mind, let's look at the tasks you need to complete *before* you insert that Windows 2000 Professional CD-ROM disc. I'll cover each task in more detail in this section.

1. Identify your hardware requirements.
2. Verify that your hardware components are certified as compatible with Windows 2000.
3. Decide whether to perform an upgrade or a clean installation.
4. Determine how you want to partition the hard disk.
5. Decide on a file system.
6. Determine your computer's role (standalone, workgroup, or domain membership).
7. Decide on your computer's language and locale settings.

Hardware Requirements

Microsoft's minimum recommendations for a Windows 2000 Professional installation are as follows:

Component	Minimum Requirement
CPU	Intel Pentium 133 MHz
Memory	64MB
Hard disk	2GB w/650MB of free space
Network	None
Display	Video adapter and monitor with VGA resolution
CD-ROM	12X (not required if installing over a network)

These minimum specs represent what Microsoft says you need to install Windows 2000 Professional. Windows 2000 Professional will install and run on a system with the minimum specifications, but you need to double these numbers at least if you want to be happy with your system's performance!

Here's a more realistic recommendation for a Windows 2000 Professional computer system:

Component	Minimum Requirement
CPU	Intel Pentium II 350 MHz
Memory	128MB
Hard disk	6.4GB w/2GB of free space
Network	Modern PCI network card
Display	Video adapter and monitor with SVGA resolution, capable of High Color (16-bit) display
CD-ROM	24X (not required if installing over a network)
Floppy Disk Drive	High-density

If your test system exceeds the recommended configuration, all the better! You can never have too fast a processor or too much hard disk space.

Hardware Compatibility List

In addition to meeting the minimal specifications, your hardware needs to be supported by the Windows 2000 OS. The Hardware Compatibility List, or HCL, is the definitive authority on whether your component is compatible with the OS. Items on the HCL have been extensively tested with Windows 2000 and are guaranteed by Microsoft to work with your installation.

If you contact Microsoft's technical support staff, one of the first questions asked is whether all your system's components are on the HCL. The HCL is located in the SUPPORT folder on the Windows 2000 CD-ROM (HCL.TXT).

Travel Assistance

Visit the Microsoft web site (http://www.microsoft.com/hcl). There, you can search for a particular component or view the entire HCL.

Upgrading Issues

Upgrading your computer system from an earlier version of Windows can be a tricky affair with its own set of pitfalls. It's important to note there's a somewhat higher risk of running into errors during an upgrade than during a "clean" installation.

Here are some travel advisories to be aware of before performing an upgrade:

- You can directly upgrade to Windows 2000 Professional from Windows 9x (all versions) and Windows NT Workstation (versions 3.51 and 4.0). To upgrade to Windows 2000 Professional from Windows NT 3.1 or 3.5, you must first upgrade to NT 3.51 or 4.0, and then upgrade to Windows 2000 Professional. To upgrade smoothly from Windows NT 4.0 to Windows 2000, boot from the Windows 2000 boot disk or CD. You can also install Windows 2000 from the Windows NT GUI by running WINNT32.EXE.
- Because of Registry and program differences between Windows 9x and Windows 2000, you might need upgrade packs (or migration DLLs) for your Windows 9x applications. That's right: not only does Windows 2000 have hardware issues, it also doesn't like a lot of Windows 9x software!

- Windows 2000 does not support applications that make use of virtual device drivers (VxDs). VxDs enable applications to access hardware directly, bypassing the OS altogether. Many older games and multimedia applications use VxDs, making this a potentially serious issue.
- Third-party disk compression applications are not supported by Windows 2000.
- Third-party power management applications are also likely to cause problems with a Windows 2000 installation.

Planning Your Upgrade

Obviously, it's worth your time to take a few extra steps before you pop in that CD-ROM! If you plan to upgrade, rather than run a clean installation, follow these steps first:

1. First and most important, run a compatibility report using the Check Upgrade utility provided with Windows 2000 Professional. The utility generates a detailed list of potentially problematic devices and applications.

   The compatibility report is generated automatically when you perform a clean installation of Windows 2000.

   You can run the utility in two ways:

   - From your current OS, run the WINNT32.EXE program off the Windows 2000 Professional CD-ROM with the CHECKUPGRADEONLY switch.
   - You can download and execute the standalone version of the utility from Microsoft's web site at http://www.microsoft.com/windows2000/upgrade/compat/default.asp.

2. Have a current backup of your data and configuration files handy.
3. Perform a "spring cleaning" on your system by uninstalling unused or unnecessary applications and deleting old files.
4. Perform a disk scan and a disk defragmentation.
5. Uncompress all files, folders, and partitions.
6. Perform a current virus scan, and then remove or disable all virus-checking software.
7. Disable virus checking in your system CMOS.

Finally, remember, that if worse comes to worst, you might have to start over and do a clean installation anyway. For this reason, Step 2 from the list above is exceedingly important! *Back up your data.*

Disk Partition Options

The first thing the Setup program does is examine your hard disk to determine its existing partition and file system configuration. You then get the option of either installing on to an existing partition (if any) or creating a new partition for installation.

By default, the active partition (typically the C: drive) is where the Windows 2000 system files are copied. The boot partition is where your OS files are located. Typically, this will be C:\WINNT for a clean installation. An upgrade installation overwrites your current OS files in their current location (that is, \WINNT if upgrading from Windows NT, and \WINDOWS if upgrading from Windows 9*x*). Microsoft recommends that your boot partition be at least 1GB in size.

You can manage your disk partitions from within Windows 2000 using the Disk Management utility. I'll cover this utility in "File Maintenance" later in this chapter.

Networking Options

As with previous versions of Windows NT, the Windows 2000 line is optimized for networking with other computer systems. By default, Windows 2000 installs the Client for Microsoft Networks, File and Printer sharing for Microsoft Networks, and Internet Protocol (TCP/IP). You are also given the option of joining either a workgroup or a domain.

Your network administrator will supply details if you're working in a networking environment. Otherwise, simply install into a workgroup and go on with the installation. (If you want to know more about Windows networking, please refer to Chapter 21.)

Language and Locale Settings

Windows 2000 can easily be configured to support multiple languages and regional input settings for such things as keyboard layout, currency, time/date display, and numbering.

Quick Review

Here's a quick summary of the preinstallation tasks and considerations we've just covered. Think of it as a checklist you should go over before installing Windows 2000 on your system.

- Your hardware is up to snuff, meaning it meets the muscle requirements and is on the HCL.
- You've decided on a partition method.
- You've selected your file system(s).
- You know what role your machine is going to play in a network.
- You know what language and locale settings you plan to use.

So far, so good. At this time, you should take a moment to decide on a unique and memorable administrative password. Windows 2000 automatically sets up an administrator's user account during the installation, and you use this account to log on and perform all administrative tasks. Losing or forgetting the password to your administrator account can be bad news indeed.

After you satisfy all the preinstallation tasks, the actual installation of Windows 2000 is almost a letdown! You truly simply insert the CD-ROM, answer a few questions, kick up your heels, and read a book for an hour or so!

File System Options

At the heart of any OS is the system by which you create and organize your files. Windows 2000 supports FAT16 and FAT32, just like Windows 9*x*, but also supports its own native New Technology File System (NTFS).

Travel Advisory

Support for FAT32 is a new feature to Windows 2000. Windows NT versions 4.0 and earlier don't support FAT32. Neither Windows 2000 or Windows NT support the HPFS file system.

If you choose to format your disk with either version of FAT, the Windows 2000 Setup Wizard automatically formats it with FAT16 if the partition is less than 2GB and with FAT32 if the partition is greater than 2GB.

NTFS

The NTFS that comes with Windows 2000 (NTFS5) has a few advancements over the older NTFS from Windows NT (NTFS4). Windows 2000 can only create NTFS5 volumes—it cannot make the older NTFS4 volumes. NTFS5 offers the most options for your Windows 2000 OS installation. Using NTFS5, you can perform the following new functions that NTFS4 could not do (or did not do as well):

- Compress data on the hard disk to conserve space
- Assign disk quotas to users to limit the amount of hard disk space they can use
- Encrypt files and folders on the hard disk
- Support Windows 2000 Dynamic Disk configurations

Unless you're configuring your system for multiple-boot options, NTFS is the best way to go. Let's look at these new features of NTFS5 in a little more detail.

Travel Advisory

Existing NTFS4 system partitions will be upgraded to Windows 2000 NTFS5 automatically during the installation. If you want to dual-boot between NT4.0 and 2000, you must first install Service Pack 5 on the NT4.0 machine. This enables NT to read an NTFS5 partition, but the advanced features won't function.

NTFS5 adds four improvements: compression, encryption, drive naming conventions, and dynamic drives.

Compression   Windows NT had a rudimentary drive compression feature that most people avoided because it enabled you to compress only an entire drive. Windows 2000 enables you to compress anything: entire drives, folders, even individual files. To compress anything, select its properties and click the Advanced button on the General tab. Then select Compress Contents to Save Disk Space, as shown in Figure 20-1. Compression is safe and powerful.

Encryption   Windows 2000 NTFS partitions now support on-the-fly encryption, which enables you to protect sensitive files or folders—even if others have access to an encrypted file or folder, they can't see it. Only the person who created the encrypted file can see it, although administrators have a method for decrypting files, if necessary. No passwords are needed.

Volume Naming   Windows 2000 lets you name a volume with either a traditional drive letter or by a directory name on an existing drive. Let's say you add

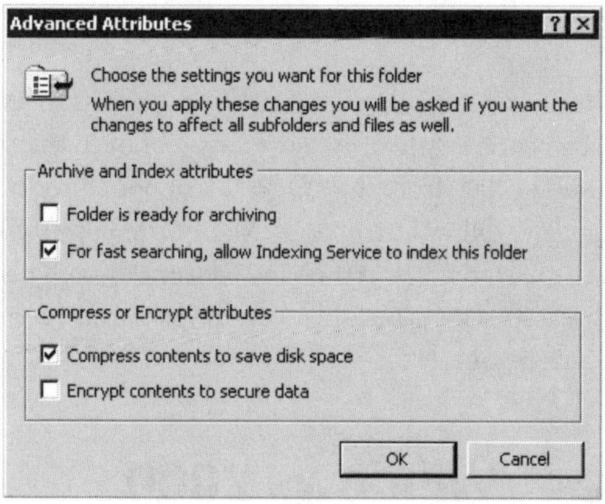

FIGURE 20-1 Compression and encryption

a 30GB drive to your Windows 2000 system. You can call that drive C:\BIG DRIVE and it will manifest itself as a folder on C:. Windows 2000 gives the volume a different icon than a normal folder to show it's actually a volume.

Disk Quotas Disk quotas simply limit the amount of disk space a particular user can take up. Virtually every other network OS has had disk quota functions for years, and competitors loved tossing NT's lack of disk quotas in Microsoft's face. Well, they no longer have anything to laugh about. Any NTFS volume supports disk quotas. Go to the drive letter's properties, select the Quota tab, and select the users for whom you want to set quotas.

Directory and File Structure

The Windows 2000 directory structure is quite different from Windows 9x. You've already seen most of this structure during earlier discussions, but here's a list of the three most important folders as a review.

- **\Winnt** contains all the files and subfolders used by Windows 2000. You'll see many folders and files are similar, if not identical, to Windows 9x.
- **\Program Files** stores installed programs, just like Windows 9x.
- **\Documents and Settings** stores all user-specific information. Note that each user gets his or her own folder, and there's also an All Users folder. This includes settings that show up for—you guessed it—all users.

Installing

After all the preliminaries, the actual installation process of Windows 2000 is pretty tame. You can choose one of two options—boot to the Startup diskettes and then load Windows 2000 from the CD-ROM, or boot directly to the Windows 2000 CD-ROM disc and follow instructions. Many techs copy the i386 folder from the CD-ROM to the hard drive and then install from there. This saves you from hunting for the disc later when you add a new device. In any event, simply follow the screens and you'll be fine.

Objective 20.02 Windows 2000 Boot Sequence

As you have read, the Windows NT/2000 OS consists of NTOSKRNL.EXE (the Windows NT kernel), the \WINNT\SYSTEM32\CONFIG\SYSTEM file (which controls the loading of device drivers), and the device drivers themselves. These files work in Windows 2000 the same way they work in Windows NT. There are some minor differences, however, in how booting is handled.

In the NT days, making a small (less than 50MB) FAT16 primary partition and a huge extended partition with one logical drive formatted as NTFS was common. This process made it possible to boot the system in case of a problem with NT. Well, those days are no more. Windows 2000 comes with a new tool, called the Recovery Console, which eliminates the need for a FAT16 partition. You'll see how to access this new tool in "Recovery Console" later in this chapter.

Dual Booting with Windows 9x and Windows NT

NT and 2000 can coexist with Windows 9x on the same boot partition, as long as the partition is FAT16 (Windows 2000 also coexists with FAT32). Although you *could* do this, the inability to use NTFS makes this idea ludicrous. The best method for dual-booting Windows 9x and Windows 2000 is to make a primary partition formatted with FAT32, and install Windows 9x on the drive. Then, install Windows 2000 on the unused portion of the drive. Both Windows NT and Windows 2000 have nice setup programs that can create a dual-boot system with ease. Many systems have Windows 2000/Windows 9x dual-boot capabilities.

System Partition Boot Files

Both Windows NT and Windows 2000 require the following four files in the root directory of the system partition:

- NTLDR (pronounced "NT loader")
- BOOT.INI
- NTDETECT.COM
- NTBOOTDD.SYS (only for SCSI controllers that don't have their own ROM BIOS)

These four files work exactly the same way in both Windows NT and Windows 2000. For more information on these files, refer to Chapter 19.

Windows 2000 Advanced Options Menu

The Windows 2000 Advanced Options menu is similar to Windows 9x systems' Startup menu, something Windows NT sadly lacked. Access this menu by holding down F8 at bootup. Although most of these settings are identical to Windows 9x settings, let's look at these options to appreciate some subtle differences.

Safe Mode   Selecting the Safe Mode option opens Windows 2000 in a mode that's as close as a high-powered, 32-bit OS can get to a Windows 9x type of Safe Mode. Safe Mode only installs basic drivers for keyboard, mouse, video, and drive access.

Safe Mode with Networking   This option opens Windows 2000 Safe Mode with basic network support.

Safe Mode with Command Prompt   This option opens Windows in Safe Mode, but with a big command prompt window running, as in Figure 20-2.

Enable Boot Logging   This is similar to Windows 9x logging. This option logs to a file called NTBTLOG.TXT.

Enable VGA Mode   This option tells Windows 2000 to boot normally, but with only a standard VGA driver. Use this option for those times when your new super-duper video card decides to cause problems.

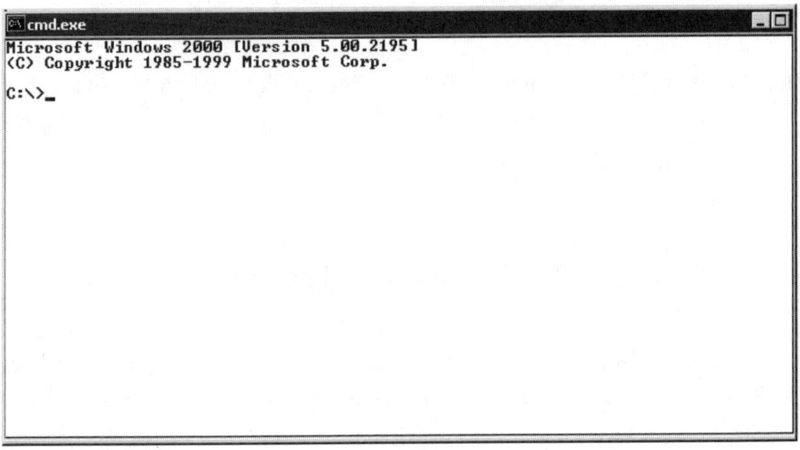

```
cmd.exe                                                    _ □

Microsoft Windows 2000 [Version 5.00.2195]
(C) Copyright 1985-1999 Microsoft Corp.

C:\>_
```

FIGURE 20-2 Safe Mode with Command Prompt

Last Known Good Configuration Windows 2000 saves a copy of the Registry at every successful startup. The Last Known Good Configuration option provides a great way to recover from bad software installs or other configuration problems. I wish Windows 9x had such a simple method!

Directory Services Restore Mode (Windows 2000 domain controllers only) This option is only for Windows 2000 Server. It's meaningless to Windows 2000 Professional.

Debugging Mode This option sends debug information to a COM port while your system boots up. This is way outside the scope of A+!

Boot Normally This option speaks for itself. You can use it if you change your mind after bringing up the Windows 2000 Advanced Options menu.

The Active Directory

Windows 2000 domains add another layer of complexity that did not exist in Windows NT: the Active Directory. The Active Directory is a common organizational database of the entire network, even when a network uses multiple domains. Network administrators can tap into powerful administrative functions by storing every user account, every shared folder, every printer—in short, *everything* that is part of the network—in the Active Directory.

While you're not required to use Active Directory in a Windows 2000 domain-based network, it makes a lot of tasks easier for administrators.

Users and Groups in Windows 2000

Windows 2000 handles users and groups a little differently than Windows NT. The administrator creates user accounts with a special program called Users and Passwords in Windows 2000, as shown in Figure 20-3. The account list has three columns: User Name, Domain, and Group. To understand domains requires extensive networking discussion, so I'll leave that for Chapter 21 and, instead, focus here on user names and groups. A *user name* defines an account for a person who has access to the PC. A *group* is simply a collection of accounts that share the same access capabilities. A single account can be a member of multiple groups.

You can access Users and Groups from the Microsoft Management Console (MMC), through the Users And Groups snap-in. From there, you can manage user accounts and the network resources that groups can use. I'll talk more about the MMC in Objective 20.04, later in this chapter.

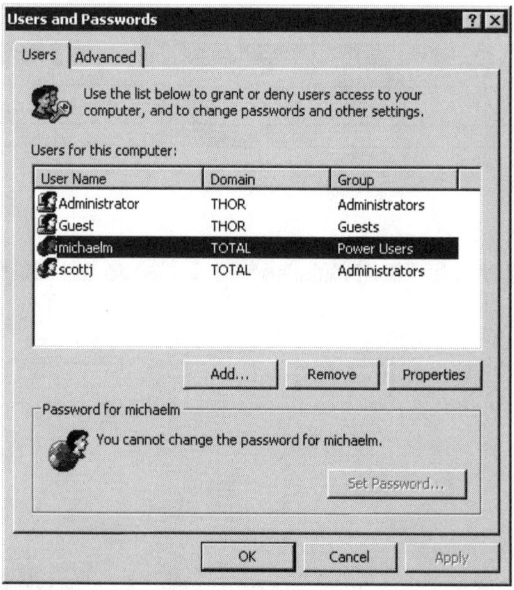

FIGURE 20-3   Users and Passwords

Additionally, you can manage users and their group membership in the Users and Passwords program in the Control Panel.

Local Security Policy

Local Security Policy in the Administrative Tools program group enables administrators to set a bewildering number of rights for users and groups. These special settings are called policies. A right, by the way, is not the same thing as a permission. *Permissions*, if you recall, enable you to access and manipulate data on an NTFS-based drive. *Rights*, in contrast, describe what you can do to a system, such as log in or restart the PC. Changing *policies* enables you to set a bunch of rights all at once.

Let's say you don't want Bob, the late-shift guy, to log on to your system at night because you're running some hairy program and he plays games, which slows down the process. The program will finish in a week, so you don't want him to delete his account—just not log on to the system for a week. Open the Local Security settings and locate the User Rights Assignment under Local Policies. Scroll through the policies until you find Deny Logon Locally.

Double-click to open it. Click the Add button to add the user Bob, as shown in Figure 20-4. Of course, if you don't have a user called Bob, this won't work!

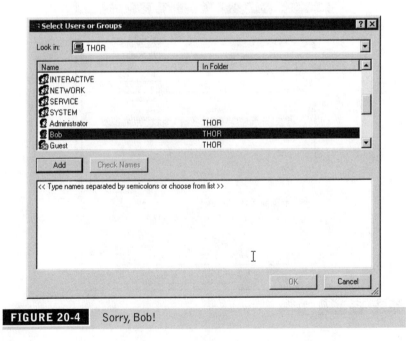

FIGURE 20-4   Sorry, Bob!

Notice the Local Setting and the Effective Setting. If the Effective Setting is checked, this means some other policy is overriding yours. For example, if you tried to deny Shut Down the System to Power Users, the Effective Setting for the policy would still show as checked because Power Users always have the right to shut down a system. It's a defined function for that built-in group.

Exam Tip

The A+ Certification exams do not ask you about particular policies. You need to understand what policies do and how they can affect you as a tech. Watch out for questions that ask, "Why can't you shut down a system?" Be prepared to answer, "Someone has set a policy that prevents me from doing it!

Objective 20.03 File Maintenance

Windows 2000 has completely redefined the concept of drive preparation, maintenance, and repair. First and foremost, Windows 2000 drops FDISK. Windows 2000 handles drive partitioning at install time. For routine partitioning and format duties, Windows 2000 comes with the amazing Disk Management utility.

You can access Disk Management via the Administrative Tools console , just as you did for Local Security Policy. Disk Management provides an attractive, intuitive view of all storage devices on your system. Work with Disk Management for a while and you'll never want to deal with FDISK again!

Basic vs. Dynamic Disks

When you install an extra drive on a Windows 2000 system, it first manifests itself as a basic disk. *Basic disks* are good old regular drives with standard partition tables and MBRs. Microsoft enables you to upgrade any drive, however, to what's called a dynamic disk. *Dynamic disks* do not use partitions as you've seen in earlier chapters. Instead, they use a unique organization that manifests itself as flexible, resizable volumes.

You should only use dynamic drives if you need to do neat things such as:

- **Spanned volume** A volume that spans multiple drives
- **Striped volume** Two drives that split the data into alternating stripes

With Windows 2000 Server, dynamic drives can also make:

- **Mirrored drives** Two drives that share identical data
- **RAID 5 drives** Three or more drives that provide redundancy in case one drive fails.

The bottom line is, in most cases, dynamic drives aren't something you'll use often in Windows 2000 Professional.

Upgrade to Dynamic Disk

To make a basic disk dynamic, first open the Computer Management MMC. You can do this in a couple of different ways, but the most direct approach is to alternate-click the My Computer icon on your desktop and select Manage. Once you've opened Computer Management:

1. Select Disk Management, under Storage, to view the drives and volumes currently set up on your system.
2. Select the disk you want to make dynamic, then alternate-click the word "Basic" and select Upgrade to Dynamic Disk. You get a verification screen, and then the drive is updated. Your only clue that this happens is a lot of grinding noise from the drive and the change of the word "Basic" to "Dynamic."

You can revert a dynamic disk back to a basic disk only by first deleting all volumes on the disk. Then alternate-click the word "Dynamic" and select Revert to Basic Disk.

Partitioning Basic Drives

Partitioning a basic disk is a trivial matter of alternate-clicking the disk and selecting a command to make a partition. You can choose to make either a primary partition or an extended partition. If you alternate-click an extended partition, you can make logical drive letters.

Unlike FDISK, you can make up to four primary partitions to support multiboot scenarios. Alternate-click the primary partition you want to make active, select Make Active Partition, and then restart the computer. Whatever OS is on that partition becomes the active one.

Creating Dynamic Volumes on Dynamic Drives

To make a volume on a Dynamic drive, alternate-click and select Create Volume. Notice only Simple volume is highlighted. Select the size and format type.

Drive Naming

The basic partitions and dynamic volumes you create are given default drive letters. Let's look at drive-letter assignment in more detail.

Changing Drive Letters You can accept the default drive letter, use another (unused) drive letter, or mount the drive to an empty folder on another drive. The last option—Do Not Assign This Drive a Letter—is used to hide drives.

Formatting Both basic and dynamic volumes support FAT16, FAT32, and NTFS formats. In fact, the Disk Management snap-in defines how drive management should truly work. Now, do you really want to go back to FDISK? Don't worry, you will at some point!

Objective 20.04

The Microsoft Management Console (MMC)

One of the biggest complaints about Windows NT and, to a lesser extent, Windows 9x, was the wide dispersal of the many utilities needed for administration and troubleshooting. Despite years of research, Microsoft could never find a place to put all the utilities needed in a way to please even a small majority of support people. In a moment of sheer genius, Microsoft determined the ultimate utility was one that support personnel could make for themselves! This brought on the creation of the amazing Microsoft Management Console.

The MMC is simply a shell program that holds individual utilities called *snap-ins*. You can start the MMC by selecting Start | Run and typing **MMC**. This brings up a blank MMC console, which isn't much to look at.

You make a blank console useful by adding snap-ins. Click Console | Add/Remove Snap-in, and then click the Add button to see a list of available snap-ins, as in Figure 20-5.

Virtually every traditional tool used by either Windows NT or Windows 9x is available as a snap-in. Even good old Device Manager is now a snap-in. Let's add the Device Manager snap-in. Once you click OK, close the Add window, and then click the Device Manager.

You can add as many snap-ins as you want—and you can choose from a long list. Many companies sell third-party utilities as MMC snap-ins. Once you add the

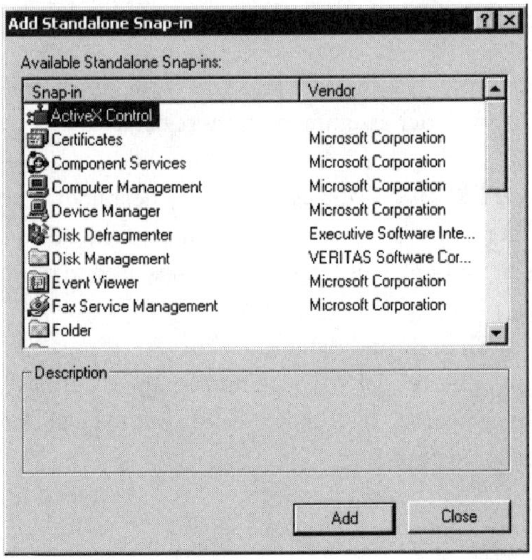

FIGURE 20-05 Available snap-ins

snap-ins you want, save the console under any name you want, anywhere you want. I'll save this console as DM (Device Manager) and drop it on my desktop. I'm now only a double-click away from the Device Manager!

If I want to, I can customize the MMC. Click Console | Options to change the icons, save it under a different name, or lock it up, so it can never be changed.

Be sure to uncheck the Do Not Save Changes to This Console check box. If you leave this option checked, when you reopen the console, the Console, Windows, and Help menu options will be gone, and the console cannot be changed.

These Microsoft geniuses also knew some folks like things the old way, so they made a bunch of prefabricated, locked consoles and dropped them in the same places—or at least close to the same places—you'd expect them to be in Windows 9x. Open the System Information Utility by clicking Start | Programs | Accessories | System Tools | System Information. It's the good old System Information utility, but notice it has a slightly different look: it's now an MMC snap-in!

If you click Tools and hold the mouse pointer over the Windows menu, however, you'll notice the MMC version has all the same utilities that came with the Windows 9x System Information utility. The snap-in versions of the old classics all look a tad different, but they still do the same job. In fact, they usually do the job better!

Control Panel in Windows 2000

The options in Windows 2000's Control Panel are much like the options in the Control Panel for Windows 9x, but some sharp differences exist between the two. In this section, you'll learn some of those differences.

Add/Remove Hardware

The Add/Remove Hardware Wizard has changed considerably from Windows 9x. While still used to detect legacy devices, this wizard now has a few new jobs. The Add/Remove Hardware Wizard is now accessible from the System Properties applet, so I'll save the new features for that discussion.

Add/Remove Programs

Microsoft completely revamped the Add/Remove Programs applet from the Windows 9x version, adding a number of handy improvements.

In my opinion, adding the size of the application approaches pure genius! So many times, people delete programs only to open space on the drives, so this helps the decision-making process. Microsoft also appreciates that a lot of folks, like me, install a gazillion programs, so adding the option to sort by name, size, and so on makes my uninstalling life much easier!

The Add/Remove Programs Wizard also has the Add/Remove Windows Components and Add New Programs tabs, which function just like their Windows 9x counterparts.

The most interesting item is what's *not* here anymore: there's no Startup Disk option. Windows 2000 doesn't have a Startup disk in the sense of Windows 9x; it's too big of an OS. You can make floppy disks for Windows 2000, but they're barely functional. Don't panic: Windows 2000 provides lots of new toys to help in recovery, as you see in "Troubleshooting Boot Problems" later in this chapter.

Administrative Tools

In the Windows 2000 Professional Control Panel, you'll see an icon labeled Administrative Tools. This group contains the most frequently used MMC snap-ins, allowing a user or administrator to be only a few clicks away from those favorite tools.

Sound and Multimedia

Windows 2000 combines the Windows 9x Sound applet and the Multimedia applet into one. There's no loss of functionality or features, just one less applet to try to find.

System

You want to see a big change? OK, let's look at the System properties. The tour begins with a quick trip to the System applet in the Control Panel. Open this applet. (Yes, you can still alternate-click My Computer to get here, although it looks different from the old Device Manager!) Here you see the System Properties dialog box, one of the most important areas to maintain and fix a system, as shown in Figure 20-6.

General Tab

The General tab gives basic information about the PC and mirrors the General tab information on a Windows 9x machine. This tab shows the current service pack, the serial number, and the amount of RAM, but it's not good for much else. The Network Identification Tab is new to the System applet, but I'll save the discussion about this tab for Chapter 21, which covers networking in detail. Of all the tabs in System Properties, Hardware tends to be the most heavily used and deserves a more thorough discussion.

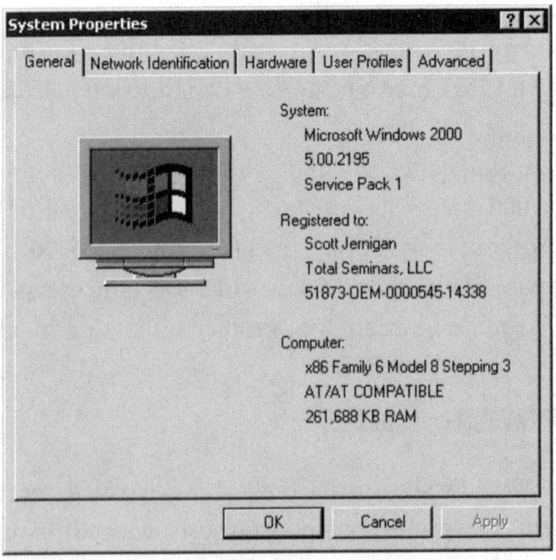

FIGURE 20-6   System Properties

Network Identification Tab

This tab contains the settings that determine how you're identified on a network. You can change your computer name here, as well as become a member of a workgroup or a domain. (For more information on domains, see Chapter 21.)

Hardware Tab

The topmost button, the Hardware Wizard, is the same Add/Remove Hardware Wizard you've already seen. In today's plug and play (PnP) world, Microsoft expects devices to install automatically. In fact, when you install a device in Windows 2000, you no longer get the famous "Windows has detected new hardware" message. Windows 2000 simply installs the device and only prompts you if it does not have a proper device driver. Microsoft no longer sees the Hardware Wizard as a primary tool for installation. Instead, it sees this as two tools in one.

Add/Troubleshoot a Device
The first tool, Add/Troubleshoot a Device, works much like the Windows 9*x* Wizard, but concentrates on PnP devices, enabling you to install or troubleshoot from a list that looks somewhat like the Device Manager. Microsoft has thoughtfully configured the wizard to place any "problem" devices at the top of the list to bring them to your attention—a nice touch! To add a non-PnP device, you must select Add a New Device, the first option. When you select Add a New Device, you get a slightly updated version of the old Windows 9*x* Add/Remove Hardware Wizard.

Uninstall/Unplug a Device
The Uninstall/Unplug a Device radio button is a new feature to the Add/Remove Hardware Wizard. This is really two new features. First, just as Windows 9*x* added the capability to uninstall applications to deal with the nightmare of removing complex software installations, Windows 2000 now adds the capability to perform thorough uninstalls of hardware, cleanly removing all the unnecessary device drivers and other support programs.

Second, this option provides support for hot-swappable devices, such as FireWire, USB, or any other device designed to unplug or eject without a reboot.

Travel Advisory

The Unplug/Eject option only works for devices designed to hot swap. Don't try removing a non-supported device like a PCI network card or a PS/2 mouse with this feature. It won't work!

Driver Signing   Badly written device drivers have plagued every version of Windows. Some device drivers simply don't work properly with their hardware. Some of them conflict with other device drivers, while others ignore basic programming rules and wreak havoc on the OS itself. Some device drivers work perfectly well, but become obsolete as service packs and new applications are created over the life of the OS.

In an attempt to reduce these issues, Microsoft instituted the Windows Hardware Quality Lab (WHQL) testing center. Hardware makers can submit their hardware and device drivers to Microsoft, and receive an electronic certificate from Microsoft stating that the drivers successfully passed a number of rigorous tests and should work perfectly under Windows 2000. The Driver Signing button on the Hardware tab enables you to decide whether to allow non-certified device drivers in the system.

A large percentage of device drivers do not possess WHQL certificates. In fact, you would find it difficult to find *any* Windows 2000 system that contained nothing but WHQL-certified drivers. Because of this, leaving the "File signature verification" setting on "Warn" is common. The Administrator option simply enables the administrator to set a default for all users.

No one knows if driver signing will become the standard. Many well-known manufacturers simply ignore WHQL because of the time and cost involved with obtaining the certificate, especially given that most manufacturers update device drivers at least yearly. Other manufacturers separate the WHQL drivers from their latest drivers, giving users the choice between a known safe driver and one that incorporates the latest features.

Device Manager   Microsoft did techs everywhere a favor by adding the Device Manager to Windows 2000. The Windows 2000 Device Manager is now just another MMC snap-in, although it works basically the same as the Windows 9*x* Device Manager.

The last option on the Hardware dialog box, Hardware Profiles, enables you to create different hardware configurations.

User Profiles

The User Profiles tab, as shown in see Figure 20-7, shows the current profiles on the system. This shows the account name, total size of all personal data, type (I'll explain this next), and the date each profile was last modified. You can glean two important bits of information from this dialog box. First, you can see how much drive space a particular user account takes up, enabling you to deal with accounts that are either taking up too much space or in need of more space.

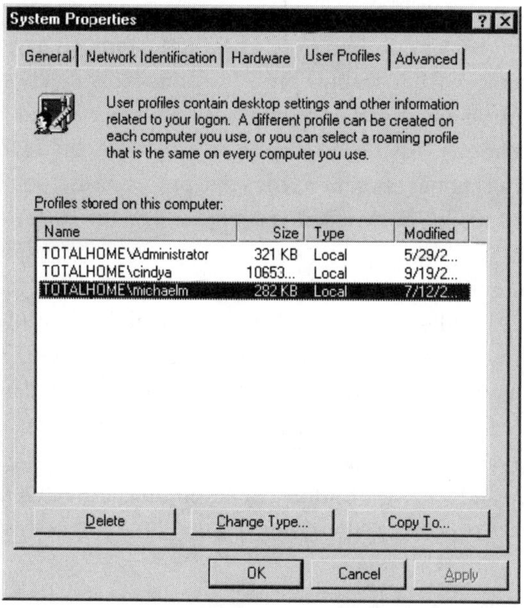

FIGURE 20-7   User Profiles tab

Second, when you delete an account, the folder tree continues to exist until you remove it here. If you notice one of the profiles showing as Account Unknown, this is a deleted account. An administrator will probably want to go through the folder tree to ensure that no important files still exist, and then return to the User Profile dialog box and delete the profile.

Windows 2000 supports two types of profiles: local and roaming. *Local* profiles, as their name implies, only work on a single system. *Roaming* profiles work on *any* system in a network. With roaming profiles, no matter what system you log on to, you can get your desktop, personal settings—what you want, the way you want it. Roaming profiles do have some downsides as well: all systems using roaming profiles must be members of a domain, and lots of large roaming profiles can put serious strain on a network. To make a local profile a roaming profile, click the Change Type button. This couldn't be easier! (For more information on domains, be sure to visit Chapter 21.)

Advanced

The last tab on the System applet, Advanced, comes in a close second to the Hardware tab for the title of Most Used Dialog Box for Techs.

The Performance Options dialog box contains a pair of radio buttons, called Applications and Background Services. These radio buttons have nothing to do with virtual memory. They set how processor time is divided between the foreground application and all other background tasks. Set this to Applications if you run applications that need more processor time. Set it to Background Services to give all running programs the same processor use. You can also adjust the size of the swap file—now called a *paging file*—on the Performance Options dialog box.

The next button, Environment Variable, provides two items, the first of which is a list of user variables used for backward compatibility with DOS and older Windows applications. You might occasionally need to add settings here. Second is a list of system variables, which are used by Windows 2000 and NT applications to provide system information to any program that might need it. Unlike the user variables, these values rarely change.

The Startup and Recovery button enables editing of the BOOT.INI and provides steps to take in case of system failure.

Objective 20.06   Ongoing Tasks for Windows 2000

After your Windows 2000 system is installed and configured, you need to perform various tasks to get the most out of your system and to keep it running smoothly. These tasks include installing new hardware, installing and managing printers, backing up the Registry, and troubleshooting boot problems.

Installing New Hardware

The processes for installing new hardware are absolutely identical to the procedures you use in Windows 9x, even down to the troubleshooting and backup utilities. Just remember, in the case of a resource conflict, you need to reserve the resource in CMOS! If you know how to install PnP and legacy devices in Windows 9x, you know how to do it in Windows 2000.

Plug and Play

Although later service packs of Windows NT provided rudimentary support for PnP, Windows 2000 packs complete PnP support. Windows 2000 now has the Device Manager and the Add/Remove Hardware Wizard, making device installation nearly identical to the methods described for Windows 9*x* in Chapter 18. Windows 2000 does do one thing differently: it doesn't show anything on the screen when installing devices unless there's a problem. I'm not too sure I like that. I miss the old "Windows has found new hardware" message from Windows 9*x*!

Printing in Windows 2000

Windows 9*x* and Windows 2000 use the Graphical Device Interface (GDI) component of the OS to handle print functions. While you *can* use an external printer language such as PostScript, most users simply install printer drivers and let Windows do all the work.

The GDI uses the CPU, rather than the printer, to process a print job, and then sends the completed job to the printer. When you print a letter with a TrueType font in Windows, for example, the GDI processes the print job, and then sends bitmapped images of each page to the printer. The printer sees a page of TrueType text as a picture, not as text. As long as the printer has a capable enough RIP and plenty of RAM, you don't need to worry about the printer language at all in most situations.

Installing and Managing Printers

Windows 2000 uses a dramatically more complex method for installing and managing printers. First, Windows sees a "printer" not as a physical device, but as a *program* that controls one or more physical printers. We call the *physical* printer a "print device." There are still printer drivers and a spooler, but in Windows 2000, they're integrated into the "printer" itself.

This arrangement gives Windows 2000 amazing flexibility. For example, one printer can support multiple print devices, allowing a system to act as a print server. If one print device goes down, the printer automatically redirects the output to a working printer. Windows 2000 also provides support for non-standard ports, enabling extra functions for networked printers.

Even though Windows 9*x* and Windows 2000 work differently beneath the hood, the general installation, configuration, and troubleshooting issues are basically identical. I'll describe a typical Windows 2000 printer installation, and point out the trivial differences between Windows 2000 and Windows 9*x* along the way.

You can choose to install either a printer plugged directly into your system or a network printer. Windows 2000 also adds the Automatically Detect My Plug and

Play Printer option, which is a nice extra touch. If you choose a local printer, Windows 2000 asks you to select the port where you installed the new printer.

Once you select the port, Windows 2000 asks for the type of printer. Select the type from the list or use the Have Disk option, just as you would for any other device. Note the handy Windows Update option to pull the latest printer driver from the Internet.

Windows 2000 then installs the printer. A small check mark appears in the corner, indicating the device is the default printer, as you can see in Figure 20-8. If you have multiple printers, you can select a different default printer by going into that printer's properties and checking Make Default Printer.

Installing printers in Windows 9x and Windows 2000 is one of the easiest processes in any version of Windows. If only everything were this easy!

Backing Up the Windows 2000 Registry

Windows 2000 approaches the Registry files differently than Windows 9x. Windows 2000 uses the term *hives* to describe a group of files that each add something to the Registry. These hive files are located in the \WINNT\SYSTEM32\ CONFIG folder

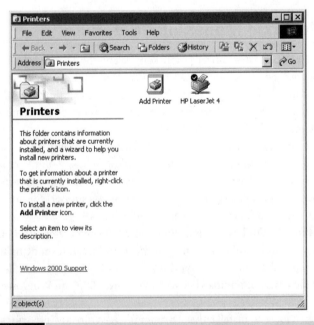

FIGURE 20-8   The Default Printer in Windows 2000

and the \WINNT\PROFILES folder. If you want to back up the Windows 2000 Registry, you need to know where these files are!

Rather than forcing you to go on a file hunt, Windows Backup lets you save vital system files automatically. In Windows 2000 Backup, you can select to save the System State, which, among other things, saves your Registry.

Troubleshooting Boot Problems

Windows 2000 boot problems, like those with Windows 9x, can be divided into two distinct areas. With Windows 2000, you can divide boot problems into system partition errors and boot partition errors.

System Partition Errors

System partition errors stand out quite readily because they are always text errors or lockups that show up early in the boot process. If an error shows, it tends to give away the problem by using errors that include the names of the critical boot files:

- NTLDR missing or corrupt
- Can't find NTDETECT.COM
- Unable to read BOOT.INI

If you get one of these error messages, don't panic until you check to make sure you don't have a diskette in your floppy drive. If this is the problem, you may want to slap yourself in the forehead. If this *isn't* the problem, try booting with the various options from the Windows 2000 Advanced Options menu. If necessary, you can boot to the Recovery Console and proceed as described in the appropriately named "Recovery Console" section later in this chapter.

Boot Partition Errors

Boot partition errors are usually harder to detect. If you're lucky, you'll get some easy error, such as "Registry is corrupt" or the stuck Windows boot screen. When these types of errors show up, first try the Safe Mode boot. Don't do anything there. Just go into Safe Mode, and then try restarting normally. If this fails, try restoring the Registry using the Last Known Good Version option in the Advanced Options menu. That usually fixes most boot problems. As a last resort, use the Recovery Console to restore the Registry folders.

If none of these processes work, use the boot diskettes to run the install procedure. When the system asks to install or repair, select R for repair.

Repairing Broken Windows

You have a choice here of manual or fast repair. Both styles essentially reinstall Windows entirely, but differ on what you'll see as an end result. Always use the manual repair because the fast repair uses an ancient copy of the Registry from when the system was first installed. You'll end up with a working Windows 2000 PC, but one without any of your applications, special settings, and so forth. With a manual repair, in contrast, everything *but* the Registry is reinstalled. Once the system finishes installing, you can then use a recent backup copy of the Registry and end up with a system similar—if not identical—to the one that crashed.

Creating Boot Disks

Windows 2000 does not have classic boot disks in the sense that Windows 9*x* does. Instead, it takes four floppy disks to start the Windows 2000 install/repair process. This is an intelligent process. It looks for a preinstalled copy of Windows 2000 and, if it detects one, it shifts from an install mode into a repair mode. Most Windows 2000 systems come with these four setup disks but, if you don't have them, they are simple to make.

Go to the \BOOTDISK folder on the Windows 2000 installation CD-ROM. There, you'll find a file called MAKEBT32.EXE. Run this file and follow the onscreen prompts to build the four floppies you need to boot the Windows 2000 installer. Be sure to label your disks!

Just as with Windows 9*x*, the secret to troubleshooting Windows 2000 is preparation. This means critical system file backup and the creation of a boot disk. Additionally, you need to set up the unique and powerful Recovery Console, a new feature in Windows 2000.

Emergency Repair Disks

You can create an Emergency Repair Disk (ERD) through Windows Backup. This disk saves critical boot files and partition information, and it's your main tool for fixing boot problems. This is not a bootable disk and it doesn't store much information, so the ERD *does not* replace a good system backup. It works with a special folder called \WINNT\REPAIR to store a copy of your Registry. This isn't perfect, but it gets you out of most startup problems. I always make a new ERD before I install a new device or program.

In Windows Backup, click the Emergency Repair Disk button and select the check box, as shown here:

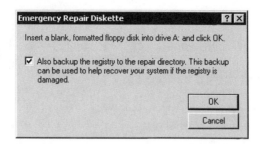

That's it! It's almost too easy. Your ERD is now ready to save your skin, if needed.

Recovery Console

While you can't really get Windows 2000 to boot to an A: prompt, you can use something called the Recovery Console. The Recovery Console is as close as Windows 2000 gets to the Windows 9x Safe Mode Command Prompt Only feature.

First, you need to install it. Log in to the system with the administrator account. Grab your Windows 2000 install CD-ROM and drop it in your system. If the autorun function kicks in, click the No button. Get to a Windows 2000 command prompt by selecting Start | Run and typing CMD. (CMD is the 32-bit super-command prompt for Windows NT and 2000. It acts exactly like the old COMMAND.COM.) When you get to the command prompt, switch over to the CD-ROM drive letter (Did you forget how to do this already? Go back and reread Chapter 16!), and then type this command and press ENTER:

```
\i386\winnt32 /cmdcons
```

Follow the instructions on the screen. From now on, every time the system boots, you'll see a boot menu like the one shown in Figure 20-9.

If you don't like looking at this screen, set the BOOT.INI timeout to some smaller number, but not too small! Reboot your system to see the Recovery Console.

Recovery Console Commands

The Recovery Console looks like a command prompt and uses many of the commands that worked in DOS, as well as some uniquely its own. Here's a list of the most common Recovery Console commands, including descriptions of commands I haven't covered previously.

```
Please select the operating system to start:

    Microsoft Windows 2000 Professional
    Microsoft Windows 2000 Recovery Console
    Previous Operating system on C:

Use ↑ and ↓ to move the highlight to your choice.
Press Enter to choose.
Seconds until highlighted choice will be started automatically: 26




For troubleshooting and advanced startup options for Windows 2000, press F8.
```

FIGURE 20-9   Boot menu after installing the Recovery Console

- **ATTRIB**
- **CD**
- **CHKDSK**
- **CLS**   Clears the screen
- **COPY**
- **DEL**
- **DIR**
- **DISKPART**   The Windows 2000 equivalent of FDISK
- **EXIT**   Exits the Recovery Console and restarts your computer
- **EXPAND**
- **FIXBOOT**   Writes a new partition table from the backup MST
- **FIXMBR**   The Equivalent to FDISK /MBR, which fixes the Master Boot Record (MBR)
- **FORMAT**
- **HELP**   Displays a Help screen
- **LOGON**   Logs on to a Windows 2000 installation
- **MD**
- **REN**
- **RD**
- **SYSTEMROOT**   Sets the current directory to the root of the system directory, usually c:\

The files that make up the Recovery Console reside on the system partition, making the Recovery Console useless for system partition crashes. The Recovery Console shines in the business of manually restoring registries (Remember where the ERD put the backup copy of the Registry? You'd better remember!), rebuilding partitions (other than the system partition), or using the EXPAND program to extract copies of corrupted files from a CD-ROM or floppy disk.

The vast majority of Windows 2000 problems manifest themselves exactly as they did in Windows 9x. The internal differences and different tools, however, make it necessary to look at alternative repair methods for the bane of the PC industry: boot problems. Otherwise, all repair scenarios work exactly the same as in Windows 9x.

Even though Windows 9x and Windows 2000 are vastly different architectures, they share so many common features—multitasking, swap files, DLLs, and so forth—that most of the errors occurring in either OS require the same fixes.

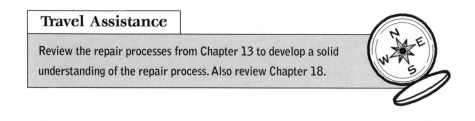

Travel Assistance

Review the repair processes from Chapter 13 to develop a solid understanding of the repair process. Also review Chapter 18.

CHECKPOINT

✔ **Objective 20.01: Installation**   Know the steps to take before Windows 2000 installation and the options you'll have during the installation procedure.

✔ **Objective 20.02: Windows 2000 Boot Sequence**   Know the Windows 2000 boot files and boot menu options, and understand the purpose and capabilities of the Active Directory.

✔ **Objective 20.03: File Maintenance**   Understand the differences between FAT16, FAT32, and NTFS, and between basic and dynamic volumes. Know how to use Disk Management to create and partition volumes, as well as to assess existing volumes.

✔ **Objective 20.04: The Microsoft Management Console**   Know how to bring up the Microsoft Management Console (MMC) and how to add snap-ins to customize a console for your needs.

Objective 20.05: Control Panel in Windows 2000   Know the differences in the Control Panel between Windows 9*x* and Windows 2000.

 Objective 20.06: Ongoing Tasks for Windows 2000   Know how to set up a printer in Windows 2000, how to create and use an Emergency Repair Disk, and how and when to use the Recovery Console.

REVIEW QUESTIONS

1. Windows 2000 provides two locations for administrators to manage all local computers' user account passwords. Which of the following are the correct places?

   A. Change Password button in Task Manager
   B. Local Users and Groups snap-in under Computer Management
   C. Security applet in Control Panel
   D. Users and Passwords applet in Control Panel

2. Which of the following is an advantage of Windows 2000 as compared to Windows 9*x*?

   A. Multimedia support
   B. Driver support for older hardware
   C. File security
   D. Support for DOS applications

3. John installed a second hard drive to his dual-boot Windows NT 4.0/Windows 2000 PC. He formatted the drive while running Windows 2000 but, when he boots into Windows NT, John can't see the drive in My Computer. Which of the following would be the most probable reason for this?

   A. The new drive was formatted as FAT32.
   B. John isn't logged in as the administrator.
   C. Windows NT cannot see any partition created in Windows 2000.
   D. The new drive wasn't partitioned using a compatible partitioning program.

4. Which of the following procedures will successfully start the process of upgrading a Windows NT 4.0 system to Windows 2000?

   A. Run WINNT from the Windows 2000 installation CD-ROM within Windows NT.

    B. Boot directly from the Windows 2000 installation CD.

    C. Use the Windows 2000 installation floppies and the Windows 2000 installation CD.

    D. Use the boot floppy and Windows NT 4.0 installation CD.

5. In Windows 2000, what is the best place to determine which devices get which system resources?

    A. Right-click My Computer and select Properties. In System Properties, go to Hardware Profiles and double-click the Computer icon.

    B. Double-click My Computer, and then right-click the C: drive and select Properties.

    C. Right-click My Computer and select Properties. In System Properties, go to Device.

    D. In Device Manager, click View, and then Resources by Type.

6. Lloyd wants to add the Windows 2000 Recovery Console option to his boot menu. He inserts his Windows 2000 Professional installation CD into drive F:. Which of the following is the correct command to run from the command prompt?

    A. `F:\WINNT32\I386 /cmdcons`

    B. `F:\I386\WINNT /cmdcons`

    C. `F:\I386\WINNT32 /cmdcons`

    D. `F:\WINNT\I386 /cmdcons`

7. Windows 2000 provides a number of ready-made MMC snap-ins stored in the _____ applet in the Control Panel.

    A. System

    B. Network

    C. Administrative Tools

    D. MMC

8. The Windows 2000 NTFS file system provides excellent features, such as Backward Compatibility and Long Filename support. Which of the following are among the other features it provides?

    A. Redundancy

    B. Recoverability

    C. Security

    D. All of the above

9. Windows 2000 can format a partition with any format type except:

    A. FAT16

    B. FAT32

    C. NTFS

    D. HPFS

10. What Windows 2000 Recovery Console command fixes the MBR?

    A. FIXMBR

    B. FDISK /MBR

    C. REBUILD

    D. SCANREG /MBR

REVIEW ANSWERS

1. **B** **D** Both the Local Users and Groups MMC snap-in and the Users and Passwords application let administrators manage user passwords.

2. **C** File security is one of the benefits of NTFS5.

3. **A** Windows NT 4.0 and below cannot view FAT32 volumes.

4. **B** Booting directly from the CD upgrades Windows NT 4.0 to Windows 2000.

5. **D** In Device Manager, you can view the resource addresses by selecting View | Resources By Type.

6. **C** The proper command to install the Recovery Console is F:\I386\ WINNT32 /cmdcons.

7. **C** Administrative Tools contains a number of frequently used MMC snap-ins.

8. **D** All of these are benefits to using the NTFS5 file format.

9. **D** HPFS isn't supported by Windows 2000. HPFS is a file system supported by OS/2.

10. **A** FIXMBR is the Recovery Console command that fixes the master boot record.

Networking
in Windows

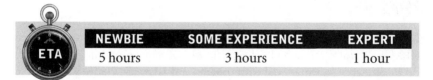

	NEWBIE	SOME EXPERIENCE	EXPERT
ETA	5 hours	3 hours	1 hour

465

PC networking involves more than just moving data from one machine to another; many other functions also need to be handled. For example, if a file is being copied from one machine to another, something must keep track of all the data packets so the file can be properly reassembled. If many machines are talking to the same machine at once, that machine must somehow keep track of which packets should be sent to, or received from, each of the other PCs.

Another issue arises if one of the machines in the network has its network card replaced. Up to this point, the only way to distinguish one machine from another was by the MAC address on the network card. To solve this, each machine must have a name, an identifier for the network, which is "above" the MAC address. Each machine, or at least one of them, needs to keep a list of all the MAC addresses on the network, and the names of all the machines so they can be correlated. Then if a machine gets a new network card, the network can make some special queries and update the list to associate the new network card's MAC address with the name of that PC.

Objective 21.01   # Network Protocols

Network *protocol* software takes incoming data from the network card, keeps it organized, and sends it to the program that requires it. When you send data out, the protocol software packages and labels the data properly so it can reach its intended destination. All networks use at least one protocol. Although many different protocols exist, the top three—IPX/SPX from Novell, NetBEUI from Microsoft, and TCP/IP from UNIX/Internet—hold a virtual lock on all networks.

IPX/SPX

Novell invented the Internetwork Packet Exchange/Sequenced Packet Exchange (IPX/SPX) protocol and built all versions of NetWare around it. The IPX/SPX protocol is speedy, works well with routers, and takes up relatively little RAM when loaded.

NetBEUI

During the 1980s, IBM developed the NetBIOS Extended User Interface (NetBEUI), the default protocol for Windows for Workgroups, LANtastic, and Windows 95. NetBEUI offers small size and a relatively high speed, but cannot be used for routing. Its inability to handle routing limits NetBEUI to networks smaller than approximately 200 nodes. A *node* is any device that has a network connection. This is usually a PC, although other devices can also be nodes. For example, many printers now connect directly to a network and can, therefore, be thought of as nodes.

TCP/IP

Terminal Control Protocol/Internet Protocol (TCP/IP) was originally developed for the Internet's progenitor, the Advanced Research Projects Agency Network (ARPANET) of the U.S. Department of Defense. In 1983, TCP/IP became the built-in protocol for the popular BSD UNIX and other flavors of UNIX quickly adopted it as well. TCP/IP is the preferred protocol for networks. The biggest network of all, the Internet, uses TCP/IP as its default protocol. Windows 98/ME/2000/NT use TCP/IP as their default protocol. TCP/IP lacks speed and takes up a large amount of memory when loaded (especially in real mode), but it is robust, well understood, and universally supported.

You need to understand a good deal of TCP/IP, but rather than dump it on you here at the beginning of the chapter, I've saved up a tasty serving of the protocol suite for you to read in Objective 21.04.

AppleTalk

AppleTalk is the proprietary Apple protocol. Similar to IPX/SPX, AppleTalk is small and relatively fast. The only reason to use an AppleTalk protocol is to communicate with older Apple computers on a network.

Objective 21.02   # Network Operating Systems

A *network operating system* (NOS) is the program that makes a network function. All network operating systems can be broken into three basic organizational groups: peer-to-peer, client/server, and domain-based. To appreciate these three groups, let's first look at the needs of a typical network.

You need to share resources across a network. How do you make that happen? Can everyone share his or her hard drives with everyone else? Should you place limits on sharing? If everyone needs access to a particular file, where will it be stored? What about security? Can anyone access the file? What if someone erases it accidentally? How are backups to be handled? Different network operating systems answer these questions differently.

Client/Server

Take one machine and dedicate it as a resource to be shared over the network. This machine will have a dedicated NOS optimized for sharing files. This special operating system includes powerful caching software that enables high-speed file access. It will have extremely high levels of protection and an organization to allow for extensive control of the data. This machine is called a *dedicated server*. All of the other machines that use the data are called *clients* or *workstations*.

In such a *client/server* network system, one machine acts as a dedicated server, with its only function being to serve up resources to the other machines on the network. These servers do not run DOS or Windows 9*x*. They use highly sophisticated and expensive network operating systems that are optimized for the sharing and administration of network resources. Currently, only one network operating system fits the client/server concept: the popular Novell NetWare.

A NetWare server is not used directly by anyone. It doesn't run Windows; it only runs Novell NetWare. NetWare has its own commands and requires substantial training to use, but in return, you get an amazingly powerful NOS. Understand that Novell NetWare only *serves* shared resources; it doesn't run programs like Excel or CorelDraw. Many network administrators will go so far as to remove the keyboard and monitor from a Novell NetWare server to keep people from trying to use it.

Client/server network operating systems such as Novell NetWare provide powerful security for shared resources. Remember the powerful NTFS permissions used by Windows 2000 Professional? Many people feel Microsoft copied several aspects of NTFS permissions from Novell NetWare because they are very similar.

Peer-to-Peer

Some network operating systems do not require dedicated servers. In these networks, every computer can act as both a server and a client. *Peer-to-peer* networks are much cheaper than client/server networks because the software costs less and doesn't require a high-end machine to be used as a dedicated server. The most popular peer-to-peer network operating systems today are Windows 9*x* and

Windows 2000 Professional. A peer-to-peer network enables any or all of the machines on the network to act as a server.

As long as the total number of machines on the network stays relatively low, there's no problem with using peer-to-peer. As the number of machines goes past 20 or 30, though, the entire network begins to slow down. If one file is being shared heavily, even five or six machines can bring the entire system to a crawl.

Security is the other big weakness of peer-to-peer networks. Each system on a peer-to-peer network maintains its own security (this is called *distributed security*). Windows 9*x* has really poor network security. When a Windows 9*x* system shares a resource like a folder or a printer, it has only three levels of network rights from which to choose: Read-Only, Full Access, and Depends On Password.

Microsoft does this on purpose. The idea is this: if you want real security, you need to buy Windows 2000. But even a network composed only of Windows 2000 machines still requires you to place a local account on every system. So, even though you get better security in a Windows 2000 Professional peer-to-peer network, system administration means a lot of running around to individual systems to create and delete local users every time someone joins or leaves the network.

Windows peer-to-peer networks organize the networked systems into *workgroups,* which is little more than a method for organizing systems in a pretty way, to make navigating through Network Neighborhood a little easier. In reality, workgroups have no security value.

Peer-to-peer remains very popular, however, because the price (usually free—it comes with Windows 9*x* and 2000 Professional), combined with its tremendous ease of use, make peer-to-peer the NOS of choice for smaller networks. After all, these networks don't need the high level of protection and the high speed provided by client/server network operating systems.

Many people believe that part of the definition of a peer-to-peer network includes the use of the TCP/IP protocol. This is not true. You can run a peer-to-peer network composed of all Windows 2000 Professional systems using only the NetBEUI protocol if you want. Windows 9*x* and Windows 2000 always assume you want to use TCP/IP and automatically install it, which is probably where this little myth originated.

Exam Tip

Understand the difference between client/server and peer-to-peer.

Domain-Based

Client/server networks, especially NetWare, dominated networking for many years. To access a NetWare server, you must have an account created on that system, and then go through a logon process. Each server system stores a database of accounts and passwords. If you want to access a server, you must log on.

When only one server exists, the logon process takes only a second and works very well. The trouble comes into play when your network contains multiple servers. In that case, every time you access a different server, you must repeat the logon process. In larger networks containing many servers, this becomes a time-consuming nightmare, not only for the user, but also for the network administrator. If an employee decides to quit the company, the network administrator must walk up to each server and delete the account—a major hassle.

A *domain-based* NOS uses a different idea. In a domain-based environment, one server holds the security database for all systems. This one database holds a single list of all users and passwords. When you log on to your computer—in fact, to any computer—the logon request goes to this single system, called the Primary Domain Controller (PDC) in Windows NT, to verify the account and password. Obviously, the PDC performs a very important task, so Microsoft allows other systems to act as Backup Domain Controllers (BDCs) that can take over in case the PDC goes down. Domain-based security saves time and effort.

In the NT world, if you wanted to use the power of domains, you needed to purchase Windows NT Server. If all the systems on your network were NT Workstations, you had to log on to each system separately. This is still true in Windows 2000. When you attempt to access another system, it requires you to log on. In a domain-based network, this will not happen.

Windows 2000 does not use the PDC/BDC. Instead, any Windows 2000 Server system with Active Directory installed becomes a domain controller. Multiple domain controllers all automatically share the security information in a process called *replication*. If one domain controller fails, the other domain controllers automatically take over.

Every Windows NT and 2000 system contains a special account called Administrator. This one account has complete and absolute power over the entire system. When you install Windows NT or 2000, you must create a password for the Administrator account. As you might imagine, anyone who knows the Administrator password has the ability to read any file and run any program. You should keep the Administrator password secret to all but the highest level of administrators. Equally important, losing the Administrator password usually requires the complete reinstallation of Windows NT or 2000—so don't lose it! (You can buy third-party "find the administrator account" packages and services, but they're all expensive and difficult to use.)

Windows 2000 assumes you'll be joining a domain, and starts making preparations for domain membership as early as installation. You probably remember being asked during Windows 2000 setup whether the computer would be part of a workgroup or a domain. Not coincidentally, a Windows 2000 installation also normally includes all the necessary components for joining a domain: the network client, file and printer sharing, and TCP/IP.

Any Windows 9*x* system may also become a member of a domain, but because Windows 9*x* uses non-NTFS file systems, its sharing security is much weaker than Windows NT or Windows 2000. A more common strategy is to add Windows 9*x* systems to a domain simply as clients. To make or change a Windows 9*x* system's workgroup membership, use the Identification tab in the Network Neighborhood properties.

Creating or changing a domain membership for a Windows 9x client takes a little more effort. In Network Neighborhood properties, select the Configuration tab, then select Client for Microsoft Networks and click the Properties button. Check Log on to Windows NT Domain (even if it is a Windows 2000 domain), and enter the domain name.

Windows 2000, as usual, makes the process a little easier. Open the properties for My Computer, and then select the Network Identification tab. This shows your current selection.

Clicking the Network ID button opens the Network Identification Wizard, but most techs just use the Properties button. Both processes accomplish the same thing but if you know what you want to do, you won't need a lot of the wizard's explanations. Make sure you have a good domain account when logging onto a domain or you won't be able to log in.

Local and Global Groups

Domain-based networks create a problem. Imagine a network of only Windows 2000 Professional systems. Each of these systems uses NTFS permissions, and each of these systems has its own local user accounts and local groups.

So what happens when you add a Windows 2000 Server system and create a domain? Do the local user accounts and local groups disappear? No! Windows domain-based networks create a second layer of accounts and groups called *domain accounts.* For a user to log in to a domain, he or she must have a domain account on the domain controller.

How do you deal with two sets of users and two sets of domains? You use them in a very special way. Here are the rules as stipulated by Microsoft:

- Each individual gets a global user account.
- Global user accounts become members of global groups.

- Each system (Server or Professional) creates local groups. Each local group gets NTFS permissions on that local system.
- Domain-based networks should not use local accounts.

The beauty of this setup lies in its flexibility. An administrator can create domain accounts and domain groups from any Windows 2000 Server system. (You cannot create domain accounts or groups on Windows 2000 Professional.) The only time the administrator would still need to run around is to change a local group on a remote system, and Windows 2000 provides remote manipulation of local groups. Lazy people must like Windows 2000 a lot!

Windows 2000 domains add another layer of complexity that didn't exist in Windows NT: the Active Directory. The Active Directory is a common organizational database of the entire network, even when a network uses multiple domains. Administrators can use this one storage area for every user account, every shared folder, every printer, everything that is the network, and can oversee powerful administration functions. Active Directory isn't required in a Windows 2000 domain-based network, but it makes many tasks easier for administrators.

Exam Tip

Don't panic about domains and domain groups and all that stuff. Just understand that a domain provides a centralized security function, and that you must have at least one copy of Windows NT Server or Windows 2000 Server to have a domain. The rest was only included for completeness. If you really want to get into networks, take the Network+ certification, and then go for the Microsoft Certified Systems Engineer (MCSE) certification.

Enough of this conceptual talk! The A+ Certification exams assume you know how to configure a Windows 9x or Windows 2000 Professional system to work on either a Windows peer-to-peer or Windows domain-based network. The process follows these steps:

1. Hardware: Cabling, installing NICs
2. Protocol: Choosing the network hardware protocol to use
3. Network: Enabling sharing, naming the system
4. Resource Sharing: Providing resources to share and accessing those shared resources

We took care of installing the hardware and protocols in Chapter 15, so what's left? You guessed it: there's still the unfinished business of joining the network and sharing resources. Without further ado, let's march on through the process of installing a Windows 9*x* or Windows 2000 machine on a network.

Network

Every computer on a Windows network, whether peer-to-peer or domain-based, gets a network name. When I discussed installing Windows 9*x* and Windows 2000, you may recall that I had you give the computer a name. Now you know why I did this: you were configuring the system for a network. I'll bet I know what you're thinking: "But Mike, we were just installing the system as stand-alone in those chapters—what good is a computer name in a stand-alone system?" You're correct: computer names in stand-alone systems *are* meaningless. Microsoft wants you to name it anyway, in case you decide to install it on a network later.

So, the first part of the network layer, the computer's name, is handled at installation. The second part—setting the system as sharing or not sharing—varies between Windows 9*x* and Windows 2000.

With Windows 9*x*, any PC can be a server or a workstation. By default, all machines are workstations. To make a PC a server, some extra software, called a *service*, must be added. There is a special service that enables the PC to share its printers, its hard drives, or both.

Once again, open the Network applet. Let me show you a second way to get to the Network applet. This time, alternate-click Network Neighborhood and select Properties. This also works for Windows 2000, although the screen is very different!

Click on Add again, and this time select Services | Locate File | Print Sharing. You can choose to share files, printers, or both. Windows 2000 doesn't give you a choice, as file and printer sharing are automatically installed. You automatically have the ability to share anything. To see this, select Properties under My Network Places (Figure 21-1).

Note that File and Printer Sharing is already installed. If for some reason you want to *stop* sharing, just uncheck the box.

Travel Advisory

Only systems that have File and Printer Sharing enabled are visible in Network Neighborhood.

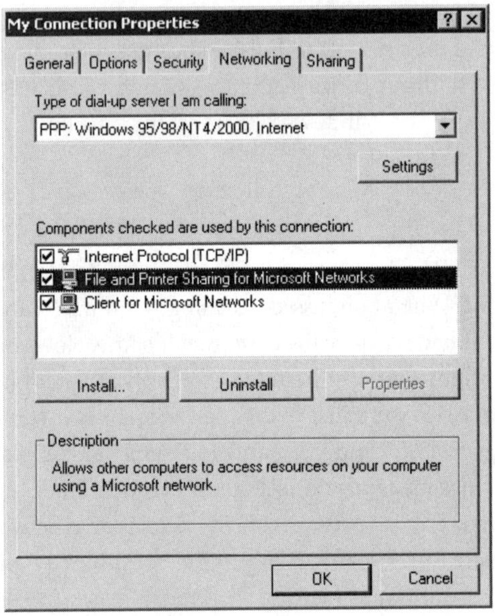

FIGURE 21-1   Network Connection Properties in Windows 2000

Super! The system has a name and you've set up the machine so it can share resources. But installing File and Printer Sharing simply gives the machine the *ability* to share. To start sharing requires the last layer of my Four-Layer Model: Sharing Resources.

Objective 21.03 Sharing Resources

Windows systems can share all kinds of resources: files, folders, entire drives, printers, faxes, Internet connections, and much more. Conveniently for you, the A+ Certification exams limit their interests to folders, printers, and Internet connections. Let's see how to share folders and printers now and save Internet connection sharing for its own section.

Sharing Drives and Folders

The various versions of Windows share drives and folders in basically the same manner. Simply alternate-click any drive or folder and select Sharing. If you don't see the Sharing option, you have not enabled file sharing on the system. By click-ing the Shared As radio button, you can add a share name. This is the name other workstations will see when they look for resources to access.

The trick here is to use a name that clearly describes the resource. For exam-ple, if the goal is to share a C: drive, sharing that drive as *C* could confuse this C: drive with other C: drives being shared around the network. Instead, try a more detailed name like FREDC or SALES3C. As a rule, try to keep the name short and without spaces.

After establishing the share name, note that you can determine *how* it is to be shared. Under Windows 9*x*, the options are simple: Full, Read-Only, and Depends On Password. This is one of the major limitations of Windows 9*x* networks. After you select the network name and the access level, click the OK button to see a lit-tle hand appear, as shown in Figure 21-2. When you see the little hand, you know the network resource is being shared.

You create Windows 2000 folder shares the same way, although the use of NTFS adds a little complexity. Access the properties for a folder in Windows 2000 and click the Sharing tab. Select Share This Folder, add a comment and a user limit (if you want to—they're not required), and click Permissions to see your network sharing permissions options.

Hey! Doesn't NTFS have all those wild permissions like Read, Execute, Take Ownership, and all that? Yes it does, but NTFS permissions and network permis-sions are totally separate animals. Microsoft wanted Windows 2000 to support many different types of partitions, old and new—NTFS, FAT16, FAT32, HPFS—Bill Gates wants everyone's business! Network permissions are Bill's way of enabling

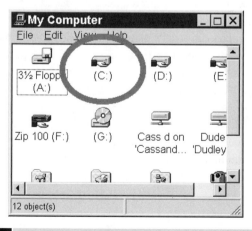

FIGURE 21-2   The little hand indicates the drive or folder is shared on the network

you to administer file sharing on any type of partition supported by Windows, no matter how ancient. Sure, your options will be pretty limited if you're working with an older partition type, but at least you *can* do it.

The beauty of Windows 2000 is that it gives you another tool—NFTS permissions—that can do much more. NTFS is where the power lies, but power always comes with a price: you have to configure two separate sets of permissions. If you're sharing a folder on an NTFS drive, as many people do these days, you must set *both* the network permissions and the NTFS permissions to let others access your shared resources.

Now for the good news: this is no big deal! Just set the network permissions to give everyone full control, and then use the NTFS permissions to exercise more precise control over *who* accesses the shared resources and *how* they access them. Click the Security tab to set the NTFS permissions.

Exam Tip

Windows 2000 has two types of sharing: Network permissions and NTFS permissions. Windows 9*x* has only Network permissions.

Accessing Shared Drives/Directories

Once you have set up a drive or directory to be shared, the final step is to access that shared drive or directory from another machine. In Windows 9*x,* you access the shared devices through the Network Neighborhood. Windows 2000 uses My Network Places, although you'll need to do a little clicking to get to the shared resources.

Network resources can also be mapped to a local resource name. For example, the FREDC share can be mapped to a local drive letter such as E: or F:. You can do this in Windows 9*x* from Windows Explorer or by alternate-clicking a share in Network Neighborhood and selecting Map Network Drive. Mapping is usually done when you want a permanent connection, or to support older programs that might have trouble accessing a drive called FREDC.

Windows 2000 supports Map Network Drive, but it adds a handy Add Network Place icon in My Network Places. This lets you add network locations that you frequently access without using up drive letters.

UNC

All computers that share, and all the resources they're sharing, must have network names. Any resource on the network can be described by combining the names of the sharing system and the resource being shared. If a machine called SERVER1 is sharing its C: drive as FREDC, the complete name would be described like this:

```
\\SERVER1\FREDC
```

This is called the *Universal Naming Convention* (UNC). The UNC is distinguished by its use of double backslashes in front of the sharing system name and a single backslash in front of the shared resource name.

Sharing Printers

Sharing printers in Windows is as easy as sharing drives and directories. Assuming the system has printer-sharing services loaded, you simply go to the Printers folder in the Control Panel and alternate-click the printer you want to share. Select Properties, go to the Sharing tab, click on Shared As, and give the shared printer a name (Figure 21-3).

To access a shared printer in any version of Windows, simply click the Add Printer icon in the Printers folder. When asked if the printer is Local or Network, select Network; then browse the network for the printer you want to access.

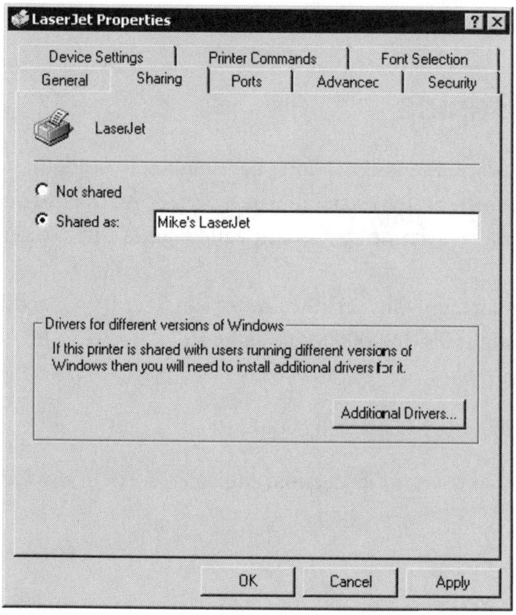

FIGURE 21-3   Giving a name to a shared printer

Windows takes care of the rest! In almost all cases, Windows copies the printer driver from the sharing machine. In the rare case where it doesn't, it prompts you for the necessary drivers.

Before Windows 95, most network printing was done via the redirection of an LPT port. A printer would be installed and an unused LPT port—like LPT2 or LPT3—would then take all the print information. This redirected LPT would send the print job over the network to the proper network printer. Although this is unnecessary in most cases today, all versions of Windows still provide this option to support older applications.

Objective 21.04 TCP/IP

TCP/IP, or to be more correct, IP, is the primary protocol of the Internet. If a PC wants to have access to the Internet, it must have the TCP/IP protocol loaded. TCP/IP has become so predominant that most network folks use it even on networks that don't connect to the Internet. While TCP/IP is very powerful, it's also a bit of a challenge to set up. So, whether you're installing a modem for a dial-up connection to the Internet or setting up 500 computers on their own private intranet—or, in fact, taking the A+ Certification exams—you must understand some TCP/IP basics.

TCP/IP Basics

In a TCP/IP network, the systems don't have names. Instead, they use four sets of eight binary numbers (*octets*) separated by a period. We call this *dotted-octet notation*. So, instead of a computer being called SERVER1, it gets a name like 202.34.16.11.

Remember, an eight-bit binary number can have $2^8 = 256$ different permutations—from eight 0's (00000000) to eight 1's (11111111). So with TCP/IP, an address like this

11110010.00000101.00000000.00001010

is shown instead in terms of its decimal equivalents. For example:

00000000 = 0
00000001 = 1
00000010 = 2

And so on, up to:

11111111 = 255

This method allows for a total of 256 different octets. So, in theory, IP addresses can range from 0.0.0.0 to 255.255.255.255. Unfortunately, certain rules in the TCP/IP world make many of those IP addresses unusable. For example, no address may use all 0's or all 1's, making addresses like 207.255.43.167 illegal (255 is 11111111 in binary and is not allowed). This significant reduction in IP addresses, combined with the explosion of new systems on the Internet, has placed a serious strain on the number of available IP addresses. This shortage of IP addresses has led to the creation of a method that enables systems to share IP addresses (see "DHCP/WINS" later in this chapter).

TCP/IP is a unique type of protocol. While it certainly supports file and printer sharing, TCP/IP adds a number of special sharing functions unique only to TCP/IP. These are lumped together under the umbrella term *TCP/IP services*. The most famous TCP/IP service is called Hypertext Transfer Protocol (HTTP), the language of the World Wide Web. If you want to surf the Internet, you must have TCP/IP.

TCP/IP supplies many other services beyond just HTTP. Using a service called TELNET, you can access a remote system as though you were physically in front of that machine. Another example is a handy utility called PING. *PING* enables one machine to check whether it can communicate with another machine. If you want to see PING in action, open a command-prompt window in a PC connected to the Internet and type **PING**, followed by a space and the name or IP address of another computer, and press ENTER. For example, **PING WWW.TOTALSEM.COM**.

Travel Advisory

Just when you thought no new command-line tools were being developed, Microsoft has come out with a new and improved version of PING, called PATHPING. For the truly detail-oriented, PATHPING gives you a breakdown of the total round-trip time in nanoseconds, percentage of data loss between nodes, and the IP address of each router or network the packet passes through.

Isn't that interesting—many TCP/IP services run from a command prompt! It's a good thing you know how to access one.

I'll show you plenty more services in a moment. The goal of TCP/IP is to link together multiple networks, called Local Area Networks (LANs), to make an entire Wide Area Network (WAN). WANs are usually linked together via some type of telephone service, ranging from basic dial-ups to dedicated, high-speed (and expensive) data lines, as shown in Figure 21-4.

The goal is to make a WAN that uses the expensive links for as little traffic as possible. The machines that connect the phone lines to each LAN are specialized computers called *routers*. To reduce traffic, each router decides which packets on the LAN should go out to the WAN. The router makes these decisions based on the packets' IP addresses.

Routers are most commonly used in TCP/IP networks, but other protocols also use them, especially IPX/SPX. There are even special routers called *brouters* (bridging routers) that can translate between different protocols, although the translation process makes them relatively slow compared with regular routers.

TCP/IP Settings

TCP/IP has a number of unique settings you must configure correctly for proper network functionality. Unfortunately, these settings can be somewhat confusing: there are quite a few of them, not all of them are used in every type of TCP/IP network, and it's not always obvious where you must go to set them. TCP/IP settings can be found in two primary locations: one for dial-up connections (modems) and one for direct (NIC) connections.

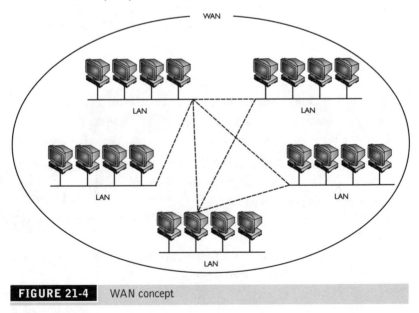

FIGURE 21-4   WAN concept

For Windows 9x computers that use a modem to access the Internet, start in My Computer and click the Dial-up Networking icon. Alternate-click the connections whose TCP/IP properties you want to set and select Properties | Server Type | TCP/IP Settings. The place to configure TCP/IP settings for direct connections is the Control Panel. Select Networks | TCP/IP, and click the Properties button.

Windows 2000 makes this much easier by letting you configure both dial-up and network connections using the My Network Places properties. Simply select the connection you want to configure, and then set its TCP/IP properties.

The A+ Certification exams assume that someone else, such as a tech support person or some network guru, will tell you the correct TCP/IP settings for the network. Your only job is to understand roughly what these settings do and to know where to enter these numbers so that the system works. Let's discuss some of the more common TCP/IP settings.

> **Exam Tip**
>
> The A+ Certification exams have a rather strange view of what you should know about networking. Take a lot of time practicing how to get to certain network configuration screens. Be prepared for questions that ask about the *specific steps you take* to change a particular value.

Default Gateway

A computer that wants to send data to another machine outside its LAN is not expected to know all the IP addresses of all the computers on the Internet. Instead, all IP machines know the name of one computer, to which they pass all the data they need to send outside the LAN. This machine is called the *default gateway,* and it is usually just the local router.

Domain Name Service

Knowing that users weren't going to be able to handle raw IP addresses, early Internet pioneers came up with a way to correlate those numbers with more human-friendly computer designations. Special computers, called *Domain Name Service* (DNS) servers, keep databases of IP addresses and their corresponding names. For example, a machine called TOTAL.SEMINAR1 will be listed in a DNS directory with a corresponding IP address, such as 209.34.45.163. So, instead of accessing the \\209.34.45.163\FREDC directory to copy a file, you can ask to see \\TOTAL.SEMINAR1\FREDC. Your system will then query the DNS server to get TOTAL.SEMINAR1's IP address and use that to find the right machine. Virtually all TCP/IP networks require you to set up DNS server names.

Internet domain names are highly regulated. If you want a domain name that others can access on the Internet, you must register your domain name and pay a small yearly fee. In most cases, your Internet service provider (ISP) can handle this for you. Originally, DNS names all ended with one of the following seven domain name qualifiers:

.com	General business
.org	Nonprofit organizations
.edu	Educational organizations
.gov	Government organizations
.mil	Military organizations
.net	Internet organizations
.int	International

As more and more countries joined the Internet, an entire new level of domains was added to reflect the country, although the original seven are still supported. It's common to see DNS names such as www.where.to or www.who.do. Recently, the Internet Corporation for Assigned Names and Numbers (ICANN) announced the creation of several new domains; given the explosive growth of the Internet, they're unlikely to be the last ones.

DHCP/WINS

The last items most TCP/IP networks require are Dynamic Host Configuration Protocol (DHCP) and Windows Internet Naming Service (WINS). To understand DHCP, you must first remember that every machine needs an IP address. In many systems, this is manually added to each machine in the TCP/IP properties menu. A permanent IP address assigned to a machine is known as a *static* IP address.

DHCP takes a different approach. It enables you to create a pool of IP addresses that are given to machines when they need them, and then taken away when they're no longer needed. This pool of IP addresses is called a DHCP *scope*, and the duration an IP address is assigned for is called a *lease*.

One of the more powerful features of a DHCP scope is that you can also include the addresses of the default gateway, DNS server, and WINS server in the IP address leases. When the client grabs a DHCP lease, it is also given the addresses of the computers it needs to contact for routing and name resolution. It's like one-stop shopping for all your client's networking needs!

DHCP is especially handy for networks with a lot of dial-in systems. Why give a static IP address to a machine that's only on the network for a few minutes a day? For this reason, DHCP is quite popular. If you add a NIC to a Windows 2000 or Windows 98 system, the TCP/IP settings are set to use DHCP. When you accept those automatic settings, you're really telling the machine to use DHCP.

Exam Tip

An interesting, but potentially confusing, new feature in Windows ME and Windows 2000 is Automatic Private IP Addressing (APIPA). With *APIPA,* if the computer can't reach a DHCP server to get a DHCP lease, it assigns itself a temporary IP address in the range of IP addresses set aside for private networks: 169.254.*x.x* to 169.254.255.254. Every five minutes, the computer tries to reach the DHCP server again. If it's successful, it takes the lease and drops the APIPA address.

Windows Internet Naming Service

WINS enables Windows network names like SERVER1 to be correlated to IP addresses, like DNS does, except this deals with *Windows* network names, not Internet names. All you need to do to set up WINS is either type in the IP address for the WINS server or let DHCP handle it for you. Windows 2000 supports WINS, but prefers to use an improved "dynamic" DNS that supports both Internet names and Windows names.

TCP/IP Tools

All versions of Windows come with handy tools to test TCP/IP. You've already seen PING, which is a really great way to see if you can talk to another system. Another way techs use PING is to see whether name resolution is functioning. For instance, if you can PING a machine by its IP address, but not by its name or URL, you know that somewhere down the line, you're not getting the DNS or WINS service you need.

Windows 9*x* provides the handy WINIPCFG program. Type **WINIPCFG** at the Run box to see something that looks like Figure 21-5.

Click the More Info button to see all your TCP/IP options. The Release and Renew buttons let you get new TCP/IP information from a DHCP server.

FIGURE 21-5 WINIPCFG in action on a Windows 98 system

Windows 2000 does not use WINIPCFG. Instead, you must go to a command prompt and run IPCONFIG. You can type **IPCONFIG /ALL** to see all your TCP/IP settings.

IPCONFIG can do a lot of other things as well, such as release and renew your DHCP lease and flush your DNS resolver cache. To get a handle on the bells and whistles of IPCONFIG, type **IPCONFIG /?** at the prompt.

TRACERT is another handy-dandy command-line TCP/IP tool you should get to know. TRACERT shows you the path that your TCP/IP data chunks, called *packets,* are taking through the Net to reach their destination. To see what I mean, open a command-prompt window and type **TRACERT WWW.TOTALSEM.COM**. You'll see every hop your packet takes, through every router and network between you and the totalsem.com web site.

For the Windows NT/2000 crowd, NSLOOKUP is there to show you the gory details about how DNS is working. NSLOOKUP puts you into a command-line environment and lets you interact with a DNS server to perform such MCSE-oriented tasks as setting a root server name, listing and transferring DNS record files, and so on. Truthfully, your life as an A+ tech will rarely take you into NSLOOKUP territory, but you should be aware of it in case you need it.

Dial-up/PPP

Dial-up links to the Internet have their own special hardware protocol called *Point to Point Protocol* (PPP). PPP is a streaming protocol developed especially for dial-up Internet access. To Windows, a modem is nothing more than a special type of network adapter. Modems have their own configuration in the network settings.

As mentioned earlier, modems also have a second group of settings in the Dial-Up Networking Settings/Properties on Windows 9*x* systems. These properties are broken into three windows: the main Properties window as shown earlier, the Server Types window, and the TCP/IP Settings window, as shown in Figure 21-6.

Note that many of these settings seem redundant to the Network Settings window. The TCP/IP dial-up settings override the TCP/IP settings to allow for multiple dial-up options. This is pretty darn handy when you're traveling with a laptop.

Most of the dial-up "I can't connect to the Internet" problems are user errors. Your first line of defense is the modem itself. Using the modem's properties, make

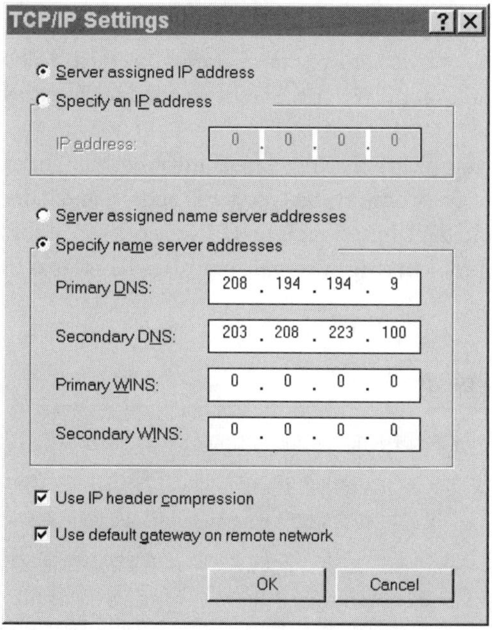

FIGURE 21-6   Internet connection TCP/IP settings

sure the volume is turned up. Then listen to the connection. Do you hear a dial tone? If you don't, check that the modem's line is plugged into a good phone jack. Do you hear the modem dial, and then hear someone saying, "Hello? Hello?" You can bet you dialed the wrong number!

If you hear the familiar mating call as the modem connects on the other side, then you'll get a failure message of some type. Wrong password failure messages are obvious. But remember, the password might be correct and the user name might be wrong. If you still can't connect, it's time to call the network folks to see what's not properly configured in the dial-up networking settings.

Setting Up TCP/IP Services

TCP/IP offers the following commonly used services: World Wide Web, e-mail, newsgroups, and FTP.

Each of these services—sometimes referred to by the overused term "TCP/IP protocols"—requires a special application with its own special settings. Let's look at all four of the services and see how to configure them.

World Wide Web

To use the World Wide Web (WWW), you need a web browser. The two most common web browsers are Microsoft's Internet Explorer and AOL's Netscape Navigator. Setting up a web browser takes almost no effort. As long as the Internet connection is working and WINIPCFG shows good settings, web browsers work automatically.

This is not to say plenty of settings aren't involved, but the default browser settings work almost every time. If you type a web address and it doesn't work, check the line, make sure the DNS server is up (PING works great for this!), and you'll know where the problem is. Browsers are pretty trivial as far as troubleshooting is concerned.

Travel Advisory

PING may be your best friend for diagnosing TCP/IP errors. PING always works. You don't need to log onto a server or even log onto a system. You can enter in either DNS names or IP addresses. You can even PING yourself—just type **PING 127.0.0.1 (127.0.0.1** is known as the *loopback address*). If you get the famous "Request timed out" message, the device you're trying to PING isn't available. When using PING on the Internet, however, "Request timed out" messages are fairly common.

E-Mail

You need an e-mail program to access e-mail. The two most popular programs are Microsoft's Outlook Express and Netscape's Messenger. E-mail clients need a little more setup than web browsers. First, you must provide your e-mail address and password. All e-mail addresses come in the well-known accountname@Internet. domain format. Figure 21-7 shows me adding my e-mail information to Outlook Express.

Next, you must add the Post Office Protocol version 3 (POP3) server and the Simple Mail Transfer Protocol (SMTP) server names. The *POP3* server is the name of the computer that handles incoming e-mail. The *SMTP* server takes care of outgoing e-mail. These two systems may have the same name. Your ISP should provide you with these settings. If it hasn't, you should be comfortable knowing what to ask for. If one of these settings is incorrect, you either won't get your e-mail or won't be able to send e-mail. If an e-mail setup that has been working well for a while suddenly gives you errors, either the POP3 or SMTP server is down, or the DNS server has quit working.

When I'm given the name of a POP3 or SMTP server, I use PING to determine the IP address for the device. I make a point to write this down. If I ever have a problem getting mail, I'll go into my SMTP or POP3 settings and type the IP address. If my mail then starts to work, I know the DNS server isn't working.

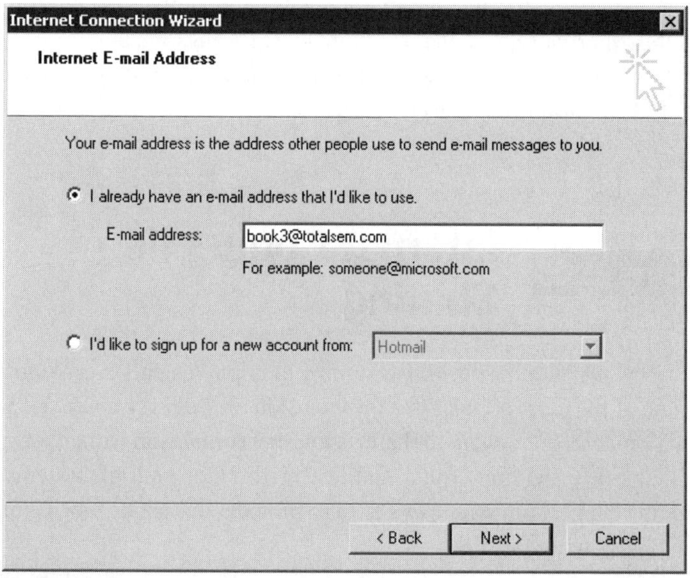

FIGURE 21-7   Adding an e-mail account to Outlook Express

Newsgroups

Newsgroups are one of the oldest services of the Internet. To access a newsgroup, you must use a newsreader program, such as the popular Forté Free Agent. Microsoft's Outlook Express is the most common of all newsreaders because it's free with most versions of Windows. To access a newsgroup, you must know the name of a news server and you must have access to it. *News servers* use the Network News Transfer Protocol (NNTP). Public news servers do exist, but they are extremely slow. Your ISP can tell you the name of its news server, and will provide you with a user name and password if necessary.

FTP

You can use File Transfer Protocol (FTP) to access systems you wouldn't otherwise be able to access, such as a Macintosh system. FTP is also a great way to share files, but you need an FTP server to do so. To access an FTP site, you must use an FTP client, such as WS_FTP, or you can fire up one of the later versions of Internet Explorer or other web browsers that provide support for FTP. Just type the name of the FTP site, such as ftp.microsoft.com.

Even if you're using a web browser, all FTP sites require you to log on. Web browsers only support the most common method, entering the user name "anonymous," and your e-mail address for a password. This is called an *anonymous logon*, and it works fine for most public FTP sites. What if you need to access a site that requires a special user name and password? In that case, I recommend using a third-party program that can store these settings, enabling you to access the FTP site more easily than a web browser. Figure 21-8 shows my personal favorite FTP application, WS_FTP.

Objective 21.05   Internet Connection Sharing

Windows 98 SE came out with a number of improvements over Windows 98; one of the most popular was the inclusion of *Internet Connection Sharing* (ICS). ICS enables one system to share its Internet connection with other systems on the network, providing a quick and easy method for multiple systems to use one Internet connection. Windows 2000 also provides this handy tool. Figure 21-9 shows a typical setup for ICS.

FT²WS_FTP95 LE ftp1.ipswitch.com						

Local System
C:\Program Files\WS_FTP

Name	Date		Name	Date
..			..	
complete.wav	961101 1		watch95.txt	960807 00
connect.wav	961101 1		WS_FTP32.exe	1001016 2
error.wav	961101 1		WS_FTP32.txt	1001016 2
license.wri	960505 1		WS_FTPLE.exe	1000314 2
prorder.wri	961219 1		ws_ftple.txt	1000314 2
whatsnew.txt	961203 1		ws_watch.txt	960807 00
ws_ftp.dll	970122 1		WSPING32.ZIP	980505 00
WS_FTP.hlp	961121 0			
WS_FTP.ini	1001212			
WS_FTP95.exe	970122 1			
[-a-]				
[-c-]				

Remote System
/pub/win32

ChgDir MkDir View Exec Rename Delete Refresh DirInfo

○ ASCII   ● Binary   □ Auto

150 Opening ASCII data connection for directory listing
Received 608 bytes in 0.2 secs, (21.74 Kbps), transfer succeeded
226 transfer complete

Close	Cancel	LogWnd	Help	Options	About	Exit

FIGURE 21-8   WS_FTP

At a bare minimum, you need the primary ICS box to have a modem and a NIC, and the other PC(s) to have a NIC as well. You'll need a hub to connect more than two PCs, or a crossover cable for just two.

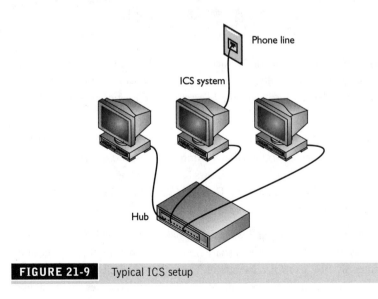

Phone line

ICS system

Hub

FIGURE 21-9   Typical ICS setup

Windows 98 SE does not install ICS automatically. Most systems require you to install ICS via the Add/Remove Programs applet's Windows Setup tab. The ICS is located under Internet Tools options. (The setting for ME is located in the Communications options.) ICS turns the sharing system into a mini-DHCP server.

As with so many other procedures, Windows 2000 makes turning on ICS even easier. Open the properties for My Network Places, then open the properties of the connection you want to share. Click the Sharing tab and select Enable Internet Connection Sharing For This Connection.

After you've installed or enabled the software, Windows requires you to jump through a few more configuration and physical setup hoops to get ICS functioning properly, but this goes well beyond anything A+ will ask.

Travel Assistance

For more information on Internet Connection Sharing, check out the Tech Files at http://www.totalsem.com/techfiles.

CHECKPOINT

✔ **Objective 21.01:** Network Protocols   TCP/IP is the most common protocol used to communicate on the Internet, but you can also use IPX/SPX and AppleTalk. NetBEUI isn't a routable protocol and cannot be used to connect computers to the Internet.

✔ **Objective 21.02:** Network Operating Systems   Domain-based networks have one or more computers that are domain controllers, through which clients log onto the network. Windows NT used Primary Domain Controllers (PDCs) and Backup Domain Controllers (BDCs), while Windows 2000 replaces this model with the Active Directory.

✔ **Objective 21.03:** Sharing Resources   Enabling File and Printer Sharing makes your computer ready to share resources. In Windows 2000, File and Printer Sharing is enabled by default. You still need to tell the system manually which files and printers to share, and who can have access to the shared resources.

Objective 21.04: TCP/IP   PING is used to test a TCP/IP connection between computers. IPCONFIG is used to test a TCP/IP configuration in Windows NT and Windows 2000; WINIPCFG is the Windows 9*x* equivalent of IPCONFIG.

 Objective 21.05: Internet Connection Sharing   Internet Connection Sharing (ICS) provides a quick and easy way for multiple systems to share one Internet connection. This feature was new with Windows 98 SE, which doesn't install this feature automatically. Installation is fairly simple in both 98 SE and 2000. Know the steps for installing it in both of these operating systems.

REVIEW QUESTIONS

1. Pick two of the following that would describe basic characteristics of a peer-to-peer network.

   A. Centralized security
   B. Bridge
   C. A relatively small number of computers
   D. Security that is distributed

2. What does it mean if a network administrator can PING a resource server using its IP address, but not its Internet name?

   A. The computer is not configured to use WINS
   B. The computer is not configured to use ARP
   C. The computer is not configured to use DHCP
   D. The computer is not configured to use DNS

3. Where do you go to join a Domain or Workgroup in Windows 2000?

   A. Control Panel | Network and Dial-up Connections | Network Identification tab
   B. Control Panel | System | System Properties | Network Identification tab
   C. Administrative Tools | Membership Manager | Domain tab
   D. Device Manager | Network Interface Card Properties | Identification tab

4. Your client wants to be able to share one Internet connection with other PCs. Which version of Windows 9*x* should he use?

   A. Windows 98
   B. Windows 98 SE

C. Windows 95 OSR2

D. Windows 95 retail version

5. A client tries to log in to her ISP and is repeatedly prompted to enter her user name and password. Which of the following are the most likely causes? (Pick two.)

   A. NetBEUI is not installed

   B. IPX/SPX is not installed

   C. The modem is not functioning

   D. Her account is no longer active

   E. She is using an incorrect user name and password combination

6. Your client reports that he is able to send, but not receive, e-mail. Which setting do you check in his e-mail program?

   A. POP3

   B. FTP

   C. SMTP

   D. HTTPS

7. Which utility should you run in Windows NT 4.0 to determine the path between your computer and another system?

   A. NETSTAT

   B. IPCONFIG

   C. TRACERT

   D. NSLOOKUP

8. If a Windows 2000 system is configured for TCP/IP and DHCP automatic addressing, but doesn't find a DHCP server when booted, what will happen?

   A. Windows 2000 won't be able to start the network

   B. The system will switch automatically to Net BEUI protocol

   C. Automatic Private IP Addressing will be used to assign an address

   D. The system will listen to the network to discover what range of addresses is being used, and then assign an address in this range

9. You have a networked PC that has File and Printer Sharing enabled, and your computer can be seen in the Network Neighborhood by other computers. However, other computers cannot connect to resources on your computer. Why?

   A. You have not shared any directories

   B. Shared directories are password-protected

    C. Other computers are using the ROM protocol

    D. Other computers do not have File and Printer Sharing enabled

10. To become a member of a domain on a network running Windows 2000, which of the following should you do?

    A. Double-click My Computer, and then select the Tools menu

    B. Open the Control Panel, and then double-click the Network icon

    C. Alternate-click My Computer and select Properties, and then click the Network Identification tab

    D. Alternate-click My Network Places and select Local Area Connection

REVIEW ANSWERS

1. **C** **D** Peer-to-peer networks have decentralized (distributed) security and can only support a relatively small number of computers.

2. **D** A system must have DNS configured in order to access systems by their Internet names.

3. **B** Control Panel | System | System Properties | Network Identification tab.

4. **B** Windows 98 SE introduces Internet Connection Sharing.

5. **D** **E** Most "can't connect" errors are the result of bad login information.

6. **A** A POP3 (Post Office Protocol, version 3) server handles delivery of incoming e-mail.

7. **C** TRACERT shows the path your data took to reach its destination.

8. **C** Windows 2000 and Windows ME use APIPA to assign themselves temporary IP addresses when they cannot reach a DHCP server.

9. **A** Enabling File and Printer Sharing makes the system ready to share resources. You still need to configure the share and share permissions manually.

10. **C** Windows 2000 makes it easy to join a domain.

About the CD-ROM

Mike Meyers' Certification Passport CD-ROM Instructions

To install the *Passport* Practice Exam software, perform these steps:

1. Insert the CD-ROM into your CD-ROM drive. An auto-run program will initiate, and a dialog box will appear indicating that you are installing the Passport setup program. If the auto-run program does not launch on your system, select Run from the Start menu and type *d:\setup.exe* (where *d* is the "name" of your CD-ROM drive).
2. Follow the installation wizard's instructions to complete the installation of the software.
3. You can start the program by going to your desktop and double-clicking the Passport Exam Review icon (you can choose between Hardware or OS) or by going to Start | Program Files | Passport | *A+ Hardware* or | *A+ OS*.

System Requirements

- **Operating systems supported**   Windows 98, Windows NT 4.0, Windows 2000, and Windows ME
- **CPU**   400 MHz or faster recommended
- **Memory**   64MB of RAM
- **CD-ROM**   4X or greater
- **Internet connection**   Required for optional exam upgrade

Technical Support

For basic *Passport* CD-ROM technical support, contact:

Hudson Technical Support
- Phone: 800-217-0059
- E-mail: mcgraw-hill@hudsonsoft.com

For content/subject matter questions concerning the book or the CD-ROM, contact:

MH Customer Service
- Phone: 800-722-4726
- E-mail: customer.service@mcgraw-hill.com

For inquiries about the available upgrade, CD-ROM, online technology, or for in-depth technical support, contact:

ExamWeb Technical Support
- Phone: 949-566-9375
- E-mail: support@examweb.com

Career Flight Path

A+ Certification generally serves as the base of origin for any number of career flight paths. Most IT companies—big and small—see A+ Certification as the entry point to IT. From A+, you have a number of certification options, depending on whether you want to focus more on hardware or go toward network administration (although these aren't mutually exclusive goals). Look at these five in particular:

- CompTIA Network+ Certification
- CompTIA Server+ Certification
- Microsoft Certified Professional Certifications
- Novell NetWare Certifications
- Cisco Certifications

CompTIA Network+ Certification   If you haven't already taken the Network+, make it your next certification. Just as A+ shows you have solid competency as a PC technician, Network+ demonstrates your skill as a network technician, including understanding of network hardware, installation, and troubleshooting. CompTIA's Network+ is a natural fit for continuing toward your Microsoft, Novell, or Cisco certifications. Take the Network+: it's your obvious next certification!

CompTIA Server+ Certification   Like Network+, Server+ Certification fits nicely as a more in-depth testing of your knowledge of PC and server-specific hardware and operating systems. If you plan to go the path of the high-end hardware tech, Server+ is the next step. Plus, Server+ is a natural lead in to Cisco certifications (see the following).

Microsoft Certified Professional Certifications   Microsoft NT, 2000, and XP operating systems control a huge portion of all the installed networks out there and those networks need qualified support people to make them run. Microsoft offers a series of certifications for networking professionals that naturally follow the CompTIA certifications. They offer a whole slew of tracks and exams, but here's what I suggest. First, take either the Microsoft 70-210: Installing, Configuring, and Administering Microsoft Windows 2000 Professional or the 70-215: Installing, Configuring, and Administering Microsoft Windows 2000 Server exam. Either one gives you the first certification, Microsoft Certified Professional (MCP).

Once you've taken 70-210 or 70-215, take the other one, because if you've followed the path I suggested, you're well on your way to attaining the Microsoft Certified Systems Administrator (MCSA) certification. To become an MCSA, you need to pass three exams (most folks take 70-210, 70-215, and 70-218: Managing a Microsoft Windows 2000 Network Environment) and one elective. The cool part is that you can substitute A+/Network+ or A+/Server+ for that elective exam. You're almost there already!

Finally, if you want to stay the course, Microsoft's ever-popular Microsoft Certified Systems Engineer (MCSE) holds a lot of clout for those looking to work in the networking field. The MCSE consists of seven exams—four core and three electives—of which you'll already have at least three. Check out Microsoft's training web site at http://www.microsoft.com/trainingandservices for details.

Novell NetWare Certification   Novell's NetWare might not be the powerhouse it once was, but a huge installed base of NetWare networks is still out there! The surge of techs toward Microsoft certifications had created a bit of a shortage of good NetWare certified techs. The Certified NetWare Engineer (CNE) is the certification to go for if you want to get into NetWare networks. Novell has a number of tracks, but most techs will go for the 50-653: NetWare 5.1 Admin and the 50-632: Networking Technologies exam. Check Novell's certification web site at http://www.novell.com/education/certinfo/cne/ for more details.

Cisco Certification   Let's face it, Cisco routers pretty much run the Internet and most intranets in the world, and Cisco provides three levels of certification for folks who want to show their skills at handling Cisco products. Nearly everyone interested in Cisco certification starts with the Certified Cisco Network Associate (CCNA). The CCNA is only one exam (640-507) and a darn easy way to slap the word Cisco on your resume! After your CCNA, you should consider the Certified Cisco Networking Professional (CCNP) certification. See the Cisco certification web site at http://www.cisco.com/warp/public/10/wwtraining/certprog for more details!

Index

INTERNATIONAL CONTACT INFORMATION

AUSTRALIA
McGraw-Hill Book Company Australia Pty. Ltd.
TEL +61-2-9417-9899
FAX +61-2-9417-5687
http://www.mcgraw-hill.com.au
books-it_sydney@mcgraw-hill.com

CANADA
McGraw-Hill Ryerson Ltd.
TEL +905-430-5000
FAX +905-430-5020
http://www.mcgrawhill.ca

GREECE, MIDDLE EAST,
NORTHERN AFRICA
McGraw-Hill Hellas
TEL +30-1-656-0990-3-4
FAX +30-1-654-5525

MEXICO (Also serving Latin America)
McGraw-Hill Interamericana Editores S.A. de C.V.
TEL +525-117-1583
FAX +525-117-1589
http://www.mcgraw-hill.com.mx
fernando_castellanos@mcgraw-hill.com

SINGAPORE (Serving Asia)
McGraw-Hill Book Company
TEL +65-863-1580
FAX +65-862-3354
http://www.mcgraw-hill.com.sg
mghasia@mcgraw-hill.com

SOUTH AFRICA
McGraw-Hill South Africa
TEL +27-11-622-7512
FAX +27-11-622-9045
robyn_swanepoel@mcgraw-hill.com

UNITED KINGDOM & EUROPE
(Excluding Southern Europe)
McGraw-Hill Education Europe
TEL +44-1-628-502500
FAX +44-1-628-770224
http://www.mcgraw-hill.co.uk
computing_neurope@mcgraw-hill.com

ALL OTHER INQUIRIES Contact:
Osborne/McGraw-Hill
TEL +1-510-549-6600
FAX +1-510-883-7600
http://www.osborne.com
omg_international@mcgraw-hill.com

ExamWeb is a leader in assessment technology. We use this technology to deliver customized online testing programs, corporate training, pre-packaged exam preparation courses, and licensed technology. ExamWeb has partnered with Osborne - McGraw-Hill to develop the CD contained in this book and its corresponding online exam simulators. Please read about our services below and contact us to see how we can help you with your own assessment needs.

www.examweb.com

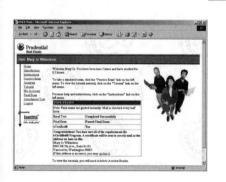

Corporate Assessment

ExamWeb can customize its course and testing engines to meet your training and assessment needs as a trainer. We can provide you with stand-alone assessments and courses or can easily integrate our assessment engines with your existing courses or learning management system. Features may include:

✓ Corporate-level access and reporting

✓ Multiple question types

✓ Detailed strength and weakness reports by key subject area and topic

✓ Performance comparisons amongst groups

Technology Licenses and Partnerships

Publishers, exam preparation companies and schools use ExamWeb technology to offer online testing or exam preparation branded in their own style and delivered via their websites. Improve your assessment offerings by using our technology!

Check www.examweb.com for an updated list of course offerings.

click. study. pass.™

For more infomation, please contact corpsales@examweb.com or call 949.566.9375